Enhancing Curricula:

exploring effective curriculum practices in art, design and communication in Higher Education

Editor: Allan Davies

Centre for Learning and Teaching in Art & Design (cltad)

2002: Ist International conference

Published by
The Centre for Learning and Teaching in Art and Design (*cltad*)
65, Davies Street
London
W1K 5DA

Enhancing curricula: exploring effective curriculum practices in art, design and communication in Higher Education
Centre for Learning and Teaching in Art & Design (*cltad*)
1st international conference 2002
ISBN 0-9541439-2-2

British Library Cataloguing-in-Publication Data.
A catalogue record for this book is available from the British Library.

Designed by Meg Richardson
megrichardson@btconnect.com

Publication 'fixer' Felix Lam

Printed in Great Britain by
Oxonian Rewley Press Ltd
Oxford

Printed on paper produced from sustainable forests.

Contents

Work in Practice

Workshops

Preface

Research into learning and teaching in higher education has been going on for over thirty years although its recent formalisation can be identified with the first 'Improving Student Learning Symposium: Theory and Practice' organised by Graham Gibbs and held at Warwick University, UK in 1993. What was significant about that conference was its emphasis on papers presented by lecturers who were using research frameworks and research tools to inform their own teaching and, hence, improve the quality of their students' learning. I attended that conference and was struck by how universal some of the frameworks and tools were and how applicable they might be to the teaching and learning of art and design. Over the years, I have experimented with a number of those frameworks and tools and have witnessed other colleagues doing likewise. Some of our outcomes have been subsequently published and, on occasions, cited but output has continued to be modest over the past ten years.

This conference sets out to address that very issue; to give colleagues who teach in art and design and related subjects an opportunity to begin to formalise their theories about learning and teaching and to share their outcomes. That this should be on a world stage is appropriate since we need to compare different cultural approaches to learning and teaching, curriculum design and assessment if we are to get the best out of what we do on a local level.

We need to make existing research outcomes and practices accessible to all practitioners in art and design subjects. Given the positive response to this conference I detect a growing enthusiasm. We look forward to meeting you again in Spring 2004.

Best wishes
Allan Davies
cltad Oct 2002

Forward

Making less do more

The challenges of a global knowledge economy on higher education place increasingly high demands on higher education. Nowhere is this truer than in the design sector, the arts, and particularly in communication. This makes the theme of the first international conference of the London Institute's Centre for Learning and Teaching in Art and Design particularly relevant to this moment in these sometimes parallel and sometimes fields. The theme of the conference was Enhancing Curricula: Exploring Effective Curricula Practices in Art, Design, and Communication in Higher Education.

While the demands on universities around the world are increasing to reflect demanding external conditions, resources are increasingly constrained. Good universities balance the tension between these forces by developing better and more effective curricula. This is true of education for the professions, as well as for the liberal arts and humanities, sciences and technology. It is true for fields such as art with a weak link to career outcomes. It is also true of many communication and design fields with their strong focus oncareer outcomes. Effective curricula are more important in these fields than elsewhere.

Until relatively recently, education in art, design, and communication has been taught by artisan and craft training in specialized academies, polytechnics, or vocational programs. Where they are taught at university, the university departments are often staffed by individuals who teach (and were themselves taught) using old curriculum models. In the United Kingdom and elsewhere, many university departments and programs have been built around the specialized academies and polytechnics that were merged into universities during the restructuring efforts of the past two decades.

Changes in the restructured UK high education sector make teaching in any field difficult. In 1961, just over 5 per cent of all 18-21-year-olds took part in tertiary education. In 2002, this has grown to just under 35 per cent. Most of this growth has come during the past decade. At the same time, resources have declined disastrously, with spending per student shrinking by 37 per cent in real terms since 1989 in a decade that saw the student population grew by 90 per cent (Economist 2002: 35-36). This creates serious problems in all fields. The challenges to art, design, and communication are more stringent for a simple reason. Other fields are being reduced from an existing university base with strong research traditions and a rich supply of graduated research scholars and well prepared doctoral supervisors. Art, design, and communication are just now being asked to develop university-level research programs and research training with comparatively fewer resources than they once had in polytechnics and academies.

Demands elsewhere are even greater. Consider China, for example, where over 200 universities have recently established industrial design programs and another 300 schools plan to launch design programs (Justice 2002: unpaged). This places incredible staffing demands on the nation. It also places significant demands on design education in the other Asia-Pacific nations where many Chinese go to study design. This will lead to even greater demands in the future. The nations that are now providing knowledge transfer for the new China must in the future compete against what will become the industrial powerhouse of the 21st century. Design education will become increasingly important in what is about to become the world's most competitive region.

These challenges must also be set against the larger global issues of resource use and human development. If the world is to survive at the same time that more of the world's give six billion people access to clean water, reliable energy, high quality health care, and a decent standard of living, we must increase productivity and output on dramatically reduced resource consumption. Design plays a role here, too.

These are merely a few of the most obvious challenges to curriculum development in one sector, design. Other, equally interesting issues affect art and communication.

The *cltad* conference was a forum for nearly 80 participants from Europe, North America, Africa, and the Asia Pacific region who came to discuss challenges like these and more. While the conference was intimate in scale, the program was large and varied. The program was nicely paced with process workshops and a low-key, interactive setting as well as a pre-conference workshop on research methods,

Plans are already under way for a second conference outside the UK. If the first is any indication, the second should be exciting. I hope to be there.

Ken Friedman

References

The Economist. 2002. "The ruin of Britain's universities." *The Economist*, Vol. 365, No. 8299, November 16, 35-36.

Justice, Lorraine. 2002. "China's Rising Design Activity." *Design Research News*, Volume 7, Number 9, September.

keynotes

Enhancing Curricula:

exploring effective curriculum practices in art,

design and communication in Higher Education

What an artist needs to know

1

Stephen Farthing, RA

New York Academy of Art, USA

Abstract

Anyone who has either originated or attempted to revise a university fine art curriculum that has embedded within it a desire to show even the slightest inclination towards satisfying students who have an ambition to become artists, will have reflected for at least a moment on the question 'what does an artist need to know?' and, if they were able to progress beyond that question, asked a second 'what kind of artists does this institution want to produce?'

This paper explores the feasibility of designing a model curriculum, then tries to establish what sort of artists universities should be aiming to train. Then, by way of a conclusion, it attempts to map a range of draft curricula.

The aim is to argue in favour of institutions defining more precisely their goals and between them offering greater diversity in what constitutes an education in fine art.

Within the detail of the argument is the question 'how important is the teaching for craft skills?' and an exploration of the relevance of even starting to educate artists at an undergraduate level. The wild cards will as always, be in the people who deliver the curriculum, but they are saved for another paper.

Introduction

My introduction is taken from the first few lines of the *Intelligent Persons Guide to Modern Art*, a book I wrote for Duckworth three years ago.

> If the title of this book were not given it would be called The Cannibals, and if it had a picture on its cover it would be a film still taken from the closing sequences of Lust for Life. My chosen image would be predominantly pale blue and golden ochre and would show the peasant driver of a big horse-drawn hay cart standing up and looking back down the stook-lined road he has been following through a recently cut cornfield. What the picture would tell us is that it is baking hot and late summer, but what it could not tell us is that it is the noise of a single gunshot that has caused the driver to stop and look back. If you have seen the film, then you will remember it is the moment just after Kirk Douglas (Van Gogh) stopped painting, walked away from his easel and his image of the crows in the sky above the field, drew his gun and shot himself. This I see as a suitable starting point for a guide to modern art [and I would add to that now a conference that sets out to reassess the curriculum we are offering to artists and designers]. The image opens the door to a consideration of the gradual loss of confidence by artists and designers in painting and drawing and in their previously held passionate belief in the need to attempt to capture and be inspired by nature. It highlights a sense of irony in the appropriations of post-modernism, as well as the obsession the audience has for the artist's biography.

This paper explores the feasibility of designing a curriculum that aims to equip aspirant artists with the skills and knowledge necessary to deal with the demands of their chosen vocation today and on into their future. In passing I ask what sort of artists universities might want to produce, then to conclude shape some space within which curricula content can be explored.

The start of the story

I started writing with one suspicion, which was that those of us currently responsible for designing the curricula of art schools may, recently have become too entangled in the teaching of the craft and the business of art and design and may not have remained sufficiently focused on teaching the art of creativity.

With this in mind I feel inclined towards the view that the art schools of the future should be places where students develop the ability to handle information creatively and inventively and within that shell focus on developing the art of 'fine' communication.

If you share this assumption, then a lengthy discussion on how creativity should or could be taught and then the practical consideration of what information we should work or play with, whilst teaching our students to handle information creatively must follow.

Art schools and academies throughout history have tended to use the history of art and design as the toy box from which students and their teachers pull examples that in their time or on the day seem relevant or important. Once out on the studio/playroom floor the art and design of the past has tended to be used as the model from which both subject matter is plucked and the art of that day is shaped.

The assumptions

The aim of this paper is to argue in favour of institutions defining more precisely their goals within art education and to encourage them to offer between themselves a greater diversity of approaches towards curriculum design and content and not to be prescriptive. In order to set the scene quickly I am, however, going to make three basic assumptions:

My first is that a goal as focused as training an artist should only be attempted at a postgraduate level.

The reason I argue from this position is that today most undergraduate fine art courses are clearly evasive about the degree to which artists can reliably be made. Reading between the lines of most course documentation you find a faculty with a clear interest in the idea that it may be possible to graduate superstar artists (as perhaps the Slade did when Martin Creed, (this year's Turner Prize winner) graduated with just a BA Hons. in 1990), but a recognition of the fact that if they are lucky they will only achieve this goal with one or two students each decade. As a result the bottom lines of most course descriptors settle to linger on the mass of transferable skills taught and skilfully avoid getting in too deep on the alchemy of making artists.

I would like to add anecdotally an observation I have made over the past two years as the head of a New York-based graduate art school, which is that the best of my students did not follow a specialist undergraduate degree course in art or design but instead completed a liberal arts degree at a good university and took a few credits in art and art history for the pleasure of it as a part of that degree. So they came to me as reasonably mature people with a rounded education, and not as young people with a highly developed sense of themselves as artists who had had their options in tertiary education shut down early.

At a post-graduate level, however, both in the UK and North America the scene is completely different, and different to such an extent that most courses feel able to articulate a mission that involves preparing their graduates to become 'professional' artists.

My second assumption is that in setting out to rethink the curriculum we offer to would-be artists and designers it seems improbable that there will be just one answer and one curriculum; instead it seems more likely either that there will be a range of distinct and different courses, or that large institutions will offer a range of modules that be can be tailored to suit the needs of the individual.

My final assumption is that if the teaching of craft skills has a place in these curricula. Then the mass of skills we could conceivably teach today is so broad that we would render it impossible to provide any depth. Remembering that we are working at a postgraduate level and going for a depth of engagement, I suggest that we can only consider courses that emphasise the acquisition of one or perhaps two skills, such as digital image handling and video, or drawing and painting, but not both.

The historical context: within living memory

In setting out to search for a curriculum that works, a reasonable place to start might be the art schools that some big-hitting artists attended in the past and look at what they were offering.

In 1956 when R.B. Kitaj, a G.I with neat handwriting, signed on to do art at 'the Ruskin' it was one of the few departments of The University of Oxford that did not offer a degree to its graduates.

What it offered instead was a humble diploma that could be got (or gotten as he may have said at the time) by attending classes in drawing, painting, human anatomy and art history then turning in the drawings and paintings he made during those classes to be marked.

Twenty-six years earlier at the Art Student's League it was a very similar deal for Jackson Pollock (who incidentally was confirmed in a working paper published last month by the National Bureau of Economics as '*America's greatest modern painter*' - he apparently won over Jasper Johns and Andy Warhol).

What Pollock, Barnett Newman, Alexander Calder, David Smith and a mass of other art world household names got once they signed on at 'the League' was not access to a finely tuned curriculum or an award at the other end, but an opportunity to practise in studios on

57th street, studios that were supervised by artists who wanted (or needed for financial reasons) to teach. For each of these artists I suspect their art-school experience was mid-way between simply finding a mentor and an opportunity to practise what were considered as the core skills of their day with like-minded people around them.

When Pollock followed his older brother Charles to 'the League' he cut his long west coast locks, then set about adopting the social and sartorial style of his teacher.

Thomas Hart Benton, who Kirk Varnedoe describes as '*a swaggering blowhard who curried an image as a no-nonsense son of the soil*', was Pollock's model, but more than providing art classes with an image consultancy thrown in free, Benson it seems inadvertently offered himself up as an establishment pillar for Pollock to urinate against.

To a bystander Benson's interest in distillation and reduction and in what he called 'fundamental principles' seems likely to have been responsible for putting the ambitious Pollock on a journey that took him chronologically through a set of art historical paradigms - Signorelli and Tintoretto, Orozco, Sequiros and Picasso - to what must have appeared at the time to be the looking glass of drip painting.

Pollock like many successful 20th-century artists never felt a need to acknowledge publicly any debt to his teacher. If you ask Ronald Brooks Kitaj (as he signed himself in his letter of application to the Ruskin School) what he did at art school, he will talk in a positive way about drawing. Day after day he tells us from the life model. Then late into the night conversations with his peers particularly David Hockney. In his articulation there are no teachers' names, no role models, just history, the life model and his native wit, intelligence, ambition, hard work and imagination. If there was a curriculum, it is to his mind: drawing, more drawing, some painting at home, reading, art galleries and deep and meaningful discussions with one of his peers. For Pollock the story seems much the same but in his case we should probably swap reading for drinking.

So to sum up

However informal it may seem by today's quality assurance standards, during the mid to early 20th century there was a curriculum, which comprised of a kind of apprenticeship.

Time was spent either in the studio practising the business of translating 'the real' from three dimensions into two dimensional illusions, or out in the bar or galleries looking at and discussing the art of the past and of the moment. But this said, some of the biggest names in 20th-century art, with hindsight believed they were more the product of the maturation of their own native wit and ambition than the product of either a finely tuned curriculum or a brilliant professor.

This of course is not a new idea but it is an important concept to hold to whilst exploring what might be a suitable curriculum for training an artist today. That is unless we believe fine art and great design is just the product of fashion, taste and slight of fiscal hand.

Today

At this point I am going to focus specifically on my subject fine art and in doing so possibly appear to step sideways some distance from design, but this is not my intention: what I want you to consider is the degree to which professional practice and other business-related subjects may be nothing more than a massive distraction if we really want to nurture creativity.

If so many successful artists are right and the business of becoming an artist is no longer about, as the Academy would have it, *absorbing a body of knowledge*, and there is no serious call from the grave for a curriculum that immerses students in the traditions of studio practice. Then it seems likely that the artists of the future will be project managers and art directors and the business studies could become not just an important subject but central to any future curricula.

With this in mind I decided to start my search for alternatives by coming at the problem from an angle that doesn't simply seek to update a tradition, but instead looks at what is expected of an artist today (and may be expected in the future) and look for new ways of preparing students for that challenge.

Geoffrey Goreman, for example, offers an approach based on a business model. I quote from his Web site:

> The art world, in fact is a very small world composed of people who have developed comfortable relationships with one another. It is no different from any other business group.
>
> Once you realise how important relationships are in your career, the sooner you will move closer to realising your ambitions. This means knowing whom the key players are, then developing working relationships with them.

In a twelve-month program based at www.artisticareertraing.com Mr Goreman helps artists build a successful career.

Fuse his approach with Sharon Dravitzki's, another Web-based trainer, and we may have a novel curriculum. She wonders if you have you ever thought that you'd like to be an artist but then shut down the idea because you felt you didn't have the talent. She advises prospective artists not to think they could be an artist but to know they are an artist. Using her mind-over-matter approach she explains that just five minutes a day if you really want to will put you on a trajectory towards becoming an artist.

She offers no discernible curriculum, just a mantra. Her technique relegates the intellect to an inconvenience and places big value on the emotions:

> Listen to our hearts, going on our gut feelings and nurturing the spark that passion and inspiration offer us ... all we have to do, once we have worked out that we want to be artists, is affirm our vision by fixing our identity as an artist.

The key to the approach is, I am told, spending a short time each day utilising short, easy-to-remember, in the first tense, spoken positive statements about us. Affirmations that will alter our energies so that we can be creative and artistic. A simple statement, that doesn't have to be true but will become part of our subconscious if we use it frequently enough. It might be, 'I am a good artist', ' I am a creative person' or 'Don't just think you could be an artist, instead know you are an artist'.

Because today, there is no serious National Academy in either the USA or the UK and the business of being an artist is one of participating in more or less unregulated self-employment, it has to be said, why shouldn't approaches of this type get results?

These alternative approaches may or may not appear to you as extreme examples but, given the way the visual arts have unfolded over the past 50 years, it seems not unreasonable to imagine that there now could be space in the art world for artists and possibly designers to graduate from business schools.

New courses could aim to graduate artists who really were engineered and ready for the market place. Course content could be drawn from an analysis of the careers and market conditions surrounding today's most successful practitioners, the aim could be to assist each student understand themselves as a product and then construct a viable market position for them self as 'that product'. A little art history could be taught to give a feel of the history of the market place, but tutors would certainly not give helpful hints on the fine detail of making things but instead look at issues relating to the evaluation of market opportunities, creating customer loyalty and branding.

The conclusion

The model I am presenting may not appeal to all or any, but I suspect it is viable and that in today's climate it could achieve its goals.

What's important to remember, however, is that it's not the answer it is just one of what I see as a cluster of possibles. No one institution can or should attempt to do everything. But our goal should be to encourage a bigger range of courses, not one narrow view of what a training or education should comprise.

Currently, to my mind, there is a depressing uniformity in the system, with just about every art school racing to become as high-tech as possible, with most having fallen over themselves on the way trying to re-write their curricula quickly and to employ a workforce that will enable them to offer a curriculum that includes the full range of electronic data and image handling related craft skills.

The fourth chapter of Tom Wolfe's book *Hooking Up* (2000) starts like this.

> The scene was the Suntory Museum, Osaka, Japan, in an auditorium so post-modern it made your teeth vibrate. The occasion was the opening of a show of work of four of the greatest American illustrators of the twentieth century: Seymour Chwast, Paul Davis, Milton Glaser, and James McMullan, the core of New York's fabled Pushpin Studio.
>
> The Show was titled 'Pushpin and Beyond: The Celebrated Studio that Transformed Graphic Design'. Up on the stage aglow with Global fame, The Americans had every reason to feel terrific about themselves.
>
> Seated facing the interpreter. The Suntory's director began his introduction in Japanese, then paused for the interpreter's English translation:
>
> 'Our guests today are a group of American artists from the manual age.'
>
> Now the director was speaking again, but his American guests were no longer listening. They were too busy trying to process his opening line. The manual age , the manual age ,the phrase ricocheted about inside their skulls bounced off their pyramids of Betz, whistled through their corpora callosa, and lodged in their Broca's and Wenicke's areas of their brains.

> All at once they got it. The hundreds of young Japanese staring at them from the auditorium seats saw them not as visionaries on the cutting edge ... but as woolly old mammoths who had somehow wandered into the Suntory Museum from out of the mists of the Pliocene past ... a line up of relics unaccountably still living, still breathing, left over from ... the manual age'

What ever happened to the hand made? Is it no longer relevant? Well I can report that at one art school in lower Manhattan it is alive and well.

At the New York Academy of Art we have no cameras, dark rooms, printing presses or computers just a lot of graduates learning to create illusions with pencils, brushes and modelling tools. What's interesting about this is not so much that we do it but that we have virtually no competitors. This of course is not a bad market position for us to be in, but it cannot be good for those students we reject or those who cannot afford to study in New York for two years.

To conclude I will throw just one more idea in the air

In his introduction to *Fields of Influence* the editor James Hamilton draws attention to the period (1820-37) in England when the Royal Academy and Royal Society were fellow tenants of Somerset House on the Strand. Hamilton argues that the influence of their neighbourly co-existence promoted a productive dialogue between the arts and sciences. It seems Humphrey Davy (the inventor of the safety lamp), Michael Faraday and Francis Beaufort (the inventor of the wind scale) regularly rubbed shoulders with Turner and Constable, shared ideas, lectured to each other and certainly informed the approaches of each other. In 1836 John Constable addressed the Royal Institution in a bid, as I understand it, for his work to be received not so much as self-expression but as research. He said:

> Why perhaps, should a painter, especially of the landscape be considered rather as a student in Natural Philosophy, and why should not his pictures be considered but as his experiments, as much so as in any other branch of study.

In Hamilton's book he argues up the influence of Beaufort on Constable's ability to paint a convincing sky and of Sommerville on Turner's painting of 'Snow Storm – Steam-Boat off a Harbours Mouth' (1842) He claims Mary Somerville's theories on magnetism must have driven Turner to impose those vortexes on his composition and not as some may imagine his observations of nature in the raw. Sommerville writes, 'Even a ship passing over the surface of the water ... ought to have electrical currents running directly across the path of her motion.' Hamilton's research on this subject makes for me the paintings of our 19th-century landscape painters even more interesting, and poses the question, why has so little really interesting landscape painting been done since?

Finally, to bring us right up to date I want for a moment to visit the Turner prize which whether we like it or not I believe must be taken as a performance indicator and to some extent our barometer of national achievement within the visual arts. But before we go there I would like to summarise where I believe I have got to. I have suggested that we have:

- placed the subject the history of art in an unrealistically important position;
- virtually ignored the possibility that it may be advantageous for artists to be educated beyond a very basic level in the sciences, mathematics, and theatre studies, music or philosophy and that these subjects and many others could well play a key role in shaping the curricula of the future;
- put IT skills and lens-based imaging at the very top of our priority list;
- relegated the hand made to a minor position on the curriculum;
- begun to envisage the possibility that business studies may have a role to play in educating artists, but are yet to fully embrace it as a large share subject; and
- made few advances in understanding how to teach creativity.

In fact I would argue that we haven't moved on much from the start of the last century. We are still delivering a variant on the experience Pollock and Kitaj had. Substitute one charismatic artist/teacher for a team of visiting lecturers and professors, substitute sitting in the Cedar Tavern arguing Arshille Gorkey up and down as an artist for an art history seminar, and swap three hours on Photoshop for a drawing class and you have it. Now what I want to conclude by saying is that either we acknowledge the art world has changed for ever and look at it as a business just like the fashion industry or the pop music industry - wrestle with market forces and teach our students how to control them - or we decide the Turner prize is not a performance indicator that we respect (I'm assuming that a winner would score big points for their institution in the RAE) and start to change the way we do it from within.

In a review published in *The International Herald Tribune* (February, 2002) Dave Barry took on the Turner Prize and in doing so seemingly effortlessly he made a mockery of the whole thing.

His opening line went like this 'We Americans tend to assume that the British are more intelligent than we are, because they speak with British accents. That is why we need to know about the Turner Prize'. He then went on to Madonna's presentation speech 'Art is always at its best when there is no money, because it is nothing to do with money and everything to do with love ... that's Madonna! Always joking' he says, then he quickly followed up with a description of the winning artist's masterpiece. Martin Creed's 'The Lights Go On and Off' consists Barry tells us of a vacant room where the lights go on and off. They go on for five seconds, then off for five seconds, and 'That's it'. Worried that we might think that blinking lights is all Creeds does he then describes another work. 'A sheet of A4 paper crumpled into a ball'. The review finishes with some praise for Creed 'Frankly, I admire Martin Creed. He can do whatever he wants, and the critics will declare it art, especially if it annoys normal people.' Finally he kicks the whole thing into touch with ' The thing to bear in mind about all this is that everyone involved has a British accent. Including more and more Madonna.'

A few weeks ago the chairman of the New York Academy of art passed me this review and said, 'Do we need art schools to produce Creed?' My reflex answer was 'No', but once on the staircase and alone I shifted ground and found myself thinking, first 'I don't know' then 'perhaps yes'. At a personal level I think his work is irrelevant but the Tate Gallery clearly does not (and because they will always be right because they don't simply record history, they make history happen) I must be wrong. Creed is important; because the advisors to the most important showcase in the UK say he is.

To conclude I would like to reflect on what I believe to be John Ruskin's most astute observation: '*Societies get the art they deserve*'. If you share my enthusiasm for Ruskin's observation then what I advocate as a response from higher education is either based on leaving everything as it is (on the grounds that the Tate in London, and MoMA and the Whitney in New York appear happy), or a reconsideration of the curriculum for artists, that sets out to build a curriculum that is less introspective and look out towards scholarship in subjects beyond art history and theory.

What I advocate is a curriculum geared to produce intellectually inquisitive artists not knowing cynics with two fingers on the economic pulse.

References

Barry, D. Turner Prize Review, The International Herald Tribune 21 February, 2002

Dravitzki, S. *How to become an artist*
URL: http://www.physicsroom.org.nz/log/archive/10dravitzki.htm
accessed November 2002

Farthing, S. (2000), *An Intelligent Persons Guide to Modern Art* , (Duckworth)

Goreman, G. Artist Career Training,
URL: http://www.artistcareertraining.com/ accessed November 2002

Hamilton, J. (2001), *Fields of Influence.* (University of Birmingham Press UK)

Wolfe, T. (2000), *Hooking Up*, (Picador)

Varnedoe, K. (1998), *Jackson Pollock: A Retrospective* Exhibition Catalogue (Museum of Modern Art, New York) J pub. pp34

Biographical note

Born:16 September 1950, London, UK

Stephen Farthing studied at St Martin's School of Art, London (1969-73) before taking his Masters Degree in Painting at the Royal College of Art, London (1973-76). Here he received an Abbey Major Scholarship, taking him to The British School at Rome for a year from 1976. His extensive teaching career began as a Lecturer in Painting at Canterbury College of Art (1977-79), after which he was a Tutor in painting at the Royal College of Art, London from 1980 to 1985. He went on to become Head of Painting (1985-87) and Head of Department of Fine Art (1987-89) at West Surrey College of Art and Design. From 1990 he was Ruskin Master at the Ruskin School of Fine Art and Professorial Fellow of St Edmund Hall, Oxford until 2000, when he moved to New York in order to take the position of Executive Director of The New York Academy of Art, Manhattan.

Stephen Farthing has exhibited extensively in one man shows since his first solo exhibition held at the Royal College of Art Gallery, London in 1977. His work, representing Britain, was shown at the Sao Paulo Biennale in 1989, leading to many further solo shows in the UK and abroad, including South America and Japan. He has also participated in many group exhibitions since 1975, including the John Moores Liverpool Exhibitions, in which he was a Prize Winner in 1976, 1980, 1982, 1987, 1991, 1993, 1997 and 1999.

Farthing was Artist in Residence at the Hayward Gallery, London in 1989. He was elected Royal Academician in 1998 and in 2000 was made an Emeritus Fellow of St Edmund Hall, Oxford. He was appointed executive director of the New York Academy of Art in 2000 and now lives and works in New York, USA.

Design curriculum challenges for today's university

2

Ken Friedman

Department of Leadership and Organisation, Norwegian School of Management, Norway, and Visiting Professor, Advanced Research Institute, School of Art and Design, Staffordshire University, UK

Abstract

Design Curriculum Challenges for Today's University

Curriculum development is a large systemic enterprise. Curriculum involves course planning, course content, pedagogical delivery, and learning objectives for the individual teacher. For the student, it involves learning styles, personal development, mastery of content, and mastery of skills. At the program level, it requires coordination among teachers and across courses. At the school and university level, it involves other issues still.

In design, curriculum development involves eight kinds of education. In university, these include undergraduate education, professional education, and research training. Many schools also offer lifelong learning, continuing education, and executive education. Some schools offer vocational training and special courses.

Design is both a field of professional practice and a research discipline. The plural dimensions of research and practice both affect curriculum needs.

To discuss curriculum effectively requires a comprehensive view of all these issues in an integrated understanding.

The keynote presentation at the cltad international conference offered a systematic overview of the many issues involved in curriculum development for design, relating these issues to the changing needs of both the profession and the discipline.

This paper is the first third of a large, comprehensive examination of the issues considered in the keynote.

This paper places university-level design education in the context of university education for professional service. Professional education at university involves four great challenges: creating new knowledge, preserving existing knowledge, training specialists, and educating citizens

To understand these challenges, it is helpful to understand the meaning and historical development of universities. This paper places professional design education in the context of these large historical issues

Introduction

Life and work in the global knowledge economy demands more of education than has ever been required in human history.

At first, what would now be called design education took place in the apprentice tradition of the artisan guilds. When formal and informal schools for craft or art developed, they took a central role in design education. Some of these became schools of art and design. In those nations where design was taught outside the apprentice tradition, these were the primary centres of professional design and craft education until quite recently.

Over the past five decades, however, design education moved into the university. While European schools of art and design remained independent, design education in North America was taught in university departments. These have generally been departments of art and design where design was seen as a form of applied art or craft skill, though some universities developed specialised design programmes in colleges of architecture, engineering, or – later – information science.

The transition of design education to university study was not merely a consequence of North American higher education, however. It was a consequence of the new needs and demands of the nascent knowledge economy. These needs and demands affect all forms of professional education. Design, as a cluster of professions, involves advice to clients. In some cases, these are internal clients within a large firm or business that employs a designer on salary. In many cases, these external clients turn to a design consultancy for help in planning, design policy decisions among alternatives, problem solving, or any other number of professional decisions. Forms, products, software, or images are often part of the solution to many design problems, but artefacts are the implementation of a design solution. Design itself is a planning process.

The increasingly clear focus on the role of knowledge in every field brings about a richer and deeper understanding of what it is that professionals do. In design, this has shaped a distinction between the planning and problem solving process common to all professional design, and the specific artistic and artisan craft skills used in any specific design solution.

So it is that the past quarter century saw many of the independent design schools of the United Kingdom first grow into polytechnics and later merge into universities. In other nations, independent design schools took on university status by government decision. In both cases, these university schools now face the challenges of all university-level professional schools.

Understanding the demands on design curricula requires us to recognise that all university-level professional schools face four great challenges: creating new knowledge, preserving existing knowledge, training specialists, and educating citizens.

The limits of this paper

As I began to write up my keynote presentation for these proceedings, I realised that I compressed many ideas into the hour we spent together. A keynote speech is often the outline of ideas that should properly be written up in a far longer paper or developed in a seminar. When I decided to write the complete paper that my keynote implied, I discovered that I had outlined a far larger inquiry than a short paper permitted. This inquiry had three parts.

The first sets all professional education in the context of the university. What universities are and what they should now be is a central policy choice for all advanced societies. These involve public policy choices by government and citizens, programmatic and development choices by university administrators, and content and pedagogical choices in the fields and disciplines.

Enhancing curricula lies in this last range of choices. For design, these choices depend on the context within which all professions now operate. To examine the challenge of university-level professional education, it is necessary to consider two large issues. The first is the past and present development of universities. The second is the knowledge economy within which universities take on new meaning.

This is the first part of the paper implicit in my cltad keynote.

The second part involves the changing nature of design education itself. The shift of design education from apprenticeship and artisan guild training to university education has many consequences. This, in turn, rests on the process and tasks of design, and the domains of design knowledge. I have addressed these issues in a series of research projects, papers, and book chapters over the past decade. I will refer to these at the appropriate point in this paper.

It is my hope later to bring these papers and the issues in this keynote together in a longer and more comprehensive view of professional design education, linking them to the third part of the keynote on specific curriculum needs.

The third part of this paper builds on the foundations I establish in the first two parts. Thus, I began at the beginning. As it is, the proceedings' deadline catches me still at work on the final third. It is there that I develop and articulate the consequences of university-level professional education in a knowledge society for the specific design school curriculum.

The challenges we face are deep enough and important enough that I wanted to develop this paper properly. For that reason, it is vital to start with the foundational issues that frame what must come next. In this way, curriculum challenges can be seen as a necessary outcome of the role that the design profession plays in a larger society. Without such a background, curriculum enhancements can always seem to be mere transitions in educational fashion as university administrators attempt to attract a proper number of students.

Nothing could be more dangerous to our conception of what university-level design education is or should be.

I apologise for delivering only the first part of my keynote in this paper, pointing to the second part elsewhere. At the same time, my apology is an apology for necessary constraints. To deliver a proper curriculum statement, we must establish a foundation that has not been clearly developed for university-level design education.

That foundation demonstrates the conditions within which we must consider the four great challenges of university education in general. To place these challenges in context, it is helpful to explore the evolution and changing role of the university over the past 5000 years.

The university today

Modern universities have many roles. They prepare citizens for life in industrial and post-industrial democracies. They train people to work in demanding jobs. They enable individuals to understand and interpret the world around them. They offer individuals the opportunity to think about fields of inquiry and study. They host research programmes that create new knowledge. They establish projects to apply the knowledge that each generates. Universities fulfil all these functions and more.

The curriculum is the mechanism through which the university meets its obligations to students. With the exception of individual faculty research – but not excepting research training and student research – delivering the curriculum is in some respects the core activity of a university.

The importance and scope of curriculum in a serious university requires curriculum development to be a large systemic enterprise. Curriculum involves course planning, course content, pedagogical delivery, and learning objectives for the individual teacher. For the student, it involves learning styles, personal development, mastery of content, and mastery of skills. At the programme level, it requires co-ordination among teachers and across courses. At the school and university level, it involves other issues still.

In design, curriculum development involves eight kinds of education. In university, these include undergraduate education, professional education, and research training. Many schools also offer life-long learning, continuing education, and executive education. Some schools offer vocational training and special courses.

Design is both a field of professional practice and a research discipline. The plural dimensions of research and practice both affect curriculum needs.

To discuss curriculum effectively requires a comprehensive view of all these issues in an integrated understanding.

This keynote presentation will offer a systematic overview of the many issues involved in curriculum development for design. It will relate these issues to the changing needs of both the profession and the discipline.

Design is changing as a professional field and as a discipline. To understand the curriculum needs of design schools today and tomorrow, the presentation will examine the larger knowledge economy within which designers are expected to work.

This analysis will lead to a model for effective curriculum development in different kinds of design programmes. Because most design is now taught in universities or university-level independent design schools, the issue of design curriculum in higher education essentially becomes a question of curriculum development in universities.

The early origins of the university

Frank Rhodes (2001) describes the university as 'the most significant creation of the second millennium'. Rhodes's (2001) recent book points to many university functions: preparing citizens, training workers for demanding jobs, enabling individuals to understand and interpret the world, encouraging inquiry and study, supporting research, creating new knowledge, and finding ways to apply knowledge. A brief review of the university places the modern university in context, and helps us to place the role of curriculum in perspective.

The remote origins of the university are found in Plato's Academy and Aristotle's Lyceum. These early predecessors of the modern university were centres of philosophy where scholars studied mathematics, logic, and geometry, as well as social and natural science as they existed at the time. Plato's Academy and Aristotle's Lyceum essentially functioned both as colleges and graduate schools, though they awarded no degrees. The great library at Alexandria was both a research centre and a graduate school.

Many scholars view Plato's Academy as the first university (Roberts, 1988, p. 207) in the vital sense of a school with regular programmes of study and inquiry. According to Boorstin (1998, p. 38), 'Some would call Plato's Academy the ancestor of the modern university, and so have distinguished Plato as "the first president of a permanent institution for the prosecution of science by original research."' The seminar was the main form of teaching. Scholars recorded lectures, conversations, and seminars, as well as recording the research results of mathematical or philosophical inquiry. At the Lyceum, scholars also engaged in empirical observation in subjects such as biology and comparative social science (Boorstin 1998, p. 51).

In the political turbulence following the death of Alexander the Great, Ptolemy I Soter welcomed Demetrius of Phaleron to Alexandria to establish the library and museum. Demetrius, the exiled tyrant of Athens, had been a student of Aristotle at the Lyceum. The Lyceum became the model for a much larger institute for research and teaching at the Museum of Alexandria. The library of Alexandria was a repository of information with an immense collection of books estimated at over 700,000 volumes and a research centre with a large staff of scholars and researchers (Fraser, 1972, p. 320; Mason, 1985 p. 149; Oxford Encyclopedia, 1998, p. 18). The Museum at Alexandria 'exercised the characteristically Greek functions of a university' (Derry & Williams, 1961, p. 16) and comprised 'a kind of institute for advanced study' (Roberts, 1988, p. 220). It was a centre for research, for documenting and consolidating earlier science and philosophy, and for supporting the work of scholars and scientists, especially in mathematics, biology, and in philosophy (Innis, 1995a, pp. 10–11, 47, 69, 111–114; Roberts, 1988: 220–1; see also: Canfora, 1989; Johnson, 1970). At one point, the Museum was staffed with roughly one hundred professors. All were paid a public salary for their scholarly and scientific work (Mason, 1962, p. 49).

The Academy endured as a teaching institution for over 900 years. Founded circa 385 BC, it survived until 529 AD, when Emperor Justinian ordered it closed (Audi, 1995: 4–5; Machlup 1982b: 89; Mautner, 1996, p. 3). The Lyceum lasted for over five centuries (Audi, 1995, p. 453). The libraries and museum at Alexandria functioned for over eight centuries from Demetrius to the 6th century AD (Brundige, 2001).

Two specialised functions of the modern university had other predecessors.

The first specialised function of the university with an early predecessor is the professional school. The earliest professional schools date back nearly 5000 years. These were the priestly professional schools and scribal schools of Egypt and the great hydraulic empires of the Tigris and Euphrates.

The Academy and the Lyceum implied a concept of democracy, as it was known in Athens. The Athenian concept of democracy was restricted to voters of the specific citizen class, and the philosophical centres were dedicated to the life of the mind as a condition of effective and wise participation in the life of the city-state. In this sense, central purposes of Academy and the Lyceum involved educating young men to be wise, responsible, and virtuous. In effect, this was an education for citizenship. Other goals more closely resembled the function of the graduate school, including research and interpretation, creating, seeking, preserving, and codifying knowledge.

In contrast, the first professional schools had nothing to do with democracy. They were the arms of church and state that helped to manage the business of the first great empires.

Much of the business in these empires was assisted or supervised by the priestly class of scribes. They undertook their studies in the clerical schools of their temples that were comparable to the cathedral schools around which the medieval universities took shape.

We have evidence of these developments from Sumeria and Babylonia in the form of documents and school exercises, especially those pertaining to mathematics and record-keeping (Ifrah, 1998, pp. 77–81; Innis, 1995a, pp. 36–39, 92–105; Innis, 1995b, pp. 326–31, 386–7, 393–4; Mason, 1962, pp. 15–24; McLeish, 1991, pp. 29–37; Roberts, 1988, pp. 64–79, 80–90). The record of Sumerian accounts goes back to 3500 BC. The excavations of the royal library at Nineveh show a library of about 650 BC that preserves 2000 years of scribal records (Hobart & Schiffman, 1998, pp. 39–45; Ochoa & Corey, 1995, p. 5).

It is impossible to date the earliest scribal schools with complete accuracy. It is reasonable to infer that they began at a relatively early stage in the process of forming organised societies. This is because of their role in preserving and transmitting the new and uncommon skill of writing in the slow, traditional societies of the Mesopotamian river plains.

Schools for scribes and imperial management specialists probably existed by 3000 BC, possibly earlier. This dates the first organised professional schools to a time 5000 years before our own.

We still use the curriculum of one such school today. Fragments of a training manual for Egyptian civil servants are still read as part of the Bible. Fragments of the 3000-year-old book known as The Instructions of Amenemopet appear in the Book of Proverbs. The book was written sometime between 1500 BC and 1000 BC as a guide to professional practice by aspiring civil servants (Proverbs, 22, 17–24, 34; Aitken, 1968, p. 3; Cambridge Annotated Study Bible, 1993, p. 557; Johnson, 1998, p. x; The New Jerusalem Bible, pp. 964–5, 997; NIV, 1995, xxiii, p. 935). It contains advice to young managers that would have been considered prudent at the palace schools and cathedral schools where medieval clerics trained for government service.

The second specialised function of the university with an early predecessor is the specialised institute or research centre. While some of the other early schools of higher education partially resembled specialised institutes or research centres, one group of institutions came even closer to the modern model. These centres for science and scholarship grew during the first great flowering of Islam.

The expansion of Islam brought with it the birth of organised institutions for research and study. Many scholars trace the specific organisational innovations of the medieval university to what they see as Islamic universities (Rueegg, 1992, p. 8), others characterise the Islamic institutions of higher education as colleges and research centres, locating the first development of universities in medieval Europe (Makdisi, 1981, p. 287; see also, Makdisi 1990, 1991).

Islamic centres for scholarship, research and teaching included colleges of medicine, law, philosophy and theology; and centres for mathematics, chemistry, and astronomy. These centres made a profound contribution to Western learning. The political and religious divisions between Islam and the West often meant that Arabic philosophers and scientists were known by Latinised names for work that was detached from the centres where they worked.

We associate Peter Lombard, Robert Grosseteste, and Roger Bacon with specific universities. This knowledge captures both our respect for the individual scholarship of great thinkers, and our understanding that their knowledge developed in the context of an important institution. The institution of a university is anchored in its culture and society, as well as in the specific time and place of any one school.

Many great Arabic scholars worked at specific institutions, and most of these institutions flourished at an earlier date than their Western counterparts, often conducting research far more advanced than anything done in the West. Al-Mamun worked at the House of Wisdom in Baghdad, for example, and Abulcasis was identified with the Cordova academy (Braudel, 1995, pp. 80–83; Mason, 1962, pp. 95–102; McLeish, 1992, pp. 137–156; Roberts, 1988, pp. 325–328, 500–501; see also, Leff, 1992; North, 1992; Siraisi, 1992). There is a relationship between a conception of higher learning, the institutions developed to promote it, and the societies within which it flourishes.

For complex reasons, the advanced research centres of the Islamic world failed to develop into full-fledged universities. It is my conjecture that the failure is anchored in the fact that Islamic societies were often theocratic. In contrast, Western universities grew and flourished precisely when Western societies accepted the necessary tension between social cohesion and the free pursuit of knowledge. Theocracy is a social and political structure that often requires agreement on a specific set of principles. In theory, these principles may also be established as a doctrine governing scientific thinking. When scholarship and science are bound by a priori dogmatic rules, free inquiry becomes difficult. Free inquiry requires the ability to consider unacceptable premises as a form of heuristic development. Free inquiry may also begin in dogmatically approved research that leads to conclusions that official doctrine rejects. In all these cases, scholarship and science slowly stop.

Western universities were engaged in this struggle since the earliest conflicts between inquiry and governance. Until the Enlightenment, church and state always won. It was only in 1798, when Emmanuel Kant (1992 [1798]) published The Conflict of the Faculties, that Western universities began to win the struggle for free inquiry. While the search for unattainable universals shaped problems for Enlightenment rationalism, the Enlightenment foundation of reasoned inquiry and democratic government continue to serve us. These goals remain foundations of the university enterprise.

If the struggle for free inquiry made the Western university what it became, however, the process was to take much of the second millennium. This growth built on earlier institutions, including ancient professional schools and scribal schools, institutions of research and study in the classical world, and the Islamic universities and research centres.

The first modern universities

The first universities that still survive were born in the Middle Ages, along with the organisational structures that now characterise the university as we understand it today (Machlup, 1982b, pp. 121–122; Pace, 1912; Rueegg, 1992, pp. 4–8; Verger, 1992, p. 35). The first of these were the cathedral schools that trained the clerics for church service and clerks for public office. Medieval Europe also saw two other kinds of institutions around which the universities of the 13th century took shape: the law school and the medical school.

The cathedral schools were the earliest and most prominent of these institutions. The early form of cathedral schools began by the 2nd century AD as episcopal schools attached to the households of bishops for training clerics. By the 8th century, Europe saw the development of the first true cathedral schools attached to working cathedrals.

Each bishop was responsible for his cathedral school. Each school had a senior scholar and administrator known as the master of the school. The master held office under episcopal supervision.

Many cathedral schools had two branches. One was an elementary school that taught the basics of reading, writing and music. The other was a higher school that taught either the trivium or the full programme of trivium and quadrivium, along with scripture and theology.

The role of the cathedral school was central to the work of the church. It was established as canon law by the Third Lateran Council in 1179, 'that every cathedral church have a teacher (magistrum) who is to teach poor scholars and others, and that no one receive a fee for permission to teach' (Turner, 1908; LeClercq, 1910). The importance of these schools is still visible in the section of modern canon law governing education (Code of Canon Law, 1983, Book III, Title III, Chapters I–III). Many of the canon rules governing Catholic education descend in unbroken line from the rules that governed the cathedral schools and the universities that grew out of them.

The universities of the Middle Ages grew in several ways. Many grew out of the cathedral schools. Others emerged from the communities of schools – including the cathedral school -- located around the great cathedrals. This was the case of the University of Paris, the greatest and most important of the early European universities.

Paris became the model that most great universities adopted. It was a university of masters and teachers organised in faculties. These were the 'lower faculty' of arts or philosophy, and the 'higher faculties' of professional study in theology, law, and medicine. Stimulated by a distinguished palace school established during the 8th-century reign of Charlemagne, the University of Paris later formed around three important schools of the 12th century: the cathedral school of Notre-Dame, the school of Sainte-Genevieve, and the abbey school of St-Victor. As was the case of most medieval universities, Paris seems to have been established and flowering well before its formal designation as a university in 1210 and 1215 (Boorstin, 1998, pp. 81–90; Feret, 1911; Hartvigsen, 1998, pp. 154–155; Oxford Encyclopedia, 1998, p. 695; Pace, 1912; Piltz, 1998, p. 107–115; Rueegg, 1992, pp. 6–7, 12, 30–34; Verger, 1992, 50–52, 60–61).

Some universities grew around the body of an earlier institution of higher learning. This took place at Salerno and at Bologna. Salerno was the site of a medical school as early as the 9th century, while Bologna was home to a school of law and several schools of the liberal arts by the 11th century. Bologna was the model of a second form of university governance, the student university. In contrast to Paris, the university was established and controlled in many important respects by students rather than by the masters. This form of university governance is now defunct, but it established many important precedents that survive in the modern university (Boorstin, 1998, pp. 81–82; García y García, 1992; Gunnes, 1991, pp.

40–50; Hartvigsen, 1998, pp. 153–154; Machlup, 1982, p. 121; Pace, 1907, 1912; Piltz, 1998, pp. 116–121; Rueegg, 1992, pp. 4–7, 24; Siraisi, 1992; Verger, 1992, pp. 47–50).

There were two other common forms of university growth. One was by migration. Migration took place when a group of masters and students departed one university to establish another elsewhere. In early academic slang, this was known as 'the swarm', comparing the birth of universities to the birth of a new hive that took place when a swarm of bees left one hive to establish another. Cambridge University was established this way. It grew between 1209 and 1214 when a swarm of masters and students left Oxford (Verger, 1992, p. 53).

The other way that universities were established was the decision of civil or church authorities to establish a university. After the Middle Ages, this was the most common way that universities were founded. While the nearly biological and often ambiguous processes of organic growth or the swarm built the first universities, conscious foundation has been the central pattern since. Emperors founded universities at Naples and Prague, for example, and enterprising city leaders established universities at Treviso, Pisa, Florence and Siena. Still others were established under the authority or the church, and many earlier universities were solidified when a pope confirmed their privileges (Machlup, 1982, pp. 121–144; Verger, 1992, pp. 53–62).

The shift to research universities

The shift from medieval universities to modern research universities was a long, slow process that involved many strains and difficulties. One typical example of conflict gave rise to Kant's (1992 [1798]) famous essays titled The Conflict of the Faculties.

The core of the dispute was a conflict between the so-called lower faculty of philosophy and the so-called higher professional faculties. The conflict raised an important question in university life: how is knowledge to be established, and which faculty shall govern? This was a conflict between the free search for knowledge and the bounded search for knowledge. The free search for knowledge was a search for pure truth that goers back to the Platonic Academy. The bounded search for knowledge involves the applied knowledge of the professions, a form of knowledge that is constrained by the obligations of service to church or state, and governed by the needs of ecclesiastical and public policy.

On the one hand, the claim of professional education is a claim of service to society. It is bounded by the oath of service that each physician, lawyer, or priest takes on entering office, and it stands for the highest professional ideals of humanity. On the other, it is subject to constraints that generally restrict the concept of knowledge to what is accepted today – or to what has been acceptable in the recent past. This is a contrast with the free search for knowledge on which new knowledge depends. Both principles represent an important social value. The challenge to universities is that each principle has at different times had superior claim. Most often, the claim of service has prevailed, linked, as it is, to the funds that establish and support the university.

Kant's discourse was occasioned by the edict of censorship imposed on German scholars when the tediously religious Frederick William II appointed a dull and bureaucratic minister of justice. King and minister joined in an attempt to shift Germany from the Enlightenment to a doctrinaire and orthodox polity. One step in this was to reduce the freedom of inquiry that scholars had enjoyed under the far more liberal Frederick the Great (Gregor, 1992, pp. ix-xi).

One of the key issues in this great debate is the understanding of the lower faculty. The idea of a lower faculty is not an idea of reduced status, but a concept of fundamental standing, for it is the lower faculty on which the university rests. The lower faculty is the first faculty, and philosophical knowledge is the foundation on which the university depends. While the higher faculties generally represent worldly power and higher social standing – not to mention better salaries – the higher faculties cannot exist without the lower.

The conflict of the faculties survives in several active debates. One is the debate between the university as a centre of free inquiry and the university as a centre of applied knowledge and social service. Another is the debate on how he university shall be controlled and governed – whether by the professorate on behalf of science, or by the founders and governors, state, church, or even private. These debates echo in important current books, such as an updated discourse on the conflict of the faculties (Rand, 1992) or Bill Readings's (1996) highly regarded critique of the university in the post-industrial nation-state.

These debates are relevant to design curriculum in several ways that I will consider later. These include the frequently conflicted relations between theory and practice and the difficulty of linking the design curriculum to the larger university curriculum. The debate over the conflict of the faculties also occurs in the insistence of many design teachers that design schools teach a special professional knowledge that must be linked to the practising profession, which they claim to represent, as contrasted to the larger body of knowledge represented by the university professorate.

When this debate touches on design schools, the claim of professional knowledge by design teachers is conditioned by three paradoxical aspects. First, it is linked to the crafts guilds that were never connected to universities. Second, none of the learned professions considers design as a profession, and most professionals regard design as a vocation connected not to the lower or philosophical faculty, but to the tradition of vocational education outside the university entirely. Third, few design teachers genuinely represent the profession of design. Few leading designers teach, and relatively few design teachers have had active careers in business or industry. Those few, interestingly, tend to have entered the university because they love research. It is a double paradox that the more successful designers to become academics are those who argue most effectively for the new curriculum. In contrast, those who argue for guild knowledge and craft traditions tend to represent the art and craft approach, and – for the most part – these art and craft designers have had no major work outside design schools.

Kant's debate set the stage for the birth of the first modern research university, the University of Berlin.

The next great advance in university development came with the establishment of the Humboldt university reform that created the University of Berlin in 1809 (Gellert, 1993, pp. 5–11). Research became a central feature of the university. In the medieval university, students once attended university to pursue a career in church or state service. Training for the professions also gave way to a vague post-medieval education in which the sons of gentry and nobility were expected to spend time engaged in a transition from childhood to manhood. While these universities followed the noble goal of training for citizenship expressed by Newman (1927) and others, universities were also places where students drank away the lazy days, learned to duel, or attempted to study with professors who rarely (if ever) taught. This was the basis of Adam Smith's famously savage critique of education at Oxford in The Wealth of Nations (Smith, 1976 [1776], v. II, pp. 283–296, 334–335).

The two final shifts in universities that must be considered came in the 1800s and the 1900s.

In the 1800s, a new kind of university emerged. In Britain, this was the new university, where such institutions as Manchester, London, or Leeds broke the earlier monopoly held by Oxford and Cambridge.

The major change, however, came in the United States, when a century-long move developed that created the great land grant universities, the major general universities, and the full-fledged research universities that have become the model for universities around the world today. This story is so long and detailed that it would require an article in its own right. The important result is that the general research university is open to all citizens based on talent. Most universities today aspire to the status of the research university and many authors tell parts of the tale (Clark, 1993; Damrosch, 1995; Readings, 1996; Rhodes, 2001; Veysey, 1965).

In the United States, the political struggles of the 19th and 20th centuries that led to the birth of the great land grant universities culminated in universal access to higher education by the late 1900s.

At the end of the Second World War, the United States made a far-reaching and influential decision. This was the Veteran's Readjustment Act of 1944, commonly called the GI Bill. The bill effectively made it possible for all returning service members to attend university. (Fenske, Besnette & Jordan, 2000, pp. 114–105). No longer was higher education a privilege of the fortunate few. While the promise of universal higher education was born in the great land grant universities, the fact that universities existed did not solve the challenge of enabling all individuals to attend them. The GI Bill and a host of successive measures made it possible for nearly any student to attend the universities built and developed with public funds. This, in turn, created rising expectations of access and knowledge, and it became a cornerstone of the coming knowledge economy. The relation between broad student participation in university life and the impact of higher education on the greater society is a central fact of academic life today (Ottinger, 2000). The result is visible in the shifting role of knowledge in modern industrial life. This, in turn, has brought about a powerful transition in every industrial democracy that strives to maintain its position relative to the other developed nations.

The creation of universities is a general democratic decision of the electorate in many places, and a strategic initiative of government in others. The result has been the same. Universities have been established more widely and in greater numbers than ever before. Some have grown out of other institutions. Some have come about by merger. Altogether, there are some tens of thousands of universities around the world. Only a small number of the universities we find today existed a century ago, and many are only a few decades old.

From the oldest to the youngest, all universities face four challenges that have been at the core of higher education for the past 5000 years.

The four great challenges of higher learning

Universities today face four great challenges. Institutions of higher learning have addressed these challenges in different forms over the past 5000 years, and they have met them in different kinds of programmes and institutional arrangement.

The four great challenges are:

1. creating new knowledge,
2. preserving existing knowledge,
3. training specialists, and
4. educating citizens.

It is immediately clear that these challenges create an inherent tension.

The requirements of new knowledge both demand a foundation in earlier knowledge and push the boundaries of what is known. This always means negotiating a delicate series of forces that draw the past into the future. At some moments, the need for preservation emphasises the past, and the love of the past often involves a tendency to preserve the past intact. At other times, the need for new knowledge can apparently overwhelm the past, and those who move forward sometimes care little for what we have known as societies and as individuals.

The first institutions of higher learning were imperial and religious centres of specialised education. These were created in vastly hierarchical societies where a few knowledge specialists served even fewer great lords and potentates, and all of them ruled a vast and oppressed majority with little thought for service to the whole.

The Greek ideal of democracy brought about a new kind of higher learning: education for the wise exercise of civic responsibility. However, this was not democracy, at least not as we know it. A few, wealthy citizens could afford this education, and only a few more were entitled to vote in societies that depended in great part on slave labour and on the subjugation of smaller and lesser cities to the great powers of the era.

The tension between education for the few and education for an increasingly large many has been a pendulum driving the growth and spread of education from the first days to our own time.

The two polarities of knowledge and citizenship also establish a subtle dimension of opposing and co-operating tendencies.

Professions require specialisation and the preservation of a coherent body of knowledge. This cements professional engagement and permits the development of practical affairs. At the same time, all professions require new knowledge to improve and grow. This demands research and a challenge to what is known. This challenge in itself can weaken the professional sodality while strengthening the profession in the long term.

Professions are by nature inclined in two directions. In one direction, they serve the larger polity. Most professions are granted specific ranges of control and social status precisely because they serve the larger polity. All professionals are in one sense citizens who act on behalf of the larger society. At the same time, the privileges and opportunities that drive professional development set professionals at odds with fellow citizens outside a specific professional group.

Any diagram of the relationships among these four challenges will reveal a series of conflicting and communicating forces that operate in an energising dialectic. At each step, we see tensions between specialisation and generalisation, between theory and practice, between research and repetition, between hierarchy and democracy, between the pull of the past and the press of the future.

These meet today in a new knowledge economy. The central virtues and challenges of the knowledge economy are simple. Societies need to know more and do more to thrive. Knowledge is an inherent property of individuals. To thrive, therefore, any society rooted in a knowledge economy must achieve two goals. The first is to grow its corps of professional specialists. The second is to widen democratic participation.

The rich web of social interactions implicit in this simply stated challenge is not at all simple, and I will not address it here. I brought this long story forward over the past 5000 years to set the stage for a few basic thoughts on the design curricula for the knowledge economy that we have see around us.

If design could still be taught or learned in artisan guilds or independent design schools, this conceptual background would not be as important as it is. The fact is that nearly every form of design that has a purpose in today's world is far too complex for the older forms of education that were considered suitable even as recently as 1975. Designers are now professionals and they must become even more professional to perform the professional services that they are now called on to perform.

Meeting this challenge requires university education and a research culture, the culture of the universities and research centres around which universities grew.

When we met in London at the cltad conference, I outlined some of these issues in a short presentation. Here, I wanted to develop a thorough background to set the stage for a few conclusions. Before moving to those conclusions, I will point to a few useful sources for detail.

Rather than draw out all the implications of the university enterprise, I will recommend Frank Rhodes's (2001) elegant book, The Creation of the Future: The Role of the American University.

Rhodes makes a good case for the importance of the research university in world affairs over the past 900 years, and he addresses issues that face us all, in Europe, Africa, and the Asia-pacific region, as well as in the Americas.

The core issues in the book are the challenges that great research universities face today. Rhodes begins by defining the nature and task of the research university. He examines the issue of professionalism in a knowledge economy, the nature of community in modern societies, and the theme of teaching as a moral vocation. He then explores undergraduate education, professional education, and research training. Finally, he examines the large social issues facing universities today. These include costs and financing, research as a public trust, social service and information technology.

Designers and design educators will find the concluding chapter particularly important. Today, we find ourselves debating the nature of research in a formerly vocational field. While most of us teach in universities, our departments and schools are relatively recent. In some places, design schools have only entered the university or attained university status quite recently. Doctoral education and research training are a central concern for the field, but some of us seek new forms of doctorate while others are not quite sure what the doctorate is. This debate can be framed in the question of the new university. This book offers a good foundation for conversation on the role of design and design research in the university.

During my talk, I presented some models and a taxonomy of issues for design education. I describe these more completely in a keynote presentation I gave at IDATER (Friedman, 2000, 2001). These follow an earlier article in which I discussed the implications of the shift from artisan training to university education (Friedman, 1997).

Before turning to the challenge of design curricula for today's universities, I want to set a background in several issues that face all forms of professional education in a knowledge economy.

The industrial revolution of the 18th century brought enormous change to the world economy. In the 19th century, the electrical telegraph ushered in the first telecommunication era while the American Civil War gave rise to the first industrialised war in a comprehensively industrial society. By the end of the century, the telephone and the railroads had reshaped societies around new communication and transport media. Soon after, Henry Ford's mass production methods and the automobiles they made possible would reshape much of the world.

Over this same period, physical science advanced from Newton's mechanics to Maxwell's equations, and then it leaped forward as Einstein developed the theory of relativity and paved the way for quantum physics.

By incremental steps and quantum leaps, these changes shifted the world from agriculture to mechanics to electrics and finally toward electronics.

Just before the Second World War, the Australian economist Colin Clark (1940) created an important classification scheme for different kinds of economies. He identified three classes: primary, secondary and tertiary. Primary economies extract wealth from nature, secondary economies transform extracted material through manufacturing, and tertiary economies engage in service. At the same time, the Canadian economist Harold Innis (1950, 1951, 1980,

1995a, 1995b; see also Acland & Buxton, 1999) was laying the foundation of a social theory based on information, while American economist Fritz Machlup (1962, 1970, 1978, 1979, 1980, 1982, 1984; see also Machlup & Mansfield, 1983) developed the first theories of information economics.

During these same years, Peter Drucker (1973, 1990, 1993, 1996 [1959], 1999) studied the managerial society. By 1959, he concluded that we were about to enter the post-modern world, a world defined by well-known social forces meeting in radical new configurations.

By the 1960s, Daniel Bell (1976, 1999) announced the coming of post-industrial society. Bell argued that a significant change in the character of knowledge was taking place, with professional knowledge elite developing to manage it.

Knowledge has always been a key factor in productivity. The earliest design and the start of manufacturing began over two and a half million years ago when homo habilis made the first weapons and tools (Friedman, 1997, p. 54; Ochoa & Corey, 1995, p. 1). The search for productivity focused on scarce material resources and the challenges of understanding the physical world. All manufacturing was handicraft until the industrial revolution gave rise to mass manufacturing in the 19th century. The wealth created in the industrialised economies of the 20th century changed this.

By the time of Colin Clark's model of societies, a focus on knowledge became inevitable. While the vocabulary of the knowledge economy is relatively new, the idea of a knowledge economy has been emerging for the past half century. For example, W. Edwards Deming's (1986, 1993; see also Aguayo 1990; Halberstam, 1987; Scherkenbach, 1991; Walton, 1989) work in post-war Japan reflects the principles of knowledge management and organisational learning. Economists such as Harold Innis and Fritz Machlup have gained increasing importance, along with sociologists such as Daniel Bell, Manuel

Castells (1983, 1989a, 1989b, 1989c, 1989d, 2001, 1999) and Saskia Sassen (1991, 1994, 1996, 1998).

This influences the work of all professionals in significant ways because effective knowledge work demands creating, sharing and distributing information as the raw material that individuals and organisations process into knowledge. The administrative principles of Henri Fayol (1987 [1916]), Henry Ford (1922, 1991) or Frederick W. Taylor (1911) restricted the flow of information and power in vertically stratified organisations. The management principles of a knowledge economy encourage the flow of information and knowledge within dynamic networks.

Since then, many thinkers have attempted to analyse and describe the forces at play and the consequences of their interaction.

Today, these forces affect university education at a time of crisis. National economies suffer under many forms of turbulence. Ageing populations and a shrinking base of workers who must pay for increasingly costly social services and pension requirements exacerbate these strains. As societies attempt to meet a greater range of demands across and increasing range of social services, the demands on higher education increase even as resources are increasingly constrained.

Good universities balance the tension between these forces by developing better and more effective curricula. This is true of education for professions, liberal arts, humanities and technology. It is even truer for fields such as art and communication with a weak link to career outcomes – and it is true of many design fields. Effective curricula are more important in these fields than elsewhere.

Curriculum development is a large systemic enterprise. Curriculum involves course planning, course content, pedagogical delivery, and learning objectives for the individual teacher. For the student, it involves learning styles, personal development, mastery of content, and mastery of skills. At the programme level, it requires co-ordination among teachers and across courses. At the school and university level, it involves other issues still.

In design, curriculum development involves eight kinds of education. In university, these include undergraduate education, professional education, and research training. Many schools also offer lifelong learning, continuing education, and executive education. Some schools offer vocational training and special courses.

Design is both a field of professional practice and a research discipline. The plural dimensions of research and practice both affect curriculum needs.

To discuss curriculum effectively requires a comprehensive view of all these issues in an integrated understanding.

Any serious inquiry into enhancing design curricula must offer a systematic overview of the many issues involved in curriculum development for design. It must relate these issues to the changing needs of both the profession and the discipline.

Design is changing as a professional field and a discipline. To understand the curriculum needs of university-level design education today and tomorrow, requires placing design in the context of the larger knowledge economy within which designers now work.

This analysis is the basis of a model for effective curriculum development in different kinds of design programmes.

The taxonomy of domains of design knowledge (Friedman, 2000, 2001) offers a basis for approaching the field. While the taxonomy is not complete or perfect, I propose it as a heuristic model describing the field of design. The taxonomy began as an approach to meeting the needs of planning a university-level design programme. As we learn more, the taxonomy will change.

At this point, I will close the background discussion. I will return to these issues again in the next part of this paper.

References

Acland, C.R., & Buxton, W.J. (eds.) (1999), *Harold Innis in the New Century* (Montreal and Kingston: McGill-Queen's University Press)

Aguayo, R. (1990), *Dr. Deming: The Man Who Taught the Japanese About Quality* (London: Mercury Books)

Aitken, K.T. (1968), *Proverbs* (Philadelphia: The Westminster Press)

Audi, R. (ed.) (1995), *The Cambridge Dictionary of Philosophy* (Cambridge: Cambridge University Press)

Bell, D. (1976), *The Coming of Post-industrial Society* (Harmondsworth: Penguin)

Bell, D. (1999) *The Coming of Post-industrial Society: A Venture in Social Forecasting* (New York: Basic Books)

Boorstin, D.J. (1998), *The Seekers. The Story of Man's Continuing Quest to Understand his World* (New York: Random House)

Braudel, F. (1995), *A History of Civilisations*, Mayne, R. (trans.) (New York: Penguin Books)

Brundige, E.N. (1991), *The Decline of the Library and Museum of Alexandria*, URL: <http://www.digital-brilliance.com/kab/alex.htm> (accessed: May 11, 2002)

Brundige, E.N. (2001), *Alexandrian Scholarship*, URL: <http://www.perseus.tufts.edu/GreekScience/Students/Ellen/Museum.html> (accessed: June 1, 2002)

Cambridge Annotated Study Bible: New Revised Standard Version (1993), notes and references by Kee, H.C. (Cambridge: Cambridge University Press)

Canfora, L. (1989), *The Vanished Library*, Ryle, M. (trans.) (Berkeley: University of California Press)

Castells, M. (1983), *The City and the Grassroots. A Cross-cultural Theory of Urban Social Movements* (Berkeley: University of California Press)

Castells, M. (1989a), *The Information Age. Economy, Society, and Culture*, Vol. I. The Rise of the Network Society (Oxford: Blackwell Publishers)

Castells, M. (1989b), *The Information Age. Economy, Society, and Culture*, Vol. II. The Power of Identity (Oxford: Blackwell Publishers)

Castells, M. (1989c), T*he Information Age. Economy, Society, and Culture*, Vol. III. End of Millennium (Oxford: Blackwell Publishers)

Castells, M. (1989d), *The Informational City: Information Technology, Economic Restructuring, and the Urban-regional Process* (Oxford: Blackwell)

Castells, M. (2001), *The Internet Galaxy. Reflections on Internet, Business, and Society* (Oxford: Oxford University Press)

Castells, M, (ed.) (1999), *Critical Education in the New Information Age with Manuel Castells, Ramon Flecha, Paulo Freire, Henry A. Giroux, Peter McLaren* (New York: Rowman and Littlefield Publishing)

Clark, B.R. (ed.) (1993), *The Research Foundations of Graduate Education. Germany, Britain, France, United States, Japan* (Berkeley: University of California Press)

Clark, C. (1940), *Conditions of Economic Progress* (London: Macmillan and Co)

Code of Canon Law. 1983. The Code of Canon Law. Promulgated by the authority of Pope John Paul II. Given at Rome, on the 25th of January, 1983. URL: <http://digilander.libero.it/gergely/cic_en.htm>. Date Accessed: 2002 October 29.
(Also see: URL: <http://www.intratext.com/X/ENG0017.htm>. Date Accessed: 2002 October 29.

Damrosch, D. (1995), *We Scholars. Changing the Culture of the University Cambridge*, (Massachusetts: Harvard University Press)

Deming, W.E. (1986), *Out of the Crisis: Quality, Productivity and Competitive Position*. (Cambridge: Cambridge University Press)

Deming, W.E. (1993), *The New Economics for Industry, Government, Education* (Cambridge, Massachusetts: Massachusetts Institute of Technology, Center for Advanced Engineering Study)

Derry, T.K. & Williams, T. (1961), *A Short History of Technology. From the Earliest Times to AD 1900* (New York: Oxford University Press)

Drucker, P.F. (1973), *The Age of Discontinuity. Guidelines to our Changing Society* (New York: Harper Torchbooks)

Drucker, P.F. (1990), *The New Realities* (London, Mandarin)

Drucker, P.F. (1993), *Post-capitalist Society* (Oxford: Butterworth-Heinemann)

Drucker, P.F. (1996 [1959]), *Landmarks of Tomorrow: A Report on the new 'Post Modern' World*, with a new introduction by the author (Rutgers, New Jersey: Transaction Publishers)

Drucker, P.F. (1999), *Management Challenges for the 21st Century* (New York: Harperbusiness.

Fayol, H. (1987 [1916]), *General and Industrial Management* (London: Pitman Learning)

Fenske, R.H., Besnette, F.H. & Jordan, S.M. (2000), 'The process of setting tuition in public university systems. A case study of interaction between governing board and campus management', in Hoffman, A.M. & Summers, R.W. (eds.), *Managing Colleges and Universities* (Westport, Connecticut: Bergin and Garvey)

Feret, P. (1911), 'University of Paris', *The Catholic Encyclopedia*, Vol. XI (New York: Robert Appleton Company), online edition 1999, URL: <http://www.newadvent.org/cathen/11495a.htm> (accessed: April 8, 2002)

Ford, H. (1922), *My Life and Work* (Garden City, NY: Doubleday, Page, and Co)

Ford, H. (1991), *Ford on Management: Harnessing the American Spirit* (Oxford: Basil Blackwell)

Fraser, P.M. (1972), *Ptolemaic Alexandria*, Vol. I (Oxford: Oxford University Press)

Friedman, K. (1997), 'Design science and design education', in McGrory, P. (ed.), *The Challenge of Complexity* (Helsinki: University of Art and Design Helsinki UIAH)

Friedman, K. (2000), 'Creating design knowledge: from research into practice', in Roberts, P.H. & Norman, E.W.L. (eds.), *IDATER 2000: International Conference on Design and Technology Educational Research and Development* (Loughborough, UK: Department of Design and Technology, Loughborough University)

Friedman, K. (2001), 'Creating design knowledge: from research into practice', in Norman, E.W.L. & Roberts, P.H. (eds.), *Design and Technology Educational Research and Development: The Emerging*

International Research Agenda (Loughborough, UK: Department of Design and Technology, Loughborough University)

Garcia y Garcia, A. (1992), 'The faculties of law', in Rueegg, W. (gen. ed.) & de Ridder-Symoens, H. (ed.), *A History of the University in Europe,* Vol. 1., Universities in the Middle Ages (Cambridge: Cambridge University Press)

Gellert, C. (1993), 'The German model of research and advanced education', in Burton, R.C. *The Research Foundations of Graduate Education. Germany, Britain, France, United States, Japan* (Berkeley: University of California Press)

Gregor, M.J. (1992), 'Introduction', *Immanuel Kant. The Conflict of the Faculties.* (Der Streit der Falkultaeten) (Lincoln, Nebraska: University of Nebraska Press)

Gunnes, E. (1991), 'Da univesitetet ble til', in Wyller, E.A. (ed.), *Universitets ide gjennom tiden og I dag: en samling Oslo-foredrag* (Oslo: Universitetsforlaget)

Halberstam, D. (1987), *The Reckoning* (New York: Avon Books)

Hartvigsen, G. (1998), *Forskerhaandboken* (Kristiansand, Norway: Norwegian Academic Press)

Hobart, M.E., & Schiffman, Z.S. (1998), *Information Ages. Literacy, Numeracy, and the Computer Revolution* (Baltimore: The Johns Hopkins University Press)

Ifrah, G. (1998), *The Universal History of Numbers from Prehistory to the Invention of the Computer* (London: The Harvill Press)

Innis, H. (1950), *Empire and Communications* (Oxford: Oxford University Press)

Innis, H. (1951), *The Bias of Communication* (Toronto: University of Toronto Press)

Innis, H. (1980), *The Idea File of Harold Adams Innis*, Christian, W. (ed.) (Toronto: University of Toronto Press)

Innis, H. (1995a), *The Bias of Communication* (introduction by Heyer, P. & Crowley, D.) (Toronto: University of Toronto Press)

Innis, H. (1995b), *Staples, Markets, and Cultural Change*, Drache, D. (ed.) (Montreal and Kingston: McGill-Queen's University Press)

Johnson, C. (1998), *Proverbs: An Introduction* (Edinburgh: Canongate)

Johnson, E.D. (1970), *History of Libraries in the Western World* (Metuchen: Scarecrow Press, Inc)

Kant, I. (1992 [1798]), *The Conflict of the Faculties* (Der Streit der Falkultaeten), trans. with an introduction by Gregor, M.J. (Lincoln, Nebraska: University of Nebraska Press)

LeClercq, H. (1910), 'Third Lateran Council (1179)' *The Catholic Encyclopedia*, Vol. IX (New York: Robert Appleton Company), online edition 1999, URL: <http://www.newadvent.org/cathen/09017b.htm > (accessed: April 14, 2002)

Leclercq, J. (1982), *The Love of Learning and the Desire for God. A Study of Monastic Culture* (New York: Fordham University Press)

Leff, G. (1992), 'The faculty of arts. The trivium and the three philosophies', in Rueegg, W. (gen. ed.) & de Ridder Symoens, H. (ed.), *A History of the University in Europe*, Vol. 1., Universities in the Middle Ages (Cambridge: Cambridge University Press)

Machlup, F. (1962), *The Production and Distribution of Knowledge in the United States* (Princeton, New Jersey: Princeton University Press)

Machlup, F. (1970), *Education and Economic Growth* (Lincoln, Nebraska: University of Nebraska Press)

Machlup, F. (1978), Information Through the Printed Word: the Dissemination of Scholarly, Scientific, and Intellectual Knowledge (New York: Praeger Publishers)

Machlup, F. (1979), *Knowledge and Information* (Princeton, New Jersey: Princeton University Press)

Machlup, F. (1980), *Knowledge and Knowledge Production* (Princeton, New Jersey: Princeton University Press)

Machlup, F. (1982a), *Knowledge, Its Creation, Distribution, and Economic Significance*. Vol. 1. Knowledge and Knowledge Production (Princeton, New Jersey: Princeton University Press)

Machlup, F. (1982b), *Knowledge, Its Creation, Distribution, and Economic Significance*. Vol. 2. The Branches of Learning (Princeton, New Jersey: Princeton University Press)

Machlup, F. (1984), *Knowledge, Its Creation, Distribution, and Economic Significance*. Vol. 3. The Economics of Information and Human Capital (Princeton, New Jersey: Princeton University Press)

Machlup, F, & Mansfield, U. (eds.) (1983), *The Study of Information* (New York: Wiley)

Makdisi, G. (1981), *The Rise of Colleges: Institutions of Learning in Islam and the West* (Edinburgh: Edinburgh University Press)

Makdisi, G. (1990), *The Rise of Humanism in Classical Islam and the Christian West: With Special Reference to Scholasticism* (Edinburgh: Edinburgh University Press)

Makdisi, G. (1991), *Religion, Law and Learning in Classical Islam* (London: Variorum.

Mason, S.F. (1962), *A History of the Sciences* (New York: Macmillan USA, Collier Books)

Mautner, T. (1996), *A Dictionary of Philosophy* (Oxford: Blackwell)

McLeish, J. (1994), *The Story of Numbers. How Mathematics has Shaped Civilisation* (New York: Fawcett Columbine)

The New Jerusalem Bible (1990) (New York: Doubleday)

Newman, J.H. (1927), *The Idea of a University* (Chicago: Loyola University Press)

NIV (1995), *The NIV Study Bible. 10th anniversary edition*, Kenneth Baker, general editor (Grand Rapids, Michigan: Zondervan Publishing House)

North, J. (1992), 'The faculty of arts. The quadrivium', in Rueegg, W. (gen. ed.) & de Ridder Symoens, H. (ed.), *A History of the University in Europe*, Vol. 1, Universities in the Middle Ages (Cambridge: Cambridge University Press)

Ochoa, G. & Corey, M. (1995), *The Timeline Book of Science* (New York: Ballantine)

Ottinger, D.C. (2000), 'Student Development. Its Place in the Academy', in Hoffman, A.M. & Summers, R.W. (eds.), *Managing Colleges and Universities* (Westport, Connecticut: Bergin and Garvey)

Oxford Encyclopedia (1998), *Oxford Encyclopedia of World History*, compiled by Market House Books, Ltd. (Oxford: Oxford University Press)

Pace, E.A. (1907), 'The University of Bologna', *The Catholic Encyclopedia*, Vol. II (New York: Robert Appleton Company),

online edition 1999, URL:
<http://www.newadvent.org/cathen/02641b.htm>
(accessed: March 20, 2002)

Pace, E.A. (1912), 'Universities', *The Catholic Encyclopedia*, Vol. XV (New York: Robert Appleton Company), online edition 1999, URL:

<http://www.newadvent.org/cathen/15188a.htm> (accessed: January 15, 2002)

Piltz, A. (1998), *Medeltidens laerda vaerld* (Skellefteaa, Sweden: Norma)

Rand, R. (ed.) (1992), *Logomachia. The Conflict of the Faculties* (Lincoln, Nebraska: University of Nebraska Press)

Readings, B. (1996), *The University in Ruins* (Cambridge, Massachusetts: Harvard University Prfewss)

Rhodes, F.H. T. (2001), *The Creation of the Future. The Role of the American University.* (Ithaca: Cornell University Press)

Roberts, J.M. (1988), *The Pelican History of the World* (London: Penguin Books)

Rueegg, W. (gen. ed.) (1992), *A History of the University in Europe*, Vol. 1, Universities in the Middle Ages, de Ridder-Symoens, H. (ed.) (Cambridge: Cambridge University Press)

Rueegg, W. (gen. ed.) (1996), *A History of the University in Europe*, Vol. 2, Universities in Early Modern Europe (1500–1800), de Ridder-Symoens, H. (ed.) (Cambridge: Cambridge University Press)

Sassen, S. (1991), *The Global City: New York, London, and Toky*o (Princeton: Princeton University Press)

Sassen, S. (1994), *Cities in the World Economy* (Thousand Oaks, California: Pine Forge/Sage Publications)

Sassen, S. (1996), *Losing Control? Sovereignty in an Age of Globalization* (New York: Columbia University Press)

Sassen, S. (1998), G*lobalization and Its Discontents* (New York: The New Press)

Scherkenbach, W.W. (1991), *The Deming Route to Quality and Productivity* (Rockville, Maryland: Mercury Press)

Siraisi, N. (1992), 'The faculty of medicine', in Rueegg, W. (gen. ed.) & de Ridder-Symoens , H. (ed.), *A History of the University in Europe*, Vol. 1., Universities in the Middle Ages (Cambridge: Cambridge University Press)

Smith, A. (1976 [1776]), A*n Inquiry into the Nature and the Causes of the Wealth of Nations* (Chicago: University of Chicago Pres)

Taylor, Frederick Winslow. 1911. The Principles of Scientific Management. New York: Norton.

Turner, W. (1908), 'Schools', *The Catholic Encyclopedia*, Vol. XI (New York: Robert Appleton Company), online edition 1999, URL: <http://www.newadvent.org/cathen/13554b.htm> (accessed: April 14, 2002)

Verger, J. (1992), 'Patterns', in Rueegg, W. (gen. ed.) & de Ridder-Symoens , H. (ed.), *A History of the University in Europe*, Vol. 1., Universities in the Middle Ages (Cambridge: Cambridge University Press)

Veysey, L.R., (1965), *The Emergence of the American University* (Chicago: University of Chicago Press)

Walton, M., (1989), *The Deming Management Method* (London: Mercury Books)

Biographical note

Ken Friedman is Associate Professor of Leadership and Strategic Design at the Norwegian School of Management and Visiting Professor at the Advanced Research Institute of the Staffordshire University School of Art and Design.

3 Curricula of collaboration: educating postgraduate students for the workplace

Teal Triggs

Faculty of Art, Design & Music, Kingston University, UK

Abstract

The intent of this paper is to explore the ways in which postgraduate curricula might be developed in order to facilitate students' understanding of and preparation for entry into graphic design practice. As industry grapples with increasingly complex design and communication problems, a new type of design studio has emerged based on a multidisciplinary framework. As such, we must ask how educational curricula might be designed to meet these new demands. Central to this is the engagement with relevant theoretical concepts and research processes (including analysis, synthesis and reflective practice). Equally, graduates must have the skills to transform strategies and concepts successfully into practical design solutions. Curricula must enable students to develop collaboration skills, as the expertise brought to any collaboration not only contributes to the group experience but also feeds back into their own specialist area.

Introduction

In the spring of 2002, the American Institute of Graphic Arts (AIGA) held their biennial national conference in Washington, DC. The title of the conference was 'Voice 2: More Than Ever' and a range of speakers demonstrated the way, according to the AIGA press release that, 'design is a necessary element of the voice of a society'. Organisers stated their intent was to provide designers with 'tools for instigating change and new ways of thinking about our roles as communicators, authors and agitators within society' (AIGA, 2002, p.1). The conference successfully provided a forum for discussions including those debates initiated a few years ago around global branding and consumer culture – many of which had emerged out of the publication of Naomi Klein's book, *No Logo* and *Adbusters*' revised version of Ken Garland's *First Things First* (2000) manifesto[1]. Equal attention was given to the debates around design for the public realm as so poignantly raised by Florida's Palm Beach voting ballots, which threw into question America's most recent presidential elections. There is no doubt that graphic designers have a heightened sense of social consciousness and indeed the AIGA's President, Clement Mok was inspired to ask designers and educators to join him in a 'call to action'. He observed 'The role and practice of design are at a crossroads; designers can either sit back and watch or become the hub of decision-making and critical discourse.' Mok continued cajoling, 'We have new responsibilities and new opportunities in shaping the character, values and sensibilities of an increasingly complex, diverse and fragmented nation. It will not be easy, but it will be infinitely rewarding' (AIGA, 2002, p. 3).

Mok's words resonate even more in the wake of the tragic events of September 11th. However, it must be noted that for many designers, concerns about the profession's immediate future preceded this period. The downfall of the highly profitable dot.com industry, for example, had already prompted a drastic review of how design studios operated and what strategies, such as diversification of a client-base, might be more suitable for economic survival. On the other hand, with the development of increasingly complex communication problems, designers have also been exploring new ways of working as a formal strategy, in order to facilitate development of more appropriate design solutions.

At the same time, the development of multidisciplinary design studios, are increasingly becoming the structural norm. Possible models for the way in which graphic designers form collaborative teams are offered up by groups such as Interbrand, Imagination and Bruce Mau Design. By drawing from a wide range of disciplines, these types of studio environments challenge the conventions of design practice and therefore, require a new type of designer who can 'free think across boundaries and naturally cross territories' (Davies, 2001, p. 116).

In this way, designers (and ultimately design students) are encouraged to develop a set of broader intellectual tools, which more readily allow them to adapt to whatever changes they encounter. The main question is to ask how educators might devise curricula at postgraduate level that begin to address the concerns of the design profession, without compromising the academic and vocational goals of students and their institutions. Within the art and design sector, a number of undergraduate programmes already have well-established links with the design profession and its related industries (such as work placement programmes, professional practice modules, and so forth). However, it may be argued that this issue of interdisciplinarity is perhaps best addressed at postgraduate level. MA and MA by research degrees, where students have already completed a specialist first degree or obtained relevant work experience, are where the real focus on industry requirements can be explored and where intellectual boundaries can be widened in the pursuit of 'free-thinking'.

Defining terms and their context

One way forward, has been to foster a better understanding and use of multidisciplinary teams and interdisciplinary research. For the purposes of this paper 'multidisciplinary' may be defined as 'a combination of disciplines coming together in collaboration for the achievement of a task'. Such a combination of specialist disciplines should operate in a reciprocal relationship. However, Julie Klein in her book *Interdisciplinarity: History, Theory & Practice*, argues that multidisciplinary activities are *additive* not *integrative*. Often, this aspect is seen in undergraduate curricula where courses struggle to achieve a balance between the teaching of a subject specialism and generalist knowledge base (Klein, 1990, p. 56). In this case, undergraduate programmes are only able to introduce opportunities for collaboration. This may be through activities, which enhance team-working skills or through the development of 'one-off' cross-discipline projects. Rarely though, does time allow for students to achieve any synthesis of their learning. Klein suggests that the process of synthesising knowledge might be developed where 'the creation of courses focused on interdisciplinary topics'. However, she warns us that this requires a greater understanding of the 'epistemologies and methodologies of other disciplines' (Klein, 1990, p. 57).

For the British-based design group Imagination, multidiscplinarity is key for such projects as 'Journey', a designated area within the Millennium Dome, telling the story of transportation. And, more recently, the Guinness Storehouse in Dublin, which is a conversion of a six-storey former brewing facility into a brand experience for Guinness, comprising an exhibition, public bars and a staff training area. For such large-scale projects a multidisciplinary team may be comprised of specialists drawn from the fields of typography, information design, psychology, fine art, 'experience' design and architecture. Imagination's Adrian Caddy, suggests the challenge is in the process of 'organising the input of ideas from all the players in a manner which optimises their talents, within a time frame and which sees a proper commercial return' (Caddy, 2002).

Interdisciplinary research, on the other hand, is by definition integrative and is the vehicle or framework used to carry out multidisciplinary work. *Crossdisciplinary* is another term, which is frequently used, but suggests working across disciplines rather than integratively. On the other hand, *transdisciplinary* has come to represent a breaking down of discipline-specific barriers in order to 'focus on a concept, theory, or method that can be applied across disciplines' (Klein, 1990, p. 66 and Lattuca, 2001, p. 92). For the discipline of graphic design, it is useful to appropriate as a framework for exploration *interdisciplinary research*, drawing on the theoretical and methodological frameworks of other fields in order to present suitable and often innovative approaches to problem solving.

While undergraduate design education has been inextricably linked to a professional or vocational model, postgraduate design education has an opportunity to examine design in context. This approach is reinforced by a number of designer/educators including Gunnar Swanson who proposes that design should become the 'liberal art for the next century'. He believes that 'the (graphic) design field is unique in that it does not possess singular subject matter. It is by definition, interdisciplinary' (Bush in Rock, 1995, p. 23). Swanson continues this argument in 'Is Design Important?', where he observes that 'design is at an intellectual crossroads where anthropology meets communication studies, art meets marketing, and cognitive psychology meets business.' Swanson advocates that design should adopt a framework, which is provided by any liberal arts programmes, and 'centres on subjects that involve integration of the traditional areas of knowledge.' By broadening out and away from the 'narrow concerns' of vocational training, Swanson argues that what is needed today is a 'general education focusing on the issues of design – form and meaning, vision and understanding …' (Swanson, 1995, p. 5). Graphic design education offers a place where industrial practices are able to integrate a range of new paradigms.

For professional practice, this is not necessarily a new approach. Industrial designers in the 1930s such as Raymond Lowey and the offices of Charles and Ray Eames a decade later, pulled together teams of sculptors, inventors, craftsmen, engineers, psychologists as well as industrial designers in order to realise their products. J. Gordon Lippincott, an engineer, outlined in his seminal book, *Design for Business* in 1947, the need for collaborations within the design profession, arguing that it was important for an industrial designer 'to be an artist, engineer, diplomat, salesman and philosopher.' However, Lippincott also believed that such a combination had to exist '... all in one personality' and was a keen supporter of a primarily vocational curriculum where students learned skills related to art, engineering, marketing, and humanities. (During this period, humanities was understood as the study of lifestyle and consumer appeal.) Equally, Lippincott believed that stronger links between industry and education were essential and surprisingly dedicated a whole chapter in his book to this subject. He reflected, 'when industry realises this fact and contributes its "know how", as well as its wealth, in guiding industrial design education, a new and even more prolific era of design will be born' (Lippincott, 1947, p. 205). J. Gordon Lippincott also argued, that it was important to for the 'American business man' to understand that 'sound education is long-range planning' (Lippincott, 1947, p. 202). Lippincott may have been writing over fifty years ago, but his message still resonates today. The industrial design profession has long recognised the benefits of educational collaboration in the same way it supports the belief that good design equals good business. Whereas for graphic design, industry believes that good design equals good marketing in terms of 'what yields profits' (Glaser, 1995, pp. 48–50). It might be argued that only now is the graphic design profession taking full advantage of collaborations, which draw upon varied knowledge bases, methods and design strategies.

Graphic design and its context

Graphic design generally has suffered from its youthful existence as a design profession, as well as the lack of understanding amongst the general public and a lack of recognition by many institutions as a bona fide academic discipline.[2] The way the profession has developed historically has also impacted the way in which graphic designers have been trained to meet contemporary needs of industry. Graphic design was once defined by the differentiation between the activity of problem solving, and that of making. In this case, making as defined by the production stages of printed communication in typesetting and printing. Andrew Blauvelt, who until recently taught at North Carolina State University, writes that 'the advent of desktop publishing fostered the reintegration of tasks (whether for better or worse), collapsing the distinct activities of designer, typesetter and printer' (Blauvelt, 1995, p. 17). Contemporaneously, the boundaries between graphic design and other disciplines have become blurred with the introduction of the computer and the opportunities for design within the digital realm. Hans van Dijk comments in 'Divergence and Convergence in the Age of Bits', that 'the introduction of the computer not only in industry, but especially in the educational process has unwittingly created a possibility or rather a necessity for convergence-designing across media' (van Dijk, 1995, p. 18).

New collaborations have emerged by necessity with the intricacies of 'new' digital technologies as well as the complexities of communication problems. Graphic designers frequently align themselves with software designers, computer programmers and interface designers. As the field of new media develops, Lauralee Alben and Jim Faris, employ the metaphor of dance to illustrate the way in which designers should take up the opportunity for developing potential partners. In 1994, they wrote in the first issue of Interact, the American Center for Design journal, that multimedia is an 'interdisciplinary dance'. This dance they argue, 'will evolve in response to the needs, concerns and opportunities of the day…our challenge is to use technology and design to empower people, and to do this collaboratively, in dance with one another.' Fittingly, Alben and Faris extend the notion of collaboration to also acknowledge that between the graphic designer and end user[3] (Alben & Faris, 1994, p.17).

Graphic design curricula, both at undergraduate and postgraduate levels, must provide opportunities where students may work collaboratively whether it is through opportunities to work in multidisciplinary teams, develop interdisciplinary research or to collaborate and 'test' ideas with end users. However, this has not always been the case. The educator and design writer, Lorraine Wild cautions us that many graphic design curricula typically base their training 'on designers maintaining their specific identity as the originators, "authors" or controllers of visual ideas' (Wild, in Heller, 1998, p. 40). This has been underscored recently by debates within the profession focussing on the place of graphic authorship within design, the development of technical skill bases, the relationship between craft and generalist knowledge, and the way in which theory informs practice. Regardless, the goal of educators should be to develop students' understanding of the collaborative process by which each member of the team contributing to the overall design process. Designers and collaborators must recognise that this is potentially a reciprocal activity where the specialist receives something back in return, such as new knowledge into the process of research and development or even client negotiation and team working skills. In any case, the value of such collaborations will last well beyond the capabilities of the technology itself.

Curricula of collaboration at postgraduate level

There are three types of collaboration that we might consider for inclusion in postgraduate curricula for graphic design. Firstly, that which takes place within the profession in the development of *multidisciplinary teams* in order to solve increasingly complex communication problems. Secondly, in an educational context where students engage with what might be termed 'learning teams', comprising an appropriate range of specialists. Obviously, where faculties are already multidisciplinary in scope, this activity may be easier to implement within an existing academic environment. Yet, it is through such collaborations where progress in developing *interdisciplinary research* might be fully realised. And, finally a *professional collaboration* fostered between industry, the design profession and academic institutions in order to fully develop and enhance students' learning experience. This potentially would foster longer-term relationships for students and collaborators as well as create a dynamic transition for students graduating and entering professional practice.

Harold Pardue and Catherine Ishino present their views on undergraduate collaborations for students in the field of interface design in a paper titled 'Interdisciplinary Interface Design: A Cross-cultural Experience' (Pardue & Ishino, 2000). Here, they explore what they believe is a 'fundamental and vital *relationship*' between the fields of Management Information Systems (MIS) and Graphic Design. Pardue and Ishino argue that the focus is not necessarily on the principles and practices of one discipline as could be useful to the other, but the discovery of fundamental and integrative relationships, which might exist between disciplines that could inform the application of those principles and practices (Pardue & Ishino, 2000). I would like to propose a similar approach in the development of graphic design curricula for postgraduate level and extend it to also include the integrative relationship between fields of experiences often designated as external to the academic institution, such as social, cultural and political forces. These should be integral to postgraduate learning positioning the field into a wider intellectual context. As the focus of graphic design broadens so too will the importance of putting in a claim for interdisciplinary study and research. Richard Buchanan writes in *Design Issues* that, 'design integrates knowledge from many other disciplines and makes that knowledge effective in practical life' (Buchanan, 1998, p. 66). This may mean the integration of critical frameworks from areas such as linguists, semiotics, anthropology, sociology and psychology.

Another consideration is the rethinking of the relationship between theory and practice. And, this relationship must also be extended to include the disciplines of history and theory as a form of design practice (Blauvelt, 1995, p. 17). Jan van Toorn, Visiting Professor at Rhode Island School of Design, writes in *Visual Communication*, 'both education and practical and academic research are the places where we should learn how to produce in the tension between the often pessimistic outcome of critical thinking and the optimistic delights of making' (McCoy, Triggs & van Toorn, 2002). We are only beginning to discover the way forward in terms of a pedagogical approach for graphic design, exploring areas where there should be an 'investment in a mentality that combines usefulness with the speculative character that is inherent to communication' (McCoy, Triggs & van Toorn, 2002).

There is a correlation to be made between the 'doer' who might reflect the group of designers who happily reinforce a hegemonic norm, while the 'makers' are those 'critical thinkers' who constantly question an existing social and cultural order. At the moment, it may be suggested that designers as 'doers' are operating on a formal and primarily aesthetic level. What actually might be required is a call for a different form of engagement in which content and meaning are central as a means of opening up a dialogical relationship with an audience. In this way, designers are asked to take on a more active role in establishing an 'open relationship', in a public sphere, which invites an argument rather than a passive reception of information (McCoy, Triggs & van Toorn, 2002). This potentially provides us with another opportunity for an effective collaboration. But one question must still be raised. How might this process be made more explicit and as a result, form a 'kit of parts' for students and designers to be more effective as critical mediators of information and as socio-communicators?

Postgraduate learning

Students enrol on postgraduate programmes for a variety of reasons ranging from an interest in deepening and focusing their knowledge of a subject to re-training for a new career to the enhancement of teaching qualifications. It may also be a result of personal development, where a professional is returning to education in order to re-examine his/her approach. The 'MAness' to such an experience is in the broadening of understanding and the critical reflection of the student on the process of research and making or theory and practice. Graphic design, like most postgraduate curricula should foster 'problem-seeking initiatives' as well as 'problem-posing inquiries'. This would allow for multiple solutions to be found rather than a single and often predictable one (Blauvelt, 1995, p. 16). Such types of solutions might also be encouraged through the process of interdisciplinary research.

Typo/graphic studies: examples of collaborations

Before we conclude, I would like to present three examples of collaboration of which I have had some involvement. They span the last three years, two different types of institutions and one educational activist group-initiated project.

The first example is from the curriculum developed for the MA Typo/graphic studies programme at the London College of Printing, exploring the opportunities provided by professional practice. The second example arises out of recent work undertaken within the Faculty of Art, Design & Music at Kingston University for the development of a cluster-based approach to postgraduate interdisciplinary research. And finally, the third example is a Web site project devised in collaboration between the Women's Design + Research Unit (WD+RU), design students and design professionals internationally.

In 1988, the graphic design educator Jim Bodoh, observed that like most courses in art and design, postgraduate graphic design programmes provided students with two kinds of learning activities. Firstly, structured learning activities, which involved '...the whole group in seminars, lectures, short courses, set projects' and secondly, independent study where students developed their own briefs related to the discipline of graphic design specifying 'complex communication problems' (Bodoh, 1988. p. 48). This last activity included working in collaboration with an outside organisation where the student was involved formally as part of a multidisciplinary team set up within the organisation itself or instead, less formally where project research was enhanced by using organisations as supporting case studies or as industrial advisors (Bodoh, 1988. p. 48).

The MA and professional practice

A decade later, the MA Typo/graphic Studies programme at the London College of Printing, set out with a similar learning commitment, to develop a curriculum of collaboration which encouraged groups of students to work together on projects as well as to develop collaborative links with professional practice and related industry. The main intent of the course was to investigate relationships – the spaces where ideas and practices collided. It looked closely at what might exist in between related disciplines and how these approaches might be applied to typo/graphic design. How does an architect, for example, describe void? How does a composer develop a graphic language for a musical score? How might a dancer or painter use form and gesture to communicate? Where does old and new technology come into play? Equally, the curriculum was about how different social, political and cultural considerations might influence design more globally.

An international advisory board of design practitioners and educators was established whose advice on current practice meant tutors could be responsive to the demands and interests of the profession. However, the collaboration was also designed to be reciprocal in nature, where students and tutors met with advisors annually to discuss ways in which their experiences might inform the development of new methods and strategies for design practice. Appropriate collaborations were also fostered with designers in professional practice or within related industry in the early stages of student research projects. These collaborations were not to be seen as work placements in the sense in which many undergraduate programmes provide their students with opportunities for industrial experience. Instead, this opportunity was viewed as a professional collaboration between student and design professionals (and with industry), in order to inform fully the formation and development of a final major project which was assessed through a written and visual outcome.

One of the successful professional collaborations took place between one of the MA students from Lebanon, Nadim Matta, and the studio of Mourad Boutros, whose principal is an internationally recognised Arabic typeface designer. Nadim's major project proposal was to examine the way in which his country, and in particular the city of Beirut, was undergoing a major process of reconstruction and how graphic designers could facilitate this. He was interested in the space in which East meets West and where the old Arab lifestyle melted into a new Western form of innovation. He was also interested in the ways in which the city also reflects the on-going clash between Arab and Western perceptions of politics and culture.

Three years after graduation, Nadim reflects on the collaborative process, 'During my industrial collaboration with Mourad, he helped me to formulate ideas about the cultural aspects regarding Arabic type; the different developmental stages and the difficulties that type developments in the Arab world have faced throughout history' (Matta, 2002). The collaboration did not end with the course. Nadim's MA thesis project and early discussions led to the development of an award-winning, Arabic typeface, Boutros 'Ahlam'(dreams), which he named as a tribute to his collaborator and mentor. The typeface is created primarily for display purposes and is inspired by the organic shapes of the flame of eternity, taking into account the traditions of NASKH, an Arabic script, and the contemporary demands of an emerging cultural force (Matta, 2002).

Interdisciplinary research methods and collaboration

This second example of collaboration is still in the early stages and concerns the development of a postgraduate interdisciplinary research methods programme for the Faculty of Art, Design & Music at Kingston University. With the validation of a new cluster of taught postgraduate programmes, the Faculty took the opportunity to review the existing research methods module for students enrolled on MA courses in Art and Space, Graphic Communication, Illustration and Animation, Screen Design for Film and Television, Production Design for Film and Television, History of Art, History of Design, Film Studies, Landscape and Urbanism, Curating Contemporary Design, and Drawing as Process.

The main aims of this module are to provide an opportunity for students within the Faculty's postgraduate modular programme to participate and contribute fully in an interdisciplinary programme of lectures, workshops, research presentations and seminars. Students are introduced to a range of research methods as well as a variety of research resources, which enable them in developing in depth their research and written skills. The module also provides a foundation for further independent as well as collaborative-based research. Delivery of the module is through a series of guest designers and theorists who encapsulate interdisciplinary practices in their own work. Small, mixed discipline seminars are also scheduled in order to enable students to continue to advance their own systematic understanding of knowledge through theory and research by engaging in discussions within an interdisciplinary context. In addition, students are introduced to more pragmatic skills to facilitate ways in which they might develop and apply research, engage with a research environment and management of their research.

The module is run by a team of four tutors and includes a creative writer who has worked extensively in film and radio collaborating with some of the UK's best-known fine artists, a journalist and cultural critic, a design historian who specialises in product and interior design, and a design critic whose interest in theory and criticism has led to collaborations with design practitioners. The programme is supplemented by a series of guest lecturers, from a range of professional practices, who engage actively with the relationship between theory and practice. The speakers and the guest lectures are bringing to the programme their knowledge of industry, other educational programmes as well as their respective professions into the classroom. Even at postgraduate level this is essential. There is an element of the 'real world' provided so that academia is not hermetically sealed off from commerce and professionalism.

The programme, of course, supplements activities already taking place on their main courses, but which may not be framed in terms of research methods or theoretical positions. Areas that are addressed include methods of critique and strategies for analysing the visual and written forms of communication, the interpretation of documents and material culture, data collection through observation and interviewing, semiotics, art and design criticism, sound and the environment, argument and creativity as well as writing as thinking, and the more pragmatic engagement with information research, retrieval and databases. Students are asked to present aspects of their own research and practice to colleagues in small seminar groups and herein lay the potential for developing not only multidisciplinary collaborations but, also interdisciplinary research. In this way students share and exchange information on specialist subjects but also bring to the group different cultural and professional perspectives. They are also encouraged to use these discussions as part of a research process, eventually synthesising the exchange into their final essay assignment. The module intent is to establish a framework in order to facilitate student learning into the exploration of the potential of collaborative relationships between different and/or related disciplines. In this way students are prompted to explore fundamental strategies, principles and practices which could be introduced and developed in their own work.

Conclusion

At the beginning of this paper, it was suggested that there are debates taking place on issue of social responsibility in graphic design. The last collaboration to mention is a Web site project developed by the Women's Design + Research Unit (WD+RU). The Web site is called www.deskwithdrawers.org and is an extension of other collaborative projects developed by WD+RU intended to raise awareness about current debates within the profession and related educational contexts. In this case, the Web site was created to highlight issues of design and social responsibility, design and sustainability, as well as business and ethical practices in design. In general deskwithdrawers seeks to:

- encourage students and professionals to be proactive and responsible designers;
- aid them in understanding the ways in which they can effect change;
- educate students about ways in which they may be involved in shaping the profession; and
- encourage networking with design professionals and active involvement within the professional organisations.

Deskwithdrawers is a collaborative venture between educators and designers, which profiles a variety of professional and student projects. These range from promoting the identity of local communities in New York City to reclaiming design for the domestic sphere and to the design of information graphics for land mine warnings. In addition, users are encouraged to contribute to the debates using the Web space as a forum for furthering ideas about education and professional responsibility.

By creating a Web site, WD+RU has begun to facilitate an international dialogue as one means of addressing social and political concerns encountered by designers and students alike. This is one way of introducing ideas and collaborative possibilities to students at undergraduate as well as the postgraduate level. Although the site itself is not currently part of any formal design curriculum, it does present an additional discursive and potentially collaborative forum. And in this way, it points to possible ways forward in the development of a more interactive postgraduate curricula for graphic design.

Notes

[1] The revised First Things First manifesto has generated spirited debates amongst the graphic design community. This is witnessed by countless letters published in the international design press and from over 1,650 signators of support found on the *Adbuster's* Web site.

[2] Despite the early efforts of Neville Brody and Jon Wozencroft whose analysis of the typeface Helvetica made the front pages of the review section of *the Guardian* in the mid-1980s, it wasn't until 2002 that the term 'graphic designer' was consciously used by *the Guardian* newspaper in order to identify the profession of an Israeli who was quoted on his views of the recent outbreak of violence in the Middle East.

[3] Even the analogy is extended to the article itself which uses the images of square dancing feet, with type copy-fitted neatly into the shape in order to rhythmically make their way though the ten pages of the journal. However, this is an example where authors and designers were unable to collaborate. In the 'authors' note', Alben and Faris object to the layout stating, 'We believe that a more collaborative approach to the designing of this article would have produced a result which would have been more agreeable to all of those involved, especially the readers' (Alben & Faris, 1994, p. 8).

References

AIGA (2001), *Voice: AIGA National Design Conference Program of Events*, Sept. 23–26, Washington DC

Alben, L. & Faris, J. (1994), 'The interdisciplinary dance (shall we?)', in Spreenberg, T. (ed), *Interact*, Issue 1 (Chicago: American Center for Design)

Blauvelt, A. and Davis, M. (1995), 'Blending bridges: a research agenda for education and practice', *AIGA Journal of Graphic Design*, Vol. 13, No, 1. pp. 14–16

Bodoh, J. (1988), 'Research, taught courses and industry', in Bougourd, J., Evans, S. & Gronberg, T. (eds.), *The Matrix of Research in Art and Design Education* (London: The London Institute and Council for National Academic Awards)

Buchanan, R. (1998), 'Education and professional practice in design', *Design Issues*, Vol. XIV, No. 2, Summer, pp. 63–66

Caddy, A. (2002), email interview with author, 18th January, 2002

Davies, M. (2001), 'A multi-disciplinary company', in Foges, C. (ed.), *Imagination* (London: Phaidon Press Ltd)

Glaser, M. (1995), 'Design and business – the war is over', AIGA *Journal of Graphic Design: The Outsiders Issue*, Vol. 13 , No. 2. pp. 48–50

Klein , J. Thompson (1990), *Interdisciplinarity: History, Theory & Practice* (Detroit: Wayne State University Press)

Lattuca , L.R. (2001), *Creating Interdisciplinarity: Interdisciplinary Research and Teaching Among College and University Faculty* (Nashville: Vanderbilt University Press)

Lippincott, J.G. (1947), *Design for Business* (Chicago: Paul Theobald)

McCoy, K. and Teal, T. & van Toorn, J. (2002), 'Undiscovered delights', *Visual Communication*, Vol. 1, No. 3 (London: Sage Publishers)

Matta, N. (2002), email interview with author, Saturday 6th April, 2002

Pardue , H. & Catherine Ishino (2000), 'Interdisciplinary interface design: a cross-cultural experience', unpublished conference paper

Rock, M. (1995), 'Talking design: educators talk about education', *AIGA Journal of Graphic Design: The Education Issue*, Vol. 13, No. 1. pp. 22–27

Swanson, Gunnar (1995), 'Is design important?', *AIGA Journal of Graphic Design: The Education Issue*, Vol. 13, No. 1. pp. 4–5

van Dijk, H. (1995), 'Divergence and convergence in the age of bits', *AIGA Journal of Graphic Design: The Education Issue*, Vol. 13, No. 1. pp. 18–20

Biographical note

Teal Triggs is Director of Postgraduate Studies, Faculty of Art, Design & Music, Kingston University. She has lectured widely and her writings on graphic design, typography, education and feminism have appeared in numerous design publications and books internationally. She is co-editor of the interdisciplinary journal Visual Communication (Sage Publications Ltd.) and has edited several books including as co-editor with Roger Sabin of 'Below Critical Radar': Fanzines and Alternative Comics from 1976 to Now (2000). She is currently working on a new book on experimental typography for Thames & Hudson. As co-founder of the Women's Design + Research Unit (WD+RU), she has contributed to the experimental typeface Pussy Galore (FUSE 12), a Web site on social responsibility in design (www.deskwithdrawers.org) and 'A WD+RU Broadcast', a short documentary film on women working in the graphic design profession. Teal is a signator of the First Things First Manifesto 2000 and a Fellow of the International Society of Typographic Designers.

papers

Enhancing Curricula:

exploring effective curriculum practices in art, design and communication in Higher Education

4 Emotions in the design studio

Noam Austerlits and Iris Aravot

Faculty of Architecture and Town Planning, Technion, Israel Institute of Technology, Israel

Abstract

This paper presents the preliminary stage of an ongoing research into the emotional aspects of the educational process, which take place in the design studio. It is assumed that because of the unique characteristics of the studio pedagogy and the meaningful student-instructor relationship, the studio has high potential for being emotionally saturated. This theoretical assumption has been followed by empirical research, examining the role of affective phenomena and particularly emotional episodes, through open interviews with instructors and students. Classification and analysis of the data enabled us to distinguish between affective phenomena and to offer interpretation for the described episodes. It is asserted that, although the variables of emotional episodes may differ from one person to another, it is possible to identify some common patterns conforming to the 'logic' of emotions. This preliminary stage of the research demonstrates that emotional episodes are researchable and that using systematic analysis put studio occurrences in a new perspective.

Introduction

The work described in this paper addresses the virtually disregarded subject of emotional phenomena connected with the educational process of architects, designers and artists. It concentrates on experiences in the design studio, since it is there that the process of becoming a design practitioner takes place. Since education is a mental process that involves both intellectual and affective functioning, it is imperative to understand better the role and mechanisms of both operational modes. While serving today as studio instructors and researchers, the writers have become more aware of emotional occurrences in the studio, in particular as regards student-instructor relationship. Therefore, a preliminary research of these aspects should examine how students and instructors experience studio occurrences and the roles that emotions play in the educational process.

Why should we look at affective phenomena in the design studio?

Sir Edmond Hillary replied when asked about the reason for climbing Mt. Everest, 'Because its there'. The question above can be answered shortly in the same way. How do we know affective phenomena 'are there'?

First by reflecting on our personal experiences as teachers of architectural design in the present as well as of architecture students in the past. This personal experience contains a variety of emotional memories such as gratitude for constructive guidance, fear of failure in explaining oneself, and even disappointments, conflicts and embarrassments. These introspections were confirmed in discussions with colleagues as well as re-appraisal of studies in architectural education.

The reason for this research is also based on the assumption that emotions, sentiments, feelings, moods etc. are normal, everyday phenomena. However, this assumption is not so obvious. Throughout the modern era affective phenomena have been considered as personal, or as a psychological disturbances that make no contribution to normal, productive, adult life (Oatley, 1992). This attitude of diminishment has caused researchers to neglect emotion research and it was left for the artist to deal with the subject. Recent decades have witnessed increasing interest in emotions and emotion research. Emotions have been examined through many approaches and perspectives. Studies have shown that emotions and emotional expression are universal phenomena essential to the survival of humans (Ekman, 1980), and that they are especially important in social functioning (Harr'e, 1986). Recent studies have tried to describe a 'logic of emotions', i.e. the typical patterns of emotional phenomena, their cause and function in everyday life (Ben-Ze'ev, 2000; De Sousa, 1987; Gardner,1983; Lazarus, 1991, 1994; Ortony et al,1988; Oatley & Jenkins, 1996; Rorty,1988). Ben-Ze'ev summarises these approaches to the nature and function of emotions as follows:

> Emotions occur when a change is appraised as relevant to our personal concerns... Emotions serve to monitor and safeguard our personal concerns, they give the eliciting event its significance.
> Ben-Ze'ev (2000, p. 18)

Such characterisations of emotions are related to the following concepts:

- emotions are an operational mode of human activity and therefore involve the entire human being, including appraisal, cognition, motivation bodily sensations etc.;
- emotions function to monitor changes in personal concern and are therefore spontaneous;
- since emotions have this important function they have to have a 'logical pattern' although it is different from that of the intellectual thought process; and
- the main concern of the emotions is the evaluated relationship between a person and his/her immediate environment, in particular the social environment.

Since emotions are everyday phenomena, it is obvious that they apply to educational situations including the studio. However, since the studio is somehow a distinct pedagogical method of higher education (Bennett, 1988), it is assumed to have a higher potential for being emotionally saturated. Its distinctiveness drives mainly from the following characteristics:

- it involves experiential learning and reflective processes;
- it involves personal creative/design processes;
- both educational and creative processes are accompanied/guided by an instructor; and
- it involves exposure and self-disclosure.

These characteristics are assumed to influence the overall psychological/emotional situation of both instructors and students, particularly with regard to student-instructor relationship. A survey into existing research (Argirys, 1981; Beinart, 1981; Boyer & Mitgana, 1996 ; Crysler, 1995; Cuff, 1991; Dinham, 1987; Dutton, 1991; Goldschmidt, 1988; Quayle, 1985; Sachs, 1999; Schon, 1987; Simmonds, 1981; Wendler & Rogers, 1995), reveal that this relationship may comprise the following:

- ambiguity and uncertainty;
- co-operation and close student-instructor relationship;
- dynamic evaluation and criticism of the other person involved; and
- dynamic changes in self-esteem.

Emotion is characterised above as a human mental mode that monitors changes. Emotion can also be seen as: '... part solution to problems of organising knowledge and action in a world that is imperfectly known and in which we have limited resources' (Oatley, 1992:3).

The aforementioned characteristics of the studio indicate that it may be an extreme kind of 'imperfectly known' situation and full of surprising changes. As a result, it is assumed that students and instructors may experience a high level of cognitive stress and a tendency to emotionality.

Emotions in the studio may be aroused by:

- the challenge of dealing with creative assignments (Averill, & Nunley, 1992) and 'wicked problems' (Buchanan, 1992);
- the challenge of experiential learning and teaching and the never-ending reconstruction of practical knowledge, concepts, beliefs etc. (Kolb, 1984);
- changes (actual or potential) in the position of the agents involved in an event ('survival' issues);
- changes in self-esteem, professional identification, social evaluation, comparisons with others etc.;
- the relationship between students (Ashton, 2001); and
- student-instructor relationship (expectations, behaviour, judgement, etc.).

These hypotheses have led us to look for valid, relevant information on emotional phenomena in the context of the design studio.

A study of affective phenomena through open interviews

A survey of contemporary studies into design education indicates that the subject of affective phenomena has been tackled relatively infrequently within the area of design studio research. Hence, empirical research to supply some information on these phenomena was required. Since the aim of the research was to describe the role and related meaning of such phenomena, as seen by its participants, the following research goals were set:

- to gather specific, first-hand, qualitative information, using empirical research that concentrated on the experiences of students and instructors in the design studio;

- to classify and analyse the empirical data, using categories obtained from existing studies into emotions; and
- to interpret specific described episodes.

This research offers new perspectives on areas of architectural education, but shows no preference for any single aspect of the emotional parameters of the studio. Lack of valid information from the studio itself induced us to conduct research that was aimed to gather specific, first-hand, qualitative information on affective phenomena as experienced by students and instructors. Emotions are hidden psychological processes, only partially known to those who experience them. However, it is essential to this research to obtain the very subjective knowledge of people about their own emotional experiences. It is asserted that this is the most valuable information, since it reflects the way reality is recognised and perceived by the interviewees. Following this approach, preliminary evidence about affective phenomena in the design studio was collected by means of open interviews with students and instructors from the Faculty of Architecture and Town Planning at the Technion (Israel Institute of Technology), during 1999–2000.

The interviews took the form of free discussions, influenced mainly by memories and associations of the interviewees. Their purpose was to expose as wide a range of affective phenomena as possible. Seventeen students and instructors were interviewed, comprising nine students and seven instructors, and the same seven instructors were also interviewed about their experiences as students.

Analysis and interpretation of interviews

The immediate result of the interviews was a wealth of impressions, memories, general attitudes etc. concerning affective phenomena related to the studio. Interviewees shared various kinds of information, often a mixture of attitudes, memories and ideas on the subject. Therefore the first analysis classified the diversified data into four categories:

- *General attitudes towards the student-instructor relationship*: for example, an instructor describes the nature of his relationship with his students:

  This is something special and sacred. We are both human beings and we do not relinquish our personality or character. There are irritating situations, so I become angry. A teacher should not be nice, he should be himself.

  Or a student reports that:

  In the early stages the relationship (with the instructor) is of accepted dictatorship ... you have to accept the instructor's opinion even if you do not agree.

- *Confirmation of the effects of affective phenomena on the educational process*: an instructor reports:

  Of course, there are those who feel that I like them and appreciate them and they like me and appreciate me. It is very pleasant having conversations with them. But there are also situations in which I feel I can't help the students. This is frustrating.

  A 4th-year student reports:

  You feel respect or anger. Both result from a situation where you are weaker. The instructor gives the mark at the end. At first you attribute to him the authority of knowledge, but later the authority is just official. Still, good criticism makes you feel good ... It is pleasant. Your confidence rises sky-high. You feel like a genius, a king, you can do anything ... But at the next meeting, you may receive deadly criticism, and then you crash.

  A 2nd-year student reflecting on his memories as a freshman said:

  I was in a bad psychological state, the studio was 80% of my life, and when someone (the instructor) keeps saying 'go on, go on' it's as if you were a rolling ball. I was in a deep depression.

Another 2nd-year student's emotional attitude was:

> I don't want to hear the instructor's idea (for the design) because it is fun to discover by yourself ... If someone says do this and do that, it embitters me.

- *Descriptions of specific emotional episodes or sentiments in the studio*: for example, an instructor reports:

> I had no patience with her. I had to take a deep breath before sitting with her and after the 'desk crit' I had to go out to refresh myself. It was very difficult.

A 4th-year student reports:

> I had once an instructor who said my project was stupid and dumb. I do not think he intended to be insulting, but I burst into tears. I was shocked. I waited for the crit to end, then I stood aside and cried, and all my friends came to comfort me.

- *Information concerning other affective occurrences within the studio*: for example, an instructor confesses that:

> I am very possessive...I tend to 'fall in love' with my students.

The content analysis of the transcripts confirmed some of our hypothetical assumptions, but it also evoked new questions such as:

- How should affective phenomena be classified?
- How should emotions be identified?
- What is the mechanism of emotional episodes?
- How should these episodes be interpreted?

Efforts have thus been directed towards locating a theoretical model of emotions that could serve as a basis for further analysis and interpretation of the content of the interviews.

In order to analyse affective behaviour in the studio we use the conceptual framework proposed by Ben-Ze'ev (2000, Ch. 4), which enables distinguishing between different phenomena within the affective realm according to two criteria:

- the occurrent or dispositional nature of the given phenomena (i.e. actual or potential); and
- intentionality (i.e. the degree of specificity of the intentional object of the phenomena).

While moods, affective traits and emotional disorders are generally continuous, potential and less intense phenomena, which have general intentionality, emotions and sentiments are intense phenomena which generally have an intentional object. Since the main interest of this research is the phenomena related to studio occurrences, it seems that intentional phenomena have higher relevancy (it can be assumed that emotional traits, for example, do not evolve from studio events, while true emotional episodes such as gratitude or anger do). Hence, at this stage of the research, it was decided to focus on analysing intentional phenomena, i.e. interviewees' descriptions of episodes containing emotions and sentiments.

Emotional episode analysis

Despite its uniqueness, there is no reason to assume that the studio is anything but a normal situation, necessarily involving the psychological mechanisms and the general logic of emotional activity. Therefore, in our analysis of emotional episodes in the studio, we refer to issues from the general framework proposed by Ben-Ze'ev as well as to descriptions of specific emotions generated in the particular episode under discussion. The following analytical features were found to be particularly relevant to our purposes:

- classification and interpretation of the described emotions;
- description of the cause of the emotional episodes (i.e. what was the significant change that elicited the emotional reaction?);

- description of the object and focus of concern of the subject experiencing the emotion; and
- analysing the variables of emotional intensity according to the following categories:

    i. the strength of the event;
    ii. the event's degree of reality;
    iii. the relevance to the agent's self-image and attaining goals;
    iv. the agent's controllability (accountability) for the emotional change;
    v. the agent's readiness for the change; and
    vi. the agent's 'deservingness', i.e. whether the agent has merited the emotional change.

The first four variables are positively (though not linearly) correlated with emotional intensity, and the fifth variable is negatively correlated with emotional intensity. Merit is related to emotional intensity in a more complex manner, but unmerited situations are typically more emotionally intense.

The analysis also refers to two other aspects of the described event, concerning:

- the effect on the participants; and
- observations on the pedagogical circumstances of the event.

The following example demonstrates that episode analysis enables three levels of interpretation:

- an accurate and concise description of the emotions involved in the episode and an interpretation of its cause and 'logic';
- an evaluation of the factors, which contributed to the emotional intensity of the described episode, which also enables to understand how one emotion predominated over other emotions; and

- a discussion of the effect and meaning of the emotion in its specific pedagogical context.

Anger and jealousy of a student (a student's memories of her sentiments in the 2nd year)

> When I was in my 2nd year, I had an instructor who really liked a project of one of the students in the studio and all the rest of us where pretty much 'unseen' by him. I was frustrated and I felt I wanted to strangle him, I really hated him (because) he showed his preferences and it was awful, it was very difficult for me.
>
> Q: The situation of not being appreciated?
>
> Yes. I had an excellent project and I got good grades, but the preferences he showed... I was not the only one. Other students were very angry with him...

- *Classification and interpretation*: a combination of two strong and continuing emotions/sentiments: one is the insult felt by the student (who is not a favourite of the instructor) which turns into anger/hate. The other emotion is the envy/jealousy of this student who feels that the instructor has abandoned her for another student. The student's psyche concentrates on the behaviour of the instructor (his unconcealed preferences) and therefore results in an overall negative appraisal of him.
- *The cause of the emotional event*: the behaviour of the instructor is evaluated as a negative change in the status of the student who is experiencing injustice and being unfairly hurt. The student also evaluates the instructor's behaviour throughout the semester as inappropriate.
- *Object and focus of concern*: the object and focus of jealousy and anger is the instructor and the object of envy is the favoured student.
- *Variables of emotional intensity*:
    - strength: the evaluated injustice is high – increased intensity;

- degree of actuality: high – increased intensity;
- relevance: high - events throughout the semester affected the student's self-esteem as well as her attitude towards the instructor - intensification;
- agent controllability (accountability): the student's accountability is low while the instructor's is high - intensified anger;
- agent's readiness for change: low - the instructor's behaviour deviates from the student's expectations - increasing intensity; and
- agent's 'deservingness': the student evaluates herself as being at least as good as the next guy, therefore the discrimination is unwarranted; the instructor's behaviour warrants condemnation and dislike.

All six variables increase emotional intensity.

- *Effect of the event*: the continuing devaluation and perceived unjustified attitude of the instructor created a growing anger which blinded the student and affected her overall attitude towards him and his pedagogy (his good grading, for example, did not have as much impact as his abandonment).
- *Pedagogical circumstances*: the pedagogical situation described in this case is of a studio in which the instructor is very dominant and his approval is very important to the student. This becomes a main issue, and the student may ultimately regard it as more important than the educational message. The student also expresses the underlying moral approach that instructors should relate all students equally.

Summary of results and qualitative observations

The initial result of each episode analysis is better understanding of the described episode as its components become clearer. Each analysis highlights the pedagogical circumstances of the event, interprets it, and suggests a logical explanation for the emotional reaction aroused. Examining the 43 analysed episodes (23 as described by instructors and 20 as described by students) as a whole enabled us to make some qualitative observations that can shed light on the nature of the emotional experience of the interviewees:

- in most of the described events negative emotion predominated (students: 15 out of 20; instructors: 18 out of 23);
- anger/insult (as a prime emotion) was the most frequently mentioned, both by students (in 7 out of 20 events) and by instructors (in 10 out of 23 events);
- most of the events contained more than one emotion; in some cases they were simultaneous, while in other cases an emotional sequence was apparent;
- the main causes of negative emotion arousal were criticism, direct confrontation, a sense of injustice and unfulfilled expectations;
- the main causes of positive emotion arousal were success in meeting a challenge and positive evaluation of others and/or their actions;
- the nature of architecture as a creative discipline and the constant demand of exposure, were mentioned by many interviewees as two of the main causes of increased emotional intensity. Many of them felt that they were being judged instead of their work;
- many of the described conflicts centred round the issue of accepting/rejecting the instructor's authority;
- some of the interviewees reported an evolution in their emotional reactions and the ability to handle emotional events; and

- the analysis indicates that the emotional intensity of the agent involved in a specific episode was mainly - affected by the following variables: the readiness for the event; the sense of controllability or accountability; the sense of deservingness.

The studio is a complex situation in which a variety of affective phenomena present. The research model enables classification of the different phenomena, as well as identification of specific emotions. Following this classification it was decided to concentrate on analysing specific and discrete emotional episodes to enable us to understand better the nature and logic of the described emotional reactions. These emotional reactions and their intensity vary in different educational situations within the studio, although there are indications that some emotional reactions are endemic to pedagogical situations in the studio.

The research indicates that both the cognitive and the social functions of the interviewees (students and instructors) were affected by the emotional dimensions of the student-instructor relationship. Interviewees reported at least two levels of effect: direct effect on mental activity itself, and overall effect on the student-instructor relationship which, in turn, affected the educational environment.

Conclusions

The studio is where students become practitioners of design through an exhausting process of learning, training and above all maturing and personal development. It is a challenging and exciting situation in which both student and instructor reconstruct their perceptions on design and of themselves as designers. This preliminary stage of an ongoing study has shown that emotions have a key role in constructing the meaning of studio occurrences and influence several aspects of the educational process (transference of knowledge, motivation, self-esteem, etc.). As a result, we can say more confidently that the emotions of studio participants play at least as important a role as their other cognitive processes. We also assert that, although the variables of emotional reaction may differ from one person to another, it is possible to identify some common patterns of its contribution to the educational process, conforming to the 'logic' of emotions. It is hoped that the systematic analysis and the suggested interpretation of the logical pattern of studio occurrences will be further developed in the following stages of the research. It is also hoped that the preliminary observations and conclusions would increase awareness about the involvement of emotions in the educational process and contribute to enhancing studio effectiveness, as well as creating a better educational environment.

References

Argyris, C. (1981), 'Teaching and learning in design settings', in Porter, W. L. & Kilbridge, M. (eds.), *Architecture Education Study*, Vol. 1 (Andrew W. Mellon Foundation)

Ashton, P. (2001), 'The social aspects of design learning: assessing the value of studio in undergraduate design education', in Swann, C. & Young, E. (ed.), *Re-inventing Design Education in the University* – proceedings of Perth international conference, 11-13 December 2001, Perth, W.A. : School of Design, Curtin University of Technology.

Averill, J.R. & Nunley, E.P. (1992), *Voyages of the Heart: Living an Emotionally Creative Life* (New York: Free Press)

Beinart, J. (1981), 'Structure of the content of design', in Porter, W. L. & Kilbridge, M. (eds.), *Architecture Education Study,* Vol. 1 (Andrew W. Mellon Foundation)

Bennett, R.D. (1988), 'Architectural education', in Wilkes, J.A. (ed.), *Encyclopedia of Architecture: Design, Engineering and Construction*, Vol. 4 (New York: John Wiley & Sons)

Ben-Ze'ev, A. (2000), *The Subtlety of Emotions* (Cambridge, MA: MIT Press)

Boyer, E.L. & Mitgang, L.D. (1996), '*Building Community: A New Future for Architectural Education and Practice*' (NJ: The Carnegie Foundation for the Advancement of Teaching)

Buchanan, R. (1992), 'Wicked problem in design thinking', *Design Issues*, 8/2, 5-21.

Crysler, G.C. (1995), 'Critical pedagogy and architectural education', *Journal of Architectural Education*, 48/4, 208-217

Cuff, D. (1991), *Architecture: The Story of Practice* (Cambridge, MA: MIT Press)

De Sousa, R. (1987), *The Rationality of Emotion* (Cambridge, MA: MIT Press)

Dinham, S.M. (1987), 'Architectural education: the possibilities for research on architecture teaching', *Architectural Record*, 175/4, 41-43.

Dutton , T.A. (ed.) (1991), *Voices in Architectural Education: Culture, Politics and Pedagogy* (New York: Bergin & Garvey)

Ekman, P. (1980), 'Biological and cultural contributions to body and facial movement in the expression of emotion', in Rorty, A.O. (ed.), *Explaining Emotions* (Berkeley, LA: University of California Press)

Gardner, H. (1983), *Frames of Mind: the Theory of Multiple Intelligences* (New York: Basic Books)

Goldschmidt, G. (1988), 'Towards a theory of design development and education', in Walter Wagner, *Education Forum: Shaping Tomorrow's Architect* Conference proceedings

Harr'e, R. (1986), *The Social Construction of Emotion* (New York: Basil Blackwell)

Kolb, D.A. (1984), *Experiential Learning* (N.J: Prentice-Hall)

Lazarus, R.S. (1991), *Emotion and Adaptation* (New York: Oxford University Press)

Lazarus, R.S. & Lazarus B.N. (1994), *Passion and Reason: Making Sense of Our Emotion* (New York: Oxford University Press)

Oatley, K. (1992), *Best Laid Schemes: the Psychology of Emotions* (Cambridge: Cambridge University Press)

Oatley, K. & Jenkins, J.M. (1996), *Understanding Emotion* (Cambridge, MA: Blackwell Publishers)

Ortony, A., Clore, G.L. & Collings, A. (1988), *The Cognitive Structure of Emotion* (Cambridge: Cambridge University Press)

Quayle, M. (1985), *Idea Book for Teaching Design* (Mesa, AZ: PDA Publisher)

Rorty, A.O. (1988), *Mind in Action: Essays in the Philosophy of Emotion* (Boston: Bacon Press)

Sachs, A. (1999), "Stuckness' in the design studio', *Design Studies*, March 1999, 195-209

Schön, D.A. (1987), *Educating the Reflective Practitioners* (San Francisco: Jossey Bass)

Simmonds, G. (1981), 'Case A: a first year studio in graduate school of architecture', in Porter, W.L. & Kilbridge, M. (eds.) *Architecture Education Study*, Vol. 2 (Andrew W. Mellon Foundation)

Wendler, W.V. & Rogers, J.S. (1995), 'The design life space: verbal communication in the architectural design studio', *Journal of Architectural and Planning Research*, 12/4, 319-335

Biographical note

Noam Ausetrlits is currently a PhD candidate and a studio-instructor in the faculty of architecture and town planning, technion, I.I.T. (Haifa, Israel). He is working as an architect in his own small practice. Noam has also 17 years of experience of teaching, in varied educational settings, such as: field guide in the Israeli nature society, teaching in guides training courses and teaching yoga. Since 1999 he has been conducting a research into the emotional aspects of design education. Principal areas of research interest are: pedagogy and theories of design learning; experiential learning; design psychology; education philosophy; education and emotion research; ethnography and culture research. Published in Hebrew and English.

Noam Austerlits
Faculty of Architecture and Town Planning,
Technion I.I.T., Haifa, Israel. 32000
noster@netvision.net.il

5 Research study drawing from visual thinking

Mike Bradshaw

School for Graphic Design, London College of Printing, The London Institute, UK

Abstract

Our research set out to explore alternative methods to the teaching of drawing in design process and visualisation skills to meet the standards required by industry. The paper is informed by practice-based research conducted over a four-year period. The text draws upon the analysis of patterns and diversity of opinion evidenced in industry and educational surveys, curriculum delivery trials, individual case studies and student feedback.

Through the selection of visual notes and sketches produced by students, the findings presented here endeavour to illustrate the importance of 'visual thinking' as a method of supporting individual development in establishing an understanding of the design process where the translation of this learning is relevant to professional practice.

> I have found the course has given me a new confidence. Since joining the course I have a new job in graphic design and when I was interviewed they loved my sketchbook from the course, and I feel it had the edge on me getting the job!
> Lewry (2000)

Starting points - drawing and the design process

In the graphics and media industries, drawing is still valued as an important part of the dialogue designers have with themselves in generating ideas, but in this context it is used as a notation or carrier of messages rather than an end in itself.

The communication technologies that are now available to designers have conversely influenced students' perceived value of the relevance of traditional drawing methodologies in the design process. Computers provide students with a powerful, sophisticated visual rendering tool, which can generate quick results and seduce them with the satisfaction of project completion. Pam Schenk, commenting on her recent study in 1998, stated that it had:

> ... also revealed a pragmatic approach from students many being convinced that working on computer provided them with a more finished and therefore a more 'professional' looking solution.
> Schenk (1998)

Sadly the achievement of this form of visual outcome in the hands of the inexperienced often lacks any depth of design process engagement or substance in problem solving. Philippe Apeloig qualifies his use of computers from a professional viewpoint. In a discussion with Michel Rozenberg he affirms that:

> ... resorting to new technologies does not modify the process of creation, in as much as the latter depends entirely on the designer's imagination ... I often abandon it in favour of pencil and paper, where I register the zigzag pattern of my thinking.
> Apeloig (2001)

We also observed in portfolio assessments that some students, depending on their prior experience of drawing, found it difficult to make the initial transition from observational studies giving an end result to the generation of sketches and notes which informed the design process. Where some students had developed technical skills with particular media rendering techniques, the perceived value they placed on this approach to drawing left them poorly equipped to tackle experimentation and self-critical evaluation.

Over the past 15 years we have seen attempts to resolve some of these issues at secondary level. There are clear pointers in the National Curriculum for Art that are designed to encourage students to look at the work of other artists and designers and to engage them in 'artists studies' to learn about the approach and context in which these 'professionals' work. It is debatable whether 'looking and reading' is better than 'doing and evaluating' in supporting an understanding of the processes involved, but their success as a key to deeper learning probably lies in the combination of these approaches and more significantly in the process of 'thinking and analysing'. Designer Alan Fletcher tells us:

> Design is not merely manipulating forms and shapes, spaces and volumes, or playing with pen and paper, mouse or screen. Design is applied thought, a sensual activity as well as a cerebral exercise.
> Fletcher (2001)

I think there is fairly wide agreement that the practical discipline of an educational drawing programme should provide students with a framework to explore freely and build on the expression of their ideas, feelings and reactions in response to both perceptual or conceptual experiences. Within the context of our research at LCP, however, we have opened a debate on the use of established drawing conventions: this has enabled us to identify alternative ways to introduce the importance of drawing to students, to challenge their approach and reinforce the transferability of these skills in design.

What approaches are used in industry?

We started with a number of questions: how could we improve our curriculum planning, and how could we support our students' learning and prepare them for professional practice? We were under no illusions as to the original nature of the study and we drew momentum from various sources (Arnheim, 1968; McAlhone & Stuart, 1996; Wentworth, 1998; and Simmons, 2000). Our motivation was in response to change. Schenk sums up some of the issues we were about to tackle in her article 'Adaptability to change: teaching drawing to designers':

> The history of curriculum planning for drawing tuition for designers indicates a sustained debate about how drawing should be taught. Although the complexity of the design process has now been well established, the most appropriate forms of drawing to support each aspect of this process have still to be generally agreed. In addition, the changes due to pressures, technological development and the shifts in philosophical emphasis that designers are required to take into account, add further to this complexity.
> Schenk (1998)

Our initial research activity, funded by the London Institute, set out to investigate and reappraise the hypothesis that there are particular approaches to 'drawing' that are fundamental to the way Graphic Designers record the generation of ideas through 'visual thinking'. In the context of this paper 'visual thinking' is defined as the process of taking visual conception to physical output and its 'interpretation' through drawing.

Having designed a survey to test out this hypothesis, we approached over 100 designers in the Greater London area for their definitions of current drawing practice and their views, recommendations and priorities for what students should come equipped with when entering 'the business'. The companies and individuals were selected at random but all focused their practice in the graphic design and media-related industries.

We were very pleased with the response rate of 56%, but more so with the 58% of these who offered additional comments and offers of support for our project. The breakdown of professional practice was mainly in the area of graphic design (86%) and typography (52%), with those who were involved in advertising, illustration, and publicity evenly represented (10%), 4% also identified TV, photo and film as an area of their work.

The majority of the respondents (74%) described the sequence to approaching drawing as:

> Image thoughts in their head, followed by drawn out rough ideas, leading to the selection and modification of ideas, for design/image solutions.

They were fairly unanimous (80%) over their definition of drawing, as 'any form of 2D or 3D media used to express or communicate ideas thoughts or perceptions'. Half of this group added further combinations to this definition to include 'mark-making in response to analytical study' and 'a process of visual research not an end in itself'. Only 12% identified with traditional objective drawing programmes.

The most dramatic result was from a question that asked them to comment on the drawing activities that they felt played an important role in developing future designers. We offered a range of traditional and non-traditional activities for them to select from and the opportunity to add to the list if they wished. 60% chose traditional life drawing classes as a first or second choice but when asked to identify the two most important drawing activities, only 14% selected this as a secondary priority. However, 96% selected drawing ideas as their first or second choice (84% of this figure were first choice) and 76% of all respondents selected this as the first most important drawing activity in their opinion.

When asked why they had singled out particular approaches in response to this question, the following statements on 'drawing ideas' were fairly typical. Michael Darby, Creative Strategy Director of Dialog, opens with:

> The most important skill ... is the ability to communicate succinctly through drawing – the drawing is not an end in itself ...There is a misunderstanding, I believe, that designers must be able to 'draw'. This is often meant that designers ought to be able to 'illustrate' – I disagree. But they must be able to communicate their ideas.

Peter Chodel, Creative Director of Addison, describes the approach:

> Nailing an idea down to a piece of paper enables the designer to share it with the team/creative director for comment. It doesn't have to be a beautiful drawing – it's the scribble on the back of an envelope type of thing before hours of development on the Mac and hunting for scrap art ... There are so many ways to make images that it's a pity that in the rush to learn the Mac we turn our backs on the richness available to us. Maybe it's the swing from paper to the digital world, but I think design would be poorer for it.

It was interesting to note that the next most popular selection was drawing on computer. 38% identified this as a secondary priority, with 76% giving this as a first or second choice. C. Kresfelder, a partner in Yellow Star Design, identified both 'drawing ideas' and 'drawing on the computer' and helpfully defined the relationship:

> The first allows ideas to develop more freely and to explore diverse and spontaneous routes. The second allows better presentation and crafting of those ideas.

It was clear from the survey that 'thinking' was a highly valued commodity in support of the design process. Tony Paras, Director of Strata, sums up:

> The ability to draw, whilst not essential to our industry, is still considered useful to be used as a means of defining an idea or concept. Finished work tends to be produced using computers – but very often the initial work is a 'hands on' approach.

What approaches are used in education?

We were curious as to whether other colleges were tackling these issues in their approach to curriculum design.

To obtain further research data and commentary for comparative analysis, we used the same set of questions used in the industry survey and sent the revised questionnaire to a range of further and higher educational institutions.

The second set of surveys conducted sought responses that would identify any innovations in curriculum design and, in particular, the emphasis institutions placed on existing methodologies and approaches to the delivery of drawing. We mapped these responses against preferred visualisation and process skills, which we had previously identified through the initial survey of design practitioners. It became evident that there were few matches and this confirmed our need to reappraise specific areas of the curriculum content in design and challenged us to consider alternative approaches to the way we were teaching 'drawing' skills.

The majority of the respondents (70%) described the sequence to approaching drawing as:

> Analytical research drawing, resulting in ideas inspiration, leading to selection and modification of initial drawings, for image composition or design solutions.

This definition places the emphasis on students experiencing drawing firstly through analysis and research before leading to ideas, which is in direct contrast to the practitioners' approach, which defines ideas and images coming first before any form of drawing. The 'education' group also differed in their definition of drawing, with all respondents agreeing that drawing included 'any form of 2D or 3D media used to express or communicate ideas thoughts or perceptions', with 65% adding further combinations to this definition to include traditional objective drawing programmes.

Unlike the practitioners, educators identified three types of drawing activity as particularly relevant. 'Media drawing' e.g. photography, collage and printmaking, was viewed by 96% as playing an important role in the students development, with 'drawing ideas' and 'life drawing' both being seen as important by 100% of respondents. We asked this group to select from the same range of traditional and non-traditional activities as the practitioners, and asked them to identify the two most important drawing activities. 56% (compared to 96% of the practitioners) selected drawing from ideas as their first choice and 43% (compared to 14% of the practitioners) selected life drawing as second choice.

These statistics raised a number of questions. Is the curriculum emphasis suitably balanced to develop a student's design creativity as well as maintain progression into the industry? Should we change the curriculum in response to the industry needs? Are the identified needs from industry really about transferability and sustainable skills or are they just a quick fix to meet current employment trends?

Jamie Hobson from Southampton University argues that:

> By favouring drawing over communication, graphic design education is missing the point ... If we are reconsidering the curriculum where does this leave drawing? Once more, the emphasis should be on appropriateness.
> Hobson (1997)

Having placed this in context he provides a solution:

> Educators need to create a drawing tool kit pertinent to – and reflecting – the changing nature of visual communication. We must consider visualisation skills that will provide 'non-drawers' with means by which they can give dimension to their concepts through simplification and visual shorthand.
> Hobson (1997)

Our existing programmes at this time provided students with a traditional vehicle in which to learn the conventions of technical handling, balanced by encouraging the use of experimentation towards the discovery of limitations, possibilities and visual qualities offered by the media and material they used. The approach was not dissimilar to the emphasis we had witnessed in our survey and we were not dissatisfied with the results. So why change?

Hobson's argument is helpful here: we sometimes fail to place drawing in an appropriate context and as a result students become more concerned with issues that are not focused within the discipline and the others who struggle with drawing, simply fail to achieve because they do not see the relevance. On reflection, if we had not responded to these findings, we would have missed an excellent opportunity to review the way we place drawing in the context of communication. As for taking a cynical view of the responses from industry, our survey findings were consistent and comments did display genuine forethought for the development of the individual.

Our consequent strategy did not pander to the notion of a quick fix for short-term gain. By maintaining some of our existing good practice we were also able to test the effectiveness of new approaches which placed the importance of drawing in a context without compromising our existing programmes.

Student progression across levels in understanding and perception

We had previously observed that, depending on their prior experience of drawing, students progressing into a college learning environment often found it difficult to make the initial transition from observational studies giving an end result to the generation of sketches and notes based on their conceptual, visual thinking. In the hope of gaining some insight into how the different levels of curriculum focus worked in supporting progression, we referred to the National Curriculum and related syllabus documents to determine the prescribed stages of progression in student learning. We also extended our research to include a survey of approaches to drawing in our feeder secondary schools and reviewed student perceptions of drawing and ideas thinking on entry to college programmes.

When we compared the survey findings that related to different educational levels, our research indicated that there were mismatches in the approach to teaching the application of drawing ideas, which did not support progression or transition of this activity from one level of experience to the next.

The first reference with direct emphasis on the development of ideas in the National curriculum occurs at Key Stage (KS) 3 where:

> Pupils should be taught to develop ideas from direct experience and imagination.
> EDEXCEL (1998)

Prior to this, 'ideas' are variously referred to in resourcing at KS 1 and 2 as pupils are developing the skills to record from observation and imagination. After KS 3 the currency of ideas is referred to in GCSE as:

> Candidates should regularly show the disposition and ability to see and understand how ideas, feelings and meanings are conveyed in visual forms and images.
> EDEXCEL (1998)

Translating at Advanced (A) level to:

> Candidates should show maturity and command in their ability to research and organise a range of evidence and information, visual or otherwise, interpreting their findings into substantial and specific ideas and responses.
> EDEXCEL (1998)

We looked again at the differences we had noted in the sequence of approach: research and analysis first, ideas to follow, or ideas followed by research and analysis. It would appear that the National Curriculum model reinforces the former and leaves transitional learning to further and higher education.

Using the same criteria as the other surveys, the returns from sixth forms (Fig. 3) indicated that six drawing activities were deemed particularly important at this level. Analytical drawing (73% of first and second choice respondents), media drawing (91%), life drawing (77%), abstraction (82%), drawing ideas (97%) and drawing from still life (94%). Although the highest return was for drawing ideas, this had to be considered in the context of the six other areas and the preferred (71% of respondents) sequence of:

Analytical research drawing, resulting in ideas inspiration, leading to selection and modification of initial drawings, for image composition or design solutions.

It was significant that given the National Curriculum framework objectives above, 72% of respondents selected still life drawing first choice as the most important drawing activity in helping individual development 10% more than for drawing ideas.

Student perceptions

We needed to test out our notional understanding of the situation and conducted a third survey to establish current, working attitudes to drawing held by learners. This information was recorded for both their attitudes to practice on entry to the college, as well as their attitude to practice on course completion. The survey confirmed that out of the students who contributed, differences of perception and approach were evident.

The evidence gathered suggested that rather than generating a more personal engagement with design through the practice of problem solving, where visualising their thoughts was essential, many students had developed their understanding of the design process through looking at existing products. This activity had in turn lead the students towards replicating superficial solutions to problems rather than being innovative in the creation of the design outcomes.

In parallel to the research survey of learners we set out to test the students' ability to challenge themselves in drawing, shifting their initial perceptions of approach from:

> Analytical research drawing, resulting in ideas inspiration, leading to selection and modification of initial drawings, for image composition or design solutions,

(as identified in the education survey) to the process of using:

> Image thoughts in their head; followed by drawing out rough ideas; leading to the selection and modification of ideas; for design/image solutions,

(as identified in the professional practice survey). The results were fascinating and a real endorsement to the imagination and effort of the curriculum teams involved. From the extensive feedback we accumulated, the following student articulated the benefits almost as we intended:

> My design work has improved greatly by being able to visualise concepts and build design around it rather than the other way round. The process has increased my confidence in drawing because I am able to draw more developed thoughts into my work.
> Hutchison (2000)

Curriculum design, trials and feedback

In 1991 Judith and Richard Wilde published Visual Literacy, a conceptual approach to graphic problem solving.

> For educators in the ever-changing visual communications field, understanding how to create these conditions is a formidable challenge. It is essential that assignments be both educationally sound and personally meaningful to the students, creating sufficient interest to

> open up the students to previously unexplored avenues of problem solving. Educators should never assume that a student's mere enrolment in design school will inherently constitute a serious interest in solving visual communication problems – this interest must be developed, through the employment of personally interesting and involving problems.
> Wilde & Wilde (1991)

Visual Literacy was a milestone in graphic design teaching. Steven Heller, Senior Art Director of the *New York Times,* wrote:

> If I had been taught through the exercises presented in this book, my skills might have been honed sooner – perhaps even better.
> Wilde & Wilde (1991)

Study of this text will show that the key to the exercises is the explanation and context in which they are placed, students are not 'left in the dark regarding intent'. In finding our way into trials for new approaches that picked up on the curriculum issues we had identified, we used some of the Wildes' exercises as a starting point to test student reception of the methodology. The response was excellent, and from this point on we began to develop our own exercises that focused on a range of cognitive problem-solving and perceptual activities

We began by introducing drawing to students through a range of exercises where the 'observation' was based on their analysis of what they produced, and their experience of producing it (Fig. 1).

Drawing introduced in this way became essential to the communication of visual thinking:

> I feel more confident in experimenting and I feel I can push myself further exploring trying different solutions I'm less afraid to make drawing if my drawings are not photographic illustrations; it doesn't bother me any more.
> Maestri (2000)

> Prior to this course I had one style of drawing, my style. Visual thinking has opened my eyes to different methods of drawing (line, texture etc.) and each method has its purpose.
> Des Vignes (1999)

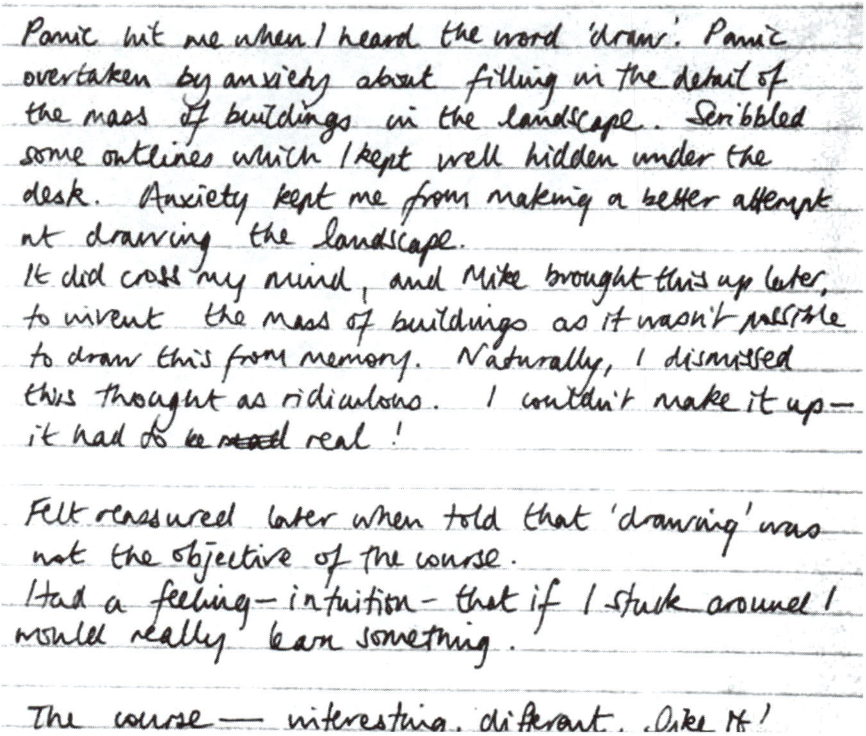
Panic hit me when I heard the word 'draw'. Panic
overtaken by anxiety about filling in the detail of
the mass of buildings in the landscape. Scribbled
some outlines which I kept well hidden under the
desk. Anxiety kept me from making a better attempt
at drawing the landscape.
It did cross my mind, and Mike brought this up later,
to invent the mass of buildings as it wasn't possible
to draw this from memory. Naturally, I dismissed
this thought as ridiculous. I couldn't make it up –
it had to be real!

Felt reassured later when told that 'drawing' was
not the objective of the course.
Had a feeling – intuition – that if I stuck around I
would really learn something.

The course — interesting. different. Like it!

Fig. 1 'Initial drawing exercises'

Interpretation could take various forms from expressive communication in the use and exploration of marks and media, to the communication of ideas through the use of diagrams, sketches and notes. All the exercises required perceptive responses based on a range of experiences from touch through to memory (Fig. 2).

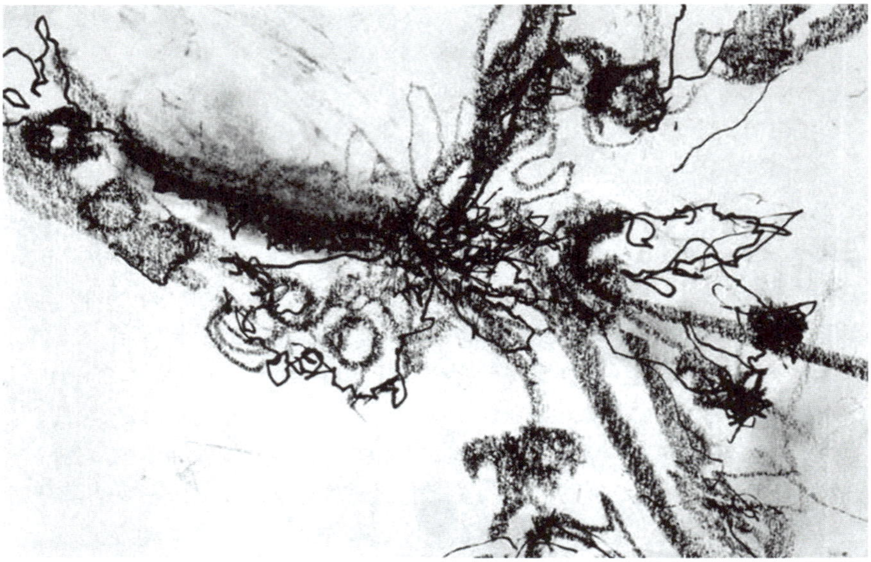

Fig. 2 'Exercises responding to sensation: touch'

One of the students described the effects of the process:

> Drawing without seeing but emphasising other senses to create a visual, visual thinking has reformed my thinking and made me more analytical.
> Des Vignes (1999)

By introducing media experimentation through this drawing methodology we were also able to help students learn to establish their own values with regard to the way media is used in graphic design, to deliberately enhance or mask communication. Through understanding these qualities in their experience of drawing in this way, students were able to develop their own visual language and codes to clarify 'the message' or evoke an abstract response in their design work (Fig. 3):

> It has opened up what is possible to communicate through drawing. It has helped me conceptualise how to approach a brief from drawings. It has allowed me to loosen up my drawing, not worry about it and therefore create a far more creative result.
> Barclay-Brown (2000)

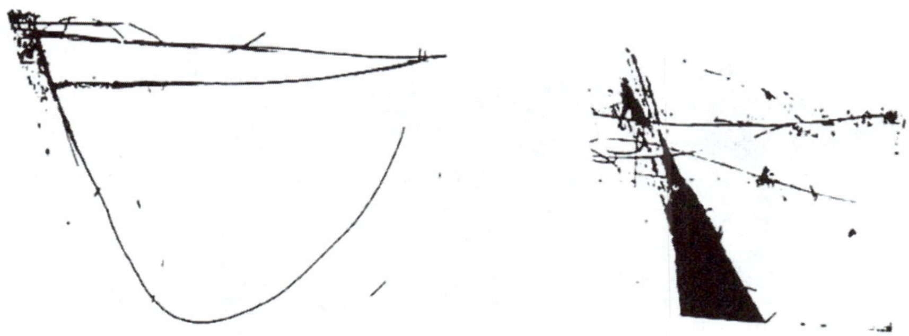

Fig. 3 'Exercises responding to material qualities'

We established a range of aims for methods of visual thinking, which helped students work more quickly whist encouraging a personal approach to the generation of ideas for use in graphic design. Through introducing students to the dynamics of composition in basic visual communication we enabled them to apply the interpretation of shape to character in the creation of layouts and letterforms (Figs. 4a and 4b):

> I enjoyed most of the projects we got, but my favourite one is been definitely the junk letterform because I felt like a child playing around with the junk that I collected and trying to give them new life and a new function. I can say that I'm very happy about this course because it helped a lot my mind to "fly" in freedom and make me see everything from a completely point of view, definitely more creative.
> Balloi (2000)

> The variety of projects has helped me to understand more fully how drawing visual thinking are related. I have realised the importance of drawing and visual thinking and now understand how it relates to commercial briefs. I think it has reawakened my confidence.
> Carey (2000)

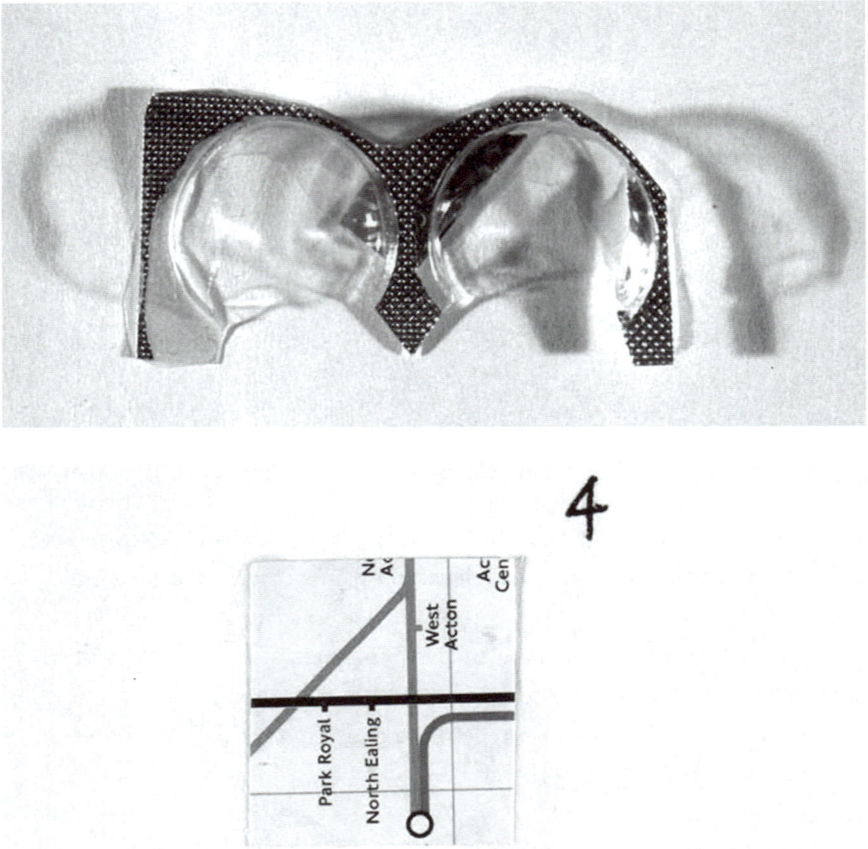

Fig. 4a and 4b 'Exercises based on letterform and composition'

We provided exercises that engaged students in investigation of the associated meanings of colour and their use in visual communication and in exploration of the qualities and potential of media for recording and expressing ideas. The exercise trials we created were a catalyst, to re-sensitise students, and to build their confidence in tackling drawing and visualisation of ideas. By providing a communication context to colour theory and introducing the cultural interpretations of colour through some very simple visualisation exercises, students began to respond and pick up on the potential of what they were learning (Figs. 5a and 5b):

It has opened up a new and vast way of drawing which I would like to pursue further.
Malewezi (1998)

It has helped me to see that actual representation in drawing is not vital but the way in which I use marks and colours is.
Brown (1999)

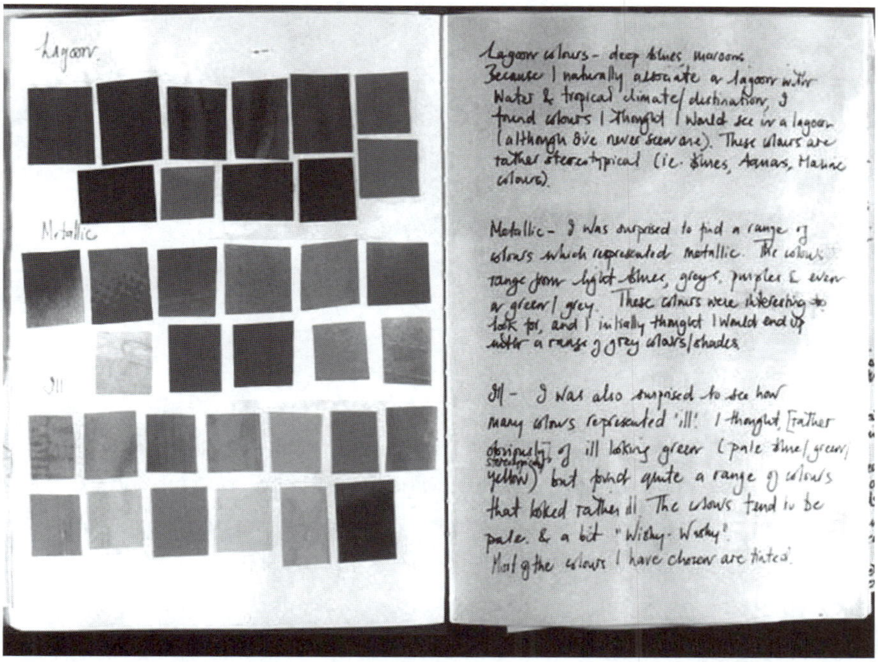

Fig. 5a 'Colour exercises'

Whereas the introduction of literal and abstract characteristics of shape received mixed reception, when we used life drawing as a focus, the same characteristics introduced through drawing in response to 'visual thinking' exercises were tackled with enthusiasm:

There is more of a message in my drawing now.
Mitrano (2000)

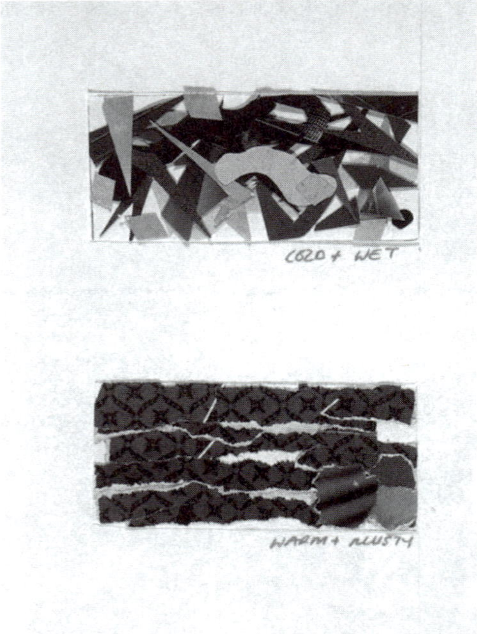

Fig. 5b 'Colour exercises'

> It views drawing from a totally different slant. I feel this involves using all our senses from memory to senses gathering reference and making notes. I think this way of working helps to probe deeper and to pull out much more than we might be capable of. This way of working enables you to loosen up and not be fearful about what marks go down on paper.
> Kinssertain (1998)

Some students did profess to find the exercises 'quite weird' but this only added to the novelty and engaged them further in their learning:

> Instead of drawing things around me I'm drawing what's inside me (feelings visual images) by first taking ideas from outside and processing them inside Its now ok to think up something draw it and say this is "something"! Getting the idea across is 90% of the point of drawing.
> Moore (1999)

> I believe this visual thinking drawing allows me to withdraw from the literal which creates opportunities in varying (my) interpretation of subjects.
> Des Vignes (1999)

As the trials involved students on enrichment courses studying full-time, as well as part-time evening class students, many of them fitted Hobson's description of 'non-drawers':

> I have learnt to think more graphic, therefore I draw better. Visual thinking has helped my projects be more well thought through, my drawing skills may-be hasn't increased dramatically, but I now feel more confident [sic].
> Torlino (1999)

> I feel that drawing from visual thinking is about mark making or producing references that may not be conventional but can be understood by everyone. Visual thinking has increased my confidence in my design work and made it more exciting and adventurous. I have also found that I am more able in my drawing skills.
> O'Leary (1998)

As the students became more confident, we introduced them to brainstorming; word, image, symbol, colour and shape associations; the use of graphic statements and visual association.

> I'm now more aware of how to begin from a brief using visual thinking methods. I feel more confident about experimental drawing than I did before.
> Bartlett (1998)

> Visual thinking is a lot of fun and it really does help to think in a more creative way and gives many benefits to the designer when answering a brief to end up with very individual exciting new ways to gain a final design solution.
> Bartlett (1998)

As trials progressed, students became hungry for more challenging activities and, three years into the development, ideas for 'visual thinking' tasks and exercises started to take on board the deconstruction/reconstruction of the visual and spoken languages used in drawing for design, by designers and clients (Fig. 6).

Fig. 6 'Construction/deconstruction language'

The resourcing of ideas opened up new areas to do with the way we interpret latent messages from materials, and the way we read the use of found objects and images in communication (Figs. 7a and 7b):

> I understand the generation of ideas from different and varied sources. It is helpful that I have now ideas about sourcing ideas. The process has increased my confidence in the generation of idea. This course has enabled me to approach the generation of ideas from fresh sources.
> Watts (2001)

> Through different tasks set I find I can think in a more visual way and help apply this principal in other aspects of my life. It helps me think of design problems in a more open minded way and to explore the potential of an image.
> Bhatinagar (1999)

Fig. 7a 'Messages from materials/Objects and images in communication'

Conclusion

As we reflect on our current status with the project, I believe we have responded to the Wildes' challenge to succeed in developing student interest "through the employment of personally interesting and involving problems" :this is reflected in their endorsement:

> Visual thinking has been one of my favourite subjects, and has really helped my Foundation year ... I've thoroughly enjoyed the course and have been surprised to find that I have frequently found spaces in my spare time to do an extra half hour here and there I enjoy being creative and this course has given me the opportunity to do so.
> Harrison (2001)

We are currently recreating clearer definitions for the parameters and conventions of drawing practice used in graphic design and, in

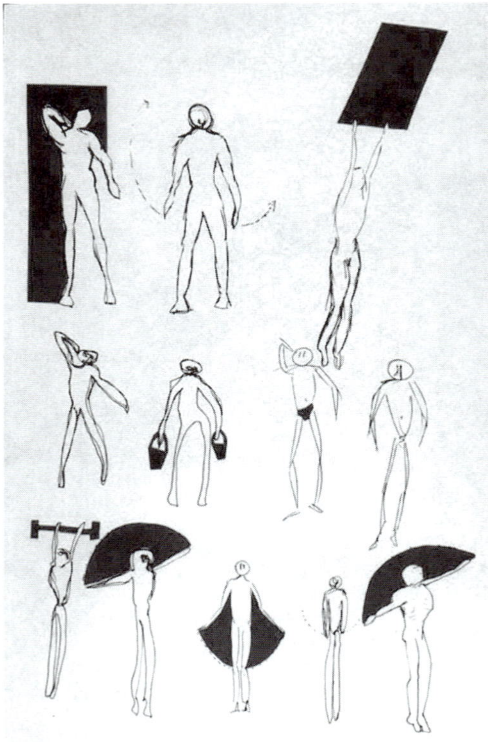

Fig 7b

this way, we are continuing to develop our revised methodology to encourage learning and build confidence in drawing. Students are learning to see and appreciate 'image' as a notation of visual thinking and understand the importance of this in relation to 'image' as an end result. In our teaching in the School of Graphic Design we are very aware that if students are not expected to challenge or have a view of what they are 'observing', their work may result in superficial outcome.

The curriculum trials have involved over six hundred students and the initial response from students progressing within the industry has been very positive. The course has recently been developed into three mainstream professional development courses validated by EDEXCEL and there are plans to convert the learning packages for online delivery.

References

Apeloig, P. (2001), *Au coeur du mot* (Inside the Word) (Lars Muller Publishers)

Arnheim, R. (1968), *Visual Thinking* (University of California Press)

Balloi, M. (2000), in 'Drawing from visual thinking', student practice survey feedback (London College of Printing)

Barclay-Brown, J. (2000), in 'Drawing from visual thinking', student practice survey feedback (London College of Printing)

Bartlett, K. (1998), in 'Drawing from visual thinking', student practice survey feedback (London College of Printing)

Bhatinagar, A. (1999), in 'Drawing from visual thinking', student practice survey feedback (London College of Printing)

Brown, D. (1999), in 'Drawing from visual thinking', student practice survey feedback (London College of Printing)

Carey, F. (2000), in 'Drawing from visual thinking', student practice survey feedback (London College of Printing)

Des Vignes, D. (1999), in 'Drawing from visual thinking', student practice survey feedback (London College of Printing)

Des Vignes, D. (1999), in 'Drawing from visual thinking', student practice survey feedback (London College of Printing)

EDEXCEL (1998), National Curriculum Continuum (for Art)

Fletcher, A. (2001), *The Art of Looking Sideways* (Phaidon Press)

Harrison, R. (2001), in 'Drawing from visual thinking', student practice survey feedback (London College of Printing)

Hobson, J. (1997), in 'The end of the line' (Eye Magazine)

Hutchison, P. (2000), in 'Drawing from visual thinking', student practice survey feedback (London College of Printing)

Kinssertain, J. (1998), in 'Drawing from visual thinking', student practice survey feedback (London College of Printing)

Lewry, S. (2000), in 'Drawing from visual thinking', student practice survey feedback (London College of Printing)

Maestri, S. (2000), in 'Drawing from visual thinking', student practice survey feedback (London College of Printing)

Malewezi, J. (1998), in 'Drawing from visual thinking', student practice survey feedback (London College of Printing)

McAlhone, B. & Stuart, D. (1996), *A Smile in the Mind* (Phaidon Press)

Mitrano, S. (2000), in 'Drawing from visual thinking', student practice survey feedback (London College of Printing)

Moore, T. (1999), in 'Drawing from visual thinking', student practice survey feedback (London College of Printing)

O'Leary, A. (1998), in 'Drawing from visual thinking', student practice survey feedback (London College of Printing)

Schenk, P. (1998), *Adaptability to Change: Teaching Drawing to Designers*, Point 6 (CHEAD)

Simmons, J. (2000), *We, Me, Them & It, The Power of Words in Business* (Texere Publishing Ltd)

Torlino, G. (1999), in 'Drawing from visual thinking', student practice survey feedback (London College of Printing)

Watts, E. (2001), in 'Drawing from visual thinking', student practice survey feedback (London College of Printing)

Wentworth, R. (1998), *Thinking Aloud* (Haywood Gallery Publishing)

Wilde, J. & Wilde, R. (1991), *Visual Literacy: A Conceptual Approach to Solving Graphic Problems* (Watson-Guptill Publications)

Biographical note

Mike Bradshaw is the Dean of School for Graphic Design at LCP. The School is a self styled educational co-operative where staff work towards the mutual aims, of reinforcing the importance of traditional design values in visual communication, alongside the development of new and personal hybrid approaches which will sustain students employability in the future.

Mike can be contacted at m.bradshaw@lcp.linst.ac.uk or 00 44 207514 6651.

6 Understanding learning styles: implications for design education in external settings

Geoffrey Caban and Jenny Wilson

Faculty of Design, Architecture and Building, University of Technology, Sydney, Australia

Abstract

This paper uses the UTS research project on designers' learning styles, detailed in the paper titled 'Understanding learning styles: implications for design education within the university', to examine how an understanding of the learning styles of designers can be applied to enhance design learning in external settings such as the workplace and museums.

Falk (2000) has identified three sectors in a learning infrastructure, namely the school, the workplace and the 'free-choice' learning sector. According to Falk, the term 'free-choice learning' refers to the type of learning that occurs when learners have control over what, when, why and how they learn. He claims that though it is a little appreciated fact, most of the learning in the United States occurs in the last of these three sectors, namely free-choice learning:

> Typically, free-choice learning refers to the type of learning regularly facilitated by museums, science centres, zoos, aquariums; and a wide range of community-based organisations including libraries, youth groups, environmental and health-related organisations and faith-based

> organisations; print and electronic media including books, radio, television and film; and the increasingly important, the Internet.
> Falk (2000, p. 4)

A research project conducted at the Powerhouse Museum, Sydney explored ways in which the Museum, with its focus upon design and the decorative arts, can enhance aspects of design learning and particularly creative learning. The researchers first developed a theoretical framework that addressed issues related to the learning styles and learning needs of designers, and also the value of museums as settings for general and specific learning experiences. In collaboration with Dr John Falk of the Institute for Learning Innovation in Annapolis, USA, they then devised a methodology to assess the effect of particular museum experiences on the design learning process.

The development of the methodology was informed by the awareness that designers have learning styles that differ from the learning styles of other professional groups (Cross, 1991), that learning styles can shift significantly during the design learning stage (Wilson, 2000), and that an understanding of designers' learning styles by both students and educators can assist the learning process.

Introduction

The research project with the Powerhouse Museum in Sydney began with our objective to know more about design learning in settings external to the traditional design school. Falk (2000) has pointed out the value of learning experiences that take place in 'free-choice' settings including museums, galleries, and community-based organisations. While there has been some general research into learning in museums, there has been no research available to museum curators on the learning needs and learning styles of specialist learning groups such as designers. The researchers decided to investigate ways in which museums can influence the development of creative thinking and other attributes that are integral to the learning of designers. The Powerhouse Museum, with its focus on design and the decorative arts, provided a useful setting for the investigation.

Underpinning our interest in the project was our view that the stereotype of the typical design graduate needs to change to embrace emerging opportunities for design thinking skills. Increasingly, designers are being recognised in the new knowledge economy as important catalysts, capable of generating new ideas and engineering economic change. Large corporations are beginning to introduce strategies for incorporating design thinking into their operational systems (Golsby-Smith, 2000). I believe that a link can be established between these new applications for design thinking skills and 'free-choice' design learning. By giving design students greater control over what, when, why and how they learn we can facilitate new applications for their design skills and broaden the scope of the design graduate.

The Powerhouse Museum, like a number of international museums, has been asking itself some questions about its general usefulness to society, including its value as an educational resource. The Museum has recently widened the scope of its 'evaluation and audience research' activities to focus on issues of generic significance to the museum, and has entered into a number of strategic partnerships with other cultural institutions and universities. The Museum is planning the establishment of a large permanent gallery to display the museum's collection of over 100,000 design objects and to highlight the Museum's profile as a major centre for exhibiting innovative design. As it is envisaged that the gallery will be of major interest to tertiary design students and other design students, the Museum became very interested in a suggestion for the collaborative research study that explored its usefulness as a setting for design learning.

The researchers aimed to explore ways in which the Museum can enhance aspects of design learning. We first developed a theoretical framework that addressed issues related to the learning styles and learning needs of designers, and also the value of museums as settings for general and specific learning experiences. In collaboration with Dr John Falk of the Institute for Learning

Innovation in Annapolis, USA, we then devised a methodology to assess the effect of particular museum experiences on the design learning process.

The study was informed by the research at UTS into the learning styles of design students (Wilson, 2000). This research showed that a key to guiding and enabling design students to become independent and effective learners is to help them to understand their own learning styles. The Wilson study showed also that this understanding can assist students to manage their own learning through access to a larger and more diverse range of educational resources.

The methodology developed for the Powerhouse study, known as Personal Meaning Mapping, was applied in a pilot study involving control groups of first-year design students. The pilot studies aimed to measure the effect of various museum experiences on the depth, breadth extent and mastery of their learning. The Wilson study had provided some expectations of the learning style preferences of these students, and there proved to be an interesting correlation between the two studies. In a Stage 2 study soon to be conducted, the same methodology will be applied to control groups of third-year design students, and it will be interesting to see if changes to their learning style preferences over a period of time result in different learning outcomes from museum experiences.

The study has attracted international interest from museum directors and curators. Mark O'Neill, Director of the new Glasgow Transport Museum, has been sufficiently influenced by the project to include in his statement of objectives for the museum:

> We'll begin by asking the visitor: 'What kind of learner are you?' None of us are observers; all of us are part of the story. So how do you fit into the story of Great Glasgow? And then we'll devise a series of hands-on experiments where, in the process of exploring other peoples' creativity, the visitor can also explore his own.

'Free-choice' settings for design learning

There is considerable evidence that most learning experiences occur in settings that are external to the university. Falk (2000) identified three sectors in a learning infrastructure, namely the school, the workplace and the 'free-choice' learning sector. According to Falk, the term 'free-choice learning' refers to the type of learning that occurs when learners have control over what, when, why and how they learn. He claims that though it is a little appreciated fact, most of the learning in the United States occurs in the last of these three sectors, namely free-choice learning.

> Typically, free-choice learning refers to the type of learning regularly facilitated by museums, science centres, zoos, aquariums; and a wide range of community-based organisations including libraries, youth groups, environmental and health-related organisations and faith-based organisations; print and electronic media including books, radio, television and film; and the increasingly important, the Internet.
> Falk (2000, p. 4)

Theories on constructivism, which are not new but are enjoying a timely revival, maintain that individuals construct their own meanings according to their personal experiences, and that they learn by accumulating experiences from a wide range of sources (Hein, 1995b). While many design education programmes have recognised that there are valuable sources of design learning outside the academy, and have made some efforts to accommodate this through co-operative education programmes and community-based projects, there is room and opportunity for a greater emphasis on non-conventional ways of facilitating design learning.

There has been some appreciation by design educators of the value to the learning process of industry and workplace experiences, and the curriculum of most design schools includes industry-based projects and some form of workplace experiences. But the magnitude of learning experiences that take place outside the academy has not been appreciated fully by design educators, many of whom continue to believe that the learning experience takes place almost totally within the design school and have developed the design curriculum on the basis of this belief.

It is in the best interests of design educators to know more about design learning in free-choice settings. In particular, we should know more about the degree of compatibility between designers' learning styles and free-choice experiences, about the potential of particular free-choice settings for design learning, and about ways in which design schools can enhance free-choice learning experiences.

Museums as settings for learning

Museum curators and design educators have access to a wide range of information on learning theory that can be applied, in general ways, to learning in museum settings.

Hein (1995a) drew upon the work of Dewey (1963), and upon Pepper's four world views (Pepper, 1981), on how knowledge is constructed, to consider four learning approaches that have relevance for museums. As well as the currently fashionable constructivism and the behaviourist learning model he discussed also the more traditional models of *traditional lecture and text* and *discovery learning*. Applying these four learning approaches to museums, Hein suggested that there could be four different kinds of museums. One is the Systematic museum, based on the traditional lecture and text model, where the content of the museum is exhibited so that it reflects the true structure of the subject matter and is presented to the visitor in a manner that makes it easiest to comprehend (Hein, 1995b, pp. 21–23).

Other kinds of museums, according to Hein, are the Discovery museum, based on the discovery learning model, and the Orderly museum based on the behaviourist learning model (p. 21). The learning features of the fourth kind, the Constructivist museum, are that the viewer constructs personal knowledge from the exhibit, and the process of gaining knowledge is itself a constructive act (p. 22). The focus is on the visitor, not on the content of the museum. Though appearing to favour the constructivist approach, Hein concedes that examples of constructivist museums, featuring a lack of predetermined sequence, use of multiple learning modalities, opportunities for visitors to make connections with familiar concepts and objects, and comparisons between the unfamiliar and new, are hard to find. However, there are an increasing number of exhibitions that are designed so that multiple paths are possible through the exhibit and the learner (visitor) is provided with a range of modalities to acquire information.

Among other research which informs learning theory in museum settings is Hooper-Greenhill's work (1999) on *transmission versus constructivist* models of communication, and also her use of hermeneutic approaches to understand the process of meaning-making in museums. For hermeneutic philosophers, according to Hooper-Greenhill, meaning-making is shaped by the inevitability of prior knowledge, the effect of tradition, the past as it works in the present, the prejudices and biases that are part of being human, and the capacity to interrogate the past and to distinguish between productive and non-productive preconceptions.

The usefulness to curators of the research on learning in museums would be enhanced by greater knowledge of visitor groups, particularly knowledge of their distinctive learning styles and particular learning needs. For museums that emphasise design, it would be useful to know more about ways in which designers make sense of the museum experience.

Learning styles of designers

While researchers into museum learning have looked at learning in some specific areas such as science, there is little or no help to curators on how they might allow for the distinctive learning styles and the particular learning needs of specialist visitor groups such as design students. Some evaluations have been carried out on the effectiveness of museums in enhancing science learning for school children, but little information is available on the ways in which museums can influence the development of creative thinking and other attributes that are integral to the learning of designers.

Empirical studies indicate that the learning styles of designers are systematically different from those of other professional groups (Cross, 1991), and this has obvious relevance to designers' ways of viewing the world and responding to different environments. A greater understanding of the ways in which designers learn should assist museum curators who are working in design-related museum settings, and should also assist students undergoing experiential learning experiences in museum settings.

Among the outcomes of the Wilson study into designers' learning styles (Wilson, 2000) were two with particular relevance for the museum project. One was the realisation that owing to changing criteria for admission to university-based design schools, students at the point of entry are increasingly displaying 'converger/ assimilator' rather than 'diverger/accomodator' learning preferences. This implies that many commencing students have strengths in critical thinking and logical systemic analysis rather than in creative thinking and experimentation. The other was the realisation that these preferred learning styles can be subject to change, and that a shift to a diverger/accommodator learning style is common and achievable. Interestingly, the study concluded that teaching and learning strategies to facilitate this change are aided if the students themselves are able to develop an understanding of their learning preferences and their capacity for change.

The Powerhouse Museum investigation

In developing and testing the methodology for the Powerhouse study, the investigators aimed to draw upon a theoretical framework of general learning in museum settings and the learning needs and learning styles of designers. Use of Falk's work on Personal Meaning Mapping (2001) seemed particularly appropriate because of its relationship to creative learning and because of some common underlying principles. These are that:

- learning in informal settings can be constructed to ensure optimal outcomes;
- the effectiveness of the learning depends on the degree of personal engagement and meaning;
- personal engagement and meaning differ from individual to individual; and
- intrinsic rewards can be incorporated as part of the museum experience.

It was decided to use the Personal Meaning Mapping (PMM) methodology and, conveniently, Dr Falk who was visiting Australia made himself available to assist with the pilot study. Personal Meaning Mapping is based on a relativist-constructivist approach to measuring learning. Each individual's prior knowledge and feelings about a particular theme or idea are compared with their knowledge and feelings after the museum experience. PMM measures learning by assessing change across four semi-independent dimensions, namely the *extent* of someone's knowledge and feelings, the *breadth* of the individual's conceptual understanding or the change in the quantity of appropriate concepts use, the *depth* of understanding or how richly and deeply someone understands the concepts they use, and *mastery* or the overall facility with which someone uses their understanding (Falk, 2001).

The investigators wanted to focus upon a particular aspect of design learning, and the theme of 'creativity' was selected as creativity is commonly identified by designers as an attribute that is essential for design practice (Caban & Trigwell, 1991). It was necessary for the investigators to specify what was meant by creativity and creative learning in museums. For example, did we mean learning to be more creative, or learning *about* the concept of creativity?

The theoretical framework developed for the study addresses a number of issues relating to creativity, and this helped us to determine our objectives. The area of creativity has been researched by numerous groups including cognitive scientists, psychologists and visual artists but, as Edwards has pointed out:

> we still have no generally accepted definition of creativity – no general agreement on what it is, how to learn it, how to teach it, or if, indeed, it can be learned or taught.
> Edwards (1995, p. 2)

Briskman (1980) argued that it is impossible to develop a general theory of creativity, pointing out that such a theory would eliminate all the mystery and miraculous nature of creativity, and would eliminate creativity itself. He argued that in order to investigate how creativity is possible, we should not be trying to look for psychological processes or traits leading to creativity, but rather for the 'aspects of products which lead us to evaluate them as creative' (Briskman, 1980, p. 91).

Other researchers have attempted to investigate how creativity is possible by identifying specific qualities and physiological factors that enhance creativity. Getzels and Jackson (1962) identified a wide range of creative qualities including playfulness, humour, variety, social concern and insight, personal introspectiveness, and inventiveness. Gruber (1981) pointed to two seemingly opposing approaches to creative work. One emphasises sudden moments of insight, dramatic reorganisations of ideas, and the other the slow construction of ideas, treating creative thinking as a growth process.

Edwards (1993) drew on the work of Roger Sperry on the separate functions of the brain's left and right hemispheres to argue that there are ways of enhancing creative thinking. Edwards interpreted Sperry's work as establishing that the right hemisphere mode is the intuitive, subjective, relational, holistic, time-free mode, in effect the creative mode. She argued that the emphasis of western culture and education is slanted strongly towards rewarding left-brain skills, and that right-brain skills – those of the dreamer, the artificer, the artist – are largely untaught and unlearned. According to Edwards, there are ways of increasing right brain activity and thereby enhancing creativity. Even though the links between creativity and physiological traits may be considered by some to be inconclusive, it is possible that Edwards' suggestions can be applied usefully towards the enhancement of creative thinking in museums.

Csikszentmihalyi (1995) provides a more direct link between creative thinking and the museum experience. His paper titled 'Intrinsic motivation in museums: what makes visitors want to learn?' refers to the *flow* experience, a 'common experiential state of mind that is spontaneous, almost automatic, like the flow of a strong current'. Csikszentmihalyi contends that painters, musicians, sportsmen (and, presumably, designers) who are willing to invest psychic energy in tasks for which intrinsic rewards are absent, do so because of the quality of experience that ensues. General characteristics of activities that produce flow are that they have clear goals and appropriate rules, avoid conflicting goals or unclear expectations, produce immediate and unambiguous feedback and accountability, and tend to occur when the challenges of the activity match the skills of the individual.

According to Csikszentmihalyi, the challenge for museums is to produce this experience so that initial curiosity and interest will grow into a more extensive learning interaction, resulting in personal growth and considerable skill enhancement. Among his suggested guidelines for facilitating the experience are:

- (guideline 3) encouraging *mindfulness*: 'a state of mind that results from drawing novel distinctions, examining information from new perspectives, being sensitive to context. An open, creative, probabilistic state of mind in which the individual might be led to finding differences among things thought different' (Csikszentmihalyi, 1995, p. 36);

- (guideline 4) providing opportunities for *deep absorption* engaged through sensory, intellectual, and emotional faculties. This guideline arises from a need to feel emotionally connected to subject area;
- (guideline 21) satisfying the need for clear goals and appropriate rules, for an awareness of what is to be accomplished; and
- (guideline 22) providing information by which visitors can compare their responses to some other standard. Successful displays tend to be those which ask visitors to make guesses, to evaluate, and to respond.

For the purposes of the Powerhouse study the investigators decided to map changes in design students' concepts of creativity as a result of a museum experience. The specific aim was to investigate how exposure to a particular museum experience affected awareness of issues underlying creativity and innovation, understanding of the relationship between creativity and innovation, and appreciation of the role that a design museum can play in facilitating this understanding.

The pilot study

The control groups for the pilot study comprised first-year design students. The Wilson study outlined above had provided some expectations of the learning style preferences of these students, and these expectations informed the approach taken and created additional interest in the results of the pilot study. The students were randomly assigned to one of four museum experiences. The students in one group were asked to visit two specific exhibitions at the Museum, while those in another group were told they could visit any exhibitions in the museum in any order. The two other groups did not visit the exhibitions at all, but were given talks by the designers of the two specified exhibitions on their ideas and approaches.

Prior to the museum experiences, each student underwent preliminary personal meaning mapping to provide some idea of their basic knowledge and understanding of creativity. Following the experience, each student was again administered a PMM to determine the changes, if any, in their understanding. The degree of change was assessed using quantitative data analysis for the statistically independent dimensions of extent, breadth, and depth, and the holistically measured dimension of mastery.

The data provided evidence that most of the students showed significant changes in their understanding of the concept of creativity and its role in design. The results showed that all groups increased the extent and breadth and mastery of their understanding of the concept. In particular, they indicated that the museum-related experiences provided the students with a concrete framework to think about issues of creativity and design.

However, the results indicated that the experience resulted in little change in the dimension of depth of understanding of the concept. This dimension looks at how deeply and richly someone understands the concepts they use and is qualitatively determined along a five point scale – shallow to deep. The researchers felt there was a link between this finding and the observation from the Wilson study that first-year students tend increasingly to be 'converger/ assimilator' learners. The planned Stage 2 study with more design students will determine whether more 'diverger/accomodator' learning characteristics are displayed.

Conclusion

It is valuable for a museum that focuses on design and the decorative arts to know more about design learning in the museum setting and how this learning might be enhanced. It is probable that a considerable amount of informal design learning occurs already in museums; many professional designers can recall museum exhibitions and exhibits that have provided inspiration for projects and design directions.

It is possible, given what we know about the learning styles and the learning needs of designers, to develop a more strategic approach to facilitate design learning in museums. This strategic approach is timely as formal learning is taking place increasingly outside the traditional educational institutions, and there is growing recognition that museums have useful and important roles as learning environments.

Design educators who develop an understanding of their students' learning styles can apply this understanding when developing their strategies for teaching and learning. Design students who develop an understanding of their personal learning styles can utilise this understanding to develop as independent learners, and to take advantage of the many learning opportunities available in settings outside the academy.

References

Briskman, L. (1981), 'Creative product and creative process in science and art', *Inquiry*, **23**, 1, 83–106

Caban, G. & Trigwell, K. (1991), 'Initiating a new design curriculum', *Designing Change*, 8–23 (University of Technology, Sydney)

Caban, G. & Wilson, J.(2002) 'Understanding learning styles: implications for design education within the university'. Paper presented at the *cltad* 1st International Conference, London, April 2002

Cross, N. (1991), 'Research in design thinking', *Design Studies*, **12**, 3–10

Csikszentmihalyi, M. & Hermanson, K. (1995), 'Intrinsic motivation in museums: what makes visitors want to learn?', *Museum News*, May/June, 35–38

Dewey, J. (1963), *Experience and Education* (1938) (New York: Collier)

Edwards, B. (1993), *Drawing on the Right Side of the Brain* (London: Harper Collins)

Edwards, B. (1995), *Drawing on the Artist Within: A Guide to Innovation, Invention, Imagination and Creativity*. (London: Harper Collins)

Falk, J. (2000). Building a 21st Century Education System: An Infrastructure for Lifelong Learning. Institute for Learning Innovation, Annapolis, Maryland, USA.

Falk, J. (2001). Personal Meaning Mapping. Institute for Learning Innovation, Annapolis, Maryland, USA.

Getzels, J., & Jackson, P. (1962), *Creativity and Intelligence: Explorations with Gifted Students* (London: Wiley)

Golsby-Smith, T. (2000), 'Building Design Culture and Practice', paper presented at the Integrated Tax Design conference held by the Australian Taxation Office, Canberra

Gruber, H. (1981), 'On the relation between "aha" experiences and the construction of ideas', *History of Science*, **19**, 43, 41–59

Hein, G. (1995a), 'Evaluating teaching and learning', in Hooper-Greenhill, E. (ed.), *Museum, Media, Message* (London: Routledge)

Hein, G. (1995b), 'The constructivist museum', *Journal for Education in Museums*, **16**, 21–23

Hooper-Greenhill, E. (1995), *Museum, Media, Message* (London: Routledge)

Hooper-Greenhill, E. (1999), 'Learning in Art Museums: Strategies of Interpretation', *The Educational Role of the Museum* (Routledge)

Pepper, S.C. (1981), *World Hypotheses: A Study in Evidence* (Berkeley, CA: University of California)

Wilson, J. (2000), 'Change, change and more change: redefining the student profile in design', paper presented at the International Conference on Design Education, Curtin University

Biographical note

Geoffrey Caban is Professor of Design Studies at the University of Technology, Sydney, and is the author of a number of books and journal papers on design education and design history.

Jenny Wilson is Associate Professor in Visual Communication at the University of Technology, Sydney. Her graphic works are in the collections of national and international galleries and museums, and her research field is design learning.

7 What to teach? Qualitative research into fine art undergraduate programmes

Frances Corner

Sir John Cass Department of Art at London Guildhall University, UK

Abstract

Questions about how fine art courses have adapted to the higher education agenda of expansion as well as the requirements to maintain excellence and increase equality of opportunity, prompted me to undertake a qualitative study into how this was affecting the fine art sector. Factors such as accountability, standardisation, increased student numbers, the diverse student body, graduateness, lifelong learning and their impact on fine art undergraduate education were all explored in a series of 12 interviews. The research aimed to identify how extensively such changes are affecting a fine art education and how fine art educators are adjusting to this new agenda. This paper sets out the stages that this research went through and indicates, briefly, a number of the major concerns, as well as possible ways forward for the fine art sector. This is a brief synopsis of what has been my doctoral study.

Stage 1: expansion equity and excellence

I began the research by looking closely at changes to the purpose and structure of the higher education sector as Government seeks to create an expanded, inclusive and highly skilled workforce. For example:

- higher education in Britain used to be an elitist system, but over the last 30 years the numbers of students has grown dramatically. The Government target, reinforced in the speech of the newly appointed Secretary of State for Education, Estelle Morris, is for 50% of those under 30 to progress into higher education by 2010. This expansion has been matched by a corresponding concern on the part of Government and other stakeholders that quality-assurance methods are sufficiently robust to ensure comparability and the enhancement of standards. In an expanded sector, many stakeholders involved with the funding and monitoring of higher education, are keen to see that the results of a higher education experience will bring direct and measurable economic, public and social benefits rather than just fulfilling individual learner's aspirations. It is for these reasons, that expansion is to be matched with both equity and excellence. How does this affect the subject?
- to drive this new agenda the Government has developed a system of funding levers, whereby institutions can only access certain monies, by responding to issues that the Government wants to see addressed. Institutions are required to demonstrate the direct actions that they are taking in relation to these specific areas in order to receive funds. In addition, the Government has commissioned a series of reports on particular issues, such as widening access, literacy and lifelong learning to help achieve this agenda. For example, in addition to accepting the findings of the Dearing report, the Government set up the Kennedy Report of 1997 ('Learning Works: widening participation in further education'), the Fryer Report of 1997 ('Learning for the 21st Century'), as well as the Moser report

into literacy and the NIACC report into creativity and the curriculum. It is reports such as these that have been used to help focus the agenda and reinforce the funding levers instituted by Government. How are Institutions managing with this changing culture?

- the social inclusion agenda and increased numbers of students studying on both pre-degree and degree courses has not always been matched with an understanding by Government of the pressures and challenges that this presents to higher education. For example, although the figures for relatively under-qualified students from lower socio-economic groups going into post-compulsory education are still comparatively low, some higher education institutions, particularly in inner London, have up to 33% of their students from socio-economic groups who have not traditionally participated in HE and they are now being caught by the Government performance indicators that measure such factors as employability, retention and progression. How are courses adjusting to a more diverse student body and negative performance indicators?

The consequence of these new objectives for higher education is an environment of constant flux and transition as higher education institutions struggle to adjust their courses to meet the new requirements of, for example, skills, employability, widening access and accountability. It is also a situation that is raising a whole series of questions and concerns amongst subject educators. Questions are being raised about just how educators meet this new agenda positively, whilst ensuring that the qualities inherent in subject disciplines are allowed to grow and develop. This formed the basis to the next stage of the research.

Stage 2: fine art as a subject discipline

The next stage set out to explore a definition for fine art and what might constitute it as a subject discipline.

I began developing my definition by referring to a term set out by L.A. Reid in his book *Meaning in the Arts* (1969). 'Embodied meaning' is a definition that sees a work of art as more than just an expression, more than just a discovery, or a representation of emotion, as it recognises that the process of creation changes the original state of the artist. The judgements of a work of art are therefore not based on the creative agonies of the artist; they are however based on the expression of a number of elements, which are embodied and articulated through the work of art to an audience. This definition signifies that the artist has brought together a broad range of complex ideas through a process of exploration, experimentation, judgement and emotion and it is through this and through the manipulation of their particular medium, that they discover meaning in and through it, for through this process the artist discovers what was not there before. There is consequently a purpose to the artist's exploration of the medium, the ideas and references to their individual life, the thoughts and responses to the world and society of which they are a part. These experiences form their content and vision and, combined with their choice of medium and their exercise of judgement, form the material reality of the work of art. Such an embodiment includes traces and evidence of the contemporary concepts and conventions, the social, moral, political ideas and issues, as well as the traditional cultural heritage that the artist is a part of and responds to. It is the artist's individual response to the world and society that they are a part of that becomes their particular vision. A valid work of art is therefore judged both on its ability to link to other works of art in the genre that it is a part of as well as the originality and uniqueness of its vision. It is consequently set within distinctly aesthetic criteria and made with aesthetic intentions. Yet, these frames of reference, the concepts and conventions behind them are formed by real life. It is therefore not possible to argue that anything can be a work of art.

There were four main areas that I investigated in more detail to support this definition. These four areas I feel form the essential characteristics of fine art, particularly in how it relates to the subject discipline. That is:

- the relationship of fine art and works of art to the society and culture from which they are formed;
- fine art as a particular means of communication;
- the discourses that surround the works of art when they are made public; and
- the transformative process that is the basis of the creation of works of art.

These four areas were looked at carefully and underpinned the definition of fine art as a subject discipline. Notably, fine art requires students to:

- learn how to shape their perception and understanding of the world; and
- to create a physical manifestation of that perception and to communicate this.

To learn how to understand and manipulate these experiences fine art students have to be taught how to:

- analyse;
- develop technical and practical skills;
- research; and
- combine these elements into a physical realisation.

Such an education develops in students an open-minded, questioning and responsive approach to their environment. They come to learn that:

- problems are opportunities;
- contemporary art echoes our complex society; and
- the creative process means we employ our skills and talents to create change, to take chances and to challenge convention.

This is an empowering process as students are encouraged to work honestly to own their success and failure. It means they come to see all aspects of their environment as well as our global culture and society as relevant and appropriate and potential elements in their creative process. This means that within fine art there needs to be an approach to teaching and learning which explores failure and that allows students to push, question and test the boundaries.

Stage 3: the current status of fine art undergraduate courses

Having explored definitions of fine art and how that might translate into a subject discipline, I wanted to gain a real picture of the fine art sector by looking at applications, course structures and graduate destinations. I hoped that this would demonstrate whether the Government agendas of, for example, employability and increased student numbers were already affecting factors such as application patterns, course structures and expectations of what defines a fine art graduate. I decided to look at how a number of institutions are currently organising the various components and elements of the subject of fine art into a curriculum. I therefore reviewed the course documents of a modularised programme, a unitised course and the more open structure of what might be termed a traditional fine art course. In doing this, I hoped to see if any one approach was better able to manage change. I also wanted to explore whether these courses were offering a degree course 'in' fine art, 'through' fine art, or some sort of balance between the two approaches.

I was also concerned to set these documents within the overall context of demand for courses by looking at the patterns of applications to fine art degree courses to judge in particular whether there are increased numbers of students studying fine art or whether there are other factors taking place. I therefore reviewed both the UCAS statistics and the National Association of Fine Art Education's 2001 Web site and 1996 Guide to Fine Art Courses. I was also interested in what happens to the graduates of fine art courses. Are fine art courses primarily preparing their students for careers as artists, or are other elements being emphasised? Do students feel that their courses have prepared them for a career as an artist or for alternative areas of employment? I therefore looked at the results of a national survey into the career destinations of art and design graduates, which has a specific category for fine art graduates and I reviewed a report on a series of focus group interviews with fine art and visual arts graduates from Cheltenham and Gloucester College of Higher Education.

Stage 4: research questions and methods

Out of the previous stages a number of research questions began to emerge. For example:

- What are fine art educators' perceptions and understanding of the effects of the move from an elite to a mass system of higher education and what do they consider the implications to be for a subject such as fine art?
- How are staff coping with increasing numbers and new audiences, and what is the nature of their student body?

The second set of questions concerned the nature and particularities of the organisation of the subject of fine art itself. For example:

- What are the core characteristics, the particular skills, attributes and philosophies associated with the subject of fine art?
- How do fine art educators identify and define the skills and abilities necessary for a fine art graduate and in what way are these definitions built into their curriculum and what teaching and learning methodologies do they use?

The final set of questions began to explore the effect of combining these two areas, as I wanted to uncover the implications and effects of change on a subject. For example:

- Are fine art educators responding to the challenge of effectively preparing their students for careers either as practising artists, arts administrators etc, or are they using the curriculum as an opportunity to prepare students for alternative careers utilising the skills they have acquired as part of their fine art education?
- How do they respond to the pressure to build skills and link with employers into academic programmes?
- Has the definition of fine art as a subject changed as a result of the recent higher education pressures?

It was out of questions such as these that I developed a set of questions and a briefing paper.

I then set about developing the methods to test the questions.

First I planned to select six institutions, representative of traditional course structures, recently modularised courses, and institutions that had modularised their courses a minimum of four years ago. I had hoped that this would enable me to construct a picture of the particular pressures both generic and specific facing these institutions. However, as it became apparent that the issues and pressures were complex I became concerned that this would in reality not provide sufficient in-depth information about what was happening across the sector.

Second, I considered undertaking three major case studies in institutions representative of a traditional course structure, a recently modularised course and one modularised some time ago. However, this approach still did not seem to reflect or match the issues and pressures that the research was revealing. I was concerned that the result would be information that was too focused on a particular institutional perspective.

I consequently decided that a more appropriate method would be to interview a number of people from across the fine art sector – in a way to treat fine art as a case study in itself.

With this approach, those selected would be chosen to represent a range of opinion and responsibilities involved with the subject of fine art. Overall, I expected that each interviewee would establish their unique understanding and perception of the current situation. This was something that I felt would enable me to construct a more comprehensive picture of the issues involved and that it would be more likely to provide in-depth answers to the questions I was preparing. Each interview would represent a small case study of expert knowledge and experience, but overall the research methodology and interview structure would enable a collective view to emerge. This was important, as I wanted the research methodology to test the notion that there are tensions between a mass system and a subject discipline, against the experience of individuals who had extensive knowledge and understanding of the issues involved. I felt that with appropriately designed research questions I would be able to gather views that would articulate the different conceptions of fine art education as well as the various experiences, ideologies and teaching and learning practices within the current higher education provision of fine art.

Stage 5: interviews

The next stage of the method was to develop an appropriate structure for the interviews. In order to do this I drew up a list of people representative of different types of fine art courses, including modularised and linear, course leaders, teaching staff and heads of faculty or institutions. I also ensured that they would be representative of different regions, urban and rural centres. As I would also need to address the relevance of the 'subject', as defined by the educators, to the reality of fine art as it exists externally to the higher education sector, I decided I would also need to interview representatives from arts organisations, as well as somebody from the Quality Assurance Agency. From this list I selected 12 individuals who would then act as case studies.

I subsequently wrote to those that I had identified, asking if they would be prepared to be interviewed. I made it clear what the purpose of the research was that they would receive a briefing paper and research questions and that they would be able to comment on their responses and the outcomes of the interview.

I then held a pilot interview to test the briefing paper and the research questions as well as the proposed interview structure. On the basis of this pilot, I revised the questions, but concluded that the method was appropriate. I then set about holding the remaining interviews.

Each interview took between an hour and a half and two and a half hours. Many of the respondents had prepared notes on their briefing paper and the overall feeling from the interviews was that they allowed much passion, commitment, and enthusiasm to be expressed about the subject as well as concerns for its future and survival. During the interviews the briefing paper and research questions were used and referred to and the areas I wanted discussed were explored. I also drew out particular issues and concerns relevant to the individuals to ensure their experiences contributed to the research. This was important, as I wanted the interviewees to emphasise the areas that they felt were particularly important.

The amount of information I collected was significant. Having completed each interview, the interviews were written up and notes sent to individuals. The majority required no alteration or clarification. Once all the interviews had been completed, I set about collating the data under the relevant categories and analysing it.

Stage 6: analysis

I began by ensuring that the interviewee's name was placed next to each paragraph. I allocated each paragraph answer to the relevant question or sub-set of questions. Such a process was necessary because each interview was inevitably discursive with every respondent taking a slightly different approach to the manner and order in which the questions were answered. The marking of each paragraph with the relevant respondent allowed me to keep track of the respondents, whilst collating data against the relevant set of answers. During this process a further theme emerged in addition to those identified in the research questions. This represented the main concerns of the interviewees from the arts boards. These responses were assigned to a new category. Once the whole categorisation process was completed, I undertook an overall analysis of each question, highlighting emerging themes. I included quotes where appropriate to ensure the main themes and issues were drawn out with the most pertinent quotes illustrating the point being made by respondents.

A number of concerns emerged as recurrent themes. What was interesting was that these concerns reflected the experiences and views of respondents working in different parts of the fine art sector and in different institutions with varied experiences and agendas. The fact that there was a consensus on the current situation and the problems facing fine art as a subject within higher education gave these concerns a validity that I hadn't expected. This therefore confirmed the central premise of the research:

- that there are problems for subject areas in adjusting to the demands of a mass system of higher education; and
- that the point about where subject areas decide to draw the line against these demands is a pertinent one.

At the heart of these concerns is:

- how to balance the needs of the individual, something that is paramount in a fine art education, with the requirements of a mass system of higher education;
- what to teach and how to teach in the context of the fragmentation of the subject and the higher education sector;
- how to maintain an holistic, artistic and educational experience in what is now a complex and fragmented higher education context;

- how to work with the changed nature of fine art practice, not only the broad range of media and approaches, but also the focus on the media and success;
- how to deal with the effects of modularity and standardisation;
- how to cope with the diverse nature of the student body with its broad range of talent and motivations;
- how to allow for opportunities for a greater crossover between subjects outside the traditional fine art area; and
- how to allow for further development of teaching and learning methods.

However, the overriding concern was that the push for greater numbers will lead to a reduction of the subject, that is a dumbing-down in the quality of exploration and experimentation undertaken by students.

Respondents felt that what needs to be protected at all costs is the development of the individual and that to do this the following needs to be considered:

- the development of a hierarchical system to encompass two approaches to the teaching and learning of fine art both in and through the subject;
- that courses should be concentrating on the development of values, manipulative skills, craft and the ability to problem solve;
- that all the aspects of learning should be made explicit to students so that they are aware of the variety of skills and abilities they have acquired and how they relate to life upon graduation; and
- that professional practice elements are crucial as is greater access to other subject areas.

Despite these suggestions respondents were also concerned:

- that the development of studio practice would become squeezed and diluted because of the inclusion of these other elements;
- that courses were finding it difficult to cope with the broad range of students' abilities, that the abilities were being stretched too far down the ladder; and
- that being explicit about learning to students and being responsive to the current political and economic climate was a priority if fine art courses are to remain a viable option both to higher education institutions and students.

Stage 7: overall concerns

In drawing together the overall analysis it became apparent that the respondents perceived one major consequence if the sector wasn't careful that, because of the effects of the massification of higher education, there will be increased numbers of third-rate artists who are ill-equipped for their futures as fine artists. In addition, the consequence of increased numbers and the inability of staff to continue with the same focus on the individual is that the educational experience for all students, not just those represented by increased numbers, is reduced and dumbed-down. The major questions facing all are 'What to teach?' and 'How to teach?'

There were a number of factors that made up this conclusion.

The first is a concern about the current state of fine art generally. The feeling is that the emphasis on the cult of the personality and the financial success of the artist is damaging the long-term future development of fine artists. The concern is that because some artists have acquired celebrity status, commanding high prices for their work and much media attention, this has shaped the aspirations of today's fine art students. Similarly, changes to the arts funding systems have encouraged museums and galleries to look to enhance their visitor numbers through crowd pulling exhibitions, the consequence of which is again that younger artists focus on publicity rather than artistic quality. This undermines the concept of fine art as an education that supports nurturing, and involves time and commitment to ensure the necessary artistic development. Respondents were concerned that the emphasis is now on youth, and the new and the latest approach to the avant-garde rather than on the long-term quality of a work of art and its power and ability to reflect society and perhaps point ways forward for us all.

Second are the changes to the nature of the teaching environment. This is made up of the increased student numbers, the emphasis on accountability, shrinking resources, the need to include new agendas such as employability and the changes in the overall nature of the student body. These are significant elements that staff are having to adjust to. Additionally, there was anxiety amongst respondents that the number of institutions offering fine art at undergraduate level has risen from approximately 60 in 1996 to over 90 in 2001. Many of these new courses are in FE colleges and there was an anxiety that these institutions do not have the physical resources to provide the students with the correct support, and that the staff are not involved with the development of their own practice to the same degree as other more established courses. Not only is it likely that these institutions are accepting weaker, less able students but they then don't have the necessary teaching and learning infrastructure to support and develop these students. In addition the changes to the teaching and learning environment have been particularly affected by the emphasis on accountability and the spread of modularity and the affects that this has had on curriculum design and assessment in particular. When all of these factors are added to the changes to the subject itself, the teaching and learning of fine art is undermined by the fragmentation of the teaching and learning environment and by what should or could form the content of the curriculum. The plethora of possible subject matter, media, theories and contexts means creating curricula that help and enable students to navigate their way through them, whilst at the same time ensuring a meaningful holistic learning environment is becoming increasingly difficult. Fine art is now a multi-variant arena with multiple possibilities – there is never one way to get there and allowing students to understand this experience is challenging, but with increased numbers of students from diverse backgrounds, it is increasingly difficult. This contributes to the pressures facing staff and increases the necessity to structure courses and ensure that teaching and learning will allow expansion, as well as ensuring excellence and equity. This all means that satisfactory answers to the questions, what to teach, how to teach it, how to assess it and how to present this when also being accountable will be critical in ensuring that the sector prevents the creation of increased numbers of ill-prepared fine art graduates.

The third factor is the nature of the student body. The Government's emphasis on widening access coupled with their changes to student funding support has meant that the student population is more diverse, it is acutely aware of the costs of their courses and that they need to prepare more effectively for their future employment. Many students are working in addition to studying and staff have to cope with a student body which is unable to devote the necessary time to their studies. Students are unable to attend their programmes in a sustained way, they are unlikely to take risks with their work, take up foreign exchange programmes and are generally are working to other goals than just the development of their subject expertise. The other related concern is the increased student body. This means that because of the increased numbers of institutions offering fine art, students are being accepted into the sector despite the fact that they lack the artistic ability and talent needed to sustain a career as an artist or in those areas of employment that fine art graduates have traditionally moved into. These students don't have the depth and breadth needed – that is, the inquiring, experimental, intellectual, risk-taking, problem-solving, boundary-pushing approach to their intellectual and artistic development. They are students who too readily accept the results of their artistic and intellectual efforts. They are students whose academic weaknesses are further emphasised by the fact that they are paying for their studies. They are consequently too concerned with achieving the grade that will form the next stage of their degree and they are not prepared to risk failure both because of the financial costs of their studies and because of the process of continuous assessment that encourages the idea of continuous progression.

Ways forward

The consequence of these and other related issues that I haven't had time to raise, is that it is now an incredibly complex and challenging teaching environment with its pressures to increase numbers, maintain excellence and achieve this with greater equity of access against a background of shrinking resources and accountability to business, Government and the students themselves. This is placing great strain on staff and the subject discipline itself. For fine art educators the subject itself has fragmented and the attempt to try and find solutions to all of these problems is causing great anxiety that in itself is deflecting staff from focusing on the subject and their students.

Nevertheless there were a number of suggestions for future directions and focus:

- that institutions should clearly develop a range of courses, that are both in and through the subject and are clear and positive about the differences – this rather than a hierarchal system should be how we protect the subject;
- that the push for regionalisation is taken advantage of, so that all parts of the country benefit from both types of courses, positive exhibitions and a range of art-related activities;
- that partnerships and collaborations are developed between courses and arts organisations to prepare students and support graduates effectively;
- that courses look at ways to include a range of subject elements outside the traditional fine art elements and improve links with other subjects to achieve this;

- that courses should be examined carefully, to ensure that assessment and courses structures support the needs of what is now a very different student body.

Reference

Reid, L.A. (1969), *Meaning in the Arts*, London, George Allen & Unwin Ltd: New York, Humanties Press.

Biographical note

Frances Corner is Head of the Sir John Cass Department of Art at London Guildhall University where she is responsible for courses in the subject areas of fine art, silversmithing and jewellery, and communications. She has also been involved with research into the career destinations of art and design graduates and has published articles on this issue. With a background in fine art (printmaking), she is currently completing a D.Phil at Oxford University that is looking at the effects of the current changes that are accompanying the massification of higher education on the subject of fine art. Frances is a member of the Steering Committees for the National Association for Fine Art Education and for GLAD. Frances is also on the editorial board for the Journal of Visual Arts Practice and is Associate Editor for the new Journal for the ADC-LTSN

Enhancing the design curriculum through pedagogic research

8

Allan Davies, The Centre for Learning and Teaching in Art & Design, UK

Abstract

Pedagogic research is becoming increasingly recognised as an important aspect of academic life. Many generic studies (Marton & Saljo 1984, Entwistle 1992, Biggs 1999, Gibbs, Prosser & Trigwell 1999, et al.), focusing on broad concepts of student learning, have found a purchase within particular disciplines. Concepts of 'deep' and 'surface' approaches to learning are now commonplace within subject-based rationales. Approaches to assessment have also benefited from research of this kind. The value of this kind of research is most pertinent when it is used at subject level to explore the learning and teaching axis.

Subject-focused research, using these established frameworks and methodologies, is only just beginning to emerge. Inevitably, the application of this new research is not so widespread. Subject-based research asks the questions about what it is that is characteristic about learning and teaching a particular subject. Recent research in creative subjects (Reid, 2000; Reid & Davies, 2000) has revealed that the quality of learning is predicated on how both students and teachers conceptualise the subject of study. In design, for instance, what teachers think design is determines how they frame the curriculum and how they go about teaching. Equally, students' beliefs about what design is underpin their intentions when they go about learning. The research reveals that there are significant qualitative differences amongst teachers as well as students as to what design is. This has an impact on the quality of the outcomes of learning design.

This paper explores the implications of the outcomes of this research on curriculum design and teaching methodologies in design education.

Approaches to learning

The concepts 'deep' and 'surface', when applied to students' learning, are becoming increasingly popular in academic contexts. Most developed learning and teaching Web sites, particularly in Australian Universities, utilise these terms in helping new teachers to conceptualise the task of promoting high quality learning. In the recent round of subject quality review by the Quality Assurance Agency in the UK, the terms were commonly seen in the Self-Assessment documents, which were prepared prior to the reviews themselves. In many instances, the terms are used atheoretically, taking for granted the inevitability that 'deep learning' is the principal aim of higher education and that 'surface leaning' is the antithesis of this. There is something almost *a priori* about the use of the terms in that the concept 'deep' offers up a much more profound conceptualisation of learning than that of 'surface'. It would be foolish, in this case, for any teacher to align themselves with promoting surface learning even if they didn't recognise the theoretical usage of the terms. However, when we ask for concrete examples of what deep or surface learning consists in, in a particular subject, then the answers are not only less forthcoming but are also wide in their range of possibilities. What one teacher means by deep can be distinctly different to another's when it is discussed at subject level.

But the terms are convenient shorthand anyway since 'deep learning' and 'surface learning' per se were never used in the early research.

Not only have the terms been appropriated from the research literature but they have, to some extent, been misunderstood. Nevertheless, they have conveniently found their way into much of the academic literature as part of the rhetoric of accountability and transparency that has emerged in the pursuit of the quality assurance of standards. However, the terms deep and surface were originally used to describe the qualitatively different *levels of processes* or *approaches* that students took to any learning situation (Marton & Säljö, 1976). There was a recognition in the early research that there was a strong, positive correlation between the quality of the outcomes of student learning and the approach (deep or surface) that students took to their learning (Svensson, 1984). Also, there was seen to be a strong correlation between students' approaches to learning and what they thought learning consisted in. Those students who believe that learning is about memorising what is put in front of them by the teacher tend to focus on the concrete and literal aspects of the task. The strategy they adopt is limited to recalling the components, usually through literal description. This is a surface approach. The approach is constrained because these students have rather limited views about the nature of learning at university.

Students who take a deep approach to learning have a focus on understanding and making sense of the material in front of them. They look beyond the literal aspects of the material through interpretation and analysis. Whilst students who take a surface approach disregard underlying structures within the material, students who take a deep approach seek out relational aspects both within the material and to other conceptual frameworks. Marton and Säljö observed that:

> We had been looking for an answer to the question of why the students had arrived at those qualitatively different ways of understanding the text as a whole. What we found was that *the students who did not get 'the point' failed to do so simply because they were not looking for it.*
> Marton & Saljo (1984)

Students who take a deep approach often do so because they see a personal benefit in learning. It enables them to see the world in a much more complex and interesting way. To this extent, the *intentions* of learners often determine the approach that they take and, consequently, the quality of the learning outcome. Whilst deep and surface approaches relate to particular learning occasions, students tend to demonstrate a predominant orientation towards either approach depending on what they believe learning consists in, in particular learning contexts.

The *prior experience* of learning in other contexts, therefore, often has a significant impact on how individuals approach learning in new contexts. Learners who have only experience of curricula and teaching that promote a surface approach are more than likely to expect this experience in any new contexts. Hence, they approach new learning situations with a strong expectation that success in learning will require the approach they adopted in the previous context. That, for them, is what learning consists in.

It follows from this that, in order to improve the quality of student learning, we must, as teachers, help those students who take a predominantly surface approach to learning in their formal studies to develop deeper, more sophisticated conceptions of what learning consists in. Indeed, the major task of education is to enable those students who 'just don't get it' to begin to think differently about what learning is for them. We need to help students who conceptualise learning as teacher-focused to experience, believe and trust that effective learning is something that they do to themselves. This requires a substantial paradigm shift in their beliefs about learning – a greater shift to the act of studying a subject than those who already take a deep approach to learning. This is the first pedagogic challenge.

In the early eighties, Biggs & Collis (Biggs & Collis, 1982) offered a taxonomy which helped to understand more clearly the *structural complexity* of student responses to tasks set. The SOLO (Structure of the Observed Learning Outcomes) taxonomy is a learning cycle, is hierarchical and has five basic levels:

1. *prestructural*: the task is engaged but the learner is distracted or misled by irrelevancies;
2. *unistructural*: the learner focuses on the relevant domain and picks up one aspect to work with;
3. *multistructural*: the learner picks up more and more relevant features but does not integrate them;
4. *relational*: the learner integrates the parts with each other so that the whole has coherent structure and meaning; and
5. *extended abstract*: the learner generalises the structure to take in new and more abstract features representing a new and higher mode of operation.

Levels 1–3 can be seen as surface approaches and levels 4–5 as deep approaches. In design terms, examples of the taxonomy might be:

- *prestructural*: the student is preoccupied with the outcomes of a previous project and is unwilling to move on; the new project is tackled by attempting to draw in the main features of the previous project despite them being inappropriate to what is required;
- *unistructural*: the student believes that there are right and wrong answers to projects set; their task is to find the answer that best suits what they think the teacher wants;
- *multistructural*: the student believes that doing lots of work is required; they are inclined to spend more time 'researching' than any other aspect of the task; they gather lots of material but do not use the material in developing and integrating their thinking;
- *relational*: the student attempts to identify different interpretations of the project and considers a range of possible outcomes; although their 'research' is focused on the project set they are open to embracing unexpected outcomes of the research activity; they are inclined to see the purpose of the project as developing their conception of the subject that they are studying;

- *extended abstract*: whilst this approach involves relational activity, a design student taking this approach might begin to question assumptions about the nature of the brief which derived from their investigations; they are likely to look beyond design principles to satisfy their curiosity.

Although these categories are hierarchical, it should be recognised that each category will involve some elements of the previous one in the hierarchy. For instance, students who take a surface approach often focus on the skills and techniques required without too much concern about their cognitive development. Students who take a deep approach, on the other hand, whilst focusing primarily on the conceptual challenge of the problems to solve, will inevitably seek to make judgements about which are the most appropriate tools and skills required to achieve their objectives. These students learn the skills and techniques by applying their understanding of design principles.

Also, whilst these categories are considered developmental in the learning cycle, students who have a conception of learning which is teacher-centred and focused on the concrete elements of design, such as learning skills etc., are unlikely to have experience of levels 4 and 5 and therefore have no intention of achieving them.

Students also hold views on the nature of the subject of study, in this case, design. In a recent study on the qualitative variation in students' conceptions of, and approaches to, the studying of design (Davies & Reid, 2000), some students expressed a quite limited conception of what they thought design consisted in. It amounted to a strong belief that design was about the manipulation of certain skills and techniques that had to be learned in order for them to be used in the industry. Their views were particularly concrete and stable about the world of design:

> ... whereas on Fridays, being the best day, because I go there, I get taught the trade, I get taught skills. That is what I want the most. Learn software programmes or any kind of craft that can help ... Because I want to become more professional, master a skill.

> I think you need to be able to step out of university and into a job and have all the skills necessary for working in the field that you have chosen.

Students holding a slightly more sophisticated conception relied heavily on the practical with the belief that doing 'research' was important if you wanted to get ideas. Research in this context amounted to gathering as much potentially useful material in relation to the project set and picking one or two ideas to elaborate:

> You have to get your research down to a 't' because it has to be correct. You do that then you do some practice runs ... and you will show your teacher and she will go: 'That is good' or 'That is bad, maybe you could do this to improve that, maybe if you go away and do this' and you will go away and you will do that two or three practice runs and try things out and then you will do your assessment.

In neither instance did these students express concern about conceptual development or expanding their conception of what design might be. For them it was taken for granted.

Some students saw design as a cognitive and interpretive activity that required a focus on solving problems set. Even so, some of these students saw problem solving as an extrinsic activity that was a skill within the nature of the subject rather than an intrinsically intellectual and personal challenge, which other students expressed:

> So I think it is probably critical to think of the equilibrium of design – like designer and user and whether you are thinking about aesthetics or function, communication or just looking pretty. I think it's important to find the balance between these two.

The most sophisticated conception was expressed by those students who looked beyond design and its principles towards greater moral and social understanding. This is a view of design that is about living in the world as a human being which requires a recognition of socio/political contexts that integrate with design principles and practice.

Students who engage in the more sophisticated conceptions will engage with the elements expressed by the less sophisticated views but in a more considered and integrated way.

We can see from this that there are two very strong perspectives – conceptions of learning and teaching and conceptions of the subject of study – that can play a major role in determining the quality of students' learning outcomes in studying design.

Factors which contribute to the quality of student learning

There are, of course, factors beyond the learner which bear upon their approach: the teaching methods used, the nature of the curriculum and, most significantly, assessment (Gibbs, 1992).

Teaching approaches

There are a number of recent studies which focus on what teachers think they are doing when they are teaching (Prosser & Trigwell, 1999). Again, there appears a qualitatively differentiated hierarchy of conceptions of teaching , ranging from intentions simply to cover the syllabus or transfer the understandings of the teacher through to helping students to change and develop their conceptions. These qualitatively different conceptions can have a marked influence on the quality of student learning. Teachers design projects, syllabi and curricula on the basis of what they believe students should learn.

In a recent study on design teachers' conceptions of teaching (Davies & Reid, 2000) some teachers expressed a commitment to teaching students their own practical expertise, explaining that, without basic skills, students were unlikely to find employment in the industry. Similarly, some teachers felt that somehow they should teach students what they thought the principles of design were through aspects of the defined curriculum. There was a strong focus on the teachers being responsible for the learning and transferring what they knew about design to the students. This approach was predominant in design education in the UK until recently, primarily through what became known as 'sitting by nellie' (Swann, 1986; Swann 1989) – a now dubious expression, taken from the practice of inducting new workers into the weaving industry in the 19th century. It assumed that learning happened on a one-to-one basis between teacher and student by seeing and doing. The practitioner passes on the relevant skills by some form of osmosis. Of recent times, increased class sizes have required teachers to abandon the one-to-one approach although the conception of teaching may not have changed.

Some design teachers believe that learning is best achieved when the students are busy doing something to solve the problems the teachers have set, normally outlined in the form of a brief which is seen to mirror practices within the design industry. There is a strong teacher-focus here with the teacher often playing the role of both senior manager (in the outlining of the brief/project) and client (in the assessment). Students are encouraged to see themselves as key participants in the process of learning design but it is essentially about them identifying problems and trying to satisfy what other people want.

Some design teachers design curriculum activities in the belief that learning is about constructing personal understandings through interpreting and experimenting. The focus for them is on helping students to develop and change their understanding of the nature of design through problem finding. The emphasis is much more on divergent thinking where the student is encouraged to find a range of alternative solutions to the brief set. These teachers tend to see the issues of learning from a student's perspective.

Finally some teachers regarded learning as helping students to become change-agents in society. They encourage students not only to reflect on the subject of design but also to become autonomous learners within the wider community.

These same teachers were also asked about what they thought was the nature of the subject they were teaching. This conception, in building on an earlier study in music (Reid, 1996), is known as the 'Design Entity'.

Some teachers regarded design as product-oriented which involves the honing and developing of the skills and techniques which contribute to the making of these objects. The objects were often seen as the principal elements in the assessment process and grades or marks awarded to the 'quality' of the object.

Other teachers saw design as solving other peoples' problems in which the criteria of success was the satisfaction of the client. Problem solving, particularly in relation to the tension between the aesthetic elements of the material outcome and its functionality, was seen as the core aspect of design practice, although some teachers looked beyond this, claiming the designer's role to be that of bringing all of these elements together and 'orchestrating' the whole.

A more sophisticated view of design was intrinsically cognitive. Not only are analytical and creative abilities required but design led to new ways of seeing the world. Often this involved an understanding of the community in which the design was operational and how design impacted on it. Some teachers considered that true designing required an understanding of human agency – who we are as people.

Each of these descriptors can be seen as qualitatively different categories, which define the limitations on how teachers regard what learning and teaching is and what the subject of study, design in this case, consists in. Not surprisingly, those teachers who held a somewhat unsophisticated view of what design is also held rather unsophisticated views about how students go about learning and how they themselves should go about teaching.

We see, then, the qualitatively different conceptions that teachers have about the job that they are doing. Teachers who believe that the basic skills of design are essential for student learning, particularly if they are to gain employment, will organise the curriculum, projects and their own teaching to emphasise these aspects of the design process. Equally, design teachers who believe that learning design is about problem solving will set their projects differently, often emphasising the challenge of establishing a balance between the aesthetic and functional values.

Given that teachers tend to teach in relation to their implicit theories of learning (Biggs, 1999), and that they are usually responsible for the syllabus, teachers with limited conceptions of teaching are more likely to promote surface approaches to learning than those teachers who hold a more sophisticated, student-centred, conception of teaching and who have intentions of deepening students' understanding of the subject of study.

In the table below, the potential relationship between teacher and student is outlined with examples of the kind of focus that might occur when the conceptions of learning and teaching and the conception of the design entity are shared. This mutuality, at whatever level of engagement, is conflict free and often leads to a productive relationship – despite the quality of the learning.

	Design entity (teacher's focus)		
Student approach	**Making/doing**	**Interpreting /experimenting**	**Living**
Uni-structural	Product/skills oriented Finding the right answer Satisfying the teacher		
Multi-structural	Collecting information Increasing skills	'Researching' Trying things out	
Relational		Making sense Choosing appropriate tools Orchestrating the parts Informed judgements	
Extended abstract		Seeking alternatives beyond design principles Teacher as facilitator	Self-authorship Seeing the world differently Change-agency Challenging design principles

Fig. 1

It is possible to make two observations from these scenarios. Firstly, students and teachers working in the same learning context and sharing the same conceptions are likely to reinforce each other's attitudes. Secondly, students and teachers who do not share this mutuality are likely to be in conflict, although the cause is rarely revealed.

Curriculum design

Understanding how students learn can help teachers develop their teaching. But understanding how students learn can also contribute to much more constructed curriculum design. When interviewed, some design teachers described how it was important to introduce students to all the basic skills in the first year, arguing that these are necessary for producing the material outcomes of the more independent, ideas-based activities in the later years. This makes sense but only from the teacher's perspective. We have already seen how some students have an already formulated view about design being about learning skills. If they have formulated this view prior to embarking on a degree programme, then the first year curriculum will be no surprise to them – it will simply reinforce their beliefs and intentions. Imagine that these skills are taught, for efficiency sake, in a strong teacher/demonstrator way. What more could encourage a surface approach? And consider the struggle (often internal and unstated) that these students have when they begin to realise that design is becoming something different to what they believed and that they have had little preparation for this new, ideas-based activity. Students who take a deep approach often take a limiting curriculum in their stride. They are able to see possibilities beyond the prescriptions of the teacher and the curriculum. Yet these teachers, because of the success of the able students, continue to believe that the curriculum is appropriate and it's the fault of the student if they 'don't get it'.

If we value the more sophisticated conceptions of design as expressed earlier and we genuinely believe that learning at university is about becoming autonomous, then these are the values that should be promoted at the beginning of the curriculum. Students need to be inducted into these values and have opportunities to experience them and, on occasions, get them wrong. There is much made of risk taking and experimentation in the learning of design, yet many students limit the risks in a context that is teacher-centred and the outcomes and assessment criteria are unclear or poorly articulated.

Assessment

Assessment is well recognised as a major driver in student learning (Gibbs, 1992). In their study, Entwistle, Hanley and Ratcliffe (1979) observed, along with meaning orientations (deep) and reproducing orientations (surface), a *strategic* orientation towards learning taken by some students. It was recognised that students with a reproducing conception, adopted a *surface apathetic* approach, and preferred teaching that transmits information and directs learning towards assessment requirements. Other research has indicated that students who show a deep strategic approach are better able to discern and utilise the aspects of a learning environment which will support their way of studying (Meyer, Parsons & Dunne, 1990; Meyer, 1991). In other words, students who are mindful of the assessment requirements of a project can take either a deep or surface approach to them. Getting high grades becomes the focus of the students' attention rather than a focus on the subject of study or their own intrinsic success as learners. Most students, at some point in a project, will ask the question, 'What do I have to do to do well in this project?' Students who take a deep approach will be able to accommodate the assessment requirements in their approach. Students who take a surface approach will be driven by the requirements. In a study of the strategic approaches taken by psychology students (Norton, Dickens, & Cook, 1996) in relation to coursework assessment, over half the students admitted to playing the role of 'the good student' with the expectation that this strategy would influence the teacher's judgement of their work.

Designing assessment tasks that promote a deep approach to learning requires that the learning outcomes and assessment are clearly defined and relate to each other. Biggs (1999) has articulated an approach to curriculum design in which all the elements of the learning context have to be 'constructively aligned' in order to encourage a deep approach.

In an attempt to explicate the observation by the Quality Assurance Agency (QAA), in their overview report on the quality of provision in the Art and Design sector in the UK, that:

> ... there is a widespread need to improve the definition of assessment criteria, to relate them to published learning outcomes and to use them consistently.

a project, funded by the Art, Design and Communication – Learning and Teaching Subject Network (ADC-LTSN) in 2001, and conducted by the author found that concern about the administrative aspects of assessment needed to be complemented by further teacher and curricular activity. Informed by the work of Price et al (2001), it recommended that:

- learning outcomes in art and design should not only be clearly written but should also promote divergent thinking (imagination, creativity, visualisation etc.) outcomes;
- the assessment criteria should be criterion referenced, related to the subject of study, and be capable of differentiating levels of achievement of the learning outcomes;
- the strategy for using the assessment criteria to determine the level of achievement of the criteria should be explicit;
- curriculum and learning and teaching strategies (e.g. socialisation events, learning teams, learning logs, learning agreements, self- and peer-assessments) should be developed within the curriculum experience to enable students to understand what is required from the learning outcomes (written material alone is not enough) and what they have to do to perform well; and

- the course team should ensure that they also understand what they are asking of the students and be able to articulate it between themselves as well as with students.

One of the key observations made during this research was that simply offering students the information on the project, no matter how well documented and 'constructively aligned' it was, was not sufficient in helping them to understand the key concepts which underpinned the tasks. It was observed that, even within projects at subject level, students' conceptions of the key concepts, such as 'analyse', 'research', 'create' etc., as well as common concepts such as 'design', varied substantially from each other's and particularly from the teacher's. Often, the terms mean different things in different subjects. Students analyse differently in sociology to the way the do in, say, psychology or business studies. The key here is to construct the introduction to the briefings, etc. so that students have the opportunity to test out their understanding of these concepts against those of other students and, of course, those of the teacher.

One of the important challenges not only in helping design students to understand the tasks in design education but also in supporting them as creative thinkers is to articulate the learning outcomes in a form that promotes this kind of thinking. One of the difficulties here is that it seems to be much more straightforward to write learning outcomes that relate to convergent thinking, which usually involves logically moving from the general to the particular or even generating theories, than to divergent thinking, which is often seeking a potential range of alternative outcomes (Hartley, 1998; Heywood, 2000). Making judgements that qualitatively differentiate the level of achievement of these learning outcomes is equally challenging for teachers. Helping students understand the assessment requirements requires as much orientation into the project as does that for the learning outcomes. Students are less likely to take a surface approach to assessment if they understand the judgements and how they are made during assessment particularly if they are rewarded for 'creativity', 'risk taking' etc. if these are the concepts which appear in the learning outcomes.

Summary

This paper has attempted to lay out just a few of the issues that emerge when we begin to recognise that there are significant differences between what students think they are doing when they are studying a particular subject, in this case design, and what teachers think they are teaching. If the conflict of intentions between students and teachers continues unexplored in any teaching/learning context then the potentiality for students taking a surface approach is significantly enhanced. Research into design education need not be profound in order to bring successful rewards. There is more than enough generic research into student learning for teachers to begin to use it to interrogate their own practice. Small-scale action research projects in relation to individual practice can often provide significant insight into specific learning and teaching contexts and help teachers design curricula, learning and teaching and assessment tasks that promote the kind of learning that genuinely does transform student understanding of the subject of study.

References

Biggs, J.B. (1999), *Teaching for Quality Learning at University* (Buckingham: Open University Press)

Biggs, J.B. & Collis, K.F. (1982), *Evaluating the Quality of Learning: The SOLO Taxonomy* (New York: Academic Press)

Davies, A. (2000), 'Uncovering problematics in art and design teaching and assessment', in Rust, C. (ed.), *Improving Student Learning (2000)*, OCSLD

Davies, A. & Reid, A. (2000), 'Uncovering problematics in design education – learning and the design entity' in Swann C (ed) Proceedings of *Reinventing Design Education in Universities Conference*, Curtin University, Perth

Entwistle, N.J. (1992), 'Student learning and study strategies', in Clark, B.R. & Neave, G. (eds.), *The Encyclopedia of Higher Education* (Oxford: Pergamon)

Entwistle N., Hanley and Ratcliffe (1979), 'Approaches to learning and levels of understanding', *British Educational Research Journal*, 5

Gibbs, G. (1992), 'Improving the quality of student learning', *TES*

Hartley, J. (1998), *Learning and Studying. A Research Perspective* (London: Routledge)

Heywood J. (2000), 'Assessment in higher education', JKP

Marton, F. & Säljö, R. (1976), 'On qualitative differences in learning – Outcome and process', *British Journal of Educational Psychology*

Marton, F and Säljö, R. (1984), 'Approaches to learning', in Marton, F., Hounsell, D. and Entwistle, N. (eds.), *The Experience of Learning* (Scottish Academy Press)

Meyer, J.H.F., Parsons, P. and Dunne, T.T. (1990), 'Individual study orchestrations and their association with learning outcomes', *Higher Education*, 11

Meyer, J.H.F., (1991) Study orchestration: the manifestation, interpretation and consequence of contextualised approaches to learning, *Higher Education*, 22

Norton, L.S., Dickens T., & Cook N.M. (1996), 'Coursework assessment: what are tutors really looking for?', in Gibbs, G. (ed.), *Improving Student Learning: Using Research to Improve Student Learning* (Oxford: OCSD)

Price, M. et al. (2001), *Strategies to develop students' understanding of assessment criteria and processes*, in Rust, C. (ed.), *Improving Student Learning Symposia 2000*, (Oxford: OCSLD)

Prosser, M. and Trigwell, K. (1999), *Understanding Learning and Teaching* (Oxford: OUP

Reid, A (1996), 'Understanding 'Music': Teachers' and students' conceptions of learning in instrumental music lessons. *Different*

Approaches: Theory and Practice in Higher Education, 19 681-685 HERDSA, Australia

Reid, A. (2000), 'Musicians' experience of the musical world: relations with teaching and learning', in Rust, C. (ed.), *Improving Student Learning* (Oxford: OCSLD)

Reid, A. and Davies, A. (2000), 'Variation in teachers' and students' understanding of professional work and teaching and learning in design' (awaiting publication)

Swan, C. (1986), 'Nellie is Dead', *Designer*

Swan, C. et al., (1989), 'On not sitting with Nellie', CNAA/CHEAD seminar paper

Svensson, L. (1984), 'Skill in learning', in Marton, F., Entwistle, N. and Hounsell, D. (eds.), *The Experience of Learning* (Scottish Academic Press)

Biographical note

Allan Davies is the Head of the Centre for Learning and Teaching in Art and Design (*cltad*). He has published articles on a range of pedagogical matters including assessment and approaches to learning and teaching.

9

Fashion variations: student approaches to learning in fashion design

Linda Drew, University of Brighton, UK

Sue Bailey, Manchester Metropolitan University, UK

Alison Shreeve, London College of Fashion, The London Institute, UK

Abstract

This paper investigates the qualitatively different ways that students approach their learning in the context of first- and second-year fashion design courses.

The central aim of the study is to explore the variation in fashion design students' approaches to learning. The focus on variation suggests that these approaches are best explored with a phenomenographic study. Fashion design students in four fashion design departments in UK universities were chosen as the subjects of the study. The phenomenographic method used commenced with semi-structured interviews focusing on student approaches to learning in the context of a fashion design project in the first or second year of study. The sample of 21 was deliberately selected to maximise the variation. The focus of analysis is to define the qualitatively different ways (but not the similar ways) in which fashion design students approach their learning.

The context explored in this study focuses on one fashion design project. The second-order nature of the research approach is concerned with talking to students about how they experience their learning (that is, to describe the experience of their interviewees, rather than to describe their own experience, which is a first-order approach). This paper also focuses on variation or on experiences that are different, in learning fashion design. The variations in approaches to learning in fashion design are constituted as a series of qualitatively different categories of approaches. These approaches move from strategies that focus on the product, through a focus on the process of design to a focus on concepts. The students' intentions in deploying these strategies vary from developing a technical competence, through the development of the design process to development of their own conceptions. These categories are described in terms of those structural and referential aspects of the strategies and intentions. This is demonstrated in the outcome space, which describes the internal relations in structural and referential terms, this enabled the construction of the hierarchy of the structural component of the study.

Introduction

Although the body of research building on Marton and Säljo's seminal study (1976) into student approaches to learning now ranges across a number of subjects and disciplines, only one such study has been conducted in art and design. A case study on the encouragement of independent and reflective learning on a graphic design course (Gibbs, 1992; Davies, 1994) touched upon student approaches but did not set out specifically to identify the range of different approaches taken, nor to define the features of the differences. This being so, teachers in the discipline have had little empirical research to inform debates on student learning. Nevertheless, the discourse that has developed around student learning has come to embrace the terms 'deep' and 'surface' without specific information about how such characteristics might manifest themselves in art and design.

It is only recently that a larger proportion of teachers in the discipline has started to recognise the role educational research can play in the development of thinking concerning pedagogical issues. This growing awareness and our own everyday observations indicate that it is very likely that students are adopting deep and surface approaches. But if they are, how do we know, and what more can we say about these approaches in the context of art and design? More specifically, what do our students on fashion design courses do when presented with the project briefs, which constitute the practical learning environments of design projects?

Biggs (1999, p. 18) and Prosser & Trigwell (1999, p. 12) have produced models of the factors that impact on learning outcomes and the relations between them. These suggest that we might develop teaching and assessment practices that encourage the achievement of higher quality outcomes if we are able to understand the learning processes students adopt in a given context and why. Knowing more about the range of variation in approach, and how the different approaches are characterised in art and design, would provide opportunities for students and teachers to reflect on how learning intentions, focus and motivation are related to the learning that has taken place. At the same time, we might develop better methods for facilitating learning if we understand more about how students variously perceive the objects of their learning.

Approaches to learning

The literature on approaches to learning encompasses what have come to be regarded as seminal studies. The first of these, conducted by Marton & Säljö (1976) was concerned with what were then termed 'levels of processing'. They found the key difference between the ways educational psychology students had read a given text rested on whether they focused on what the text was about (deep processing), or on the text itself (surface processing). Svensson (1977) also working on how students read texts found similar results in what he termed students' 'approaches', but he referred to the two approaches as 'atomistic' and 'holistic', the former describing a focus on parts of the text, and the latter a focus on the meaning of the text. Over time, elements of the terminologies adopted in these two early studies appear to have merged to give us the 'deep/surface approaches'. Research undertaken by Laurillard (1979) confirmed that the two different approaches were adopted by students working on problem-solving tasks on a combined science course, and also identified that students would change approach according to the learning context. Thereby it was established that an approach is not a fixed characteristic of the student, although there may be a preferred approach. Studies conducted by Entwistle and Ramsden (1983) again supported the early findings but identified that students could also take a 'strategic' approach. This resonated with the 'cue-consciousness' first observed by Miller & Parlett (1974), and accorded with Ramsden's (1979) earlier investigation into the effect that the learning context, for example heavy workloads, could have on approach.

Deep approach	**Surface approach**	**Strategic approach**
Intention to understand	Intention to complete task requirements	Intention to obtain highest possible grades
Vigorous interaction with content	Memorise information needed for assessments	Organise time and distribute effort to greatest effect
Relate new ideas to previous knowledge	Failure to distinguish principles from examples	Ensure conditions and materials for studying are appropriate
Relate concepts to everyday practice	Treat task as an external imposition	Use previous exam papers to predict questions
Relate evidence to conclusions	Focus on discrete elements without integration	Be alert to cues about marking schemes
Examine the logic of the argument	Unreflective about purpose or strategies	

Table 1 Features of student approaches to learning (Source: Entwistle, 1987)

Features of approaches are summarised in Table 1. Many of the features describe or relate to learning, teaching and assessment practices that are not part of the learning environment common to most art and design institutions i.e. project based, problem based or experiential and independent learning. The majority of learning time is spent through practice of the design processes and would include a number of stages of the process which are perhaps not readily identified in the descriptions elicited here.

The re-contextualising of such research into a language familiar to art and design practices is perhaps undertaken on an intuitive basis by teachers, the terminology certainly having resonance to our experiences as teachers. Further illumination may be provided by references to the aspects or dimensions, rather than the features, of deep and surface approaches and these are outlined in Table 2. Drawn from Marton and Booth's (1997) detailed analysis of the experience of learning and from the later interpretation by Dall'Alba (2000), both take a phenomenographic perspective. All three dimensions appear to have a more universal application to analysing approaches to learning than the previous example.

Methodology

The study was modelled on a brief that focused on finding out about approaches to learning, conceptions of learning, and contextual factors that had influenced approaches. From this brief a framework was constructed relating to the conduct of the interviews and on how to present the data (Drew, Bailey & Shreeve, 2001).

> The phenomenon used as a focus for eliciting the students' experiences of learning for this study was the taught design project, which equates with the assignment or essay used to facilitate learning in text-based disciplines. First-year students and students in the first term of the second year were the focus for the study. These students are past their introductory studies and into their first design projects, but not at a stage of concentrated specialisation. This context was a constant

for all the interviews. Additionally, as 2000) assessment is a key factor that affects approach, students were asked to describe a project that had been completed and assessed. The students were selected so as to maximise the variation; in other words, students with different approaches to the fashion design project were sought.

Aspect	Deep approach	Surface approach
Direct object of learning (Marton & Booth) *or* Student's focus of learning (Dall'Alba)	On underlying purpose and meaning of task or learning material	On the task or learning material itself
Indirect object of learning (Marton & Booth) or Student's intention (Dall'Alba)	To understand	To reproduce
Act of learning (Marton & Booth) or Way in which the student engages in learning (Dall'Alba)	Organising and integrating	Memorising the content of what is being learned

Table 2 Aspects of approaches to learning (Sources: Marton and Booth, 1997; Dall'Alba)

The defining features of approaches to learning, the terms deep and surface approach to learning (Marton and Säljo, 1976), and the description of those defining features (further elaborated and summarised by Entwistle, 1997) were understood by the researchers not to fit neatly with their experience of design education. With this as the main underpinning feature of the aim of the enquiry, to redefine the features of approaches to learning in the context of design, the research question can be framed as:

What is the qualitative variation in approaches to learning adopted by design students, and how does that range of approaches relate to research results in other disciplines?

And further defined as:

> What is the qualitative variation in approaches to learning adopted by fashion design students within the framework of the design project?

This study embarked on in this paper contributes toward the further articulation of approaches to learning in design by testing the research questions within the context of first- and second-year fashion design.

> Phenomenography is the empirical study of the limited number of qualitatively different ways in which we experience, conceptualise, understand, etc, various phenomena in and aspects of the world around us. These differing experiences, understandings etc are characterised in terms of categories of description, logically related to each other, and forming hierarchies in relation to given criteria. Such an ordered set of categories of description is called the outcome space of the phenomenon in question. Participants in the study are encouraged to reflect on previously unthematised aspects of the phenomenon in question. The analysis is carried out in an iterative manner on those reflections. Distinctly different ways of experiencing the phenomenon discussed by participants are the units of analysis and not the single individuals. The categories of description corresponding to those differing understandings and the logical relations that can be established between them constitute the main results of a phenomenographic study.
> Marton (1992)

This research approach has been articulated more fully by Marton and Booth (1997).

One example of a set of results (outcome space) from the study on learning instrumental music (Reid, 1997) contains three ways of conceiving of the music object (an outcome of the learning of a musical instrument). The three ways are qualitatively different in meaning, with the focus being on the instrument, on the music, or on the musician:

> [Music] as technique relates to the physical aspects of playing the instrument as well as notational elements such as phrasing, accents or articulation.
>
> [Music as] sound and communication [is] related to the belief that each piece of music has an inherent meaning that is constituted by such things as style, period, harmony and composers' intent. It is the [inherent meaning of the music] that is communicated to an audience.
>
> Music as personal meaning ... involve[s] aspects of [technique and sound and communication], but these aspects were reinterpreted by the participants through the notion that music is a way of expressing personal meaning and understanding of the world through music performance. It is the musician's ideas that are expressed through the music's inherent meaning.
>
> Reid (1997, p. 204, in Trigwell, 2000)

There is, however, also a structural differentiation present here in the form of logically related hierarchies. (An outcome space is far more than a 'list'.) The playing of music as a way of expressing personal meaning (a focus on the musician) is still seen to be achieved through the development of technique and the communication of sound. And communicating the meaning of the music (a focus on the music) is still accomplished through the playing technique and an awareness of phrasing, accents and articulation. The category that focuses on the musician is structurally related to the other two and would therefore appear to be the most inclusive and complete. In other words, there are internal relations in the outcome space (Trigwell, 2000).

Findings

In this study of 21 university students of fashion design we have identified four different approaches to learning. These approaches are constituted in terms of the students' strategies and intentions in the context of one of their first- or second-year fashion design projects.

The approaches are briefly described below.

Approach A

In this approach students adopt a product-focused strategy with the intention to demonstrate technical competence.

Students focus on making a technically competent artefact (garment, drawing, pattern etc.) Information is collected with the intention to reproduce elements in the making of the artefact. The visual aspects of the design process focus solely on remembering procedures and techniques.

Approach B

In this approach students adopt a product-focused strategy with the intention to develop the design process.

As with approach A, students adopting this approach also have the intention to develop technical competence, but they aim to do so through strategies focused on experimenting with design processes. Part of their development occurs in interaction with a tutor, technician or peers. Students collect and review information in order to develop the process of design in the making of an artefact. Practice and repetition of design and making skills are an important part of the learning process.

Approach C

In this approach students adopt a process-focused strategy with the intention to develop the design process.

Students focus on the process of visualisation through experimental design and making. Students make connections and relate ideas in the process of visual research. The design process is interactive with tutor, technician or peers in order to further develop ideas. Experimentation in this approach is a strategy used for discovery and development of design processes rather than a means to making an artefact more competently.

Approach D

In this approach students adopt a concept-focused strategy with the intention to develop own conceptions.

Students focus on the process of visualisation of concepts through experimental design processes and making. Visual concepts are developed through relating ideas in the research process. The development of visual concepts is considered to be fundamental in this approach and therefore is more important than the final execution of the product. The design process is interactive with tutor, technician or peers in order to develop critical abilities and conceptual thinking skills.

The strategy and intention dimensions of the student approaches as described in the categories above are summarised in Table 3.

Strategy	**Intention**		
Focus of the learning	Developing technical competence	Develop design process	Develop own oconceptions
Making an artefact (product focus)	A	B	
Experimenting with process (process focus)		C	
Visualising of concepts (concept focus)			D

Table 3 The structural and referential aspects of the categories of approaches

Discussion

The interview data collected was framed within the context of particular projects that had been assessed and thus formulated a past experience which students recounted to the interviewer. The analysis and findings must be interpreted in the context of this situated learning experience and do not necessarily represent a fixed approach to learning in each of the students responding. All the accounts reflected a similar pattern of experience, the framework of project or problem-based learning, which most art and design programmes undertake.

The outcome space represents the hierarchical relationship of approaches. Each approach encapsulates those below it. For example, a student who demonstrates a concept focus may also demonstrate strategies that concentrate on processes and experimentation. This can be illustrated further by reference to particular approaches.

Approach A

For students adopting a product focus with the intention to demonstrate technical competence, the key traits are their desires to 'get it right', to reproduce a product or technique and to do as they are instructed. The tendency in their accounts is to expect the tutor or the technician to show them or tell them how to do something and then to reproduce this with a professional finish.

> Student (S): It's scary at first because you're thinking 'I don't want to get it wrong.' 'Don't do this wrong'. The amount of time you've got you need to get this done by. You're kind of scared but then you kind of go into a rush - 'I have to get it done, I have to get it done.' You just don't think about anything else but getting that shirt done.

> S: You always learn, you know, you always learn something, so it's never a waste of time. S: You always learn, I mean I learnt, you know, having to do the fabrics in big sections made you learn a lot about how to make a fabric professionally and you know how to finish something off professionally because you can't have bad, botched-up fabric in a full garment, you know. So I suppose it did help to learn and focus that these are real garments and they should be finished to a professional standard and so yes I suppose you did.

Students adopting this approach perceive the process of designing, visualising and making to be one of memorising and applying techniques and procedures, as illustrated overleaf:

> S: Firstly you have to get a book which has patterns and that and you read it and they give you examples and you actually are able to try them out. So that's how I learnt by reading and learning every day. It's easier for me that way. Sort of learning and doing something, for me memory wise it's easier for me to learn every day so I can remember it. I can visualise it in my head – 'I remember doing it this way' so that helps. That's how I learn anyway through doing that.

Students gather information with the intention of identifying within it elements that can be copied and reproduced:

> Interviewer (I): When you say 'thinking about' what does that involve, 'thinking about pockets'?
>
> S: Just drawing a few different examples of pockets and maybe having a look at some real trousers and having a look at real pockets, then going back to sort of the paper and just drawing out some ideas of different pocket shapes and things like that.

Interaction with tutors or technicians is for the purposes of being instructed or shown techniques and procedures:

> S: I just went down into the knit room and I spoke to one of the technicians, told them that was what I wanted to do - and they just showed me how to do it and I just went ahead and did it, so - I mean I had done a workshop in the first year but that was using the small, sort of hand machines, these were the bigger machines - so, you know, it was just sort of show - this is how you do it and then you try it yourself.

Approach B

As with approach A, the intention of approach B is on the production of the artefact, on developing technical competence, but the student adopts strategies of experimenting with the design process.

> S: Started off in the library with visual research, lots of sketchbook work. Photographs and general playing around with denim as well, making little samples, ways of making it stiff. Thinking about exaggerated body

form and how I was going to make something that had to be wearable, only in terms of going down the catwalk. Whilst we were doing our visual research we had pattern cutting tuition for I think three mornings. Had various little projects to do for that as well. Then just making the garment.

S: On one hand [the sketchbook] is there to sort of store the information that you have collected, but also it is there to use the information you have collected and play with it before you have the final idea.

I: So is play important in your learning?

S: Yes I think so.

I: You think so?

S: It is. A lot of the stuff, in relation to this project, a lot of the bits that I did earlier on, I didn't really know what I was doing but I was just playing around, experimenting really and finding out was doesn't go right, which is more important, and what does go right. Making mistakes and finding out how to go about trying to change them or leaving them as they are. Experimenting.

The acts of rehearsing and evidencing design and technical procedures are important aspects in these approaches.

S: ... thinking about it is more unrealistic than actually doing it. I think when you think about ideas they can often be - once you put them into practice you can push those areas more but I definitely used that in the past two projects, I have been a bit more active in things rather than just talking about how things are going to look. I just do them. Especially when you are talking to a tutor there is not point in saying what you are going to do. They can't tell you that is great when they haven't actually seen it. I think it is the evidence of how you are working that is important.

Approach C

Students who adopt approach C focus on the processes, include experimentation, trial and error, but use these strategies to develop the design process, rather than concentrating on producing the artefact more competently. They see interaction with others as opening up opportunities for further development of ways of seeing things differently.

> S: And then just went on to selecting items, garments and stuff.
>
> I: And when you're doing that what do you do?
>
> S: Lay everything out and go through it, sort of see what jumps out at me. Usually the tutor sort of will maybe, you know, say something to ... and usually I think it already. A lot of the time I ask my flatmates or friends. More than - em, flatmates because they're all design students too, so.
>
> I: How have you found out about doing that?
>
> S: Trial and error, I think, mostly. And, obviously tutors and uni mates a lot of the time. Definitely helps.
>
> I: They're helping you to learn how to do things?
>
> S: Yeah. Yeah just - the procedure you go through. And then trial and error because it doesn't always work. It's different for everybody.

Discussions with peers, tutors and technicians are seen as opportunities to identify and develop new ways of manipulating ideas, materials and techniques:

> S: Yes, I did but I also kept my mind open. I mean if my teachers were to suggest something, then I would definitely do it and I would definitely try it out. Or even if my peers suggested something then I would definitely try it out.

Approach D

Student adopting approach D will also use experimental approaches. Visual concepts are developed through relating and developing ideas through research. The focus of their intention however, is on the concept of their work and not the process, finish or the perfection of technique. This student describes her attempts to express an abstract concept:

> I: What did you find most difficult?
>
> S: Matching the reality of the garment with what was in my head and in my design. Not the cut part but the concept – does it convey the idea - what I wanted it to be? ... People look at a garment and think about whether they or anyone would wear it. It's not the point. I want people to think about the idea, not whether it's a 'nice' frock or if anyone would walk down the street in it.

Students adopting this approach use research to make connections and to develop concepts to a wider world view.

> S: So, I spread out what I had and what I'd found out – information and stuff I'd got from the library and the net. I liked the idea of the stuff I'd picked up from the street, the non-fashion materials that she'd mentioned in the brief. They were dirty and raw, about time and decay and experience – do you know what I mean? They'd kind of lived and died. Christmas was in the middle of the brief and my brother was talking about violence and fights near the university where he is, and in the town. I realised I wanted to do something that kind of linked the nearness of violence and chaos and fear in cities now with ideas around apocalypse – you know that we do have apocalypse now, all the war – that stuff in Yugoslavia, that was apocalypse for the victims, wasn't it, I mean. And fires, tornadoes, floods – I mean the chaos everywhere....

Interaction with tutors and peers is to develop critical and conceptual thinking skills:

> S: I like feeling that a tutor is there when I need help to get me through to the next stage, not to tell me – that's so much better here, where I was before she used to make too many suggestions and it was like to follow them was 'to do it right'. Here, she gets me to think and to answer my own questions.

With all these different approaches to learning occurring within a first year cohort of students one needs to understand that learning is not simply a straightforward activity in which all parties undertake a programme of work and arrive with the same outcomes. There are implications for structuring and clarifying exactly what the focus of assessment is, when students have been through the project process. Where students do not see learning as a relating to an abstract concept, for example, but tutors do, they will not succeed and will probably find it difficult to understand why they do not achieve high marks. There is a challenge for tutors to devise ways to enable students to adopt approaches which relate to the development of concepts in a relational way, if indeed this is what the aim of the curriculum is to be.

Conclusion

There are similarities between the original approaches to learning studies outlined earlier, but in attempting to redefine the features of approaches to learning in the context of design, the differences between the original research results and the new context must be evaluated. In examining these earlier, seminal studies, the focus is on learning using a text (even though the term 'text' can take on a metaphorical meaning), or of learning in text-based study. At the extremes of deep and surface approaches to learning, this study illustrates a resonance between the intention to reproduce, memorise facts and procedures, and at the opposite extreme, the intention to relate ideas to previous knowledge and experience. These two approaches in this study appear to parallel the deep and surface approaches in some elements. Text and design can be freely interchanged with these descriptions of the features of approaches to learning. The findings expressed in the outcome space developed for this study indicate a greater area of variation between these two extremes. It is within the development of the design process that the difference appears. The approaches reflect neither a strategy for reproduction, nor one of making connections and relations in the learning, but one of experimenting with designing, making and material processes in order to engage with the learning of design.

The implications for learning, teaching and curriculum design are situated in the recognition that for different students, and quite possibly, for different teachers (Prosser & Trigwell, 1999), the focus of learning can be at odds with curriculum, assessment criteria and stated outcomes.

Acknowledgements

We acknowledge the contribution made to this study by Keith Trigwell, Rowena Pelik, Carmel Kelly, Polly Kenny and Suzi Vaughan.

References

Biggs, J.B. (1987), The Study Process Questionnaire (SPQ) Users' Manual (Hawthorne, Victoria: Australian Council for Educational Research)

Biggs, J.B. (1999), *Teaching for Quality Learning at University* (Buckingham: SRHE and Open University Press)

Dall'Alba, G. (2000), 'Reflections on some faces of phenomenography', in Bowden, J.A. & Walsh, E. (eds.), *Phenomenography* (Melbourne: RMIT University), pp. 83-101

Davies, A. (1994), 'Identifying and working with student expectations of learning', in Gibbs, G. (ed.), *Improving Student Learning* (Oxford: Oxford Centre for Staff Development)

Drew, L., Bailey, S. & Shreeve, A. (2001), 'Phenomenographic research: methodological issues arising from a study investigating student approaches to learning in fashion design', *Higher Education Close Up 2, 2001* Lancaster University (available from: hhtp://www.leeds.ac.uk/educol/documents/00001770.doc)

Gibbs, G. (1992), *Improving the Quality of Student Learning* (Bristol: Technical and Educational Services Ltd)

Entwistle, N.J. (1987), 'A model of the teaching-learning', in Richardson, J.T.E., Eysenck, M.W. & Warren Piper, D. (eds.), *Student Learning : Research in Education and Cognitive Psychology* (Milton Keynes: SRHE and Open University Press, 13-28)

Entwistle, N.J. (1997), 'Contrasting perspectives on learning', in Marton, F., Hounsell, D. & Entwistle, N.J. (eds.), *The Experience of Learning: Implications for Teaching and Studying in Higher Education*, 2nd ed (Edinburgh: Scottish Academic Press)

Entwistle, N.J. & Ramsden, P. (1983), *Understanding Student Learning* (London: Croom Helm)

Laurillard, D. (1979), 'The process of student learning', *Higher Education*, **8**, 395-409

Marton, F. (1992), 'Phenomenography and "the art of teaching all things to all men"', *Qualitative Studies in Education*, **5**, 253-267

Marton, F. & Booth, S. (1997), *Learning and Awareness* (Mahwah, NJ: Lawrence Erlbaum)

Marton, F. & Säljö, R. (1976), 'On qualitative differences in learning: I – outcome and process', *British Journal of Educational Psychology*, **46**, 4-11

Miller, C.M.L. & Parlett, M.R. (1974), *Up to the Mark: A Study of the Examination Game* (London: Society for Research into Higher Education)

Prosser, M. & Trigwell, K. (1999), *Understanding Learning and Teaching* (Buckingham: SRHE and Open University Press)

Ramsden, P. (1979), 'Student learning in context – the relationship between student learning and perceptions of the academic environment', *Higher Education*, **8**, 411-427

Reid, A. (1997), 'The meaning of music and the understanding of teaching and learning in the instrumental lesson', in Gabrielsson, A. (ed.) *Proceedings of the Third Triennial European Society for the Cognitive Sciences of Music Conference* (Uppsala: Uppsala University)

Svensson, L. (1977), 'On qualitative differences in learning: III – Study skill and learning', *British Journal of Educational Psychology*, 47, 223-243

Trigwell, K. (2000), 'Phenomenography: discernment and variation', in Rust, C. (ed.), I*mproving Student Learning: Improving Student Learning through the Disciplines* (Oxford: Oxford Brookes University, Oxford Centre for Staff and Learning Development)

Biographical note

Linda Drew is the Subject Centre Manager of the Learning and Teaching Support Network for Art, Design and Communication (ADC-LTSN) based at the University of Brighton. Professional experience includes appointments at the London Institute, as Programme Leader for the SEDA/ILT accredited programme in Learning and Teaching for staff at the London Institute colleges and Wimbledon School of Art and as Quality Assurance Manager at Chelsea College of Art and Design. Teaching appointments include the London College of Printing and the London College of Fashion, latterly as principal lecturer with particular responsibility for developing the BA (Hons) Fashion Studies. Teaching experience includes fashion design, forecasting, marketing and fashion related cultural and design historical studies. Currently registered for a PhD in Educational Research at Lancaster University with a research focus on conceptions of teaching and approaches to teaching situated within the context of practice based teachers of art, design and communication.

10

Can the use of computer-mediated communication for distance collaboration enhance the design curriculum?

John Fraser

Richmond American International University (RAIUL), UK

Abstract

Researchers argue that design's essential discipline lies in the way designers both engage with and process externally derived information. The increasing impact of computer-mediated communication (CMC) is having an enormous effect upon information flow. This paper describes an international collaboration between students from Richmond American International University in London and the University of Nebraska at Kearney in the USA working on a CMC-based joint graphic design project. The study compares the communication that took place between co-located pairs of students working on the same campus and distributed pairs who were assigned to work 'at a distance'. The study examines the attitude and behaviour of the students and the effectiveness and efficiency of their social interaction and collective performance when engaged in the project. The paper presents some of the data emerging from the study and assesses the outcome of introducing an element of international collaboration into the design curriculum.

Introduction

Computer-mediated communication (CMC) makes international collaboration more feasible in joint design projects by 'collapsing' space and allowing students who might otherwise be unable to meet, share ideas and work together. This research investigates design students design-making while using CMC for communicative interaction. In order to reflect the contemporary design context as well as the increasingly global nature of teaching and learning, the students were drawn from internationally disparate educational institutions. While acknowledging the importance of cultural difference on international collaboration this research focuses on how design students go about negotiating meaning and making decisions as they generate ideas and develop artwork for a design brief. The research investigates the collaboration between design students when working on joint projects at a distance via technological interfaces.

Cross et al. (1994) suggest that certain aspects of cognitive behaviour can be identified in successful design practice. Among these is the ability to tolerate uncertainty and to work with incomplete information while making decisions. Design is concerned with how things ought to be and is produced through a process of developing novel forms. Designers apply imagination and constructive forethought to practical problems, while using drawing and other modelling mediums as a means of problem solving (Cross et al., 1994). However, while emphasising design's co-ordinating role as a context for the re-association of a range of other subjects, design's essential discipline lies in the way designers collaboratively engage and process their externally derived information (Thistlewood, 1990). In a collaborative situation this means negotiating meaning and making decisions appropriately to arrive at a joint solution. This study introduced a collaborative project into the graphic design curriculum at the two collaborating universities to see what differences students might report in how they went about making decisions and problem solving and whether it affected their flexibility in formulating ideas and handling information. Initial analysis of the results seem to indicate that one of the ways design students can develop their cognitive skills is by participation in collaborative projects using CMC. This would support Scrivener and Vernon's (1998) assertion that this group activity offers a rich context for learning to design.

Scrivener and Vernon (1998) argue for the potential of information and communication technology (ICT) to support both co-located and distributed design teams. There is a significant body of research dealing with collaborative group work and this has obvious implications for research into computer-supported co-operative work. This work has come from a variety of disciplines and includes work related to the psychology and sociology of groups, the sociology of organisations and the psychology of media as well as collections of original papers on groupware and computer-supported co-operative work (Greenberg et al., 1993, McLuhan, 1988). CMC technology is being developed which supports and sustains new and effective channels for international communication and research interest in ICT is now beginning to address the use of pedagogical studies to evaluate the different scenarios that might present themselves in an education setting (Mumford, 1996).

The business of both processing information and collaborating has been fundamentally affected by the widespread take-up of information and communication technology. The growth and accessibility of the Internet can benefit designers by giving them access to myriad databanks of multi-disciplinary knowledge while the development of CMC allows distributed design teams an opportunity for interactive communication and a group social dynamic that the research suggests may be enabling to the designing process. Eggleston (1976) writing about designing describes a process that begins with a detailed preliminary identification of a problem and a diagnosis of the needs that have to be met by a solution, and goes through a series of stages in which various solutions are conceived, explored and evaluated until an optimum answer is found that appears to satisfy the necessary criteria as fully as possible within the limits and opportunities available. At the same time, the very fact of using CMC might alter design practice behaviour during the processes of exploration, conception, problem solving and testing. It might be argued that this has tended towards a creeping globalisation of attitudes, ideas and cultural identity.

ICT is not a value-neutral technology and the trend towards a growing use of ICT in education is the subject of much professional debate. Some theorists are sceptical of the claims made for ICT's enfranchising and educational benefits citing security issues, the privacy issue, and problems to do with access and the democracy issue (Rheingold, 1993, Lengel, 2000). However, Marsland (1995) would suggest that design practitioners should take responsibility for their own professional self-renewal by exercising independent judgement in trying to meet the educational needs of their students. The potential of ICT for teaching and learning is exciting. However, design educators must strike a balance between using technology appropriately in the classroom and communicating the values of their domain knowledge.

The 'added value' of computer-mediated communications?

The study investigates the use of CMC for international collaboration in the design classroom and the implications this might have for design curriculum development. CMC technologies have been developed to support and sustain effective distance learning. Video conferencing, multi-user domains, special interest groups and electronic mail are all the subject of increasing interest in education and training (Schnurr & Smith, 1995). Research is going on into the development of interactive databases, multimedia course materials and vocational courseware built to meet the specific needs of learners and delivered using the technology of the World Wide Web. There is a growing commitment to the use of ICT in training, teaching and learning generated through many initiatives in the UK (Howard et al., 1996). Virtual reality technology is developing rapidly and before too long we should be accessing sites on the Internet that allow us to interact in audio-visual shared spaces in the same way as we now communicate using e-mail and newsgroups (Gulbransen & Rawlings, 1996). Virtual environments are one emerging technique for interacting with online information. Contemporary examples are: virtual art and design studios (designnet, virtuosi); virtual laboratories (cite, ou); medical training facilities; and foreign language laboratories (saeln). They hold out exciting possibilities for creating experiential scenarios, visual, auditory and tactile (Lemay et al., 1996). If developing technology is to impact successfully on educational design practice then design teachers need to adopt a professional attitude towards the use of ICT, and students will need to develop skills and abilities to deal with it for learning and research. Developments such as computer conferencing already offer alternative pathways for collaborative activities, and group-to-group collaboration is now possible at a distance and encourages shared experience and co-operation. Incorporating aspects of this technology into design education could develop students' cognitive abilities (Goodfellow & Kukulska-Holme, 1996).

This study investigates students' design making while using CMC for communicative interaction. While acknowledging the importance of cultural difference on international collaboration, this study focuses on how design students go about negotiating meaning and making decisions as they generate ideas and develop artwork for a design brief. Specifically the investigation assesses the effectiveness and efficiency of the students' social interaction and collective performance when using CMC in their project work. Communicative interaction can be thought of as the changing relationships that occur between internal states and sets of intentions as the students gather information, discussion and ideas are generated, sketching and reflection takes place and solutions are arrived at by the design groups. The online record of group discussions is analysed to elicit students' understanding of their own communicative interaction while decision making and their descriptions of how they negotiated meaning collaboratively through their actions and behaviour.

Designing involves brainstorming sessions, group discussions and general playing around with the most unlikely of ideas. Can designers being able to access online information and participate in online discussion forums using the Internet enable the process of abductive reasoning? Can decision-making strategies be enhanced through the collaboration of different minds from different positions in virtual space by resolving their different definitions of the problem and working together to come up with a joint solution? It could be considered that contemporary designers have obvious advantages in researching sources via the Internet and then engaging creatively with their material through collaborative use of digital technology to produce design solutions. One could question the influence of the development of virtual interactive and collaborative spaces on this secondary solution-focusing stage of the design process. Can the nature of non-verbal modes of reasoning be altered by interaction with design group members in online environments and collaborative working through shared online use of ICT?

Ontological and epistemological approaches to researching design and designing

The criteria for selecting suitable research methods and the process of analysis are often influenced by the researcher's basic set of beliefs in the nature of reality and how we know and gain knowledge of the world. Mitcham (1995) while suggesting that the act of making resulting in a final material product is realised by mental intention, is of the opinion that this is not necessarily through any systematic anticipatory analysis or modelling. He contends that design has emerged historically alongside modern science and technology either from an artist-architect viewpoint as embodied poetic thinking or from an engineering perspective emphasising the quantitative, analytic and iterative character of a multiphase process. Cross (1995) highlighted the different problem-solving strategies of designers and scientists and described Lawson's work suggesting that these different strategies could be traced back to their education. Designers concentrate on solutions to the problem – a solution-focusing strategy – whereas scientists concentrate on the structure of the problem – a problem-focusing strategy. Yet again design can be considered either as problem solving explainable in behavioural terms, or as a technical process where problem solving is more empirical and explained by law-like relationships governing mental relationships. The 'behavioural' approach and the 'technical' approach have their roots in two opposing traditions. If the design process is intuitive then the designed object is there not in consequence of any order, planning, deliberate forming or control but as a consequence of fortuitous circumstance or spontaneity. If on the other hand the design process is cognitive, logical and a knowledge-producing affair then one could derive a set of principles or procedures that permit effective control over it. Each of these viewpoints assumes a different ontological and epistemological perspective.

A staged process model

This approach to the study of the design process assumes problem solving can only be adequately explained by observing measurable and replicable patterns of physical behaviour and supports the development of phase or rigid-state models of creative problem-solving behaviour conforming to an episodic process of distinct and almost discontinuous phases of activity. One such model incorporates four fundamental phases of activity. These are: preparation for the task at hand; incubation; illumination or inspiration; and finally verification, involving the testing of proposed solutions (Wallas, 1926). Developing these ideas, Asimov (1962) identified two structures in the design process: a vertical structure involving a similar sequential phasing of activities and a horizontal iterative structure in the form of a decision-making cycle common to all phases incorporating synthesis, evaluation and communication. Feedback loops were incorporated to account for the observable tracing back through the process in order to respond to new information or difficulties. Archer (1963) proposed a similar operational model of designing.

These models of the design process discriminate between distinct phases of activity and assume such distinctions will advance our understanding of design. Advocates of this approach hold out the prospect of a totally objective approach towards design education, where the previously esoteric and subjective realm of design can be emancipated and made accessible to many by the adoption off various staged-process models of design education. In this tradition while acknowledging the realm of mental processes the research is strongly based on structured observation of human behaviour. A criticism of staged-process models is that while they illuminate certain commonly observable features of design activity it is at a comparatively low level. However, similar models which clarify the design process have been used for educational purposes (Thornley, 1963).

An information processing model

Research associated with information processing theory is fundamentally mechanistic and mentalistic in doctrine. Creative problem solving is considered as essentially purposeful and the task is seen to be the controlling mechanism in problem-solving behaviour. Creative problem solving is considered to be directed behaviour that involves a schema or organisational framework for structuring information. Systematic introspection can be used as a means for describing problem-solving behaviour where subjects are asked to reconstruct their sequence of thoughts during some problem-solving exercise. The information processing theory of problem solving reasserts the primacy of essentially cognitive processes in explaining creative problem-solving behaviour. This theory incorporates the concept of a problem space whose elements are knowledge states, some of which represent solutions to a problem. Basic mechanisms process the information contained in these knowledge states allowing complex problems to be solved. Experimental research is usually conducted through the use of elaborate protocol analysis in which subjects engage in a problem-solving task and communicate what they are doing as they work through a problem. The results from these experiments are then carefully examined to discern which fundamental information processing mechanisms appear to be involved (Rowe, 1991).

A protocol model

Cross et al. (1994) suggest that certain aspects of cognitive behaviour can be identified in successful design practice. These are: the production of novel and unexpected solutions; the ability to tolerate uncertainty and work with incomplete information; the ability to apply imagination and constructive thought to problems; and the ability to use drawing and other modelling media as means of problem solving. They adopted a quasi-experimental approach in protocol study experiments they undertook on some aspects of design expertise. The design solutions were assessed for overall quality, technical feasibility, ergonomic suitability and creativity of the concept. They argue that design educators should develop programmes that develop these abilities more consciously and deliberately. Rowe (1991) in his investigation of design thinking examined three case studies of designers in action and asserted that there is no such thing as an ideal step-by-step design process. Rather he identified common characteristics within different styles of decision making. Designing he suggested is a complex business incorporating individual styles of decision making often influenced by the constraints of the initial setting of the problem and sometimes by the personal attitudes of the individual designer. This type of approach would seem to share a common ontology with contemporary responses such as critical theory, rejecting the idea that the world is objective and independent of the observer and by arguing that social and cultural reality is already interpreted by participants as a cultural and symbolic meaning system which can be changed over time (Blaikie, 1993). Structuration theory is another contemporary approach that attempts to construct an ontological framework incorporating agency and structure. This approach perceives the study of human social interaction as the study of social actors engaged in both producing and reproducing their social world.

Rowe's investigation involved lengthy periods of observation and documentation, where designers described their activities in detail with the aid of drawings. Through these interview sessions Rowe was able to reconstruct the sequence of steps, moves and other logical procedures that were employed. The advantage of this sort of reconstruction or protocol is that it does record the sequence of major events although it omits minute-by-minute detail and other real-time variations in design behaviour. More importantly it allows the designers the opportunity to give detailed explanations of their rationale thus providing greater insight than simply observation of surface activity (Rowe, 1991).

Methodology

The research compared the communication and collaboration that took place between co-located pairs of students working on the same campus and distributed pairs who were assigned to work 'at a distance'. The programme's curricular objective was to give design students the opportunity to produce artwork for a five-week course project while working collaboratively across national and cultural borders. The brief for the graphic design project required each team to collaborate to gain approval for their proposal, organise logistics, communication and individual responsibilities, and develop final artwork. Each group collaborated using proprietary computer-conferencing software called 'Blackboard' set up on Richmond's server. This allowed them to e-mail, use discussion lists, use a whiteboard and exchange graphic files. A Web page on the RAIUL Web site was set up to serve as a portal for the project. This page included a hyperlink that connected the student design groups to the London–Nebraska link.

The research is interpretative and involves a detailed analysis of aspects of the social interaction that the students engage in while working on their collaborative projects. The approach that was adopted is intrinsically linked to the aims for the study and the research questions and is influenced by Rowe's approach. An adaptation of Asimov's iterative design-process model was used as a template for identifying critical negotiation and decision making for analysis. The methodology focuses on context and meaning and uses a holistic approach that recognises that what happens in the classroom generally has complex layers of meaning, interpretation, values and attitudes. However, it has been suggested that there is no single best description of what might be happening in the design studio and that the selection of what is seen or recorded might be influenced by the purposes which the description is to serve (Croll, 1986). Therefore participant observation through reflective journals and semi-structured interviews was used. This allows for qualification of actions, ideas, values and meanings through the eyes of the participating students. The research stance hypothesises that the reality of designing is subjective and multiple as seen by the participants in the study. Consequently the research adopted a basically qualitative and ethnographic methodology. Interaction is an important element in this research and the relationship that exists between the tutors and the students is informal, value-laden and biased. This approach lends an essentially interpretative ontology to the research in which the act of designing is regarded as the product of processes through which the students together negotiate the meanings and understandings that underpin their design actions and processes.

The research focus is on the way design students go about negotiating meaning and making decisions as they generate ideas, develop artwork and focus on solutions to a design brief. Each student group records: the means and extent of their collaboration; the amount, type and quality of their communication; and the contribution and integration of their design ideas. The initial questionnaire established each student's past experience, skills and attitude toward using Blackboard as a communication medium. The final questionnaire concentrates on concrete details of their experience while working on the project. The videotaped interviews focus on encouraging the students to reflect on the meaning for them of the project experience. Each of these three stages provides a level of detail that helps to illuminate the next stage. Epistemologically knowledge about designing is derived from the students' re-descriptions of their role in the design process. Participant observation is used to gain insight into the activities taking place through students' descriptions of the sequence and timing of their activities. Qualitative discourse analysis through structured interpretation of language is made of recordings of 'online' and taped discourse to evaluate the communications stratagems developed by the groups and how meaning is negotiated. An initial analysis of the data focused on identifying common themes and categories related to periods of negotiation and decision making. The identified material was further analysed and coded and compared to the information obtained from a quantitative analysis of the questionnaires. Methodological triangulation was used to ensure some substantiation of the data collected from the different instruments.

Findings

The responses from six distributed groups and six co-located groups were analysed. On comparing the distributed groups to the co-located groups certain significant differences were apparent. The distributed groups were in agreement that CMC was of most use during the later stages of verification and finalising the artwork while being negative about its use in the early stages:

> We couldn't just sit down face-to-face and talk to each other. It took maybe about two or four or five e-mails back and forward – 'do you like this' or 'do you want to do this' – which made it kind of difficult. Maybe a five- or ten-minute conversation took us about two weeks.

They talked about the difficulties, particularly at the beginning of the project, of being able to establish a necessary relationship and get across their varying points of view:

> I think definitely at the end. That's when it works out the best when you sit down and exchange thoughts. At the beginning, at the very raw stages – just a pain.

A frequent comment from distributed groups was the difficulty in fixing meeting times owing to time differences, different class times on each campus and so the different deadlines. One student eloquently described the excitement that most of the students reported about being involved in the project:

> File Exchange – oh yeah, that was a big help with us because it's so much faster and easier than e-mailing. Just drop the image in and it comes right up on her screen and she can see it. Oh yeah and we had the chat on at the same time. The virtual chat room chat. Oh yeah, 'I like that one that you did' or 'No maybe that could be changed a little bit'. Just back and forth. We had so many images. Like I'd alter one, drop it in. She'd look. Alter it. Alter it a little bit more and drop it back to me. That was very convenient, very fast.

By contrast the co-located groups felt it was most useful during the initial stages of problem identification and idea generation. A Richmond co-located group member, asked about when CMC was of most use during the project, said:

> I think maybe at the beginning stages where you're coming up with ideas and you're both (sic) are coming from two separate ideas. At the end we ended up working together side by side and that was our most productive time (sic) is when we were sitting at two computers side by side working together.

This was typical of most co-located students who found CMC very useful for communicating their ideas in the time between classes and for research but used it less and less in the later stages of their work. At the same time the co-located groups did not have the problems of time differences and benefited from initial communication being verbal and face-to-face. Another co-located student said:

> During the week Deidre and myself we don't have any other classes together, we don't live in the same dorm, so we would be able to communicate by going on to Blackboard but we found ourselves on it for a good amount of time. I think it worked well. It helped us out a lot.

This student went on to say that in the later stages they spent most of the time face-to-face finalising the work

The results from the survey indicate that many students considered the lack of face-to-face contact most problematic. This was confirmed as a major concern during the interviews. Most students were not concerned about showing themselves up when using the equipment and felt positively about sharing Internet research and very positive about working jointly on the artwork. This contrasts with many studies where the fear of not being able to cope with the equipment and looking stupid to your peers is often quoted as a reason for enjoying anonymity. Surprisingly, given the popularity of the Internet for researching information, only a minority of students used this facility during the projects. This might however simply reflect the tight time-scale and subject matter of the project. Interestingly both the co-located and the distributed groups felt the project was very exciting, not in the least frightening or a waste of time. They felt the CMC application was easy or very easy to learn and was of positive benefit in improving their designing skills. Generally, however, they were less positive about the notion that CMC provided 'easy communication'. The distributed groups were much less confident initially in their computer skills which might indicate a concern about using CMC. After working on the project 85% agreed that using CMC would improve their design skills. Interestingly 80% of both co-located and distributed groups would use ICT even when collaborating in teams on the same campus.

What was most striking was the similar attitudes that all students held, whether working together or at a distance. Most agreed that CMC was neither frightening nor a waste of time and were supportive of the idea of using CMC in design work. They felt positive and excited about the benefits CMC might have for developing and communicating ideas. In general they all felt that using CMC benefited their design skills and supported incorporating CMC into their design studies. Some students indicated that they were not too concerned about having immediate feedback on their ideas. However, this was at odds with most students who said that their greatest difficulty was not being able to communicate directly with their partners. This attitude was confirmed by students expressing frustration about a lack of immediacy and the difficulty with CMC when trying to develop their ideas together. They were much happier about facilities for exchanging artwork. The file exchange being identified as both one of the most used as well as the most preferred facility. E-mail was the other popular facility. However, these are both generally asynchronous methods of communication and one extra facility that many students identified as necessary was some form of easy-to-use synchronous chat device. For reasons mainly to do with time differences and different class days most students found the chat room facility unhelpful. However, some managed to use it quite well.

Conclusion

Students from both Richmond and Nebraska describe an increase in their levels of interest and motivation when working on the collaborative projects. This is supported by findings from a range of research including surveys and evaluation studies undertaken in the early 1990s evaluating the use of CMC in education in the UK (Starling, 1994; Schnurr & Smith, 1995; Mumford, 1995; Howard et al., 1996; Laurillard, 1996). These studies found that changes reported after the introduction of communication software into the classroom included a lessening of problems of social isolation and students being keener to participate. The interviews did not seem to support some findings from previous reports which indicated that students will often erect resistance barriers when dealing with CMC in an attempt to avoid the fear of looking stupid to their peers when encountering problems with the interface. Similarly the students did not report worries about breaking the equipment, or being spied upon when they were effectively in a private study situation as other studies have suggested (Durbridge, 1996).

Gregory (1966) suggests that problem solving can be adequately explained by observing the participants measurable and replicable patterns of physical behaviour. His model of the design process discriminates between distinct phases of activity and assumes such distinctions will advance our understanding of design. An analysis of the time sheet graphs did not support this. Rather the random and different sequences of activity recorded by the students in this study would support Rowe's (1991) assertion that designing is a complex business influenced by the initial constraints of the problem and sometimes by the personal attitudes of the designers.

The results obtained from this study indicate that the introduction of international collaboration into the design curriculum, bringing with it a global and multicultural perspective, motivated design students. CMC may make international collaboration more feasible in joint design projects by allowing students, who might otherwise be unable to meet, to share ideas and work together. The results so far indicate the potential of ICT for giving design students practice in negotiating meaning and decision making. Results so far indicate the positive benefits of introducing an element of international collaboration into the visual communication and design curricula at both universities. Consequently this study provided the impetus for a series of collaborative design group projects called 'Designlinks', involving design departments in the UK, the USA, South America and Canada which are currently underway.

References

Archer, B. (1963), 'Systematic methods for designers', *Design*, pp. 172-188

Asimov, M. (1962), *Introduction to Design* (New Jersey: Prentice Hall)

Blaikie, N. (1993), *Approaches to Social Enquiry* (Cambridge, MA: Polity Press)

Croll, P. (1986), *Systematic Classroom Observation* (London: Falmer Press)

Cross, N., Christiaans, H. & Dorst, K. (1994), 'Design expertise amongst student designers', *Journal of Art and Design Education*, Vol. 13, No. 1

Cross, N. (1995), 'Discovering design ability', in Buchanan, R. & Margolin, V. (eds.), *Discovering Design: Explorations in Design Studies* (London: The University of Chicago Press Ltd)

Durbridge, N. (1996), 'Whose dream? A case study of educational multimedia design and art explorer (1)', *Program on Learner Use of Media 53* (Institute of Educational Technology, The Open University, http://www-iet.open.ac.uk, Dec. 1996)

Eggleston, J. (1976), *Developments in Design Education* (London, Open Books Publishing Ltd)

Goodfellow, R. & Kukulska-Hulme, A. (1996), 'Evaluating new technology in learning and teaching', *Centre for Information Technology in Education Report 225* (Open University, http://www-iet.open.ac.uk)

Greenberg, S., Roseman, M. & Webster, D. (1993), 'Issues and experiences designing and implementing two group drawing tools', in Baecker, R.M. (ed.), *Readings in Groupware and Computer-Supported Cooperative Work* (San Fransisco, CA: Morgan Kaufman)

Gregory, S.A. (1966), *The Design Method* (London: Butterworths)

Gulbransen, D. & Rawlings, K. (1996), *Creating Web Applets with Java* (Indianapolis: Sams.net)

Howard, T., Hubbold, R., Murta, A. & West, A. (1996), 'Survey of virtual reality activity in the United Kingdom', Advisory Group on Computer Graphics, T*echnical Report Series, No. 27.* (Loughborough University, UK, for the Advisory Group on Computer Graphics Technical Report series, an initiative of the Joint Information Systems Committee of the HEFC's and the Research Councils)

Laurillard, D. (1996), 'Multimedia and the changing experience of the learner', *Program on Learner Use of Media 44* (Institute of Educational Technology, The Open University, http://www-iet.open.ac.uk, Dec. 1996)

Lengel, L. (ed). (2000), *Culture and Technology in the New Europe* (Westport, CT: Ablex)

Lemay, L., Murdock, K. & Couch, J. (1996), *3D Graphics and VRML 2* (Indianapolis, Sams.net)

Marsland, D. (1995), *Towards Teacher Professionalism* (York: Campaign for Real Education)

McLuhan, M. (1988), *Laws of Media* (New York: McLuhan Associates)

Mitcham, C. (1995), 'Ethics into design', in Buchanan. R. & Margolin, V. (eds.), *Discovering Design:Explorations in Design Studies* (London: The University of Chicago Press Ltd)

Mumford, A. (1995), 'Support for the use of IT in graphic art and design in UK', in *Conference Proceedings CADE 95 Brighton*, UK, pp. 242-247.

Mumford, A. (1996), 'The potential of virtual reality for UK higher education', in *Support Initiative for Multimedia Applications Report Series*, No. 19, March 1996 (Loughborough University, UK, for the Advisory Group on Computer Graphics Support Initiative for Mulitmedia Applications Report Series an initiative of the Joint Information Systems Committee of the HEFC's and the Research Councils)

Rheingold, H. (1993), *The Virtual Community* (New York: Addison Wesley)

Rowe, P.G. (1991), *Design Thinking* (London: MIT Press)

Schnurr, C. & Smith, C. (1995), 'Video conferencing in education. Meeting teachers' and learners' support and training needs', in *Support Initiative for Multimedia Applications Report* Series, No. 11, March 1995 (Heriot Watt University, UK)

Scrivener, S. & Vernon, S. (1998), 'Design net: transitional design project work at a distance', in Millsom, H., Taylor & Francis (eds.), *Technology and Social Science: A Researcher's Guide*, pp 75-84 (London: Taylor & Francis)

Starling, M. (ed.) (1994), 'The use of IT in art and design. Case studies', Advisory Group on Computer Graphics, *Technical Report Series*, No. 26 (Manchester Metropolitan University, UK)

Thistlewood, D. (1990), 'The essential disciplines of design education', in Thistlewood, D. (ed.) *Issues in Design Education* (London: Longman)

Thornley, D.G. (1963), 'Design method in architectural education', in Jones, J.C. & Thornley, D.G. (eds.), *Conference on Design Methods* (Oxford: Pergamon)

Wallas, G. (1926), *The Art of Thought* (London: Jonathon Cape)

Biographical note

John Fraser, Associate Professor of Design and Communications, Richmond, The American International University in London
214 Pacific House, 7-17 Ansdell Street, London W8 5BN
tel +44 (0)20 7368 8409 e-mail fraserj@richmond.ac.uk

The author is interested in using Information and Communication Technology for collaboration in design work in international educational contexts. He is currently involved in a research project called DesignLink, which aims to examine students' decision-making procedures when using ICT in computer-supported co-operative work and involves distributed teams of design students drawn from Universities in the US, the UK, South America and Canada.

11

Students' understanding of the relationship between theory and practice

Annie Grove-White

School of Art and Design, University of Wales, Cardiff, UK

Abstract

This paper explores photography students' understanding of the relationship between theory and practice. The research was undertaken during 1999/2000 with third-year students from Newport School of Art and Design and Surrey Institute of Art and Design. Semi-structured interviews were carried out with seven students and videoed.

Aims of the research

To understand the ways in which our subjects are understood or misunderstood by students

As teachers we need to know how our individuals experience the subject. As Laurillard writes:

> Teachers need to know more than their subject. They need to know the ways it can come to be understood, the ways it can be misunderstood, what counts as understanding: they need to know how individuals experience the subject.
> Laurillard (1998, p. 3)

In particular, we need to be aware to what extent do we make the implicit discourse of the subject explicit to our students. By 'implicit discourse' I mean for students to be able to interpret a complex academic discourse as having a particular meaning or relevance, they must first of all be able to perceive or understand the implicit structure of that discourse. Meaning is given through structure. Since meaning is given through the structure of the discourse presented in any one course - module descriptors and learning outcomes should identify these in a formal and pragmatic way. But to what extent do students grasp the full implications of these? To what extent do lecturers make the implicit discourse explicit in a more meaningful way?

To begin to identify a typology of these understandings particularly in relation to the relationship between theory and practice in art and design

While there is not a lot of research into this area within art, media and design, a number of other studies (Marton & Säljo, 1997) show that students taking text-based studies failed to get the point of the article or extract because they were not looking for it. This, it was argued, leads to a surface approach which focuses on the product. It is also atomistic and fragmented and very different from those who took a deeper approach to learning which focused on the process which can be characterised as holisitic and searching for meaning. Students in this instance saw themselves as creators of knowledge.

Certainly, the kinds of goals a student arrives with, can influence their approach to learning (surface or deep). If, however, the purpose of higher education is to encourage a deep approach as students progress through the course, then if students fail to understand what they are being asked to look for in any one project, then they will misinterpret the implicit discourse of any course of study and make alternative meanings.

Scope and framework

The research is influenced by a phenomenographic approach, in that the focus is on the student experience. It does not aim to be judgmental in terms of describing students as good or weak. The paper will present extracts from the interviews, but it is important for the reader to be aware that they are selected and edited by the author.

Laurillard (1998, p. 58) identifies academic knowledge as being fundamentally different from everyday knowledge in that it is to do with the world of descriptions. In relation to theory, academic learning is different from other kinds of learning in everyday life because it is not directly experienced but is necessarily constructed and mediated by the lecturer. Undergraduates are not learning about the world directly, but about descriptions of the world devised by others – hence the idea that teaching is mediated learning and 'a rhetorical activity' (Laurillard 1998, p. 25) where the lecturer seeks to persuade the student to acquire knowledge of someone else's way of experiencing the world.

Because academic knowledge has this second-order character, it relies heavily on symbolic representation as the way in which it is known. This is usually through written or spoken language, but can also be through other symbolic systems that can represent a description of the world - mathematical symbols, diagrams, musical notation etc. Students have to learn to handle the representation system as well as the ideas they represent. In the case of photography, which involves the making and reading of images, students are required to move between two languages: the verbal and visual.

What is understood by theory?

Given this complexity, our expectations of our students are high. There is an assumption that the work should be informed by theoretical considerations and that the student somehow should be able to move seamlessly between these two systems of representation. Such learning outcomes as the following give some idea of what we expect:

- an ability to demonstrate a critical understanding of techniques and theories as practised; and
- an ability to reconsider assumptions about the activity of looking and its relationship to knowledge.

However, I would argue that while we can perhaps be more precise with language (as a commonly agreed system of communication) it is more complex in relation to visual codes in terms of expressing ideas. Not all visual codes are commonly agreed on, or even understood in terms of references and so on.

Semiotics has gone some way to providing a way of reading images, but in this post-modern world meanings are by no means fixed. This paper does not claim to have unravelled this complexity. Rather, it attempts to map out some paradigms as well as explore how learning approaches and styles influence these interpretations of what theory means and is useful for. Säljö's conceptualisation of the learning process (1979) demonstrates the developmental progression and provides a useful way in which to map approaches in relation to the interviews. They can be briefly summarised as:

- the increase of knowledge;
- memorising;
- the acquisition of facts, procedures for use in practice;
- the abstraction of meaning; and
- an interpretative process for understanding reality.

The nature and value of theory

The first most basic notion of what constitutes theory is that of a specific quantifiable amount of knowledge which is essential to the vocational nature of becoming a photographer.

> I think that the theory side is something you should know about before you come here. I mean if you're going to do a degree, you should know a fair bit about photography before you come ... knowing all your film speeds, which formats to use, flash workshops - all that sort of theory.
> Student A (male)

Here the student is acquiring purely technical facts and procedures for making a photograph. In light of this quote, we have to ask ourselves how this student still held this idea of theory after three years of undergraduate study. It certainly questions the effectiveness of our own teaching and clarity of positioning. Other than this example, many students found it difficult to talk about what they understood by theory:

> No, theory doesn't play a part - not in the creation of my images ... it's probably because I haven't found a connection. Someone who can understand theory could look at my work and say 'blah, blah, blah', but I wouldn't be able to see it.
> Student B (female)

> A theory is, I don't really know how to put it into words - a part of history, a style or why? ... Theory is a very hard thing to describe, but I think whereas before if you said 'I like that, I don't like that', you wouldn't be able to say why. Once you understand the theory, you can give an explanation of why.
> Student C (female)

Although these are slightly different interpretations, theory does not seem to have much to do with the making of images for either of these students, although it can be useful in giving a verbal explanation to the products of photographic practice. While second student (Student C), feels she has developed the ability to apply theory to the image, this mid-level cognitive ability seems to elude the first student (Student B). It is also interesting to note that Student C mentions history as having something to do with theory, and indeed it comes to provide her with a vocabulary of styles which she adopts for her work. Here, history, in the sense of a history of styles, becomes something external to her from which she can pick and choose. She goes on to say:

> You have to come up with different ideas all the time, you do get a bit brain dead in the end... I like so many different styles and subject matter, I make it harder for myself in a way...I mean the last four or five projects... one was colour and people in a village... very formal, then I did a black and white clear sepia toned landscape project ... very arty ...
> Student C (female)

Again this is an example of a student acquiring facts and establishing procedures within the externally motivated situation of needing to produce something different each time to meet the project brief.

So what do students have to say who feel they draw on theory in some way to produce their images, not just in relation to the consumption of images. As this integrated process develops, so the feelings and attitudes of students become more complex and sophisticated:

> (Theory is) the thought processes behind things, the ideas people come up with to produce the work... looking at how other people had applied them (theories), other people's opinions and ideas, so I had a more well rounded idea of where I was coming from.
> Student D (female)

This student focuses on the process of constructing images by drawing on theory and the way she believes other photographers have used it. This suggests a more active and internalised approach in which the parts of the whole are separated until relationships are clear. They are then recombined to form a new set of values within which she positions herself. Perry (1970) notes that the ability to position oneself personally demonstrates a high level of cognitive and affective thinking. Thus learning is more intrinsically motivated and displays an ability to abstract meaning from the learning experience.

While this may seem a fairly clear rational process of stages and method, other students expressed a much more dynamic exchange between theory and such processes as imagination, past experiences and randomness, intuition, risk.

> For my process, what's important is my attitude towards photography. I somehow try to explore or create accidents ... provoke new situations and just take photographs of everything, and let's say the theoretical part, the response to these photographs comes afterwards. I first take loads of photographs and then I work with them, but I kind of like to give opportunities to intuition... Of course, you've got a certain knowledge and experience already and that is going to work on the image, so I'm not denying theory before the image somehow ....
> Student E (male)

This approach allows for different kinds of understanding based on knowledge and intuition. This more global approach produces a more fluid and flexible process to occur. And more importantly, as the following quotes illustrate, it becomes a way of seeing the world beyond the specific project in hand at any one moment:

> If you're trying to separate theory from practice, I think I have a problem with that, or practice from theory ... You can't have any practice without theory - it's just part of it.
> Student F (male)

> I approach things differently because of it (theory). It taught me how to work. It's been completely enriching now that I search more. I couldn't go back to not knowing ... it's not just research like you get from some books and periodicals from the library, it's about what's around me, my own children and my empathy if you like. It's my feelings that make my work. The theoretical thread is what's helped me understand my own feelings ... as an artist it becomes more a way of life.
> Student G (female)

The integration of theory and practice as central to interpreting and understanding reality leads to a more total personal commitment. As Kolb (1991) argues, this is an important feature of adult learning.

Theory as manifest in practice

Is it possible for theory to be manifest explicitly in the final piece of work? For those students who had come to believe theory was valuable in some way, they reported how they had passed through a very particular stage during their second year of study. This stage can be characterised as one where the student takes deliberate steps towards orientating her/himself to engaging with the 'implicit structure' of the discourse between theory and practice – if a bit literally as they themselves note:

> I was quite aware that I stopped exploring with the image as a language and that I was trying to illustrate my ideas which is the part I don't like about theory – when it comes before the image – and then photography is beginning to lose the only thing that's specific to it ... When you make that theory obvious I think it kills the possibilities for the audience to make their own connections and I think there needs to be some kind of openness.
> Student E (male)

This is what we might call a first attempt at a theorised image or we might say that the image illustrates the theory. As the student implies, the verbal is prioritised over the visual. The photograph illustrates the text rather than being used as a symbolic language in its own right. He also identifies three disadvantages to producing this kind of work: exclusivity of audience, closure of meaning and restraint on the creative potential of the individual.

However, students continue to suggest that somehow text somehow makes manifest the theoretical aspects that lie behind a piece of work, if in a rather contradictory way:

> They're a lot better thought out. There's a lot more gone into these ... you can tell the ideas that have gone on behind it, and the work involves text as well. So they're self explanatory, the images, but there's text to back them up.
> Student D (female)

Here the theory is made visible through either the caption or other form of verbal anchoring.

Another student suggested that theory could be articulated visually through historical reference – particularly if the history of photography is as much to do with the history of ideas. But of course, the audience in this case, needs to be aware of those references and have sufficient cultural capital to make these connections.

> I've chosen to take the inspiration from my immediate environment and then develop it and go and search for people that have done similar work and decide to push it in a different way that suits me. I mean I'm inspired greatly by Sally Mann: the ideas, the theories behind her photography, so it's not just the visual but also the reasons for her doing it. But then Sally Mann was inspired by Margaret Cameron – so there's many components that make the whole work that's mine.
> Student G (female)

Theory through research

Since theory, as academic knowledge, is a set of abstract concepts, one would expect students to undertake independent reading and study as a central means of gaining theoretical knowledge. Much course documentation suggests that research (like theory) provides the backbone and substance to a successful piece of work and lecturers stress the importance of research in many teaching situations. However, in spite of this apparent explicitness on the part of many lecturers, interviews revealed significant differences in the students' perceptions of the value of research and of what kind of research was important for practice.

Interviews showed that research is often discussed by practice lecturers - particularly in the tutorial situation – with reference to the canon of photography. Students are asked to 'look at' the work of well-known photographers, rather than being explicitly asked to read around the theoretical/historical ideas and contexts which might lie behind a photographer's approach. It is almost as if, in the eyes of the tutor, the photographer's name or set of images themselves become a shorthand for certain theoretical ideas. However, that isn't always understood by the student to be the case.

Many of those students interviewed referred to 'looking at' rather than 'reading about'. Of course this is unsurprising in many respects since photography is clearly concerned with the visual and the process of looking. But again, students display a variety of different motivations behind the process. 'Looking at' is far easier for many students who avoid or experience difficulty with reading academic texts. Research in this case provides a student with a set of visual and technical devices or approaches which she can pick and choose from:

> I look at other people's work. I try ... It's hard cos you don't want to look at it to copy, to reproduce what they've done, so you look at it to take a little snip out of what they've done ... I look at them, I don't know why I look at them, maybe because I'm told to look at them ... in the weekly tutorials ... Reading 10% out of 100%, I do learn a little bit, but if I didn't have to do it, I probably wouldn't do it.
> Student B (female)

Ironically for other students, research was seen to stifle their creativity and imagination. Indeed, the acquisition of knowledge itself can become problematic for such students who assume a surface approach to learning:

> I love landscape photography and I can't do it for toffee - whereas I used to try. I looked at so many wonderful landscape photographs but now I've given up basically ... maybe if I hadn't seen their work, I would have seen how my work had progressed a bit and perhaps I wouldn't have given in.

> Because you know so much about other photographers, it's very hard to find something that hasn't been done before ... and in a way it's a handicap cos if you didn't know all the other stuff, you'd go out and do it your way without being prejudiced in any way. The need for students to feel they should be wholly original was significant in other ways as well. Research became a means by which you could ensure that you were not 'copying' others.
>
> Because I feel so strongly about what I produce, I need to find out why – so I go to research other people and what their opinion of the subject is ... looking at other photographers, maybe theorists ... It's researching other photographers to make sure you're not going over old ground. You're producing a completely new and unique piece of work.
> Student D (female)

The emphasis on 'doing something different' may be interpreted as an attempt on the part of the students to be original and avant-garde in the modernist sense of the word – of creating a new work that distances itself from the past or what has been done before. Research here is seen as an instrumental and transferable skill that provides a way of working to create the unique and creative visual statement.

This approach to research differs significantly to Student G, earlier, who referred to the ideas and approaches of Sally Mann and Margaret Cameron underpinning her work. Here the student manipulates the two kinds of academic knowledge that Laurillard identifies as central to the university experience:

- an understanding of the representational system of photography; and
- an understanding of an ability to interpret the ideas that the representations represent.

From the above, it is possible to see that research can be perceived positively or negatively by students, depending on how they approach their learning.

Theory as dissertation

Traditionally the dissertation is seen as the place where a student's theoretical (and historical) understanding can be demonstrated, without any of the complexities alluded to in the previous sections. This reflects the conventional division within art and design education: practice equals creativity, self-expression and professionalism, and writing equals intellectual and academic processes and outcomes. This view overcomes the difficulties in expecting students' ability to move across the two languages of representation – at least in terms of the making of the images. The range of responses to the dissertation reflect the different learning approaches as suggested earlier

> ... [ideas] do play a part in the dissertation but not in any way with my work... The theory's really the dissertation ... which is on war photography. I was scared at first - 10,000 words - but it's been okay and I've enjoyed it.
> Student B (female)

> I love landscape photography but ... I've given up now basically and I did a dissertation on landscape photography which I thoroughly enjoyed doing... I just kept them very separate.
> Student C (female)

As we have already seen, theory has little relevance for these students in their practical work and the dissertation is seen as the arena where that is to be found. In the case of Student C, the dissertation has become a substitute for an area of perceived self-failure in her practice. She has been unable to reflect this knowledge back to the experience of making her own images. In spite of this, the experiences of writing a dissertation clearly gave both students a sense of achievement in being able to manipulate verbal systems of representation.

The ease with which students experience the dissertation depends on their understanding and ability to manipulate forms of representation, and lecturers bear a lot of responsibility in facilitating this understanding. In relation to her theory lectures, Student B recounted:

> If I was in a lecture and they were talking about semiotics, when I'm sitting there I haven't really got a clue about what they're talking about. The past two years, it's not been taught at a basic level so everyone can understand ... it's as if they're talking another language to you. Roland Barthes is a very strange man! ... I know they have to teach what they do, but it needs to be fun. It's down to the way you're taught ...
> Student B (female)

While we may acknowledge, from previous interview extracts, that this student taken a more surface approach to learning, she does accept that 'they have to teach theory'. So, she has not completely rejected it but has failed to find a way of understanding the language of description or, as discussed earlier, she has failed to find the point.

Other students were able to take fuller advantage of what a dissertation offers in relation to their practice. Here a closer relationship between the different languages of representation is found, not only in understanding other photographer's work but also in creating their own.

> My dissertation was very much about my practical piece of work, so I kind of unconsciously wove the two together. I suppose it became one huge piece of work really ...
> Student G (female)

> ... it (dissertation) was directly related to my practical work but I decided to take it in a different direction ... it shares the same interest with my practical work, but is not about it.
> Student E (male)

Above and beyond this, there is the argument that writing the dissertation itself is a form of practice, but this notion came from some interviews with theory lecturers rather than from students.

Conclusion

This paper has attempted to map out what value theory is seen to have for students and how it manifests itself in the making of images and the writing of the dissertation. If any of these conceptions that students have expressed here, surprise or worry us and do not always reflect what we thought we were doing, then we, as the mediators of ideas, need to identify more precisely exactly what changes in a student's learning we wish to encourage. This requires a process of self-aware reflection on our own practice as teachers. In particular, we should ask ourselves to what extent do we make our own position and understandings of the relationship of theory to practice explicit through dialogue.

Laurillard (1998, p. 85) argues that one of the prerequisites of the learning process is that lecturers reveal their own concept and positions clearly. This notion certainly challenges some traditional art and design practice within a crit or tutorial situation, where a lecturer may pronounce 'it works well' 'it doesn't work' or 'it's good', without any justification. This way of being presents the lecturer in a powerful and dominating position which does not encourage sharing and dialogue. Part of the learning process is also to do with staff taking responsibility for helping students develop 'the way they believe they come to know' (their epistemology). In other words, encouraging students to identify what do they think learning is, within a discourse that is made explicit.

References and further reading

Barthes, R. (1990), *Image-Music-Text* (London: Fontana)

Biggs, J.B. (1994), 'Student learning: research and theory – where do we currently stand?', in Gibbs, G. (ed), *Improving Student Learning - Theory and Practice* (Oxford: Oxford Centre for Staff Development) (accessed from DeLiberations Web site)

Biggs, J.B. & Collis, K.F. (1982), *Evaluating the Quality of Learning: the SOLO Taxonomy* (New York: Academic Press)

Boud, D., Keogh, R. & Walker, D. (1999), in *Supporting Open Learners: Theoretical Reader* (Milton Keynes: Open University)

Burgin, V. (ed.) (1982), *Thinking Photography* (London: Macmillan)

Entwistle, N. (1998), 'Motivation and approaches to learning', in Brown, Kolb, D., Rubin, I.M. & Osland, J. (1991), *Individual and Organisational Learning, Organisational Behaviour: An Experiential Approach* (New Jersey: Prentice Hall)

Laurillard, D. (1998), *Rethinking University Education: A Framework for Effective Use of Educational Technology* (London: Routledge)

Marton, F. & Säljö, R. (1997, 2nd ed), in Marton, F., Hounsell, D., & Entwistle, N. (eds.), *The Experience of Learning* (Edinburgh: Scottish Academic Press)

Perry, W.G. (1970), *Forms of Intellectual and Ethical Development in the College Years* (New York: Holt, Reinhart & Winston)

Ramsden, P. (1996), *Learning to Teach in Higher Education* (London: Routledge)

Schön, D. (1999), in *Supporting Open Learners: Theoretical Reader* (Milton Keynes: Open University)

Biographical note

Annie Grove-White teaches across theory and practice in Graphic Communication at Cardiff School of Art and Design, University of Wales Institute Cardiff. She is also Director of Learning and Teaching for the School. Her research interests cover cultural studies, as well as learning and teaching.

12

The act of sketching in learning and teaching the design of environments: a total skill for complex expression

Richard Hare

Department Landscape Architecture, Leeds Metropolitan University, UK

Abstract

In the words of the Swedish Architect Lennart Nord, ‘Sketching is a path into the many possibilities of the complex word’ (Nord & Birgestam, 1998) and this paper hopes to examine something of the pedagogy of sketching as a means for students to begin to engage with that ‘complex world’.

Some of the theory of sketching will be examined with particular reference to sketching and IT. Some suggestions will be made as to ways of improving skills in both, simultaneously rather than exclusively. The paper will use an outline of some of the pedagogical approaches to sketching at the beginning of the Landscape Architecture and Garden Art and Design undergraduate courses at Leeds Metropolitan University (LMU) to suggest some working practices for debate. A recent questionnaire intended to discover something of current students’ relationships to drawing is also considered.

Introduction

Sketching is used in this paper to refer to a subset of drawing, including observational drawing, idea generation, diagramming, design working drawing and doodling. Sketching does not here imply that work is necessarily incomplete or ill formed, though it may be both.

> In effect the process of developing pictorial and diagrammatic representations has traditionally been treated as a skill rather than an essential part of the process of thinking about a design problem and developing a design solution
> Purcell & Gero (1998)

Sketching is still commonly regarded simply as a skill. Kimbell, Saxton and Miller, have created a model of design that puts drawing firmly in a functional skills domain for their 'Distinctive Skills and Implicit Practices,' a review of their investigation 'Design Skills for Work' carried out for the Design Council (Eggleston, ed., 2000). They say 'we do not believe that the functional skills domain best captures the essence of design because this domain essentially comprises the tools that give external form to our thoughts, and all disciplines use such modes of expression.' They conclude that design is special because of the operational strategies designers use.

I hope that this paper helps to show that the separation of the operational strategies from skills is perhaps a little simplistic in understanding designers and designing. It is more likely that we use strategies that are consequent on our ways of knowing the world and that sketching and drawing are means of extending and simultaneously transforming our understanding, rather than simply means to let others know what we think or even ways of revealing to ourselves what we think. It is not unreasonable to suggest that those who sketch are thinking and acting differently (even when not actively sketching) from those who don't. Here I hope to explore this and draw a relationship between this and the curricula of Landscape Architecture at LMU.

Drawing as a contemporary issue in art and design education

There has been a resurgence of interest in drawing within art and design education in recent years. However, the introductory notes to the new PhD and MPhil 'Research in Drawing', at the RCA, 2002, tell us that 'Drawing is at present an under-theorised discipline, especially in relation to its technological applications.' The Drawing Research Network has been established to act as a conduit for research. Kingston University has entered the arena with an MA in Drawing as Process, first recruited September 2001, and there is an MA in drawing at Wimbledon College of Art.

Others are set to follow and we can look forward to drawing becoming more fully theorised. hopefully there will be some useful work on learning and teaching as a result.

Across many design disciplines there is widely expressed concern at a perceived shortfall in drawing skills amongst first-degree-level students.

In a short article by Robert Bevan in *Building Design* (Bevan, 2000), Christopher Egret, a director of Alsop and Stromer Architects, is quoted 'I am finding a lot of things in the city; architecture and furniture don't look right because [the designers] don't know how to draw.' This heralded the start of Drawing Power from The Campaign for Drawing. This is a 3-year initiative aimed at encouraging us all to draw and refocus attention on drawing as a thinking tool. It has resulted in the Big Draw events of 2000, 2001 and forthcoming events in Oct. 2002, which are taking place nation-wide.

One premise on which Drawing Power is based is that too many children are giving up on drawing around the age of 10 when they move into a more self-critical stage of their development. If this is so there must be an impact on higher education and in addition those tutors who are convinced that drawing skills are useful for design students often express the opinion that drawing is also under attack from IT. They see CAD (and other software) eating into curriculum time that may have been used for sketching.

At the same time some tutors are concerned that students might be seeing the use of computers as a substitute for sketching.

Perhaps a lack of theory has made sketching a difficult subject to discuss and therefore champion in curricula where the functional needs for CAD et al. are easy to communicate. Perhaps tutors assume that everyone simply knows that sketching is important, and why, and perhaps students are often simply expected to know this too.

Students' perceptions

To begin to understand something of student conceptions of, and their relationships with drawing, a pilot questionnaire has been put to groups of students at LMU on design of environments courses Architecture, BAHons (Arch.), Landscape Architecture, BAHons (BALA) and Garden Art and Design, BAHons (GAD) at levels 1 and 2 full time. Initial findings based on a sample of 90 students (self selecting by virtue of the fact that they were the ones who turned up to scheduled teaching on given days) suggest that drawing is certainly on the students' agenda.

It must be stressed that this questionnaire is intended as a pilot to suggest possible areas of further study and these results are regarded as no more than indicative.

- 86% of the group agreed or agreed strongly with the statement 'I enjoy drawing for its own sake';
- the highest percentage for any single cohort was 100% for GAD level 2;
- 87% of same group agreed or agreed strongly with the statement 'I have enjoyed drawing since childhood';
- the highest percentage for any cohort was 94% jointly for Arch. level 1, Arch. level 2 and BALA level 2;

- these figures suggest, rather unsurprisingly that we have 'drawers' on our courses;

  16% of the group agreed or agreed strongly with the statement 'Designing is possible without drawing skills';
- the highest percentage for any single cohort was 55% for GAD level 1 (6 of 11 students);
- 8% of the group agreed or agreed strongly with the statement 'The use of computer software has replaced the need to develop drawing skills';
- the highest percentage for any single cohort was 22% for Arch level 1 (4 of 18 students) and 0 or only 1 student from each other cohort;
- 13% of the group agreed or agreed strongly that 'I have found ways to avoid having to draw on my current course';
- the highest percentage for any single cohort was 27% for GAD level 1 (3 of 11 students) and between 0 or 3 student from each other cohort;
- 68% of the group agreed or agreed strongly with the statement 'Learning to draw on my current course has made me feel more creative'; and
- the highest percentage for any cohort was 91% jointly for GAD level 1 and GAD level 2.

It appears then that generally our students enjoy drawing, have enjoyed it since childhood and do not think that computer software obviates the need to develop drawing skills. There seems to be a prevalent belief that designing is actually not possible without drawing and most students feel that learning to draw on their current course has made them feel more creative.

The questionnaire obviously gives us no idea of the practical drawing abilities of our students but we can begin to see that drawing is viewed as important by these students. In fact their conception of design could be being severely restricted by the primacy they give to drawing.

My own experience of students from a number of institutions on design of environments courses, across Europe, is that there is often a hunger for drawing instruction, particularly for sketching. Students appear to consider there are good reasons to be able sketch well, whether they know what those reasons are or not, and after teaching sketching for 7 years and using drawing as the medium of an MA I still feel there is a lot more to it than there seems.

Psychology of sketching

Over recent years design as a process has begun to attract the attention of psychologists, intent on unlocking the secret workings of the creative minds of designers, and inevitably sketching has been a key puzzle to them.

A number of experiments have begun to inform a fledgling literature on the subject with some of the wild swings of prognosis consequent on a small potential sample of studies.

There is, however, evidence from Verstijnen and Hennessey (1998), and others, to support the thesis that sketching is a means by which tasks can be undertaken that are beyond our capabilities of mental imaging. This mental imaging is done within what has been called the visuo-spatial sketch pad, a facility of cognition within the short-term memory. When our short-term memory is faced with a complex task it cannot cope and, so the argument goes, we need to externalise some of this. Design tasks have been dubbed 'wicked' tasks because of their complex, multi-faceted and unfolding nature, and it is precisely this sort of complexity which seems to be beyond us without externalisation. Here, it is important to stress the representational aspect of sketching: it is for a large part about projecting visual information in a visual form and designers generally appear to prefer visual communication to written forms. Sketching is often a means to engage with the un-sayable, in an un-sayable way, not a shorthand for words but a different realm altogether.

Another key aspect of sketching in design is expressed by Purcell and Gero (1998) through their explanation of the work of Geol:

> He argued that sketching constituted a particular form of symbol system, which is characterised by syntactic and semantic, denseness and ambiguity and it is these aspects of sketching which allow lateral transformation to occur.
> Purcell and Gero (1998)

Geol's lateral transformations are as those in which an idea develops tangentially while vertical transformations are those which are linear modifications to an idea. It could be seen that making our rectangular building a little longer in one axis is a form of vertical transformation while making it circular is a form of lateral transformation.

This complex aspect of sketches and their potential for simultaneously divergent meanings makes sketching a useful working method for the designer and a problematical one for researchers and particularly those engaged in developing IT means of replacing or even just augmenting sketching in design. As Purcell and Gero (1998) go on to say, 'In contrast to sketching, the computer based drawing system is non-dense and unambiguous and should consequently make lateral transformation difficult.' Obviously this lateral transformation is the key move in a well-developed design process. It could be seen that 'non-dense and unambiguous' sketching on paper also inhibits the design process, the familiar problem of 'tight' drawing. As will be discussed later, however, computer software and hardware exists that allows extremely dense and ambiguous work to be undertaken: it's just that it isn't CAD.

So sketching appears to offer a pretty good working method in the design process. In *How Designers Think*, Lawson (1997) is a little cautious, however:

> The disadvantage of designing by drawing is that problems, which are not visually apparent tend not to come to the designer's attention.

> Architects could not 'see' the social problems associated with new forms of housing by looking at their drawings.
> Lawson (1997)

Here perhaps Lawson does not allow for the notion of diagramming as a subset of drawing. There is evidence that diagramming is not a design specific drawing methodology, the disciplines of physics, biology and economics have all revealed a sophisticated use of diagramming (Verstijnen and Hennessey, 1998).

The way that diagramming and sketching are inter-linked in a design process can obviously extend Geol's 'denseness and ambiguity' into yet another dimension.

Lawson (1997) describes the design process as one of 'interwoven analysis and synthesis', analysis of the design brief, and its situations, and subsequent situations envisioned through the process of design. It seems only sensible to use a working method that allows the easy movement between analysis and synthesis. This process is particularly significant to the design of environments where a specific site must be explored by the designer. Here, sketching as part of site exploration acts to begin the process of design by putting site analysis into the realm of the sketch from the beginning. Having a means to transcend words in this way allows for complex analysis – not simply a means to express that analysis but in fact a means to carry it out.

In this site analysis through sketching the learning process is not at all simple, learning is happening through a number of actions, including prolonged presence on site, studied observation and the physical act of sketching. The last of these is a physical learning of the site, learning through gesture, in the way an athlete learns a movement. A colleague and I often mime a particular sketching gesture to draw the other's attention to an aspect of the landscape, often to the raised eyebrows of new students. Lawson (1997) gives an interesting illumination of this phenomenon at work within the design process in a description of the architect Robert Venturi as '... having a facility between hand and mind ... sometimes the hand does something that the eye re-interprets and you get an idea from it.'

This facility can be viewed through Howard Gardner's model of multiple intelligences between what he calls bodily/kinesthetic and visuo/spatial intelligences. There are many years of research to be done to clarify the potential relationships between these intelligences, but it would seem clear that the physical actions (bodily/kenesthetic intelligence) called on in drawing are significant in the type of learning which they foster. If the physical actions and effects of sketching on site are considered, walking, climbing, enduring/enjoying the weather etc. an even more fulsome engagement of the bodily/kenesthetic intelligence will take place. This is learning through doing and as Schank (1995) tells us 'Learning by doing works because it teaches implicitly rather than explicitly.'

Beyond site exploration the action of sketching can also be seen as creating a store house of ideas, drawing gestures and reference points for the designer as inspiration. Obviously the physical record created is a primary resource.

If sketching is likened to a language, which it often is, it is all too easy to loose the sense of it as an inherently creative action and to regard it simply as a process of externalising cognition. Sketching can be more or less creative, but it is essentially about creating (even with limited skills) and therefore puts the sketcher immediately into a creative position. Birgerstam states that 'Sketching gets its substance from experience, brought forward by intuition' (Nord & Birgerstam, 1998).

Additionally, sketching offers an extremely useful methodology for reflective practice. Sketching obviously allows us to reflect on our sketching methods, but it importantly allows us to enquire into our ways of seeing. It self evidently provides a focus for enquiry into the sketching methods and ways of seeing of other sketchers.

Sketching is obviously a complex business and to make it comprehensible in an educational context its functionalities are often disentangled. In ‘Sketching as a didactic phenomenon’, Nord and Birgerstam (1998) state that ‘Sketching to a landscape architect seems to be a working method that has at least five different functions:

- to collect sensory impressions;
- to create a whole;
- to discover and formulate problems;
- to try and solve the problems, the ‘organising’; and
- to communicate with others.

Even without the explicit inclusion of analysis and synthesis (which may be regarded as implicit in the formulating and solving of problems) and the omission of recording and reflecting on the individual’s process their list begins to yield some key learning activities.

Biggs’ Structure of the Observed Learning Outcomes (SOLO) taken from *Teaching for Quality Learning at University* (Biggs, 2002) is perhaps a useful measure of the potential for sketching method in education.

SOLO rates learning as falling somewhere between:

- *uni-structural*, which is essentially perceived as being ‘done to’ the student: it is about memorizing but not transforming;
- *multi-structural*, which is the acquisition of facts, skills and procedures which are to be used later, again without transformation;
- *relational*, where students are making sense of and finding underlying principles in what is learnt; and
- *extended abstract*, where learning enables a transformation in a student’s perception of the world and enables a student to contextualise and value their work in the world.

With an emphasis on relational and extended abstract methodologies within student learning a deep approach to learning can begin to be fostered. This deep approach is perhaps typified by the abilities to understand, analyse and synthesise, and transfer thinking and practices between situations.

Sketching as a methodology almost entirely precludes a uni-structural approach to student learning and at the same time obviously facilitates multi-structural, relational and Extended Abstract approaches. There are dangers of an emphasis on an approach to sketching where students see sketching simply as a means to an end and despite the inherent transformative nature of sketching, students must be conscious of this if deep learning is to take place. Progression through a course of study must allow students to become aware of what they are already doing (and its significance) i.e. comprehending through the transformative act of sketching, thus enabling analysis and synthesis.

Sketching in practice at LMU

In common with many design departments, Landscape Architecture at LMU began within a college of art, was absorbed into a polytechnic and now exists within a 'new' university, Leeds Metropolitan University (LMU). At LMU Landscape Architecture sits at present in the School of Art, Architecture and Design.

Within its field Landscape Architecture at LMU has a reputation as a creative course which puts a strong emphasis on sketching and graphic skills.

Sketching has historically been important to the pedagogy of the department of Landscape Architecture at LMU, and rather than IT threatening sketching it is being seen as increasingly useful to designers to extend the scope and forms of sketching.

As the questionnaire appears to suggest, our students do not believe that an either or relationship exists between drawing skills and IT (a little contrary to the views of some academics) and as we design curricula for students we can find an increased variety of ways to develop sketching activity.

'The process of drawing is one of the best ways we know to absorb design ideas', Lawson (1997) tells us, and for those with strong visuo/spatial and bodily/kinesthetic intelligences this would seem to be true, and not just of design ideas. If we are dealing with these visuo/spatial and bodily/kinesthetic intelligences amongst our students, it would seem logical to be employing this distinctive intelligence in their learning. Sketching offers ways of approaching, analysing and synthesising a whole range of ideas and simultaneously developing communication and design skills. This is not to say that important aspects of students other intelligences should not be developed simply that the visuo/spatial and bodily/kinesthetic intelligences will perhaps offer students their core learning methods whether through sketching, model-making, physical interventions within a situation or site, etc.

Within the first level of the courses of BA Hons Landscape Architecture (BALA) and Garden Art and Design (GAD) the use of drawing/sketching is established for the students as a key activity.

This takes place through the structure of modules aiming to develop drawing/sketching abilities and to develop further learning strategies through drawing/sketching.

Site exploration through sketching and intervention

Module 101 for both BALA and GAD is an introduction to their subject through direct experience of landscape and through their expression of that experience, primarily through sketching and annotation. The emphasis is on understanding through observation and direct experience. Annotation of sketches is considered vital from this early stage giving voice to observations beyond those that a student can sketch. This may mean non-visual observations or observations that are beyond the ability of the students to capture successfully through sketching.

The teaching at this stage is dependant on direct tutor-student contact, short presentations on techniques of observation, sketching skills and on-site tutorials. Tutor input is concentrated at the beginning of this module through intense on-site exercises with students working at times in groups and at times individually but in close physical proximity to one another. Tutor guidance is regarded as vital at this stage, students can have difficulties reconciling what is perceived as a purely creative act, that of sketching, with critical observation.

The initial phase of this module employs an intensive week-long visit to Lindisfarne. In addition to sketching as an engagement students are also involved in creating an intervention in the landscape. Students are introduced to the key concepts of the module here before returning to Leeds, to employ them further in urban and peri-urban locations. This is important because students gain a conception of the scope of their subject and begin immediately to transfer skills between situations.

After this initial stage, the sequential sketching techniques of Cullen (1961) are explored by the students, in groups, as a means of understanding space and progression through space. This was recently introduced very successfully by means of a walking lecture through Durham city centre during which the students created their own sequential sketch record as lecture notes.

The culmination of this module is the creation of 180 degree panoramic sketches individually by students which are intended to synthesise the practices of observation and analysis developed through sketching (with annotation). The panoramic format is itself a synthesising device, bringing more than a single view into consideration. Students choose a viewpoint within their site that gives the opportunity to record varied spatial arrangements through elements of foreground, middle ground and back ground and again annotation is essential. Tutorial support on site is less important at this stage and many students can independently produce excellent work.

This module is almost entirely based on site. Assessment of this module is synoptic, covering all aspects of the project work presented through a notebook containing a drawn and written record of all work undertaken and a presentation of the panoramic sketches.

Designing through sketching, sketch modelling and intervention

The module BALA/GAD 102 Design and Communication follows 101 and is generally referred to as the 'Music Module'. Here a scenario is created for the students within which they are required to create a sensory space in response to a chosen piece of music.

In contrast to 101 this module is almost entirely studio based and the studio environment is used to record and reflect the process of the module, through an evolving exhibition of work.

Abstract sketching is used as the starting point for the student's response to the music but is then used as a process to run alongside sketch modelling. The module introduces the notion of design processes with tutors using sketching as a primary means of communication with the students at the drawing board. The result is that often students' own sketches will be interspersed with those of tutors, and ideally those of other students.

It is here that students are introduced to Adobe Photoshop as potential part of their process. This has been done by using Photoshop to extend the possibilities of their sketching, taking a sketch generated from a response to the music and manipulating it further. This method appears to work well for the majority of students and the use of relatively intuitive and accessible software allows a smooth process of integration into their process.

Because IT is used at such an early stage in the design process, when the process demands a phase of abstract development, and because Photoshop is used in preference to a drafting tool like CAD, it is possible for students to develop images that manifest Goel's 'syntactic and semantic denseness and ambiguity ... which allow lateral transformation to occur'. With the methodology currently used however the student work using Photoshop demonstrates a great deal more vertical than lateral transformation of ideas, though it does facilitate lateral transformation in further sketching and sketch modelling.

Again, intervention in the landscape is employed, in this context as a means to extend the design process. These interventions are individually conceived by students through propositional sketches, then created by a group of students and then recorded by the group under the direction of the proposer using sketching. This process is an important means by which students can use sketching to develop and explain ideas and demands that students communicate not only how their ideas should be realised but how they can be most effectively recorded through sketching.

The assessment of this module is synoptic covering all aspects of the project work presented in part through a design notebook containing all paper work with clarifying comments and a storyboard, which is a graphic presentation of reflection on the design process and usually includes reproductions of sketches and photographs of sketch models. Students are using increasingly sophisticated IT skills to create these storyboards.

Plant study through sketching

Concurrently with these modules BALA/GAD103 Natural Processes involves students in the study of plant materials for use in landscape and garden design. The study of plants has a long history of investigation through drawing and specimen illustration has traditionally been a useful study method for botanist. However, for the designer, knowing the character and context of plant material is as important as understanding its biology. As students develop skills of site exploration through sketching in their introductory module they apply these to the study of plant material which aims to explore the characters and contexts for a variety of plants.

The assessment for the plant study component of this module is through a plant study notebook, which is periodically reviewed through the module. It is anticipated that students will, through sketching, develop their relationship with and understanding of plant materials.

Summary of LMU sketching pedagogy

Sketching is regarded as a primary learning motor at LMU. Through its role in site exploration, idea generation, development and resolution and communication, it serves the academic aims of the curricula, but importantly it serves as a means for students to strengthen their learning methods, physically action their 'connectedness' with the world around them and experience their own creativity at work. This happens because sketching, on site and in a stimulating studio environment, engages students' visuo/spatial and bodily/kinesthetic intelligences, sketching is used in tandem with model making and landscape interventions which further employ these intelligences. IT is used in the intuitive form of Photoshop engaging the visuo/spatial intelligence and giving students a chance to develop their ideas freely, without constraining them to the 'undense and unambiguous' requirements of CAD.

Tutoring involves a lot of sketching, because to question a student's intention with a sketch is effectively 'speaking their language'. If inquiry into students' sketching is wholly verbal then students are being required constantly to approximate what can be necessarily complex and ambiguous expressions. For tutors to allow parts of the analysis and synthesis that is the design process to remain unvoiced seems vital. Preben Skaarup (course leader of Landscape

Architecture at Aarhus Architecture School, Denmark) says that 'Sketching is to bring the elements of a project together. To create the chaos from which a solution is to be found.' (Lund and Stenholm, eds., 1994) (author's translation).

Conclusion

Sketching requires a great deal more investigation before we can be sure why it is so important to designers, but the evidence is slowly building to suggest it is inextricably linked to cognition. It seems to offer us working, teaching, learning and reflecting methods rather than being a functional skill to apply to other activities.

Educators must value the multiple intelligences of design students and develop learning situations that allow students to grow their experience, knowledge and creativity through non-verbal/linguistic routes. Sketching on bits of paper, crude though it seems, is still extremely effective in doing this, increasingly IT is offering ways to extend sketching rather than limit it and creative educators must use new technology to offer ways to expand students' creativity. The idea that drawing skills are somehow 'traditional' and incompatible with new technology is a sure-fire way to avoid the potential for both. For a number of years cheap desktop graphics tablets have been available, linking sketching skills to any drawing software and recently the D-Board has been developed by Nemetschek. This is a tablet and screen combined. Perhaps the prospect of portable sketching tablets and e-carbon paper is not so far off. It seems that technology is morphing itself to meet the needs of the designer and it is up to colleges to capitalise on this. The future of sketching in a world of technology is encouraging if we can come to understand both and help to create a demand for technology that is truly an aid to learning and designing. Kavakli, Scrivener and Ball in conclusion to their Structure in Idea Sketching Behaviour:

> Sketching, then, is likely to remain a key behaviour in the early idea generation stage of design until its role in supporting creative discovery is properly understood. Indeed such understanding may simply confirm a continued need for sketching.
> Kavakli, Scrivener & Ball (1998)

Bibliography

Bevan, B. (2000), 'Drawing skills "lost"', *Building Design*, Sept. 8., 2000, p. 6

Biggs, J. (2002), *Teaching for Quality Learning at University* (Open University Press)

Cullen, G. (1961), *Townscape* (Oxford: The Architectural Press)

Eggleston, J. (ed.) (2000), *Teaching and Learning Design and Technology* (Continuum)

Kavakli, M., Scrivener, S. & Ball, L. (1998), 'Structure in idea sketching behaviour', *Design Studies*, 19 Vol. 4

Lawson, B. (1997), *How Designers Think* (Oxford: The Architectural Press)

Lund, A. & Stenholm, S. (eds.) (1994), *Strief i dansk havekunst*: Køge (DK), (F. Henriksens Eft.A/S)

Nord, L. & Birgerstam, P. (1998), 'Sketching as a didactic phenomenon' *Sveriges Lantbruksuniversitet*, Internal Report (unpublished)

Purcell, A.T. & Gero, J.S. (1998), 'Drawings and the design process', *Design Studies*, 19 Vol. 4

Schank, R.C. (1995), 'What we learn when we learn by doing', Technical Report No. 60 (Institute for the Learning Sciences Northwestern University)

Verstijnen, I.M. & Hennessey, J.M. (1998), 'Sketching and creative discovery' *Design Studies*, 19 Vol. 4

Biographical note

Richard Hare, Grad.Dip.LA, MA, is an associate lecturer in Landscape Architecture at Leeds Metropolitan University (LMU) and The Royal Veterinary and Agricultural University, Copenhagen (KVL). Studies have been in Landscape Architecture at Heriot Watt University, LMU and University College Dublin and in Art and Design at Hull College of Art and LMU. Research work covers issues of cultural landscape, participatory design processes in landscape architecture and the pedagogy of drawing as process. Teaching covers graduate programmes in Landscape Architecture, Architecture and Interior Design specialising in drawing and design.

13 A relationship between thinking styles and design degree student motivation

K. H. Hilton

The Centre for Design Research, Northumbria University, UK

Abstract

This paper deals specifically with the relationship between intrinsic motivation and learning styles, for design degree students, and originates from a larger, ongoing, programme of research investigating self-developmental behaviour.

The increase in student numbers over recent years, as a response by higher education to commercial changes has meant that there is an increasing need to encourage and develop the intrinsic motivation of students, so that they may perform better in their educational development. In order to achieve this it is proposed that students need the opportunity to understand the merits of different cognitive strategies by way of a variety of experiences. This paper therefore investigates the proposition that motivation is the expression of a number of influencing factors, of which an individual's 'thinking styles' could be a contributor.

An opportunistic approach was taken to sampling, where e-mail was used to contact a mixture of design graduates and undergraduates in their second year or above. Respondents came from a number of design courses including: industrial, multimedia, and communication design. The Universities included: Northumbria, Teesside, Glasgow and St. Andrew's. The total size of the sample group was 24, and composed of 6 females and 18 males, of which 14 were undergraduates and 10 were graduates.

The respondents were supplied with a two-part questionnaire. Part I was composed of a series of questions requiring them to *reflect* upon their course and their motivational influences *during* their degree. Part II provided respondents with the Sternberg-Wagner 'Self-Assessment Inventory for Thinking Styles'.

The findings of this investigation suggested that the cognitive traits which would enhance design student motivation would include:

- understanding and holding to the incremental theory of intelligence;
- greater intrinsic motivation; and
- a higher-level liberal thinking style (Sternberg, 1997).

Individualised styles of learning are viable, but the delivery of individualised teaching in respect of learning and thinking styles, generally is not. Instead, it is suggested that all courses should remain focused upon developing their core intellectual potentials, to satisfy the demands and opportunities of the professions they service. In order that the majority of the students are encouraged and motivated towards self-development then, they must be provided with the opportunity to understand and develop their personal learning strategies through regular meta-cognitive experiences. Therefore, as a step towards this aim, this paper aims to increase interest in the issues of intrinsic motivation and meta-cognitive (Nickerson, 1994), approaches to the encouragement of self-developmental behaviour.

Introduction

In order to attain sustainability of resources in changing circumstances, higher education has increasingly looked to develop more commercial business strategies, but with mixed results in the short term. Many degree courses have had to increase student numbers in recent years to compensate for cuts in government funding, and the resultant staff:student ratio has led to a need to change the allocation of time to students. In addition to this and other resource-related challenges, we see industry is now keen to employ graduates who are not just bright but innovative and self-motivated. For the degree courses, these commercial desires ally with the academic needs to encourage self-developmental behaviour in students.

> In the constantly evolving global employment market, it is essential that graduating students are equipped to be flexible, adaptable and prepared to take on responsibility for their own learning and their own continuous personal and professional development.
> Stefani et al. (2000)

Student motivation is a logical influence upon their success. It is the observation of this programme of research that the biggest obstacle to self-developmental behaviour appears to be a common attitude of '*What is the least I need to do to get by*?' Two major reasons have been identified for this attitude, regardless of age:

- approaches developed during an individual's schooling, e.g. surface learning, where the effort involved in their educational experiences may not have proved sufficiently rewarding, in part due to ineffective cognitive strategies; and
- a time-management issue, where many students these days have to work part-time in order to help fund their education, resulting in their full-time studies suffering.

However, the level of student motivation at any one point in time must be understood as an expression of a number of influencing factors, one of which could be an individual's 'thinking style'.

The personal inventory and order of thinking styles are specific to the individual, as are their responses to everyday situational influences, including the degree of success from learning experiences. Some students may have preferences that have led them to take control of their learning experiences whilst others may have preferences for learning through highly supervised lessons and assignments. In the present academic and commercial climate these latter individuals are highly likely to find that their educational and professional lives provide less motivating experiences and opportunities for success than the former, deeper learning individuals.

Context

Any discussion of the motivational influences of an individual's learning experience may itself be influenced by our various choices of approach towards contextualising a learning and motivation system. An initial understanding of the learning-motivation context is influenced by the individual's 'nature v nurture' belief.

> People who believe that intelligence is fixed, possess what is called an *entity theory* of intelligence. People who believe that intelligence is modifiable by experience subscribe to an *incremental theory* of intelligence.
> McCormick & Pressley (1997)

To encourage the self-developmental behaviour of students, a wider belief in the incremental theory of intelligence needs to be developed, through experiential learning.

> It is the responsibility of higher education teachers and tutors to develop teaching and learning methodologies which actively encourage students to become autonomous, independent and self-motivated learners.
> Stefani et al. (2000)

There have been a number of approaches taken to develop thinking and learning styles including the works of Gregorc (1982) and Sternberg (1997) and whilst they have proposed differing style forms they have adhered to the principle of individuality. In view of this, the advice to educators has been to build an awareness of thinking and learning styles and to decide what approach would be most effective for the lesson or course they are required to deliver. However, it has been warned that they should *not* attempt to accommodate the learning styles of all potential individuals within their strategy.

> It would be naive to expect that adult educators could systematically design and deliver a course to fit the learning style needs of their students.
> Tennant (1997)

However, an approach for the incorporation of thinking and learning styles into course design would be to discuss with students the individual differences and merits of these styles. This 'learning about learning' has been termed meta-cognition (Nickerson, 1994).

For this investigation, Sternberg's (1997) 'Self-Assessment Inventory for Thinking Styles' was used. Whilst his original text should be referred to for the complete description of each of these styles, for the purpose of this context a brief outline of each follows:

- *Legislative*
  These people like to do things their own way. They like creating, formulating and planning things. In general, they tend to be people who like to make their own rules. They prefer creative and constructive planning based activities, such as writing papers, designing projects and creating new business or educational systems.

- *Executive*

  These people are implementers. They like to do and generally prefer to be given guidance as to what to do or how to do what needs to be done. Executive people prefer problems that are given to them or structured for them and take pride in being doers, in getting things done.

- *Judicial*

  These people like to evaluate rules and procedures and to judge things. They prefer problems in which they can analyse and evaluate things and ideas.

- *Monarchic*

  These people tend to be motivated by a single goal or need at a time. They tend to be driven by their single-mindedness. They often attempt to solve problems full speed ahead, damn the obstacles. They can be decisive and occasionally too decisive. If they cannot see how something relates to a preferred issue, they may find the thing lacking in interest.

- *Hierarchic*

  These people tend to be motivated by a hierarchy of goals, with the recognition that not all of the goals can be fulfilled equally well and that some goals are more important than others. They thus tend to be priority setters who allocate their resources carefully. They tend to be systematic and organised in their solutions to problems and in their decision making.

- *Oligarchic*

  These people share power equally. They tend to be motivated by several, often competing goals of equal perceived importance. They have trouble deciding which goals to give priority to. The result is that they may have trouble allocating resources.

- *Anarchic*

  These people tend to be motivated by a wide assortment of needs and goals that are often difficult for others, as well as for themselves, to sort out. They tend to be not so much asystematic as antisystematic. They tend to take a random approach to problems. They have a certain potential for creativity that is rare in others.

- *Global*

  These people prefer to deal with relatively larger and often abstract issues. They tend to focus on the forest, sometimes at the expense of the trees. Their constant challenge is to stay grounded and not get lost on cloud nine.

- *Local*

  These people tend to prefer to deal with details, sometimes minute ones, and often ones surrounding concrete issues. They tend to focus on the trees, sometimes at the expense of the forest. Their constant challenge is to see the whole forest, and not just its individual elements.

- *Internal*

  These people tend to be introverted, task oriented, sometimes aloof, and socially less sensitive than other people. At times, they also lack interpersonal awareness, if only because they do not focus on it.

- *External*

  These people tend to be extroverted, people oriented, outgoing, socially more sensitive, and interpersonally more aware.

- *Liberal*

  These people like to go beyond existing rules and procedures and seek to maximise change. They also seek or are at least comfortable with ambiguous situations, and prefer some degree of unfamiliarity in life and work.

- *Conservative*

  These people like to adhere to existing rules and procedures, and minimise change, avoid ambiguous situations where possible, and prefer familiarity in life and work (Sternberg, 1997).

Those individuals who hold to the 'incremental theory' of intelligence are more likely to experiment with, and to benefit from, thinking and learning styles, if brought to their attention. However, in order that an individual may determine the degree of benefit facilitated by a chosen approach, they will need to be clear on their personal assessment criteria. The chosen criteria will be dependent upon the individual's type of motivation:

- extrinsic: opportunities or threats of an external nature, e.g. money;
- social: influenced by family or peer relationships, e.g. honour;
- achievement: improving career opportunities, e.g. qualifications; and
- intrinsic: activities which provide personal reward, e.g. see Thomas (2000).

Whilst individuals may be seen as motivated by a mixture of these types, it is proposed that the more intrinsically motivated an individual is, the more likely they are to experiment with and benefit from the thinking and learning styles as part of a self-developmental programme. The criteria for assessing intrinsic motivational benefits can be viewed as sources of reward.

The four intrinsic rewards:

- meaningfulness;
- choice;
- competence; and
- progress (Thomas, 2000).

This is supported in part by the findings of Drew's (2001) investigation of support and provision for the self-developmental behaviour of students:

> Student views support the writings of those who emphasise the personal meaningfulness of education (e.g. Rogers, 1983). Motivation towards the course was influenced by their perceptions of the relevance of discrete aspects of the course to the whole, the appropriateness, and relevance of teaching and learning activities for a topic, and by relevance to '*the real world*' and to their needs.
> Drew (2001)

Method

The context for this paper initially indicated that a highly self-developmental individual in design education would appear to:

- hold to the incremental theory of intelligence;
- be more intrinsically motivated; and
- indicate a slew towards the 'legislative' and 'liberal' thinking styles.

An opportunistic approach was taken to sampling, where e-mail was used to contact a mixture of design graduates and undergraduates in their second year or above. Respondents came from a number of design courses including: industrial, multimedia, and communication design. The universities included: Northumbria, Teesside, Glasgow and St. Andrew's. The total size of the sample group was 24, and composed of 6 females and 18 males, of which 14 were undergraduates and 10 were graduates.

The respondents were supplied with a two-part questionnaire. Part I (see Appendix), which was composed of a series of questions requiring them to *reflect* upon their course and their motivational influences *during* their degree. Part II provided respondents with the 104 question, Sternberg-Wagner 'Self-Assessment Inventory of Thinking Styles' (Sternberg, 1997).

The Sternberg-Wagner Self-Assessment Inventory was selected for this investigation on two counts:

- this inventory covered a breadth of thinking styles; and
- where feedback to students is potentially important, the ease of interpretation and visualisation can be key, and whereas many style inventories may be broad, a number lack the ease of visualisation, appearing to have been intended for academic professional end users.

Considering the length of the whole questionnaire the response was better than had been predicted, but it was paradoxical that this investigation would have further benefited from the participation of those potential respondents who were not motivated to fill in questionnaires. However, the sample size obtained did provide a usable range of thinking styles and motivational response levels.

The approach taken with Part I of the questionnaire, was to use 25 questions for the motivational rating, plus some additional questions to provide the opportunity for highlighting other situational influences upon motivation. Some respondents' comments indicated intrinsic or extrinsic motivation and preferences for divergent or convergent thinking. The value of this was to act as a cross-check to the Sternberg-Wagner Self-Assessment Inventory results.

Sternberg (1997) provided reliability calculations for the Inventory within his text, possibly as a reaction to the controversies over the credibility of thinking and learning style inventories in general. It was predicted, for this investigation, that a usable sample size of general public would slew towards an even spread of individual thinking styles so that when averaged out the results would show 'middle low/middle high' results. Further to this, any specific samples, such as 'designers', may be identified as having a slew towards some subject process-related thinking styles.

The intention was to compare the results of Part I and Part II to see if a reasonable link was indicated between motivation level and preferred thinking styles, and to discuss the implications for design in higher education.

Results

The results, presented under this heading, in graphical form, reference the Sternberg-Wagner thinking styles and ratings:

A = legislative	G = anarchic	6 = very high
B = executive	H = global	5 = high
C = judicial	I = local	4 = middle high
D = monarchic	J = internal	3 = middle low
E = hierarchic	K = external	2 = low
F = oligarchic	L = liberal	1 = very low
	M = conservative	

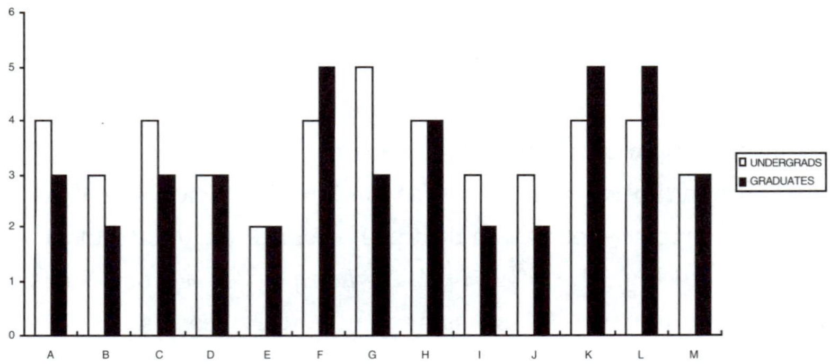

Fig. 1 Undergraduates/graduates mean rating analysis

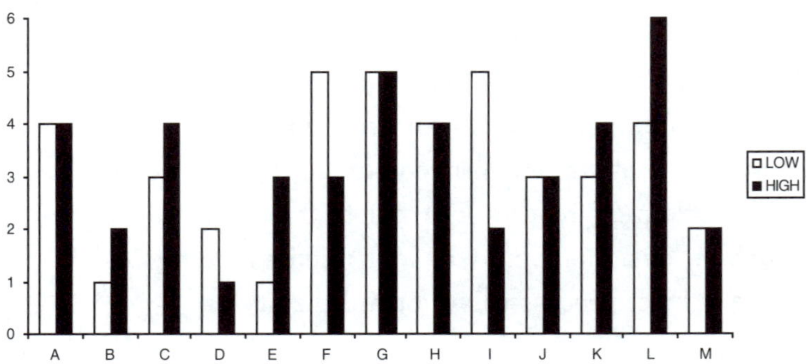

Fig. 2 Low/high motivation mean rating analysis

In addition to the responses used for the motivational rating, a number of respondents provided deeper insight into the situation surrounding potential motivational influences. Typical comments of the undergraduates were:

- low motivation:

  'I assumed my chosen subject would be enjoyable'; 'The briefs de-motivated me'; 'Tutor support was lacking'; 'I don't believe that exam results have any importance'; 'Peer support was there when I needed it'; 'As a designer I see myself as a cynical realist.'

- high motivation:

  'I enjoyed design at school'; 'I wanted to improve myself. Stand out from the rest'; 'I want to make people go "Wow!"'; 'I place quite a lot of importance on exam results'; 'Peer group support was good'; 'As a designer I'm getting there.'

Discussion

Most of the Sternberg-Wagner thinking style results were found to be mid-range, an outcome thought by the researcher to be predictable for a reasonable size general-public sample. However, there was a low rating for the hierarchic style and a high rating for the liberal style. This suggested that the designers as undergraduates generally preferred going beyond existing rules and procedures to maximise change, whilst generally tending not to be so good at setting priorities or allocating resources.

The total sample group was initially composed of undergraduate and graduate samples and although the questionnaire requested that everyone reflect upon the period of their design degree, there was a chance that such reflective activity might prove difficult for some of the graduate respondents. Therefore a comparison was made between their results and a difference was indeed indicated (see Fig. 1). Whilst both samples still shared the same ratings for the hierarchic and liberal style, the undergraduates indicated a high preference for the anarchic style, while the graduates indicated low preferences for the executive, local and internal and additional high preferences for the oligarchic and external. This suggested that whilst graduates had been requested to respond in a reflective sense, they may have projected their professionally matured preferences into their responses, possibly unaware that their thinking styles had actually changed. Sternberg (1997) had indicated that styles can change as individuals develop more effective cognitive processes. Unfortunately for this investigation, it was decided that the graduate respondents had to be dropped from the sample group in order to gain a clearer picture surrounding the core question of *student* motivation.

Next, the upper and lower limits of the motivation results were assessed against the thinking styles. The motivation level was determined by the number of positive as opposed to the number of negative or neutral responses, made towards each individual's course. It was found that the students with lower motivation had very low-hierarchic and high-local styles, whereas the highly motivated students were very high-liberal and low-local styles. This was interpreted as indicating that students with a lack of motivation towards a design degree tend to be poor at setting priorities and allocating resources, whilst also tending to become fixated on details and not stepping back often enough, in order to see the global picture. Whereas, the highly motivated students indicated a tendency to avoid much of the detail, whilst highly likely to go beyond existing rules and procedures to maximise change. Also being comfortable with ambiguous situations, and in fact preferring some degree of unfamiliarity in life and work, a thinking style which certainly lends itself to certain professional roles in design.

In addition to these results the further comments made by the students (see above), suggested that those with low motivation had a degree of dependency, a lack of confidence and direction – outcomes that are indicative of relying upon ineffective cognitive strategies.

However, some of their comments were in near agreement with the highly motivated students. Motivational influences of peer groups and parents were generally commented upon favourably. At the higher end of the motivation scale, students communicated a degree of independence, confidence and clearer direction, indicative of individuals using more effective cognitive strategies.

However, it cannot be claimed that individual effectiveness of thinking and reasoning is the sole influence of individual levels of motivation. The correlation here though, between thinking styles and motivation, and the polarised student responses to the design and delivery of design degrees, certainly suggests that effective thinking could be a major influence.

Degree courses should remain focused upon developing their core intellectual potentials, to satisfy the demands and opportunities of the professions they service. In order that the majority of students are encouraged and motivated towards self-development, the students must be provided with the opportunity to understand and develop their personal learning strategies through regular meta-cognitive experiences. It is suggested here that this approach should be facilitated by all tutors, but initiated as early as possible in Higher Education, by first-year degree tutors, or even by foundation course tutors, for maximum effect. Such a strategy should be viewed as an investment – one that is intended to encourage self-developmental behaviour, towards an individual's lifelong-learning.

Conclusion

The findings of this investigation suggested the traits that students should be encouraged to develop would include:

- understanding and holding to the incremental theory of intelligence;
- greater intrinsic motivation; and
- a higher level liberal thinking style (Sternberg, 1997).

Students need to be intrinsically motivated before they can develop themselves. Therefore, it is suggested that the meta-cognitive approach to self-development must attend to individual sources of motivation prior to styles of thinking. An appreciation of the mechanisms of learning and the identification of opportunities to make intellectual tasks and desires easier to attain, should inspire students to take on greater challenges and gain greater rewards.

Appendix

Reflecting on your motivation questionnaire

Name:

1. Course name:
2. Have you now graduated from the named course?
3. Why did you decide to do a degree?
4. What encouraged you to choose your field of design for a degree subject?
5. What motivated you the most during your degree?
6. What de-motivated you the most during your degree?
7. What motivates you the most about the profession you have chosen to pursue?
8. Do you have a role model?
9. Do you feel a need to do what your peer group wish, much of the time?
10. Do you do as you please much of the time?
11. How would you describe to a friend, a person off your course who:

    11.1. Has done well?

    11.2. Has not done so well?

    11.3. Was highly motivated towards the course?

    11.4. Seemed to be de-motivated by the course?

    11.5. Never skipped lectures?

    11.6. Frequently skipped lectures?

12. What was your favourite design project?

13. Do you have a favoured piece of designer's work?

14. What part of the design process do you enjoy the most?

15. What part of the design process do you enjoy the least?

16. What rewards do you seek from your profession?

17. Do you intend to stay in this profession throughout your career?

18. If you could start your education again from the beginning, are there any elements you would wish to be different?

19. During your course, how much did you need the following:

    19.1. Financial support?

    19.2. Parental support?

    19.3. Tutor support?

    19.4. Peer support?

    19.5. A social life?

    19.6. Recreational activities?

20. During your course, how well did the following meet your requirements:

    20.1. Financial support?

    20.2. Parental support?

    20.3. Tutor support?

    20.4. Peer support?

    20.5. A social life?

    20.6. Recreational activities?

21. How much importance do you place on exam results?

22. Describe yourself in just two words as:

    22.1. A designer....

    22.2. A person....

    22.3. A student....

References

Drew, S. (2001), 'Student perceptions of what helps them learn and develop in higher education', *Teaching in Higher Education*, Vol. 6, No. 3

Gregorc, A. (1982), *An Adult's Guide to Style* (Maynard, Mass: Gabriel Systems)

McCormick, C. B. & Pressley, M. (1997), *Educational Psychology: Learning, Instruction, Assessment* (New York: Longman)

Nickerson, R. S. (1994), 'The teaching of thinking and problem solving', in Sternberg, R. J. (ed.) *Thinking and Problem Solving* (San Diego: Academic Press)

Rogers, C. (1983), *Freedom to learn for the 80s* (Columbus, OH: Merrill Publishing)

Stefani, L.A.J., Clarke, J. & Littlejohn, A.H. (2000), 'Developing a student-centred approach to reflective learning', *Innovations in Education and Training International*, Vol. 37, No. 2, pp. 163-171

Sternberg, R.J. (1997), *Thinking Styles* (Cambridge: Cambridge University Press)

Tennant, M. (1997), *Psychology & Adult Learning* (London: Routledge)

Thomas, K.W. (2000), *Intrinsic Motivation at Work: Building Energy & Commitment* (San Francisco: Berrett-Koehler)

Biographical note

Dr. Hilton is a Design School Director at Northumbria University. His field of research is the 'Psychology of Innovation'. Working from the Centre for Design Research, his particular interest is individual differences and influences, affecting and enabling positive change.

14

Independent learning in art and design masters courses: the development of an electronic learning contract

Robert Jerrard, Jeannette Luczkowski, Marie Jefsioutine and Darren Newbury

Birmingham Institute of Art and Design, University of Central England, UK

Abstract

This paper draws together two areas of teaching and research that have been developed over a number of years at Birmingham Institute of Art and Design: the development of contracted learning within masters courses in art and design, and research into the uses of new teaching and learning technologies, specifically for work/practice-based learning.

The paper contains the following elements: (i) a brief discussion of the learning and research contexts in which the project was initiated; (ii) a discussion of the issues involved in work-based and contracted forms of learning - for example, the integration of the educational agendas of student and institution in an industry context; (iii) a rationale for the development of an electronic form of the learning contract and discussion of the user-based research that underpinned specific decisions about its construction; and (iv) a discussion of the future development of work in this area.

Introduction

Birmingham Institute of Art and Design (BIAD) at the University of Central England has during the last five years pioneered the development of learning contracts within masters courses. This initially helped Teaching Company Associates gain dual outcomes from funded collaborative projects in small firms. A review of this experience and the associated research into work-based learning shows that a particularly novel student learning experience has been introduced. The operation of such contracts has provided high levels of scholarship and facilitated the collaborative interaction between university, student and employer. In particular, the inclusion of work-based assignments and the credit accumulation of elements at work, in parallel with course assignments in the university, provides an unusual but realistic and stimulating learning environment. Individual learning strategies appear to centre on aspects of shifting 'learning domains' where design professionals, usually working in areas of professional group allegiance, appear particularly adept at mapping personal learning ambitions onto work agendas. In a cultural sense, 'stolen' time appears to provide the essential common ground between ambition and expectation. It was also noted that students have been able to conflate career and intellectual domains easily.

The particular focus of this paper is the development of an electronic form of the contract, based on our previous experience, and together with a close analysis of the personal pedagogic agendas and domains of those students involved. The 'Electronic Learning Contract Project' (ELC) is part of BIAD's 'Framework for Research into Electronic Teaching and Learning', which is centrally involved in the development of digitally based learning and teaching in the faculty. Linked to the 'Framework' is 'User-Lab', a centre for research into the user experience and user-centred design. The development and testing methodology for ELC, carried out by User-Lab, has been based upon definitions of usability and user-centred design (UCD) derived from ISO standards (including ISO 9241-11 and ISO 13407 Human-Centred Design of Interactive Systems), and has involved both learners and teachers, at all stages of design and production.

Learning in the workplace

The origin of the current system of undergraduate and postgraduate education in art and design in the United Kingdom lies in a practical philosophy derived by the Council for National Academic Awards (CNAA). Degree-level study was designed to include exemplar experience. Art and design courses have particularly relied on professional engagement in the form of visiting staff or sandwich course arrangements. Work experience and live projects have also connected learning with the professional world, thereby preparing and motivating an understudy generation. For example, the CNAA (1983) expected courses that involve an element of supervised work experience to consider the following selected aims:

> ... to place students in an environment where they may see some of the opportunities which may become open to them, and be helped to establish their choice of career.
> CNAA (1983: 20-21)

and

> ... to give students an opportunity to acquire some of the skills which are a normal requirement of the careers to which the course relates.
> CNAA (1983: 26-27)

Developing the capacity in students for reflection on real-world events holds much for career education in art and design. However, the involvement by a student in professional work alone may not allow for the appropriate learning to occur in order to satisfy qualification requirements. The conflation of a variety of personal goals within an experience of higher education increasingly requires additional learning and teaching styles. Garawon et al. (1994) suggest that experience-based reflection through small discussion groups should be central. According to Guedella et al. (1997) 'a focus on the group reference point rather than on the individuals' suggests that individual problem focus is linked to understanding how a variety of people focus on the same problem. A motivated art and design student may be said to be one who learns not only from problems, but also from fellow students. It is clear therefore that an external work involvement requires a close and careful consideration of the traditional values of scholarship, as well as a considerable extension of the natural altruism of teaching.

Contracted learning and learning contracts

Contracted learning is a means both of recognising that learning takes place in a variety of situations outside of the lecture hall or seminar room, including the workplace, and of structuring and facilitating the learning process. It also allows students to take an active part in the design of their own programme of study, signifying a move away from the tradition where the learner is a passive receiver of a preordained curriculum. In turn, this leads to a shift in the balance of the relationship between the student and tutor, whereby the student and tutor enter into a partnership of equal standing.

Learning contracts provide a negotiated form of study, a study structure and a record of achievement. The origins of contracted learning are outside the art and design sector and are often linked to professional outcomes as well as intellectual ones, for example, the original learning contracts used at BIAD were derived from Teaching Company Schemes. Thus, contracts have formed the basis for the accreditation of work-based elements and independent study. The following represent the key elements, in the authors' experience, involved in running learning contracts and work-based learning:

- formal agreement between an individual student and an institution comprising: time, project/milestones, learning outcomes and course modules;
- collaboration with an exterior organisation;
- exterior curricula;
- the provision of assignments at work; and
- partnerships between employers, students, universities and examiners.

As stated, contracted learning has largely been developed outside of the art and design sector. However, the importance of practice- and work-related experience to art and design education leads the authors to suggest that the scope of this mode of learning can be extended to many areas. In some instances there may be no need for an employer to be part of the equation. For example, a practitioner carrying out commissioned work, or a designer/maker sited in her own studio space, may also wish to exploit the learning opportunities these contexts can provide.

Additionally, owing to the flexible and consultative nature of contracted learning, it can be viewed as responding positively to current trends in the educational environment, towards individualised learning, co-operative learning and partnering (Vogel & Klassen, 2001).

Five key elements in a learning contract can be identified:

- the development of learning objectives – providing a specification of individual elements within the overall aims of the course and contributing to the student's 'personal learning agenda';
- the specification of strategies and the location of resources – linking and integrating the diversity found at work or in the studio, and at the university;
- defining evidence of accomplishment of objectives and their recording – ensuring that the contracts are clear and accessible to the student and staff involved;
- validating evidence of accomplishment of objectives – linking remote learning to the existing course regulations and expectations of the university; and
- Accredited Prior Learning and Accredited Prior Experiential Learning.

Why learning contracts, why the Web?

The development of Web-based forms of the learning contract recognises the changing nature of studentship, in particular an acknowledgement of the changing geography of learning and an acceptance of where it might take place. It is also aligned to a wider strategy, fulfilling two of the goals stated in the University of Central England's teaching and learning strategy:

> Create opportunities for developments in learning and teaching, including the use of ICT, by stimulating innovation and linking teaching with research;

and

> Encourage curriculum innovations designed to increase the employability of UCE students.
> UCE Teaching and Learning Strategy

The establishment of the dual motivations surrounding educational experience and professional future may be interestingly enriched by much more adventurous course design. For example, a more student-centred and career-related taught course might be increasingly collaborative and necessarily linked to a wider learning environment. The provision of Web-based access to higher education should provide effective forms of communication and a rich but different learning experience, not a mere lecture or workshop replication. Preparatory research clearly indicated that the nature of existing subject delivery should not be weakened by merely re-broadcasting course content. A commitment to the development of the contract as a form of curriculum carrier is likely to prevent the disappointment and inflexibility often found in other Web-based material, as highlighted by English & Yazdani (1999).

An electronic version of the learning contract allows for the embedding of contracted learning within any number of art and design programmes thereby broadening the scope for learning. It also has the potential to reach out to a diverse range of learners who have not been able previously to consider gaining higher qualifications, because of conflicts between external commitments and programmes of study with set timetables. Contracted learning also allows for a reasonable adjustment to be made to a programme of study in accordance with the United Kingdom Special Educational Needs and Disability Act (SENDA) 2001.

The Web-based contract offers flexibility both in terms of negotiation and in maintaining a holistic overview of the individual programme of study. The potential exists to increase one-to-one contact between student and supervisor, without the need to organise mutually acceptable times in order to communicate. Students involved in the paper-based contract have expressed how important it was to have one-to-one contact in the initial stages of negotiation in order to help build confidence when drafting the contract.

Learning contracts should also be seen as part of broader interdisciplinary view of educational environments, Banathy (1993), suggests four levels of an educational system, each with a different focus:

- the four levels are: the learning-experience level; the instructional level; the administrative level; and the management level;
- when the instruction is the focus, the teacher teaches the subject matter;
- when learning is the focus, the learner masters the learning tasks and the instructor becomes the manager of the learning environment.

Adapted from Banathy (1993)

The development of the Web-based contract has implications at all four levels. The deliberate shift of focus from supporting teaching in the university, to supporting learning in the workplace has implications for educational managers and administrators, as well as students and teachers. It was important therefore that the new Web-based form of the contract was based on a careful analysis of existing practice and subject to evaluation during its development, taking a broad educational view rather than focusing simply on the software.

Developing the electronic learning contract

The electronic form of the contract includes all the features of the paper-based form. Additional features allow for interactive use by the student, with specific features for dialogue within the cohort of contracted students, and with staff. The paper version of the contract was tried and tested, and received enthusiastic support from those students who used it. In order to ensure that the electronic version fulfilled all the functions of the original it was necessary to map out not only the structure of the paper contract, but also the process of constructing and completing a contract. There were five aspects to the design process:

- establish the aims and objectives of learning contracts – the links between all the facets of structured learning and the expectations and achievements of students who have used contracts;
- identify the aims and objectives of the electronic version – the differences and particular advantages of the electronic form;
- map out the form and structure of the existing contract – in particular the relationships between different parts of the contract and the way in which key elements are negotiated;
- analyse the process of completing a contract from the point of view of each party involved – the order of completion, its use and perception by students, staff, the university and external examiners; and
- draw up a design specification – a contract for asynchronous use by students and staff with a variety of access protocols.

What has come before

As a starting point the form and structure of the existing contract were examined. This was done by looking at a blank contract as well as at a number of completed contracts. Although the completed contracts had been created from the same blank proforma, it was important to be aware of any inadequacies with the format, which would show up as structural alterations made during completion. It would not be possible for a student to alter the structure and layout of an online, database-driven form should it prove to be inadequate.

Each of the current contracts were broken down into the component parts, namely:

- statement of the overall aims;
- personal details page;
- supervisor and assessor details;
- summary of learning activities to be undertaken with start and finish date and grade achieved; and
- detailed page for each learning activity containing specific objectives, assessment criteria, start and finish dates and grade.

Analysing each section in detail revealed some inconsistencies in terminology (e.g. the words 'milestones' and 'objectives', 'aims' and 'goals'), particularly between work-based activities and university modules. It was important to establish whether the differences in terminology actually reflected semantic differences. This would be important in the design of the database, where different types of information would have to be stored in different fields. Similarly, differences in structure and layout were analysed in terms of those that could be standardised and those that were variable and must remain flexible. Whilst standardised page structures would enable a more efficient and coherent system, it was important not to compromise the learning process by limiting flexibility.

In addition, a number of paper-based contracts from other departments and institutions were analysed, from both art and design and from other disciplines. Thus a variety of contract experiences and regulatory environments were surveyed, although the design of the electronic version was constrained by the fact that it had to conform to the established and accredited format.

Simply making an electronic version of the paper contract would not in itself be of much value, nor would it be successful if it did not integrate with the whole process of study. Moore and Kearsley (1996) point out that changing one component of a complex system like education will have implications throughout. For example, changing the communications medium will have an effect on the nature of instruction, interaction, and the learning environment. Any attempt 'to design or implement distance education without taking into account these interdependencies will likely fail or be ineffective' (Moore & Kearsley, 1996).

It was important, therefore to analyse the whole process of using a learning contract and to understand the wider context of its use. This was done through detailed interviews with tutors and students.

The student experience

The interviews involved mapping out the entire process from initial negotiations between employer and university, to signing off a contract and completing a course of study. Interviewees were asked to describe the process from the beginning of their involvement, being prompted for further detail where needed.

Discrete stages were identified for further discussion, noting whether they were sequential or parallel activities, and to what extent they overlapped. Each stage was then analysed against the following factors:

- the parties involved and their responsibilities;
- the amount, duration and type of communication between parties;
- any guidance sought and by whom;
- any guidance provided and by whom;
- knowledge needed and how it was obtained;
- difficulties and misunderstandings encountered and by whom; and
- how difficulties were resolved and by whom.

During the interviews each interviewee was also asked what benefits or disadvantages they might expect from an electronic version of the contract, and what features they would find useful.

Some of the interviews were retrospective; some were run concurrently with the student's experience of completing a paper contract, both provided useful reflections on the process. For example, the experience of contract negotiation was elicited together with the required tutorial frequency and information requirements. Compared with non-contracted learning this shows greater concentration of both staff support and supporting information at the early stages of the contract but considerably less in later stages.

Students who were unable to attend interviews were asked to complete a questionnaire about their experiences with the contract, requesting details of the experience of the contract at work and its 'life' in the workplace.

Designing the user experience

The results from the interviews, questionnaires, and the analysis of the paper contracts, were used to draw up a design specification for the electronic version. In keeping with a user-centred design approach, the priority was to design the users' experience. An early and continual user focus has been maintained centring on ease of use.

Potential users of the system would include academic supervisors, employers, students/employees, and external examiners, each of whom may or may not have had experience of using computers before, and may or may not have been part of a learning contract before. Any of these users would need to be able to access the contract and understand immediately how to use it. El Bacha et al. (1990) have found that systems that take time to master do not get used by teachers. The interface, therefore, had to be clear and simple to use. Furthermore, since all users were likely to be from an art or design background, it was considered important that the interface reflected good contemporary design rather than be a clumsy form filling activity.

It would have to work both as a viewable document and an easy to fill out form. The contract had to work at two levels, as a viewable and printable document and as an editable online form.

The results of the interviews and questionnaires revealed that the printed guidelines were only of limited use during the contract negotiations. In fact, much of the guidance came through interactions with the supervising tutor. Brookfield (1986, p. 81) warns that writing contracts is a learned skill involving considerable input to help students choose realistic activities. This has important implications for students primarily using an online environment, where contact with the tutor may be limited, or conducted asynchronously at a distance. Moore & Kearsley suggest that 'distance educators need to pay a lot more attention to student motivation and feelings than in a traditional setting' (Moore & Kearsley, 1996).

It was clear from the interviews that the process of completing a contract is very much about negotiation. There was a danger that by working electronically, students would get the impression that they were working independently. In order to emphasise the need for continued communication with their tutor, it was felt that a communication device should be built into the interface, and that it should be the focal point. As a student logs on, the first thing they come to is the message board, containing any recent communication from their tutor. It was felt initially that an off-the-shelf message board system would meet the needs of the contract. Initial feedback from early prototypes showed, however, that the look and feel, poor usability and unnecessary functionality of the package distracted users from the contract itself. It was decided instead to design and implement a tailor-made system.

There is also the possibility that the message board could be used for communication between students using contracts. It was felt that a separate area should be reserved for student communication.

The interviews revealed that many students had difficulty with some of the key concepts behind the learning contract, such as setting effective learning objectives, and recognising learning at work. Many studies have emphasised the need to clarify to the student the rationale behind the contract (e.g. Greenwood 1995, Anderson et al. 1994). It was essential therefore to include clear guidelines for the student, not only on how to use the Web site, but also on how to construct an effective contract. Anderson et al. (1994) point out that it is equally important to identify which elements of the contract are not negotiable. The existing paper contract is supported by printed guidelines and these were used as a basis for the online guidance. Additionally a number of other guidelines were consulted.

Guidance

A well as guiding the learner, it is important to ensure that the tutors feel comfortable with the system too. Moore and Kearsley argue that 'the effectiveness of a distance educator is closely tied to their mastery of the particular media/technology involved' (Moore & Kearsley, 1996). If the tutors do not use the contract or the message board then the student will soon learn that effective communication can only occur outside of the electronic environment. Looms (1993) cites a study by El Bacha et al. (1990), which found that one of the main reasons for teachers not using interactive media was a lack of guidance, and that pedagogic guidance was as important as technical support.

The electronic contract also involves an additional user of the system, one that the paper-based version did not require: the administrator. Responsibility for initially setting up the system and entering academics' details into the database falls within the remit of the administrator. In entering these details a user ID and password is automatically generated and e-mailed to the recipients. Contract supervisors then supply the administrator with the student details (i.e. name and student number). The administrator creates an account for the student that is in effect a blank contract. Guidance in performing these tasks and any other in respect of administering on a data level is given by two methods: screen by screen or via a guidance section.

Software design

Whilst the design of the users' experience was our starting point, it was important to approach the design of the software in parallel. Indeed, designing the database structure flagged up a number of issues of detail that were not apparent in designing the functionality. Access and editing rights for the different parties involved had to be carefully and thoroughly specified. For example, who should be able to enter grades? Currently the student is responsible for adding grades to the paper contract, but the electronic version offers the potential for the supervisor to do this, or for the grade to be automatically entered by the course or module tutor. Each individual involved in the contract process would need to be entered into the database, together with their status, which would then determine their editing and access rights. This raised the issue that one individual could potentially be a student on one contract, an employer on someone else's, and a tutor on a third. It became apparent that each individual would need a home page in which they could select the contract they wished to view, and then be given the appropriate access rights depending on their role in that particular contract. This meant that one person should be represented as one person, not three.

Conclusions and future directions

A number of issues have arisen during the design of the electronic contract and its evaluation in use during the pilot phase. Two points are worth highlighting here in conclusion. First, it has become increasingly apparent during this project that supporting learning and teaching using electronic media requires a clear and in-depth understanding of the whole learning and teaching process. In order to design appropriate software it has been necessary to articulate aspects of the process, which in conventional practice remain tacit or hidden from view. For example, deconstructing the tutor-student dialogue that takes place around the development of a learning contract, and sharing this across the development team has been an important element in the project. Without this shared understanding of the process, the design of the electronic contract would have been less effective.

Second, we were aware at the outset of the danger that, once completed and signed, the contract becomes a dead document. However, initial evaluation suggests that the electronic version has the potential to become a useful planning and management tool; and one that, with the addition of feedback and reflective notes associated with each learning activity, becomes a useful document of the learning process. The fact that students can produce a self-determined programme of study using the contract as a personalised curriculum carrier greatly assists in the whole learning process, particularly as it is a learning experience in itself. This is supported through an online environment offering guidance and flexibility in undertaking such an activity. Both students and supervisors are able to treat the Web-based version in its initial stages as a working document, which can be amended without difficulty. This enhances the experience of embarking on such an undertaking. The learning process, in this remote form is more dynamic and less strictly timed, and supports the argument for Web-based material to present structure rather than content.

Looking to the future, it seems likely that this form of the learning contract will not reach its full potential until it is possible to integrate it with administrative systems and other online educational material. This is often the experience of such projects where Managed Learning Environments emerge as natural partners for hosted learning and teaching software. Nevertheless, a great deal has been learnt from the operation of the contracts, the development of their electronic form and the associated research into learning and teaching. With the increasing availability of the Web in a variety of art and design settings, including the studio, this approach to learning and teaching has something important to contribute to the future of art and design education.

Notes

The Electronic Learning Contracts Project Website can be found at: http://www.biad.uce.ac.uk/research/framework/projects/inprogress.html

The ELC project represents part of the Teaching and Learning in Art and Design cluster of research at BIAD. Two other research clusters that are supported are Design and Virtual Design and Fine Art Practice. Further information on research projects, including the Research Training Initiative, can be found at: http://www.biad.uce.ac.uk/research.

User-Lab focuses on exploring usability issues pertinent to art and design, innovative digital media and electronic learning and teaching tools. As a practical outcome, User-Lab provides usability support for the research projects within BIAD: http://www.user-lab.com

National Centre for Work-Based Learning Partnerships: http://www.mdx.ac.uk/www/ncwblp/

UAce Work Based Learning Network: http://www.uace.gcal.ac.uk/

A Review of Work-Based Learning in Higher Education: http://www.dfee.gov.uk/heqe/wblindex.htm

References

Anderson, G., Boud, D. & Sampson, J. (1994), 'Expectations of quality in the use of learning contracts', *Capability: The Higher Education Capability Journal*, 1(1), available from url: <http://www.lle.mdx.ac.uk/hec/journal/1-1/2-1.htm> (accessed 22nd March 2002)

Banathy, B.H. (1993), 'Comprehensive systems design in education: designing education around the learning experience level', *Educational Technology*, 33(1): 33-35

Brookfield, S. (1986), *Understanding and Facilitating Adult Learning* (San Francisco: Jossey-Bass)

Council for National Academic Awards (CNNA) (1983), *Handbook* (London: CNAA)

El Bacha, N., Fuchs, E., Lampe, B., Malige, F., Monteiller, L., Riou, A. & Thiriez, M. (1990), *IBM: European Marketing* (Paris: Ecole Supérieure de Commerce de Paris)

English, S. & Yazdani, M. (1999), 'Computer-supported cooperative learning in a virtual university', *Journal of Computer Assisted Learning*, 15(1): 2-13

Garawon, T. & O'Cinneide, B. (1994), J*ournal of Industrial Training*, 18(8): 3-12

Greenwood, S. (1995), 'Learning contracts and transaction: a natural marriage in the middle', *Language Arts*, 72 (2): 88-96

Guedella, M., Herlan, H., Bash, P. & Shabram, A. (1997), 'The KUBUS System – the holistic approach to entrepreneurship', *Enterprise Development in Education: Nurturing Bright Ideas*, Conference Proceedings, Coventry University, 10th June 1997

Looms, P.O. (1993), 'Interactive multimedia in education', in Latchem, C., Williamson J. & Henderson-Lancett, L. (eds.), *Interactive Media: Practice and Promise* (London: Kogan Page)

Moore, M.G. & Kearsley, G. (1996), *Distance Education: A Systems View* (Belmont, CA.: Wadsworth Publishing Company)

Vogel, D. & Klassen, J. (2001) Technology-supported instruction: status, issues and trends', *Journal of Computer Assisted Learning*, 17(1): 104-114

Biographical notes

Dr Robert Jerrard is Professor of Design Studies, Birmingham Institute of Art and Design, University of Central England. His research interests include design theory, technology diffusion and work-based learning. He is a Council member of the Design Research Society and has published widely; recently in new product development, social observation of design and consumption, and human-computer interaction.

Jeannette Luczkowski is Research Assistant for Curriculum Development Research in Art and Design: Electronic Learning. She is currently working on the research and development of Electronic Learning Contracts within art and design work-based learning environments.

Marie Jefsioutine is Senior Research Fellow in Digital Media, Birmingham Institute of Art and Design, University of Central England. She is currently working with research groups across the faculty to develop and evaluate electronic teaching and learning activities. She has worked in multimedia development for ten years and has recently set up User-Lab, a Digital Media Usability Laboratory.

Dr Darren Newbury is Research Co-ordinator for Visual Communication at Birmingham Institute of Art and Design, University of Central England. He has special responsibility for the development of electronic learning within the faculty, and is currently working on the Research Training Initiative, a project developing and publishing research training resources for postgraduates in art and design in both print and electronic formats.

Paul Hammond is Design Manager at Birmingham Institute of Art and Design's Digital Media Centre. His work currently involves both commercial and research multimedia production, and he has worked in new media production for five years. His current interests lie in e-learning technologies and converging media.

Yu Zhang is a Web-based information systems programmer. He is currently involved in existing systems analysis, and web-based database applications design and implementation linked to commercial and academic projects. He is interested in Object-Oriented Web-DBMS application.

15

Theory in practice: practice in theory – strategies for integration

Ken Marsden,
Faculty of Technology, Southampton Institute, UK

Abstract

This paper seeks to identify and describe ways of establishing and/or further developing (i) creative synergies between the theory:practice interface within the higher education design curriculum and (ii) effective collaboration between colleagues teaching on both undergraduate and postgraduate design courses.

A short review of current attitudes and debates on the topic, from leading theorists and practitioners, is followed by a description and analysis of various teaching and learning strategies that offer opportunities for improving and developing the integration of theory and practice.

The paper concludes that design must, in order to take up its rightful position within the Academy, embrace the notion of integration, in order to provide and further enhance a cohesive and balanced curriculum, conducive not only to higher education, but also the profession itself.

Introduction

I started my lecturing career, primarily as a studio-based practitioner. But gradually over subsequent years, began to realise that the theoretical and practical components should not lead separate and exclusive lives (although in my experience, this tended to be the case in practice).

This interest took on a new poignancy when I became the *critical discourse co-ordinator* at Southampton Institute, 35 years ago. My chief role was to take ownership and responsibility for the organisation and management of the common theoretical units of all the art and design undergraduate courses in the faculty. Up until then, this part of the curriculum had been exclusively serviced out to another faculty.

For a significant number of design students, the position of theory within the predominantly practice-based degree courses, has been a difficult one for them to comprehend. This is, I believe, apparent for a number of reasons, which include:

- *non-traditional entry* – typically art and design students tend to derive from a wide variety of non-traditional routes, and consequently don't possess the conventional academic qualifications necessary to achieve a place on a traditional academic honours degree course;
- *practically orientated skills* – their skills and attributes are predominantly in the practically orientated creative processes and production areas;
- *time-management priorities* – students prioritise their time between theory and practice work, particularly when assignment deadlines are due; they choose the easier option and perhaps, more importantly, the one they perceive as being of more benefit, in terms of career aspirations and credit weighting; and

- *psychological barriers* – many students do not, or aren't willing to, fully engage and/or participate in the study of design history and/or theory; most perceive it as difficult, annoying, time-consuming and at the very best a necessary evil – students have often told me that they 'didn't come on to a design degree course to spend my time writing essays', and 'don't have enough time to undertake theoretical work – our workload is too demanding'.

This paper will attempt to identify and describe ways of establishing and/or further developing effective collaboration between staff teaching on both undergraduate and postgraduate design courses, and creative synergies between the theoretical and practical components of the design curriculum.

When students are able to appreciate fully the relevance and purpose of the theory:practice interface, they should then be in a stronger position to participate more effectively in all aspects of the course curriculum. This will not only enhance their learning experience, but also improve their overall performance.

Current thinking

The Subject Benchmark Statement for Art and Design, Consultation Document (Third Draft), May 2001 states:

> In engaging with the contextual setting of their discipline(s), students also engage in the various related theories within historical, contemporary and cultural settings which inform that context ... As a consequence, students develop their own critical disposition in relation to their discipline(s).
>
> QAA for HE (2001, Defining Principles 2.4)

It is very encouraging to read that the Benchmark Statement formally recognises the importance of incorporating theory within practice, although exactly to what extent is rather unclear.

Some design educators have called for the diversification of the design curriculum, to include, for example, theories of perception and communication, semiotics, cultural history, anthropology and visual rhetoric.

Cal Swann, in his paper for the conference 'Foundations for the Future: Doctoral Education in Design', presented at La Clusaz, France, July 2000, entitled 'Meanwhile Back on the Ranch…' believes that design educators have been too concerned with meeting the demands of the design profession, and that design students should:

> … discover and develop their talents within a broad learning environment … University design schools need to look for students with all-round academic abilities, especially those associated with reading and writing and the capacity to understand culturally situated knowledge related to design and production.
> Swann (2000)

Richard Buchanan states that:

> Design offers the opportunity to reconstruct a vision of university education that may someday lead to a new kind of university, one that prizes a new balance of theory, practice and production that is suited to the circumstances of a world that is strongly shaped by the imagination and creative ability of designers.
> Buchanan (2001, pp. 21-2)

Ken Friedman believes that design requires a theoretical framework in order to engage fully with, and provide or support knowledge and understanding of, the practice.

> The issue of knowledge revolves around the relationship between theory and practice … Theory must be linked to working practice to be shown as useful.
> Friedman (1997, pp. 54–72),

Johanna Drucker, associate professor at Yale University, believes that theory is important in the teaching of art and design because:

> ... it lets you see that there are ways to talk about things at a level that articulates the ways in which meaning is produced, not just what meaning is produced ... As structure and information interpenetrate, the designer's task requires *more rigorous theoretical skills*.
> Drucker (1998, p. 139)

She doesn't 'think that design needs theory', but thinks 'designers need theory' (ibid, pp. 141-142).

I would now like to outline a number of strategies that could be adopted and developed within course programmes. These are divided in to two sections: Curriculum Content and Curriculum Delivery.

Curriculum content

Theoretical assignments incorporated within practical projects

Where a practical project is set (for example, 'Design a poster'), the student could be asked to present their theory-based assignment on an aspect of research directly related to their poster design. This could include biographies of designers, analysis of their key works, contemporary examples and influences, social, political and cultural histories, contexts, and/or theories, technological developments, images and illustrations (including their own sketches, plans, diagrams, flow charts, etc.), data, analysis and critical reflection. This aspect of *design research* will directly support and inform the student's practical work.

This work could be presented in a number of different ways – for example, as a report, file, folio, article, display panel or oral presentation – and assessed by both theory and practice-based tutors. For group presentations, each seminar group could be divided into three or four smaller groups, which could make one or more presentations on a rotation basis, throughout the duration of the project or assignment. During the first session or seminar, each group would have to identify the key areas of research required in order to undertake the assignment or project successfully and allocate roles and responsibilities to each group member. (N. B. Alternatives to the traditional essay could be offered – for example, a diary entry, client report, short story, job application letter, journal article, etc.)

> It has been argued that skills are learned much more effectively when the student is aware of the need for them, and has a personal interest in acquiring them, and the equality and depth of the learning experience is usually found to be enhanced when technique and theory are taught within the framework of a project.
> Cobb (1999)

Integrated approaches

The MA Design course at Southampton Institute (S.I.) places a strong emphasis on developing critical synergies between theory and practice. The theoretical and practical units run concurrently and serve to regularly inform and support each other throughout the duration of the course. For example, the 'Design in Context' theory unit is undertaken alongside the 'Design Production 2' practical unit and requires the student to locate and analyse their practice within the current design profession and reflect upon its potential influence and impact on culture and society. This is formally assessed – students produce a seminar paper and presentation, followed by a written critique at the end of the unit.

On one of the design degree courses at S.I., the Level 3 'Major Project' and the 'Research Exposition' units run concurrently throughout the final session of the year. The Major Project represents a 'showcase' demonstrating the creativity, knowledge, technical skills and intellectual maturity acquired during the course. The nature of the project will vary according to the individual student's interests and aspirations, but should normally incorporate the multi-disciplinary elements of the course. The Research Exposition unit provides students with the opportunity to produce a comprehensive written critical analysis, evaluating the research, design development, synthesis and contextual environment of the Major Project. Both theory and practice, production and reflection, regularly inform and support each other during the design process

Text as design

The text journal or critical diary could be seen as the equivalent of the sketchbook for visual practice, i.e. foster the notion of reflective learning and compile a record or file of research, generate and formulate ideas, critique events/visits/exhibitions, etc. It could also form part of the assessment process (e.g. under the research criterion) within either the theoretical and/or practical units.

The design process shares many similarities with the writing and thinking processes. A project that asks students to present an academic text in a creative and aesthetic form could provide an interesting blend of design-related processes and knowledge which reinforce the theory:practice interface. Writing can and perhaps should be seen as a *design activity*.

Mike Sharples in his book entitled *How We Write: Writing as Creative Design*, believes that:

> The time is ripe for a re-integration of illustration and text design with writing, not just an aspect of visual literacy but as an essential part of the process of writing as design".
> Sharples (1999, p. 131)

He suggests that text and images can be organised to create emotional and informational effects on the reader, assist in the communication of information and express the language of the imagery. A good example of this, he suggests, can be found in the guidebooks of the author, illustrator and mountaineer, Alfred Wainwright.

Graziella Tonfani, in her book, *Writing as a Visual Art*, believes that text can be formed into various shapes, according to the specific function of the text, rather than the traditional A4 rectangle. For example, a square shaped text could identify the text as a story, triangular shaped text could embody a memory or a personal experience, a circle could describe a general concept, etc. She refers to these textual signs as being 'like traffic signs whose specific shapes immediately and unambiguously alert you' (Tonfani, 1994, p. 91), and as being designed to inform the reader about the general nature of the text.

Bryan Lawson (1990) describes several qualities or characteristics of the design process that could equally be applied to the thinking/writing process:

- Design problems cannot be comprehensively stated' (Lawson, 1990, p. 88) - the outcomes of the design evolve during the process;
- The design process is endless' (ibid, p. 90) – designers are rarely satisfied with the outcome;
- 'There is no infallibly correct process of design' (ibid, p. 91) – there are an infinite number of solutions;
- 'The process involves finding as well as solving problems' (ibid, p. 91) – a significant amount of time is spent on identification and reflection;
- 'Design inevitably involves subjective value judgement' (ibid, p. 91) – the quality of the design outcomes can only be subjectively assessed; and
- 'Design is a prescriptive activity' (Ibid, p.92) – unlike science which describes the world, design prescribes and helps to create the future.

The thought processes involved in creating texts and designs are similar, because they can be reshaped and revised. These links between the design and the thinking process, could be established from the outset of the course or programme and regularly reinforced throughout via seminars, workshops and tutorials in both the theoretical and practical units.

Apply design thinking processes to theoretical work

- There are a number of creative design processes that can be utilised for generating and developing concepts, issues and directions for theoretical work, in exactly the same way that one would do, if setting a studio or practice based project, e.g. brainstorming, mind-mapping and concept fan exercises. Further, utilising the sketchbook will help the student to reflect on, and visualise, their theories and ideas and provide an opportunity to explore it as a visual stimulus for writing.

  > We don't need to be creative for most of what we do, but when there is a need to *think something different* our own attitudes can get in the way.
  > Von Oech (1992, p. 20)

  Roger von Oech (1992) examines how these 'mental locks' can be opened and unleashed in a series of exciting and entertaining ways.
- Sometimes two or more previously unconnected or unrelated concepts of thought can result in a new, different solution. For example, Johann Gutenberg, combined the functions of both the wine-press (which applies force over a large area), and the coin punch (which leaves an image on a small area) to produce the printing press and movable type.
- The purpose and function of objects and artefacts can be redefined to break the mould. For example, take an everyday household object, such as light bulb, toothbrush, hair-grip, bottle etc., and try to think of as many different practical and non-practical uses that could be associated with the object.
- It helps to identify likes and dislikes (e.g. music, arts, food, clothes, books, etc. etc.), strengths and weaknesses, significant events that have been witnessed or experienced, and so on. Who are you?;
- Group brainstorming activities emphasise intuitive action rather than reflection or evaluation – quantity breeds quality;

- The pattern of continuity can be broken by deliberately disrupting routine patterns of thought and action;
- Too much information can create 'mind-sets'. Gaps in information can stimulate a questioning approach and create a sense of ambiguity, which can force the problem solver to explore other directions;
- *Student exercise* - in order to generate other possible directions of the students' intended research topics, students could be asked to write down three key words associated with their topic under three separate columns. Then the students should write down as many different words associated with those three key words, followed by a comparison and discussion of the results in the seminar groups. This activity could then be continued by utilising a Web-based teaching and learning resource e.g. Learnwise, Web CT, etc. Each student should post up any three key words associated with their topic, on the notice board for all students and staff to view, but only those students from each group can respond to each other. Each student from each group, on a first come first served basis, would select and post up another three words they would most associate or link with the last three words posted up, and so on.

Design metaphors and approaches

Graziella Tonfoni (1994) suggests that determining the textural metaphor will provide a valuable visual context for the process of writing. This directly refers to the clarity of communication, e.g. smooth is clear and concise, whereas coarse is unclear and fragmented. Different kinds of writing is for different communication purposes - fine texture for detail, course texture for thick bold application:

> A writer needs to decide how much 'texture' the text will have ... the density of information conveyed by it. Depending upon the communicative purpose of the text ... the texture of the text may be more or less dense.
>
> Tonfani (1994, p. 40)

She also suggests that text is like musical composition and words are like musical notes. Therefore one can construct visual symbols or icons that can enhance the communication and co-operation between writer and reader. This is because visual symbols can establish a level of communication and harmony between the writer (composer) and the reader (musician), as in the use of a clef to indicate pitch, scales to indicate the key, etc.

It is helpful to outline and clarify to students the many different approaches to writing, by first initially identifying various types associated with other creative professions or activities:

- *Beethovian* (discoverer or holist);
- *Mozartian* (serialist or planner);
- *Architect* (focuses on planning overall structure, but may not start at the beginning); and
- *Sketcher* (works on drafting, tries different approaches to text)

Students can be asked to identify these and others and to which they would most closely associate.

Designers as authors

There are a growing number of designers who have expressed more than a passing interest in becoming authors. For example, *Fuel*, a three-man design team (Miles, Murray and Sorrell) based in London, see the connection between content and form (theory and practice) as one and the same. *Fuel Three Thousand* is their latest book, and contains images and text working together in a visual form under specific concepts e.g. anatomy, etc.

The designer Bruce Mau states that he is interested in:

> ... expanding and extending the role of the designer to include the substance of the message itself ... The content – what is being said — is the trigger for form. Our goal is produce an environment of collaboration for the development and integration of content and form.
> Mau, quoted in Poynor (2000)

According to Rick Poynor:

> [Mau] believes that restructuring the working process could generate ideas and possibilities, new cultural objects, and products, that will never arise from established patterns of work ... Such projects require a designer to possess a considerable depth of cultural knowledge, or a willingness to engage in a process of continuous research and learning, and most probably both.
> Poynor (2000)

Assessment and presentation

- Where appropriate, identical assessment criteria for both theory and practice work could be used. Some of the wording may have to change but essentially the requirements could be the same – for example, criterion such as: clarity of communication, innovation/imagination, research, synthesis, etc.
- Presentation of both the theoretical and practice-based work could be submitted *together*, at the appropriate assignment deadlines (and returned together). Also, the degree show/presentation should contain all components of work produced at level/year 3 *together*.

Curriculum delivery

Course team involvement

Course team staff, including full and part-time, could participate fully in the teaching and assessment of both the theoretical *and* practical units. The national picture appears to indicate a wide variance of participation within design degree courses, for a whole range of reasons, some of which are partly historical. It is still perceived to be a highly contentious issue amongst studio practitioners and design historians/academic theorists. There is a degree of unwillingness on the part of some studio-based staff to become involved with the delivery of the theoretical units, which has led to an undermining of its role and significance, not only within the overall course curriculum but also on the student's attitude and performance. Their position could be due to a lack of understanding and experience of, and/or confidence with, the subject. However, some of these could be addressed by undertaking staff development activities – short courses, workshops, seminars, mentoring, etc. – to enable staff to gain the necessary skills and expertise. However, this will be an evolutionary process and can only be achieved with willing and able participants and managed in a sensitive and sympathetic manner.

Course teams need to adopt more flexible work practices by teaching across common or core units and courses, and in particular, on both the practical *and* theoretical units, (e.g. design research, IT skills, creative and/or critical thinking skills, etc.). Increased staff interaction between course teams could also lead to cross-course initiatives and synergies. Further, by fully utilising staff expertise and experience across all the courses, the efficiency levels within the department / subject group would increase significantly.

The significant increase of student numbers in design degree courses in recent years, has meant that the traditional *atelier* method of teaching studio-based subjects has been severely threatened. This was due, in part, to the merging of the polytechnics and traditional universities, c. 1992. According to the Fieldwork Report on a project conducted for the Design Council, produced by Richard Kimbell, John Saxton and Soo Miller (1999), this has changed the role of the traditional subject-specific courses and led to more unitised and modular types of courses.

> In many of the courses we observed we see a focus directed toward the external world with a requirement to understand and manage design processes; to recognise the needs of clients; to develop the capabilities of working within teams; and to recognise the strengths and weaknesses that students can bring to the professional team. Kimbell, Saxton and Miller (1999, p.5).

These characteristics form a significant part of *both* the practical and theoretical curriculum, and consequently would lead to greater cohesion and more effective re-enforcement, if delivered by all of the course team.

Mix 'n' match

- Tutors from other subjects and disciplines who are not normally involved in the teaching of a project could contribute towards the seminar and tutorial programmes. This can generate lively discussion and offer new and different dimensions to the creative process. Tutors could also participate in the cross-disciplinary assessment of students' work.
- Students could undertake project work for both practical and theoretical units of study in mixed subject cohorts, which would allow for greater opportunities to learn from each other's approaches, experiences and methodologies.
- Library and study support staff could be asked to work alongside studio staff in conducting tutorials in the studio, as well as delivering lectures on research methodologies and library/IT skills etc. to help reinforce cohesion.

Support and guidance

- Staff could offer workshop seminars and tutorials on developing writing skills – funding for extra study support input may be available if there is evidence of, for example, low retention and/or poor results for theoretical work.
- *Study/reading groups* could be established, facilitated by tutors and/or students for both students (and staff), with regard to theory and practice, historical and contemporary key texts, debates, issues, etc.
- Other curricular activities and events could be included to reinforce the integration of theory and practice, e.g. educational visits, visiting lecturer programme, conference weeks, etc. These may or may not be linked to formally assessed assignments. Part of the event could involve each small cross-disciplinary group being required to make a group presentation (consisting of visual and textual material), to the whole student cohort. All presentations could be peer assessed.

Integrated course models

The three fundamental stages of the learning process at the S*chool of Design, Carnegie Mellon University*, Pittsburgh, U.S.A. are:

1. *Studio experience* – emphasis on practice, creation and synthesis;
2. *Ideas and methods in design practice* – emphasis on investigation; and
3. *Design studies* – emphasis on design history, theory and criticism and reflection

Richard Buchanan believes that the purpose of this third element is to help students 'understand the cultural and intellectual foundations of design, the place of design in society and business, and the qualities of effective thinking and communication that are essential for reflection and practice' (Buchanan, 2001, p.24). He also believes that this form is a radical departure from other design schools and departments, because it is based upon a 'humanistic' approach or vision of design education. They teach design as an 'integrative discipline that allows students to synthesise the insights afforded by aesthetics and the fine arts, engineering and the natural sciences, and the social and behavioural sciences' (ibid, p. 24).

Over the past five years members of the St. Joost Academy in Breda, Holland, have been devising strategies to overcome what they see as the 'unteachability' of design. They believe that design, unlike for example, law, economics and sociology 'has no isolated object for research ... design is a project not an object' (Staal and Gruson, 2000, p. 4). They wish to liberate the designer from specific objects, styles and media, and focus on the design process or method and the creation of models. This is achieved by developing knowledge and skills in 'generating, applying and manipulating signs, images and symbols ... but most of all ... methods of inventing form' (ibid, p. 9).

Three inter-related themes – identities, urban space and accessibility, and proposal and counter proposal – form the basis of the curriculum throughout the two-year programme.

> Thinking in terms of models, has proven applicable to both the educational situation and in professional practice. It embraces a logically planned, process orientated and focused resolution of design problems that, from the moment of the initial briefing, can never again be seen as simple linear problems.
> Staal and Gruson (2000, p. 18)

Conclusion

Esther Dudley believes that the designer will gain more credibility if they can make 'words and images perform on comparable conceptual levels'. She fears that 'despite the recognition of its importance, pressures may be brought to bear on studio-based courses which could threaten the continuation of the dissertation as an essential element' (Dudley and Mealing, 2000, p. 59).

This is already happening, I know of an institution, where all design courses agreed to a 50% cut in the credit weighting of the dissertation unit. This was based on the belief that, as the weekly taught hours were being reduced, this then increased the demand for extra hours in the studio, in order to make up the difference.

The Field-Work Report entitled *Design Skills for Work* (Kimbell, Saxton and Miller, 1999) suggests that interpersonal skills, such as flexibility and good communication skills, and personal qualities such as commitment and responsibility are as important as acquiring the technical skills associated with design. These necessary skills can be most effectively developed when applied in both the studio and seminar room. A tutor commented in the report:

> The general feel within the industry seems to be that broader based students, less discipline-specific students, people with analytical skills

> and enquiry skills, who aren't necessarily tied to one vocation seems to be the way the industry is going.
>
> Kimbell, Saxton & Miller (1999, p. 15)

Design courses must be careful not to assume that all design students will become designers. The report concludes, 'If other employment options for graduate designers are not being recognised, explored and celebrated, what is the point if worrying about transferable skills?' (ibid, p. 20).

If design education is to become a liberal art of contemporary culture, as Richard Buchanan proposes, programmes and courses will include students who have no desire to enter the design profession at all. 'They will study design as a preparation for many other types of careers, in the same way that students study literature or natural science or history or social science' (Buchanan, 1998, pp. 65-66).

Whether design students pursue a career in design or another related discipline, become authors, and/or initiate their own projects, it is important they develop their critical and analytical skills in tandem and within all components of the design course curriculum.

References and further reading

Blauvert, A. (1998), 'Building Bridges Between Theory and Practice', in Poynor, R. (ed.), *Design Without Boundaries: Visual Communication in Transition* (London: Booth Clibborn Eds.)

Buchanan, M. (1995), 'Making Art and Critical Literacy: A Reciprocal Relationship', in Prentice, R. (ed.), *Teaching Art and Design: Addressing Issues and Identifying Directions* (London: Cassell)

Buchanan, R. (1998), 'Education and Professional Practice in Design', *Design Issues*, Vol. 14, (2)

Buchanan, R. (2001), 'The Problem of Character in Design Education: Liberal Education and Professional Specialisation', *International Journal of Technology and Design Education* 11 (Netherlands: Kluwer Academic Publishers, pp. 13-26)

Cobb, J. (1999) 'Overview of the Teaching and Assessment Practices Commonly Used in Art and Design Education', paper delivered at the I*mproving Student Learning: Through the Disciplines Conference,* University of York, 8th September, 1999

Davies, A. (1996), 'Exploration of Evaluation and Research Methods for Improving Student Learning in Art and Design', in Gibbs, G. (ed.), I*mproving Student Learning: Using Research to Improve Student Learning* (Oxford: Oxford Centre for Student Development)

Drucker, J. (1998), in Heller, S. & Pettit, E. (eds.), 'Design theory' in *Design Dialogues* (New York: Allworth Press)

Dudley, E. (2000) in Dudley, E. & Mealing, S., (eds.), 'Intelligent Shape Sorting'*, in Becoming Designers: Education and Influence* (Exeter: Intellect Books)

Friedman, K. (1997), 'Design Science and Design Education', in McGrory, P. (ed.), *The Challenge of Complexity* (Helsinki: University of Art and Design, Helsinki)

Kimbell, R., Saxton, J. & Miller, S. (1999), *Design Skills for Work: Distinctive Skills and Implicit Practices*, Fieldwork Report on a project conducted for the Design Council (Technology Education Research Unit, Goldsmiths University of London)

Lawson, B. (1990), *How Designers Think: The Design Process Demystified*, 2nd Edition (Butterworth Architecture Press: Oxford)

Lupton, E. & Miller J. Abbott (1996), *Design/Writing/Research* (London: Phaidon)

Maclear, K. & Testa, B. (eds.) (2000), *Life Style: Bruce Mau* (London: Phaidon)

McCoy, K. (1998), 'Design Education', in Heller, S. & Pettit, E. (eds.), *Design Dialogues* (New York: Allworth Press)

McCullagh, K. (2000), 'Design Praxis:Towards a Design Context Rooted in Practice', in Dudley, E. & Mealing, S. (eds.), *Becoming Designers: Education and Influence* (Exeter: Intellect Books) Poynor, R. (2000) 'Is it Art? Is it Photography? No Actually it's Graphic Design', The Independent, November 19, 2000

QAA for HE (2001), *Subject Benchmark Statement, Art and Design*, Consultation Document (Third Draft), May 2001

Rand, P. (1993), *Design, Form and Chaos*, (New Haven CT and London: Yale University Press)

Sharples, M. (1999), *How We Write: Writing as Creative Design* (London: Routledge)

Staal, G. & Gruson, E. (eds.) (2000), *Copy U Proof: A New Method for Design Education*, (Rotterdam: Uitgeverij 010 Publishers)

Swann, C. (2000) 'Meanwhile Back on the Ranch ...' , conference paper for *Foundations for the Future: Doctoral Education in Design*, presented at La Clusaz, France, July 2000

Tonfoni, G. (1994), Writing as a Visual Art (Oxford: Intellect Books)

Von Oech, R. (1992), *A Whack on the Side of the Head* (Creative Think: Mento Park, California)

Biographical note

Ken Marsden is Principal Lecturer in Teaching and Learning (Design), and course leader for the M.A Design, in the Faculty of Technology at Southampton Institute. He joined the Institute in January 1999, after leaving Blackpool and the Fylde College, where he had taught on the BA (Hons) Photography/Design courses for many years. His photographic work has been exhibited at several galleries and museums in England and his current pedagogic research interests include the relationship between theory and practice and assessment practices within art and design.

Nurturing an intelligence of seeing

16

Howard Riley

School of Art & Design, Swansea Institute, Associate College of the University of Wales, UK

Abstract

> Even the most obvious occurrences of everyday life might appear utterly transformed if we were inventive enough to construe them differently.
> Kelly (1970, p. 1)

This paper probes the possibility that a new approach to the teaching and practice of drawing may develop, in first-year fine art undergraduates, an inventiveness for construing those everyday occurrences, to which Kelly refers, in ways previously unimagined.

Specifically, the possibility explored is whether students may come to recognise that their understanding of everyday perceptual occurrences may be construed differently, and expressed through a drawing practice based upon an increased awareness of perception theory and communication theory.

For the purposes of this paper, drawing is defined as the making of any hand-wrought response to the experiences of perception, emotion and imagination through the use of dry media or pens upon a two-dimensional surface.

Alternative philosophical bases for the teaching of drawing

Underlying the history of change in the organisation of art education, there is a history of change in the pedagogical methodologies adopted by teachers of drawing.

The two histories may appear dissimilar, since the former is driven by the perceived educational needs of a social formation, the latter by a series of competing philosophical positions defined by ontological and epistemological parameters. Since the two are rarely explicitly discussed in art schools, few teachers of drawing are fully conversant with both. However, it is suggested here that there is a connection between the two histories, which is important for drawing teachers, since any philosophical attitude toward the teaching of drawing is constructed in response to an educational need, and the social nature of such need conditions philosophical attitude. A dialectical relationship is evident between the two.

Four broad philosophical bases from which a variety of pedagogical methods may be derived are identified in Fig. 1.

A relativist ontological position may be aligned with an epistemology of semiological interpretation so as to justify a pedagogical methodology which addresses cross-cultural drawing practices. Such a methodology, through recognising the other three appears to be worthy of exploration, since it allows students to be increasingly conscious of their own and others' social formations, and to be aware of how their drawing practice is affected by their inherited habits of perception and their conventions of visual communication.

What I am proposing here is a pedagogy of drawing built upon an explicitly-articulated review of perception theories and communication theories, and which identifies the range of ontological, epistemological and methodological parameters that define philosophical stances towards visual representation.

Philosophical base	Ontological attitude to drawing	Epistemological attitude to drawing	Methodological approaches to the teaching of drawing
1.Rationalist 2.Empiricist	'OBJECTIVE' Reality as absolute	Analytical Observational	Assumption of viewer position Application of anatomical knowledge, perspective techniques. Distance-values emphasised. The Academy approach Application of measurement techniques based onthe natural sciences. Ruskin's 'innocent eye'. Coldstreams's 'measured verification'. Haptic and proximal values.
3.Pragmaticist	'SUBJECTIVE' Reality as an individual experience	Psychological	Exploration of emotional responses. Emphasises the 'individual eye'. Distortion of drawn elements, to induce disturbance of emotional response (e.g. Kandinsky & Itten)
4.Constructivist	'RELATIVIST' Realities recognised as social constructions including the above categories	Semiological	Cross-cultural visual studies. Explicit experimentation with both viewer centred and – object-centred representations. Ecological relationships. Distance, haptic and proximal values.

Fig. 1: Philosophical bases for the teaching of drawing

Perception

Many of the salient positions adopted by theorists of perception may be construed as responses to what William Epstein has termed 'the inverse projection problem':

For any given three-dimensional (3-D) structure, event in three-dimensional space, or spatial layout, if the physical dimensions of the structure, event, or layout are known exactly, then application of the appropriate mathematics will allow the occurrent retinal spatiotemporal structure to be computed. Solving the direct projection problem, that is, going from the distal state of affairs to the proximal affairs is a straightforward task.

> The circumstances are drastically different when the inverse projection problem is assayed: When the occurrent retinal state of affairs is known, it is impossible to pick out a unique distal property, object, or event as the source. In contrast to the direct projection problem, going from the occurrent proximal state of affairs constitutes an ill-posed problem. The difficulty arises from the fact that while a specific distal event or arrangement is compatible with only a single retinal state, a given retinal state is compatible with countless distal states.
> Epstein & Rogers (1995, pp. 1–2)

Advocates of the computational theory of vision, such as David Marr (1982), may be analysed in terms of their attitude to the inverse projection problem. Marr's colleague Tomaso Poggio expressed the problem thus:

> In classical optics or in computer graphics the basic problem is to determine the images of three-dimensional objects, whereas vision is confronted with the inverse problem of recovering surfaces from images.
> Poggio, Torre & Koch (1985, p. 314)

Their response is to seek out constraints on the environment that may allow a correlation to be made between events occurring in three-dimensional space and the patterns occurring on the retinae.

James J. Gibson (1979) insisted that the inverse projection problem was a misconstrual of the actuality of seeing. His advocacy of an ecological approach to understanding perception was based on the premise that we see not objects via retinal stimulation, but the whole environment mapped by the visual perception system. For Gibson, stimulation and the environment are linked, providing direct information about the world. However, it may be argued that the availability of such information is contingent upon environmental constraints.

Marr recognised some degree of compatibility between their positions:

> Gibson's important contribution was to take the debate away from the philosophical consideration of sense-data and the affective qualities of sensation and to note instead that the important thing about the senses is that they are channels for perception of the real world outside, or, in the case of vision, of the visual surfaces. He therefore asks the critically important question. How does one obtain constant perceptions in everyday life on the basis of continually changing sensations? This is exactly the right question, showing that Gibson correctly regarded the problem of perception as that of recovering from sensory information 'valid properties of the external world.
> Marr (1982, p. 29)

The two differ over their explanations of how our physiological apparatus deals with the incoming light.

Gibson claimed we resonate directly in response to the ecologically structured information contained within the arrays of light arriving at our eyes. Some invariant aspects of the structured arrays specify lower-order information about surfaces – their distance and slant for example. Other invariants are supposed to specify higher-order information about objects and what they may afford us. There is therefore no requirement in Gibson's theory for an intermediate level of information processing. The reception of affordance information leads automatically to active response. The theory does not address how resonance is accounted for physiologically.

Marr's theory proposes three levels at which perception needs to be explained; the ecological and the physiological, with a level of mediation in between, an *algorithmic* level, in Marr's term, which organises the ecologically-conditioned information arriving at the eyes in a way suitable for representation by the physiological system.

In Marr's opinion, the omission of such a level of mediation – information-processing – invalidates Gibson's theory of direct perception:

> Gibson's...fatal shortcoming...results from a failure to realise two things. First, the detection of physical invariants, like image surfaces, is exactly and precisely an information-processing problem. And secondly, he vastly underrated the sheer difficulty of such detection.
> Marr (1982, p. 30)

Detecting physical invariants may be difficult. However, we *are* able to do it. Marr's difficulty was in demonstrating *computationally* how it is done.

His important distinction between a viewer-centred representation of a scene and an object-centred representation allows interesting insights into the ways people have developed systems of geometry in order to make visual descriptions of these various perceptions.

Both of these theorists' relevance to the practice and teaching of drawing is acknowledged in the proposed new teaching programme.

Communication: the social semiotics of drawing

In the materialist sense, drawings are produced through the selection and combination of particular surfaces, drawing tools, and the marks resulting from their interaction. However, *semiotically speaking*, both producers and viewers of drawings take up positions, adopt attitudes and points of view which are influenced by their positions within their sets of social relations. Such an ideological positioning involves a specific way of using signs (a semiotic), and a structured sensibility (an aesthetic) both grounded in a particular system of social relations. The way the producer selects and combines the compositional elements of the drawing, and how the viewer relates to that drawing, are both functions of the social contexts in which the work is (re) produced. But to say that drawings simply reflect social structure is too passive. *Drawing not only expresses the social context but is part of a more complex dialectic in which drawings actively symbolise the social system, thus producing, as well as being produced by, the ideological framework of a society.*

This dialectical relationship is what Michael Halliday (1978, p. 183) discusses in the phrase 'social semiotic'. Halliday makes use of the concept of *register*, referring to the variation in selecting and combining visual elements according to the purpose for which the drawing was produced, and according to the situation of its display. A social system can be represented as a construction of meanings – as a semiotic system. The meanings that constitute the social system are exchanged through the rich variety of semiotic codes developed by humans, of which drawing is one.

From this social semiotic perspective, any social context may be understood as a temporary construct, mapped in terms of three variables Halliday et al. (1964) called *field*, *tenor*, and *mode*:

- *field* of social process – what is going on at the time of production of the drawing;
- *tenor* of social relationships – the type of drawing we produce varies according to the level of formality, of technicality, of need for clarity of communication, etc; it is the role relationships – the drawer, the subject matter, the viewer and their inter-relationships – that affect the variations; and

- *mode* of symbolic interaction – in the sense that how we draw varies with our attitude: an attitude of objective observation may produce drawings in a realistic mode; emotional disturbance may be realised in an expressionist mode; absentmindedness in doodling mode.

Halliday (1973) also proposed that communication has three main functions: firstly, to convey some aspect of our experience of the world; secondly, to express our attitude or mood regarding our experience, and also to position the receiver in terms of mood and attitude; and thirdly, to structure these two into a coherent, perceptible form. The first two functions may be labelled the *experiential* and the *interpersonal*. The third may be termed the *compositional* function.

The parameters of social context – field, tenor, and mode – are systematically related to the functions of the semiotic system. In fact, those meanings that constitute our understanding of any particular social situation are made visible through the selection and combination of elements within the semiotic system.

Parameter of social context	Function of drawing through which a social situation is realised
Field (what is happening)	Experiential function
Tenor (who is taking part)	Interpersonal function
Mode (what part the semiotic code plays)	Compositional function

This may be adopted as the basis of a model that may theorise how drawings operate within a social context.

Halliday (1973) elaborated upon this basis to provide a model that identified the systems of choices from which specific selections may be related to the functions of language in specific social contexts.

Subsequently, Michael O'Toole (1994) demonstrated the versatility of Halliday's model by adapting it to theorise how painting, sculpture and architecture may be understood in relation to their social contexts. Following these pioneers of a systemic-functional semiotics of the visual, this paper proposes just such a theoretical framework within which drawings may be discussed.

Such a model is presented in Fig. 2 where the *Experiential* function of drawing relates to a drawing's ability to represent some aspect of our experience of the world. The *Interpersonal* function deals with how drawings may express the maker's attitude to their experiences, and may position the viewer in terms of attitude and mood. The *Compositional* function deals with the systems of available choices of media, surfaces and marks that combine to make visible, to realise, the other two functions. The heading '*Levels of engagement*' in the chart refers to the hierarchical layering within which engagement with the drawing is possible. The '*Matrix of systems of choices*' emphasises the *systemic* nature of the model: these ranges of available choices do not simply allow meanings to be negotiated at any single functional level, but affect all functions as a whole.

Social meanings to do with the drawer's and viewer's experience within the field of the real world, and also the tenor of the relationship between drawer and viewer are all realised simultaneously through the systems of *Theme*, *Modality*, *Geometry*, etc. Choices from these systems are realised as particular modes of drawing which are themselves realised as appropriate combinations of drawn marks upon a surface.

In this chart, the varieties of geometries derived from the variety of ways of seeing, become some of the systems available to the compositional function in order to realise – make visible – the interpersonal and the experiential functions. Also, John Willats' (1997) denotation systems made up from selections and combinations of picture primitives, may be integrated within the systems of choices available.

Levels of engagement		FUNCTIONS OF DRAWING		
		Compositional	Interpersonal	Experiential
The drawing as displayed in context	Matrix of systems of choices	• Inter-textuality • Systems of geometry: persp. orthographic, oblique, inverted persp., & topological • Size and format • Framing devices • Location options	• Systems of modality, mood, attitude, positioning: viewer centred, object-centred • Public/private • Intimate/monumental	• Systems of theme: physical, emotional, imaginative experiences.narrative, historical genre • Realistic/abstract • Interplay between objects, poses, events
Sub-divisions of the drawing's surface		• Secondary geometry • Gestalt relationships: horizontal, vertical, diagonal axes • Proportional relationships • Tonal passages (aerial persp.)	• Systems of gaze: eyepaths; focus points • Dynamic/static • Calm/excited • Balance/unbalanced	• Primary geometry • Actions, poses, events, objects • Awareness of distal and proximal perceptual values
Combinations of drawn marks		• Relative size of marks • Relative orientation of marks • Relative position of marks • Colour, tone and texture contrast – boundaries • Pattern • Rhythm • False attachments	• Deep/shallow range of depth illusion • Foreground/background range of positioning • Stability/instability • Scale • Heavy/light	• Distance between surfaces • Edges: occlusion of one surface by another • Direction • Transparency/opacity of surfaces • Atmospheric conditions • Quality of light • Time of day • Awareness of haptic perceptual values • Weight
A drawn mark		• Size relative to picture surface • Orientation relative to picture surface • Position relative to picture surface • Combination of surface texture and drawing medium • Picture-primitives	• Psychological orientation • Range of textural meanings: wet/dry; hard/soft;matt/gloss • Denotation level of meaning	• Spatial depth • Effects of gravity and other forces • Effects of light and water upon material surfaces • Scene primitives
		Matrix of systems of choices		

Fig. 2

Combinations of selections from the available systems of compositional choices allow the drawer to give visible material form to modulations of their physical, emotional and imaginative experiences of the world. Reciprocally, those combinations are modulated through and related to the viewer's own experiences of the world. Thus the proposed model may facilitate both a means of putting sense into drawings, and making sense out of drawings. Crucially, the inclusion of the variety of levels of perception within the systems of choices available in the experiential function acknowledges the variable foci of perception of both drawer and viewer.

The model is the organising principle that structures the proposed new teaching programme in drawing. It enables the design of drawing exercises that focus students' attention upon specific problems of visual representation, as well as being a means of assessing the resultant drawings. For example, the student who is able to derive the world-view of another culture from the analysis of its drawings becomes increasingly aware of ontological possibilities other than their own. Such awareness empowers the student to deconstruct their own, taken for granted, beliefs about time and space, and affords the possibility of elaborating more sophisticated ontological constructs through drawings.

The teaching programme: structure and content

From the outset, studio projects were designed to encourage students to notice natural phenomena at the various levels of perception: the haptic values within the scene, the distance values, the proximal values. The possibility of looking without language is explored through drawing exercises.

As these exercises begin to nurture an intelligence of seeing, the fundamentals of visual communication are addressed. Compositional relationships between figure and field, for example, may be discussed in terms of their effects upon the viewer; dynamic and static, stable and unstable compositions may be totally altered in mood by the selection of the mark-making medium and how it is physically applied to the support.

The ambiguities within the notion of 'accuracy' are addressed through studies of proportion.

Whilst traditional methods such as the 'Coldstream measuring method', the 'invisible grid method', and the 'observation of negative spaces' method are applied, they are discussed in terms of the assumptions implicit in their use: assumptions to do with the relationship between the primary geometry of the scene and the secondary geometry of the drawing; assumptions to do with the relationship between viewer-centred representations and object-centred representations.

Students are encouraged to consider the social functions of drawing when making selections from the range of projection systems. Of course this only becomes possible when the student is aware of the functions of drawing and the variety of geometries at their disposal. As well as the activity of drawing, slide talks held in studio allow these issues to be elaborated through examples of work from a variety of periods and cultures. However, it is emphasised here that the students' own practice is paramount in the learning process.

Ultimately, drawing is presented as a means of transformation. Transformation from scene to picture via systems of geometry; transformation of individual perceptions into social communication; transformation of cultural values into material form; and finally, the transformation of the student's personal ontological and epistemological constructs so as to inform and empower future practice in the visual arts.

Structure of proposed new drawing programme

Semester 1

Weeks 1–3 *Visual studies workshop*

An introduction to the vocabulary of the drawing class for those students with no previous experience.

Weeks 4–6 *Looking through the prism-house[1] of language*

Exercises to explore how language affects the way we see the world. Introduction to the three levels of perception; haptic values, distances values and proximal values. Stereograms illustrate how further information may be discovered through changing our way of seeing.

Weeks 7–10 *Welcome to Plantasia*

A project conducted among the exotic flora and fauna enclosed in the large glazed structure known as Plantasia. The three levels of perception are explored, as are the three functions of drawing. These functions are introduced and illustrated in a studio slide-talk prior to the visit.

Weeks 11–15 *Seeing and believing*

An exercise designed to increase student awareness of ontological constructions, and how these may be made visible in drawings.

Semester 2

Weeks 1–5 *Geometries of vision*

The variety of drawing systems, including projection types, is introduced in a slide talk. Primary geometry and secondary geometry are explored, as are viewer-centred and object-centred representations.

Weeks 6–9 *Gesture and empathy*

A closer look at the Interpersonal function of drawing.

Weeks 10–15 *Transformation from scene to picture*

An introduction to scene primitives and picture primitives, denotation systems. T-junctions and Y-junctions are explored in relation to the concept of fractal geometry.

Evaluation of students' drawings

The drawing, Fig. 3, is from a series of studies carried out during *Plantasia* project. It displays a high level of intelligence of seeing, affording the viewer ample information about textural qualities of the various plants represented, as well as a strong illusion of depth.

The Golden Section proportion of the vertical and horizontal axes which sub-divide the drawing's surface, and the smoothness of the eye-line from the focal point of the intersection of those axes, the Bird of Paradise flower at left foreground, through to the complexity of forms at right background, may be read by the viewer as metaphor for the complex harmonies to be found in the structures of natural forms.

Fig 3

Fig 4

A variety of realisms was discussed in the *Seeing and Believing* project, and the ways in which those realities have been expressed through the drawing conventions of different cultures in different periods were studied. Students were encouraged either to analyse and, if necessary, adapt an existing convention from the range, or invent from first-principles their own means of visually representing forces and forms which constitute reality.

A world in which *forces* are codified and made visible is displayed in Fig. 4. At the level of engagement *The drawing as displayed in context*, a framing device has been invented, with a fragility susceptible to the slightest force of air movement. Here, the drawing (i.e. the combination of 28 parts) moves in response to the viewer's movement, emphasising the experience of interplay between viewer and viewed. At the level of engagement *Sub-divisions of the drawing's Surface*, the 28 sub-sections are arranged in a regular grid

Fig 5

which flutters in response to air movement. In this way the viewer is confronted with a work that is both dynamic and static, both calm and excited, both balanced and unbalanced. At the level of engagement *A drawn mark*, each of the twenty eight components bears a mark, visible indications of a variety of forces which were applied to the paper: compression, tension, torsion and shear. Here is evidence of the student's ability to move away from conventional representations of the visible world, towards a fresh representation of the *forces that form* the visible world. Here too is evidence of the efficacy of the new teaching programme in empowering a student to discover new directions of visual research.

In contrast to the fragility of the work illustrated in Fig. 4 is the robust solidity of a large-scale (six feet square) heavy gauge drawing paper completely rendered with graphite stick (Fig. 5). Engaging with this work at the level of *A drawn mark*, each hand-made scribble of the graphite is standardised in terms of size and orientation, producing a grain structure across the surface. The rough surface texture of the paper is compressed by each mark to produce a polished sheen of graphite. The viewer is able to interact visually with this surface, since any movement of viewing position sets off a shimmer of surface reflection and illusions of spatial depth.

Upon this shimmering, deep surface, four totemic columns have been stamped from a wooden plank routed with patterns of linear marks.

The liveliness of the light, small-scale irregular linear marks contrasts with the large-scale, heavy, regular rhythm of the four columns spaced evenly across the whole drawing. Engaging with the drawing as a whole, the viewer may discern another contrast, that between the intimacy of each hand-cut mark and the (relative) monumentality of scale of the overall work. This drawing on display becomes a very public statement about a developing private code. A code which may not be fully systematised, but which recognises its need to articulate oppositions and one which invites viewers to ponder upon the arbitrariness of their own cultural conventions.

Fig 6

The Geometries of Vision project afforded students the opportunity to relate the concepts of primary geometry and secondary geometry to those of viewer- and object-centred representations through their drawing practice. The series of drawings, Fig. 6a and 6b illustrates a systematic approach to the exploration of a possible transition from a viewer-centred representation to an object-centred one. Fig. 6 was drawn from a (relatively) fixed position and indicates the student's grasp of the transformation process from primary geometry to a viewer-centred secondary geometry. As the series progresses, lines and contrast-boundaries between tones representing the salient edges in the scene become interlocked, producing a complex web of compositional axes. This pictorial device enables the viewer to see relationships between those edges defining the space which are not available from a fixed viewing position. As more information about spatial relationships is added, less is revealed of the viewer-centred representation of the figure within the space. Finally, in Fig. 6b the figure is transformed through geometry into pure organic form.

Fig 6a

Fig 6b

One of the considerations suggested to students in the *Gesture and Empathy* project concerned the vulnerability of the unclothed life-model within the potentially harmful environment of the drawing studio.

Fig. 7 illustrates one student's attempt to communicate his empathy with such vulnerability. At the level of engagement of the whole drawing, the viewer is positioned close to the foot of the drawing-donkey which supports the life-model, within reach of the slippers acting both as a focal point and an entry point into the compositional space. At the next level of engagement, *Sub-divisions of the drawing's surface*, the slippers act as a full stop to the diagonal axis formed by the upper leg of the drawing-donkey, and the dash-lines which pierce the model's head and connect to the top edge of the drawing. Another diagonal axis, an even stronger one, emanates from the same top connection point, grazes the model's back, and pierces the floor close to the slippers. The angle of this second axis is repeated across the surface of the whole drawing, at different scales of length and tonal density, representing one leg of the tripods

Fig 7

supporting the easels. This combination of sharp, angular elements appears cutting across the thighs of the model, and cutting into the model's right elbow, shoulder, and back.

At the level of each drawn mark, the consistency of sharp-edged linearity throughout every single mark not referring to the model pointedly contrasts with those marks that do refer to human flesh; indeterminate soft smudges of tone.

At each level of engagement, compositional decisions make visible the empathetic experience of the drawer, and invite the viewer to share the feeling of such experience.

The '*Transformations from scene-primitives to picture-primitives*' project offered an opportunity for students to consider the process of drawing as a transformatory one. Having already been introduced to the concepts of primary geometry and secondary geometry, and having explored the possibilities of transforming the former into the latter through their own studio practice, students were receptive to the study of the scene-primitives that generate a primary geometry and the picture-primitives that constitute drawings.

Observing the life-model at every level of scale from the whole figure to the study of a finger reveals a commonality in the appearance between surfaces, somewhat akin to fractals.

Students were encouraged to notice T and Y connections at all scales. These terms refer to the pattern of the contrast boundaries at the place where two surfaces occlude one another, and both occlude a third. The transformation of such scene-primitives as corner, edge and surface into the picture-primitives dot, line and tone was explored in this exercise.

Fig. 8 emphasises the T and Y connections which have been noticed by the student, both on the surfaces of the figure and between the figure and its surroundings. If this approach were taken at a smaller scale, observing surface connections apparent on an individual limb, for example, then a drawing may be produced which is entirely constructed of T and Y junctions at a variety of scales and tonal weights.

Fig 8

Conclusion

The research presented here is undertaken in response to a perceived need for a theoretical mapping of the domain of drawing.

Visual perception and visual communication (the latter driven by the uniquely human desire to share our experiences of the world) are two activities fundamental to the existence of this domain, and are here construed as dialectically entwined. The synthesis of their theoretical bases is shown to be effective in the development of a new pedagogy of drawing.

The central aim of the new teaching programme presented in this paper is to *empower* students by expanding their awareness of the whole domain of drawing: the inter-relationships between ways of seeing, ways of drawing and social belief-systems.

It is argued that providing students with the means to negotiate such a mapping of the domain of drawing empowers them more effectively than a pedagogy which prescribes conventions of seeing and of drawing construction, as in the case of many of the pedagogical methods tabled in Fig. 1.

Notes

[1] The pun on Nietzsche's term 'prison-house' attempts to encompass the myriad of meanings that may be refracted when looking through language.

References

Epstein, W. & Rogers, S. (eds.) (1995), *Perception of Space and Motion* (London: Academic Press)

Gibson, J.J. (1979) *The Ecological Approach to Visual Perception* (Boston, Mass: Houghton Mifflin)

Halliday, M.A.K. (1973), *Explorations in the Functions of Language* (London: Edward Arnold)

Halliday, M.A.K. (1978), *Language as Social Semiotic* (London: Edward Arnold)

Halliday, M.A.K., McIntosh, A. & Strevens, P. (1964), *The Linguistic Sciences and Language Teaching* (London: Longman)

Kelly, G.A. (1970), 'A brief introduction to personal construct theory', in Bannister, E.D. (ed.) *Perspectives in Personal Construct Theory* (London & New York: Academic Press)

Marr, D. (1982) *Vision: A Computational Investigation into the Human Representation and Processing of Visual Information* (New York: W. H. Freeman)

O'Toole, L.M. (1990), 'A systemic-functional semiotics of art', *Semiotica* 82 (3/4) 185–209

O'Toole, L.M. (1994) *The Language of Displayed Art* (London: Leicester U.P./Pinter)

Poggio, T., Torre, V. & Koch, C. (1985), 'Computational vision and regularisation theory', *Nature* 317, 314–319.

Willats, J. (1997), *Art and Representation. New Principles in the Analysis of Pictures* (New Jersey: Princeton U.P.)

Biographical note

Howard Riley PhD MA(RCA) is Co-ordinator of Postgraduate Research in the School of Art and Design at Swansea Institute of Higher Education, Wales, U.K. His professional experience includes: Senior Lecturer in Drawing, Curtin University, Western Australia; Visiting Lecturer in Drawing, Malaysian Institute of Art, Kuala Lumpur; Member of the Eastern Arts Research Centre. Exhibitions: Australia, Malaysia, Finland, U. K. Research interests: the relationships between perception theories, communication theories, and the practice and teaching of drawing. Dr Riley has publications in the areas of drawing pedagogy, visual semiotics, and generative art.

17

Teaching creativity – a systemic viewpoint

Pradeep Sharma

UNITEC Institute of Technology, Auckland, New Zealand

Introduction

An informal study of art and design schools within New Zealand indicates that the teaching of creativity is dealt with at a rather simplistic level with the focus being predominantly on the individual. Experience of design schools within the United Kingdom would indicate a similar level of attention to the subject of creativity.

There are generally four approaches to creativity, which are dealt with individually or in combination. The first and oldest is the belief that creativity comes from God and that we are empty vessels waiting for the Muse to pour the creative suggestion into us – the creative leap. The second tends to focus on natural abilities and personality traits, the effect of which is to encourage students to behave in certain pre-conceived ways. The third is socio-dynamic, which emphasises the importance of the social and environmental factors around the individual. Once again, the result is a tendency for students to behave in certain ways to encourage their own creativity. The fourth approach is the pragmatic generative approach, which encourages the use of new techniques.

Over recent years, creativity and innovation have also been taught in management programmes. Once again, there are only a limited number of approaches to the teaching of creativity. These tend to be based on personality traits and pragmatic generative techniques. The latter have gained perhaps the most ground in these institutions owing to the work of authors such as Edward de Bono, Roger von Oech, Michael Michalko and Arthur van Gundy. The teaching of innovation is generally dealt with at the individual, creativity level or at an organisational bureaucratic systems level.

A study of the literature on creativity would indicate that there are many more documented approaches to the study of creativity, especially in recent years. However, none of them appears to deal adequately with the socio-political aspects of creativity in real life contexts.

The purpose of this paper is to present some of the thoughts being developed in the School of Design at UNITEC Institute of Technology, New Zealand as part of the design management programme. The aim has been to develop a systemic viewpoint of creativity that will take into account the aspects of diffusion of ideas into social groups. This is a work in progress and has been addressed from a perspective of 'how does one manage creativity and innovation?'

Research approaches to the study of creativity

The study of creativity has a long history. However, serious research into creativity, certainly from a western perspective, only really took place from the middle of the 20th century. Many believe the trigger to be Guildford (1950) who in his APA Presidential Address challenged psychologists to pay attention to what he found to be a neglected but extremely important attribute in human behaviour, namely creativity. The focus at the time was from a psychological and behavioural point of view. As knowledge and experience developed, other frameworks for research into creativity started to emerge.

Prior to Guildford's plea, the earliest accounts of creativity were based on divine intervention. The creative person was seen as an empty vessel that a divine being would fill with inspiration. The individual would then pour out the inspired ideas. These mystical approaches dominated the study of creativity for many thousands of years and still have a major influence today.

The psychodynamic approach can be considered the first major twentieth-century theoretical approach to the study of creativity.

Based on the idea that creativity arises from the tension between conscious reality and unconscious drives, Freud (1908/1959) proposed that writers and artists produce creative work as a way to express their unconscious wishes in a publicly acceptable manner.

Later, the psychoanalytic approach introduced the concepts of adaptive regression and elaboration for the study of creativity (Kris, 1952). Adaptive regression, the primary process, refers to the intrusion of un-modulated thoughts in consciousness. Un-modulated thoughts can occur during active problem solving, but often occur during sleep, intoxication from drugs, fantasies or daydreams, or psychoses. Elaboration, the secondary process, refers to the re-working and transformation of primary processes through reality-oriented and ego-controlled thinking.

Soon after the psychoanalytical approach, process models of creativity started to be developed. One of the earliest models of the creative process is attributed to Graham Wallas, based on the work of the mathematician Poincaré. Wallas (1926) proposed that creative thinking proceeds through four phases:

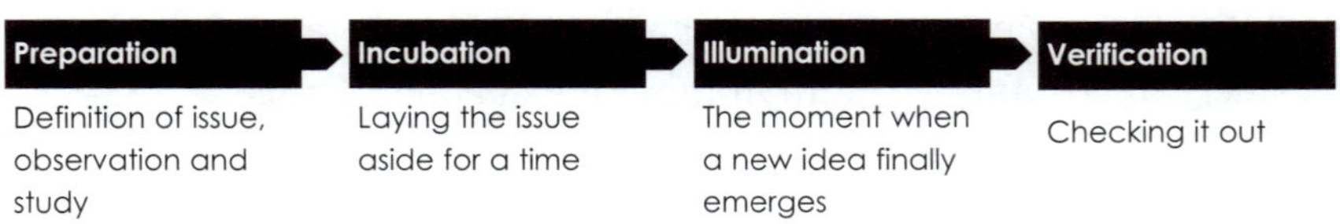

Source: Wallas (1926)

The inclusion of incubation followed by sudden illumination in this popular model may explain why some people view creative thinking as a sub-conscious mental process that cannot be directed.

Many other models further expanded on the theory of subconscious and uncontrollable events. These models went on to present the theory that creative ideas emerge from a largely uncontrollable Darwinian process of random variation and natural selection.

In contrast to these models Perkins (1981) argued that subconscious mental processes are behind all thinking and therefore play no extraordinary role in creative thinking. Just because we cannot fully describe our thought processes does not mean that we are not in control of them. Further, Perkins argues, just because random events play a part in some acts of creation, this should not be taken to imply that they are the only source of all acts of creation. He coined the term 'ideate' to imply the sub-conscious and conscious generation of ideas.

Source: Perkins (1981)

While some models still lean towards this magical process, the predominant models lean more towards a theory that novel ideas emerge from the conscious effort to balance analysis and imagination. The systematic combination of techniques for directed creativity and techniques for analysis continues as a strong theme in several more recent models.

In his APA address, Guildford (1950) proposed that creativity was in all of us and could be measured with a psychometric approach using paper-and-pencil tasks. Building on Guildford's work, Torrance (1974) developed the Torrance Tests of Creative Thinking. The predominance of the psychometric perspective is surprising considering the widely held belief that creativity is undefinable and unmeasurable (Callahan, 1991); Khatena, 1982).

Creativity tests tend to be of two types, those that involve cognitive-affective skills and those that attempt to tap a personality syndrome.

The cognitive approach to creativity seeks to understand the mental representations and processes underlying creative thought. Finke, Ward & Smith (1992) proposed what they called the Geneplore model, according to which there are two main processing phases in creative thought: generative phase and an exploratory phase. In the generative phase, the individual constructs mental representations, which have properties promoting creative discoveries. In the exploratory phase, these properties are used to come up with creative ideas. A number of mental processes may enter into these phases of creative invention, including the processes of retrieval, association, synthesis, transformation, analogical transfer, and categorical reduction.

Work in the social-personality approach has focused on personality variables, motivational variables, and the socio-cultural environment as sources of creativity. Researchers such as Amabile (1983), Barron (1968, 1969), Eysneck (1993) have noted that certain personality traits often characterise creative people. These traits include independence of judgement, self-confidence, attraction to complexity, aesthetic orientation, and risk taking.

Proposals regarding self-actualisation and creativity can also be considered within the personality tradition. According to Maslow (19 68), boldness, courage, freedom, spontaneity, self-acceptance, and other traits lead a person to realise their full potential. Focusing on motivation for creativity, a number of theorists have hypothesised the relevance of intrinsic motivation, need for order, need for achievement, and other motives.

The most recent practitioner perspective has been taken by pragmatics who have taken a generative approach aimed purely at producing more and more ideas (De Bono, 1971, 1985, 1992; Osborn, 1953; Gordon, 1961; Adams, 1974, 1986; Von Oech, 1983; Michalko, 1998). This perspective has been of particular interest to the business and management schools.

Towards a systemic viewpoint

Most of the research into creativity has had a focus on the individual and how they can become more creative. In some reference framework, all the approaches and explanations have validity and there is plenty of data and evidence to support them. However, from an innovation point of view, they do not take into account the actual use or uptake of ideas.

More recent scholarly works on creativity hypothesise that multiple components must converge for creativity to occur (Amabile, 1983, 1996; Csikszentmihalyi, 1988). At the level of explicit theories, Amabile (1983) describes creativity as the confluence of intrinsic motivation, domain-relevant knowledge and abilities, and creativity-relevant skills.

The creativity-relevant skills include:

- a cognitive style that involves coping with complexities and breaking one's mental set during problem solving;
- knowledge of heuristics for generating novel ideas; and
- a work style characterised by concentrated effort, an ability to set aside problems, and high energy.

Csikszentmihalyi (1988, 1996) takes a different, systems approach and highlights the interaction of the individual, domain and field. An individual draws upon information in a domain and transforms or extends it via cognitive processes, personality traits, and motivation. The field, consisting of people who control or influence a domain, evaluates and selects new ideas. The domain, a culturally defined symbol system, preserves and transmits creative products to other individuals and future generations.

Csikszentmihalyi (1999) further argues that if creativity is to have a useful meaning in management terms, it must refer to a process that results in an idea or a product that is recognised and adopted by

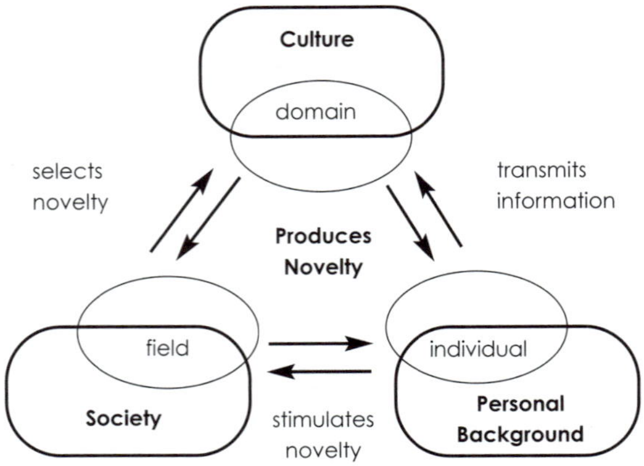

Csikszentmihalyi (1999)

others. The sole act of creation is not enough to be useful in a business sense. Creativity is not the product of single agents but of social systems making judgements about the agent's offerings. The concept of creativity in a business sense has to be grounded in what the social system is willing to accept. It is therefore necessary for a creative idea or product to be accepted (Simonton, 1988, 1991, 1994).

If the purpose of creativity is to generate ideas, then we must not only look at the 'stock' of ideas, but also where those ideas go and how they get there:

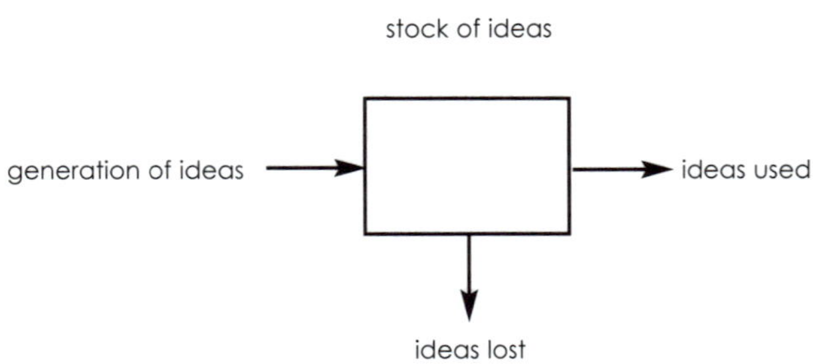

For ideas to be used they must be externalised and articulated to others for acceptance. For the purposes of the Master of Design Management programme at UNITEC Institute of Technology, design is defined as the process that gives form to ideas. Hence, ideas are developed through a design process.

In the process of design, ideas are generally developed into conceptual models, then prototypes, then products which are then accepted, or rejected, by the consumer/society. To complete the picture, these ideas, now embodied as products, diffuse into society where they go on to take on a meaning and function perhaps different to that intended at the start.

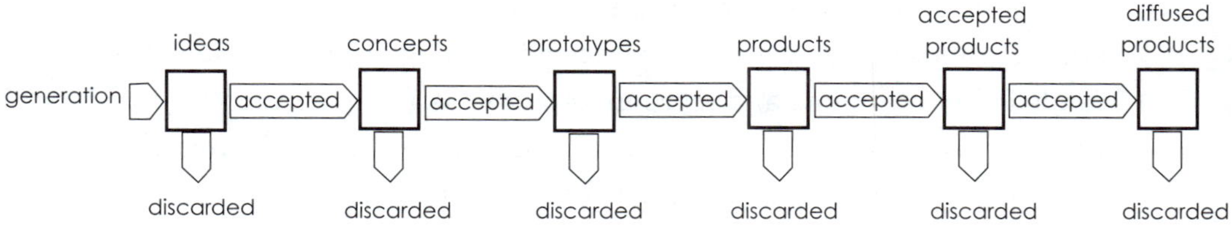

For the purposes of this model, concepts are defined as loose models that have been grounded in some form of reality. They may still be metaphoric in character and intangible. Prototypes start to become tangible and have some physical reality to them. Accepted products are products that are successfully commercialised. Diffused products are those that start to develop a longer-term meaning in society. This is also the area where brand value starts to develop and the consumer develops a deeper relationship with the product and the organisation.

From a management perspective, an understanding of the dynamics at each stage is essential for innovation, especially if it is to be sustained over a period of time, for example, in terms of feedback, the use of ideas encourages creativity – nothing succeeds like success. Conversely, ideas getting lost, for whatever reasons, not captured, ignored, quashed, is a huge demotivator, which will also reinforce behaviour.

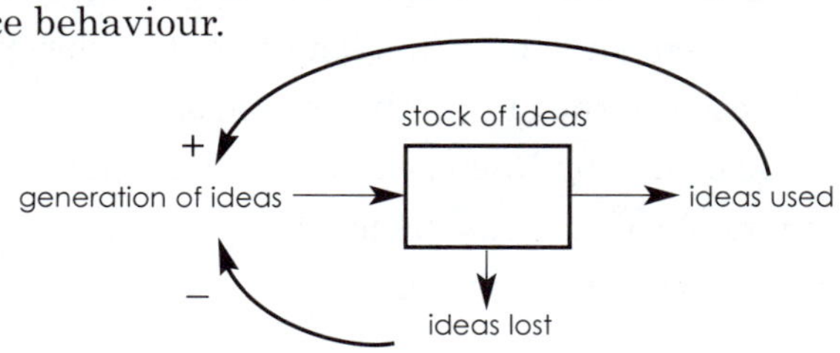

The way ideas are used is through a process of persuasion. Persuasion comprises of the following components:

persuasion = communication + validation + acceptance + influence

There are other factors that also come into play which have been omitted at this stage, including timing, luck etc.

Communication takes many forms and changes depending on which stage it takes place. At the ideas/conceptual stage the communication tends to be intangible and more metaphoric. It relies on the communication skills of the presenter, perhaps even the theatre of presentation for the acceptance of the idea. At the prototype/product stage there is a tangible mediate in the form of a hard model which does a lot of the communication. When it gets to the product acceptance and diffusion stages, the communication changes once again to intangibles and story telling.

The validation and acceptance components include the traditional metric based decision matrices based on measurable facts. However, they also have to take into account the intangibles such as the vision and values of the people and the organisation – what meaning does the idea have to those people? This starts to bring in concepts of mental models, capabilities, ethics etc.

The influence component is about the socio-political nature of the decision making process. Generally decisions are made not only of tangible facts but on political issues, egos, politics etc.

Managing creativity and innovation

The Master of Design Management programme at UNITEC Institute of Technology is concerned with the management of the 'design' stages of projects. These are the stages that are usually ill defined – the fuzzy front end as coined by Reinerstein (1996). Design is defined as the process of giving form to ideas, hence it could be the design of an organisation, a new type of strawberry, a research project. The focus is from a knowledge creation, knowledge sharing and knowledge application perspective. The programme is essentially about the management of creativity and innovation.

Systems thinking forms a core philosophy of the programme and the management of creativity and innovation are viewed as a socio-political system. The core modules are based on the management competencies of Boyatzis and Burgoyne:

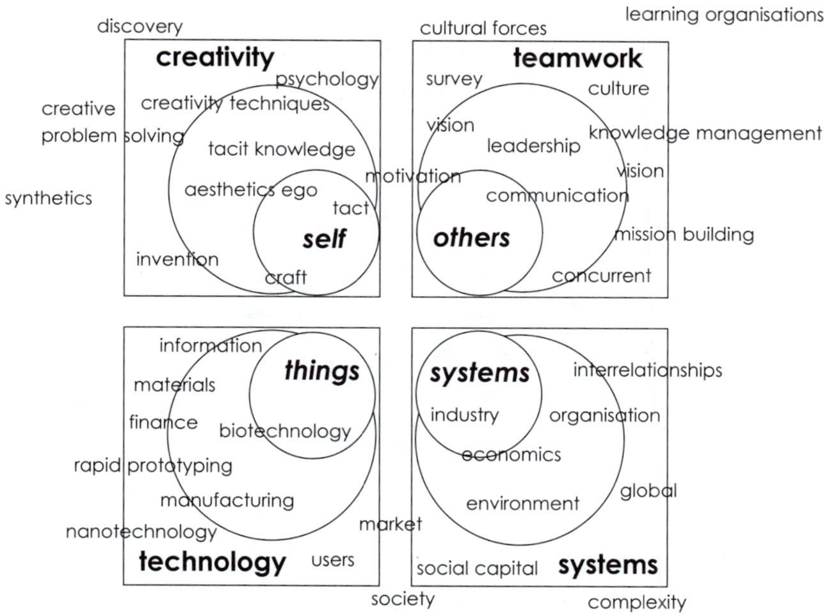

The fourfold division into 'self', 'others', 'things' and 'systems' is derived from the work of Boyatzis and Burgoyne on management competencies.

Creativity looks at the aspects of *knowledge* creation with a study of the various perspectives on creativity. Teamwork or people management looks at the processes of *knowledge* sharing and addresses the issues covered above. Leadership, culture, vision, values, motivation, communication all form a major part of the curriculum. Technology looks at the tools and techniques for *knowledg*e application. The systems course not only provides a philosophical way of looking at the world, but also allows us to look at the whole and where the ideas go, society and ethics.

The programme is still in its early stages and the arguments, conjectures and thoughts presented above are being constantly reviewed.

It is believed that the teaching of creativity with an understanding of the supporting context or an understanding of the willing market will help in the management of creativity and innovation. The supporting context provides an understanding of the individual and organisational competencies and capabilities as well as the aspirations and values, whereas the willing market indicates an understanding of the process of the ideas, concepts and products becoming accepted.

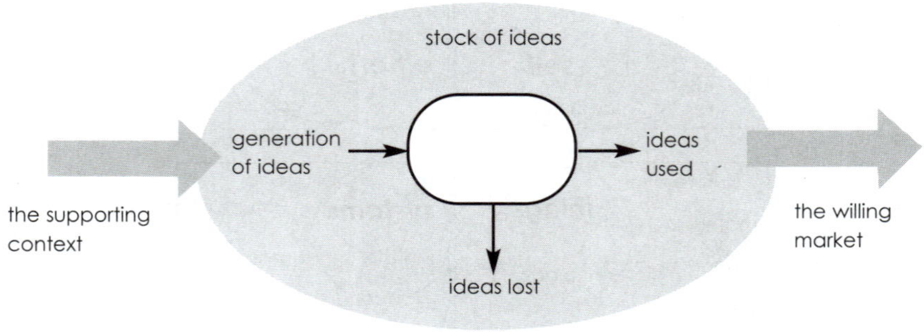

Selected bibliography

Amabile, T.M. (1983), *The social psychology of creativity* (Springer-Verlag)

Amabile, T.M. (1996), *Creativity in Context* (CO: Westview)

Argyris, C. & Schon, D. (1980), *Organisational Learning: A theory of action perspective* (Addison-Wesley)

Arthur, W.B. (1989), 'Competing technologies, increasing returns and lock-in by historical events', *Economic Journal*

Barron, F. (1963), *Creativity person and creative process* (New York: Holt, Reinhart & Winston)

Boden, M. (1994), *Dimensions of Creativity* (MIT Press)

Brown, S.L. & Eisenhradt, K.M. (1998), *Competing on the Edge: Strategy as Structured Chaos* (Boston: Harvard Business School Press)

Burgelman, R.A., Maidique, M.A. & Wheelwright, S.C. (1996), *Strategic Management of Technology and Innovation* (McGraw Hill)

Csikszentmihalyi, M. (1988), 'Society, culture and person: a systems view of creativity', in Sternberg, *The Nature of Creativity* (Cambridge University Press)

Csikszentmihalyi, M. (1996), *Creativity* (HarperCollins)

Clark, K.B & Wheelwright, S.C. (1993), *Managing New Product and Process Development, Text and Cases* (New York: Free Press)

Dosi, G. (1984), *Technical Change and Industrial Transformation* (MacMillan)

Eysenck, H.J. (1993), 'Creativity and personality: a theoretical perspective', *Psychological Inquiry*, 4, 147-178

Finke, R.A., Ward, T.B. & Smith, S.M. (1992), *Creative Cognition: Theory, Research and Applications* (MIT Press)

Imai, K., Nonaka, I. & Takeuchi, H. (1985), 'Managing the new product development process: how Japanese learn and unlearn', in Clark, Hayes & Lorenz, *The Uneasy Alliance: Managing the Productivity-Technology Dilemma* (Boston: Harvard Business School Press)

Kotler, P. (1992), *Principles of Marketing* (Prentice Hall)

Krugman, P. (1996), *The Self-Organising Economy* (Blackwell)

Leonard, D. & Sensiper, S. (1998), 'The role of tacit knowledge in group innovation', *California Management Review*, Spring 1998

Maslow, A. (1968), *Toward a Psychology of Being* (New York: Van Nostrand)

Maturana, H. & Varela, F. (1980), 'Autopoiesis and cognition: the realisation on the living', *Boston Studies in the Philosophy of Science*, Vol. 42 (Dordect: D.Reidel Publishing Company)

Nelson, R., & Winter, S. (1982), *An Evolutionary Theory of Economic Change* (Cambridge: Belknap Press)

Nonaka, I & Takeuchi, H. (1995), *The Knowledge-Creating Company* (Oxford: Oxford University Press)

Prigogine, I. (1967), *Introduction to Thermodynamics* (New York: Interscience)

Reinerstein, D.G. (1997), *Managing the Design Factory* (New York: Free Press)

Rich, B.R. & Janos, L. (1994), *Skunk Works: A Personal Memoir of My Years at Lockheed* (Boston: Little Brown)

Rogers, E.M. (1995), *Diffusion of Innovations* (New York: Free Press)

Simonton, D.K. (1994), *Greatness* (New York: Guildford)

Stacey, R.D. (1993/1996/2000), *Strategic Management and Organisational Dynamics: The Challenge of Complexity* (Prentice Hall)

Thonke, S.H. (1995), *The Economics of Experimentation in the Design of New Products and Processes*, Ph.D. thesis (Massachusetts Institute of Technology)

Weisberg, R.W. (1986), *Creativity Genius and Other Myths* (Freeman)

Wheelwright, S.C., & Clark, K.B. (1992), *Revolutionising Product Development* (New York: Free Press)

18

More than seeking model answers to predetermined problems: enhancing students' problem-finding capabilities in design subjects

Kin Wai Michael Siu

School of Design, The Hong Kong Polytechnic University

Abstract

Many educators point out that critical minds are important in finding problems to tackle, rather than only seeking model answers to predetermined – well-defined – problems. However, compared to other skills in the design process, such as analysis and solution generation, problem-finding is an area in which today's students are weak. To enhance their capability in problem-finding, a design subject has been offered to engineering students in Hong Kong. According to the performance and feedback of students, this paper argues that problem-finding is not an in-born capability that students need to practise. Design curricula should thus provide more opportunities for students to identify problems, instead of only proposing solutions, particularly model solutions.

Problem-finding: a key aspect of creative thinking and performance

The great scientist Albert Einstein (Einstein & Infeld, 1938) asserted the importance of problem-finding. He pointed out that the formulation of a problem is often more important than its solution. He reminded us that to raise new questions and new possibilities, to regard old problems from a new angle, requires imagination and marks a real advance in science. In *Productive Thinking*, Wertheimer (1959) also pointed out that the function of thinking is not just solving an actual problem but discovering, envisaging, probing into deeper questions. He further pointed out that envisaging and formulating the productive question is often a more important and greater achievement than the solution to a set question. Regarding the topic of creativity, in C*reativity's Compass*, Jay and Perkins (1997) state that the act of finding and formulating a problem is a key aspect of creative thinking and creative performance in many fields, an act that is distinct from and perhaps more important than problem-solving (see also Bunge, 1967; Fischer, 1970; Osborn, 1963; Polya, 1965; Rossman, 1931; Starko, 2000; Subotnik & Steiner, 1994).

Therefore, we should agree that a person good at generating creative solutions to defined problems is a creative thinker. However, if neither this person nor any other can find any problem for this 'creative' person to solve, his or her creative talent will never be expressed. In other words, without people who discover problems, there would be no creative solutions. Thus, a good thinker can be the person who is able to solve problems creatively, but can equally be the person who can critically identify problems using his/her initiative.

Current situation

New job requirements

Since the mid 1990s, several studies have been carried out in Hong Kong on the problem-finding capability of design and engineering students, as well as industry's need for this capability (Siu, 1994, 1997a, 1997b, 2000). The findings of these studies indicate that there has been a slight change in the job requirements for design and engineering students, especially the latter (Siu, 2000, 2001). In the past, the role of designers has been more on generating solutions by using their claimed creative minds, while the role of engineers has been mainly in problem-solving based on their technological and engineering knowledge and experience. Today, designers and engineers are more often required to initiate directions for design and production, even when not working at the supervisory level. In current post-industrial societies, such as Hong Kong with its high competitiveness and rapid changing of the direction of development, employees are more often required to initiate 'What should be done?' rather than 'How should it be done?'

Limitations of problem-finding experience provided in curricula

However, the findings of the studies also state that the current curricula have placed relatively less attention on enhancing students' capabilities in identifying problems. Although curriculum planners today always emphasise the importance of teaching students to be more creative, the focus is still mainly on training students to be more creative in generating solutions to predetermined problems. Most of the time, the only problems students have addressed at school are those already defined, so that problem-finding behaviours are not likely to emerge there.

The findings further show that, compared with other capabilities necessary in the design process (such as analysis and solution generation), students are relatively weak at problem-finding. One of the reasons for this is that many students lack the opportunity to identify problems for their work/assignments, for example, to define project titles or topics. In order to ensure administrative convenience in supervision or assessment, many teachers and examination boards prefer to provide one project title or a set of titles for students to tackle, instead of asking them to identify titles by themselves. This situation appears not only in basic education such as at primary and secondary school, but also at tertiary level. The cases in Hong Kong illustrate that undergraduates lack the opportunity to identify their project titles until the final year, that is, in the final project (Siu, 2000). In fact, Hong Kong is not an atypical case. When we review the curricula of many countries, like Getzels (1964, 1982, 1987) and Starko (2000) we find that the problem-finding capability of students is considered relatively infrequently.

A design subject for enhancing students' problem-finding capabilities

Since 2000, a new programme co-organised by design and engineering departments has been offered to non-degree graduates who are interested in furthering their study. The programme aims to train students to be more creative and innovative. In it, a design subject is offered to the students. Unlike other subjects in the programme, instead of only encouraging students to be creative in generating solutions to predetermined problems (which we shall also call 'provided' or 'well-defined' problems), the subject aims to enhance students' problem-finding capabilities. The subject requires each student to tackle a design project by identifying a problem, fixing a title/brief, and then conducting research and proposing solution(s). The students are encouraged to use their imagination to recognise, discover or invent problems. Unlike general project requirements, which focus on idea development, solution, evaluation and presentation, the assessment criteria of the project include the students' performance in problem-finding.

Students' feedback on the subject

Method

A study on the design subject was carried out to evaluate the problem-finding experience of the students. The activities included a questionnaire and in-depth interviews. All of the students were part-time students who had full- or part-time jobs. In total, 19 students responded to the questionnaire, and several (volunteer) students were invited for the interview. There were 14 males and 5 females. Six of them had certificate or diploma qualifications, 9 had higher certificate and higher diploma qualifications, and 3 had degrees. Most of the students came from an engineering background, while 3 of them came from a design background.

The major objectives of the questionnaire were to study the students' (a) previous experience in problem-finding for a project, (b) perceptions of problem-finding, and (c) comments on the problem-finding process and experience (for example any difficulties or advantages). The reason for holding interviews in the format of a casual discussion was to clarify the collected data and seek more in-depth data.

Results

Regarding the responses for the questionnaire, there was no significant difference between male and female students. There were differences in the responses to some questions among students with different education levels and backgrounds. Details of the differences will be given in the following paragraphs.

The responses to the questionnaire and interviews can be summarised as follows:

(A) Students' previous experience in problem-finding

1 Apart from those with a design education background and 2 with higher certificate or higher diploma qualifications, none of the students had experience in problem-finding in a design process by themselves before studying the design subject.

2 Some students had gained problem-finding experience only in extra-curricula activities.

(B) Students' perception of problem-finding

1 As few of the students had any problem-finding experience in projects (that is, experience in the regular curricula), their experience was in tackling just one provided title or selecting a title from a set of titles. Regarding the most important factor for the students in selecting project title(s):

- 2 out of 3 design background students stated that the most important factor for them in selecting their project titles was 'interest'; both of these design students had previous experience in identifying project titles; and
- 4 out of 16 students with engineering backgrounds stated that it was 'easy to find a solution'; they preferred to 'play it safe' in fulfilling the requirements of their assignments.

2 Regarding the suitable time for students to gain experience in identifying problems in a project, more than half of the students stated that it should be 'as early as possible'.

3 Regarding the ways of obtaining problem-finding capability and experience:

- 17 out of 19 students strongly disagreed or disagreed that 'identifying problems is a conceptual skill, and it is not necessary to gain practice in it'; and
- 11 out of 19 students strongly disagreed or disagreed that 'the experience of identifying problems can be obtained in the workplace and thus there is no need to have this kind of experience at school'.

(C) Students' comments on the problem-finding process and experience in the project

1 11 out of 19 students ranked the most difficult stage of the design process as being 'identifying the issue' or 'confining the problems to a project title'. That is, more than half of the students found it difficult to identify and fix project titles. The major reason for this difficulty was that:
   - the students had limited experience in problem-finding; and
   - some students did not know 'what is a problem' or, to put it another way, found that 'everything seems to be a problem'.

2 Regarding how many weeks the students had spent on identifying the problems and fixing their project titles in the 13-week project:
   - the mean value was 5 weeks;
   - two students responded that they had spent 8 weeks fixing their project titles, and
   - some agreed that problem-finding was much more difficult than they thought when they really attempted to do it.

3 Some engineering students agreed that they were really thinking about the grades of their assignments/projects. Commenting on the requirements of the design subject, they agreed that although the assessment criteria for the project included 'problem-finding', they still focused most of their attention on the solutions. Therefore, to meet the minimum requirements of the project, they preferred to 'recognise' problems that already existed, instead spending time 'discovering' or 'inventing' problems. Some students also pointed out that it was difficult to ascertain what was a good 'problem', but relatively easier to judge whether a solution was good or bad.

4 Regarding the importance of problem-finding ability:
   - about half of the students strongly agreed or agreed that 'experience in identifying problems is useful for their current job'; and
   - about two-thirds of them strongly agreed or agreed that 'experience in identifying problems will be useful for their future jobs'.

5 However, in responding to another question asking whether the students preferred to identify project titles by themselves or simply address those

assigned by their teacher, fewer than half of the students preferred to identify project titles by themselves. This contradictory response in their understanding of the importance of early experience in problem-finding (see items (B)2, 3, and (C)4) and their preference in fact appeared similar to other studies in which the students always agreed with the advantages and importance of experience in identifying problems. However, when they faced the difficulties and increased workload involved in finding their own problems, they preferred to give up this opportunity and expected the teachers to provide title(s) for them (Siu, 1994, 1997a, 1997b).

6 The major difficulties encountered by students in finding a problem can be summarised as follows:
   - The students had difficulty identifying problems at the beginning of the project; the major reason was that many of them had no previous experience;
   - Many of the students preferred to identify existent problems; they agreed that:
   - it was difficult for them to distinguish between existent, emergent and potential problems; and
   - it was difficult for them to identify emergent and potential problems, particularly the latter. (In explaining the nature of problems, Dillon (1982) distinguishes among levels of problems: existent, emergent, or potential. That is, with an existent problem, it is evident that a problematic situation exists, and the appropriate activity is to recognise it and solve it. An emergent problem is implicit, so that it must be discovered before it can be solved. A potential problem does not yet exist as a problem whose elements exist, and may strike the discoverer as an unformed problem, interesting situation, or idea worth elaborating. As further elaborated by Starko (2000), regarding potential problems, by combining the elements in some way, the observer creates or invents a problem where no problem previously existed.)
   - Some students pointed out that they had tried to discover and invent a problem that was implicit. However, this 'implicit' nature resulted in difficulties for them in ascertaining whether the discovered and invented one 'was a problem'. Moreover, such kinds of questions were too implicit, which made it difficult for them to propose solutions to them. Many of the students agreed that, once they had had difficulty proposing solutions to the problems (that is, to finish the project), they would give up and try to find another more explicit problem, to which the solutions would also be more explicit.
   - Some students agreed that they had been satisfied with some problems. However, these questions were difficult for them to solve owing to the nature of the problems. For instance, they might identify

the problems related to social and cultural issues. These problems were difficult for them to solve in a way directly related to design and engineering activities.

- The students sometimes felt frustrated, since it was difficult for them to judge whether a problem was good (identified/defined) or not. In other words, there was no systematic way to allow them to judge whether a problem was good or not. Some students also found difficulty in 'fixing' the project title (that is, making a decision/selection on one out of several problems). This means that they had difficulty deciding whether an identified problem was the right one to tackle. Most of the time, they relied heavily on the judgement (that is, feedback in tutorials) of the teacher and the project tutors.

7 The students' positive feedback on the project (regarding the problem-finding experience) are as follows:

- They gained more experience in problem-finding. They understood the difficulty in problem-finding not only in a theoretical way, but also through practical involvement. They recognised that problem-finding was not an in-born or easy skill.
- Although understanding and recognising the difficulty in problem finding, the students also indicated that they had gained more confidence in problem-finding. Like the students with design backgrounds, 3 out of 16 engineering students stated that they would prefer to identify project titles by themselves in the future. Some students who disliked identifying project titles by themselves also pointed out that, if the problem-finding activity was not related to 'marks', they would like to have more experience in problem-finding in order to enrich their experience.
- Some students stated that finding problems by themselves provided them with more space to develop their thinking and imagination. They stated that if a problem (a project title or a set of titles) was determined by their teachers, the latitude for thinking would be narrower. However, in the design subject project, since the students were required to identify the problem by themselves, they had to refine the problem step by step before they started thinking about the solution.

8 With reference to 7, some students agreed that the project allowed them to achieve a greater balance of development in skills in the different stages of the design process. For instance, if the problem was identified by teachers, the students would pay more attention to the solution. On the contrary, if the problem was identified by the students themselves, the attention was more balanced: 'all' the stages of the design process – problem-finding, title fixing, idea development, implementation, and evaluation.

9 To meet the requirements of the project, the students pointed out that they needed to pay more attention to conducting investigations, or at least asking themselves the reasons for the surrounding events. Some students agreed that this increased their social and cultural awareness, and encouraged them to practise their thinking in a more critical way.

Enhancing problem-finding capabilities

To enhance students' problem-finding capabilities, three major areas should be considered: first, the background and experience of students; second, their original perceptions of problem-finding; and third, the curriculum and learning environment required for students to gain problem-finding experience.

It is obvious that the first area affects the latter two areas. As mentioned before, many students nowadays are still unable to gain experience in problem-finding through their regular curricula. The students' feedback in the design subject indicates that they had gained problem-finding skills only in extra-curricular activities. As current curricula still emphasise the ability of students to provide 'solutions' and 'answers', in particular to some conventional subjects which still expect students to provide model answers to predetermined problems, many students are unable to develop problem-finding skills until the undergraduate level, or even until they go out to work.

In fact, like other problem-solving skill activities, problem-finding experience should be provided as early as possible (Department of Education and Science, 1989, 1990; Jay & Perkins, 1997; National Curriculum Council, 1990). The only difference should be in the level of guidance provided by supervisors, the nature of activities, and the difficulty of requirements. We believe that problem-finding ability should be obtained by practice and the accumulation of experience of such kinds of practices.

According to the results of the design subject project, students' difficulties in problem-finding come from two levels: the ideological level, which relates to the students' original perception of problem-finding, and the practical level, which relates to the curriculum and the learning environment necessary for students to obtain experience.

At the ideological level, with reference to the students' feedback mentioned above, many students do not consider problem-finding as a necessary skill. In particular, students studying subjects that conventionally only require model answers or well-predetermined/defined solutions seldom think that it is important to discover or invent 'something to do' or 'something to think'. Compared to science students taking conventional experiments in laboratories in which they are required to find out well-defined outcomes, or engineering students taking conventional examinations in which they are required to present their mathematical and engineering skills, skills in problem-finding seem relatively less important. Even though some of the students may realise that problem-finding skills are essential for their future study and work, some of them still think that it is easy for them and that it should not be necessary for them to have this kind of practice (that is, experience) in their learning.

On the other hand, students and even teachers often associate 'creativity and innovation' only with solutions, and not with problems. The major reason for this is that in the thinking process, we always emphasise the 'end'. In other words, we would call a student unsuccessful if he or she could only get the 'start' but had no guarantee of a satisfactory 'end'. It is clear that this kind of thinking is deeply implanted in students' as well as teachers' minds. In addition, we have made little effort to establish a kind of assessment that can seriously and effectively evaluate students' performance in problem-finding (for example, the performance in conducting research and in turn recognising, discovering or inventing a problem, and finally in identifying a project title or direction).

At the practical level, the problem can further be sub-divided and seen in two ways. Firstly, most of the time, as mentioned at the beginning, for convenience of project administration and assessment, teachers prefer to set a title or set of titles for students. Even in tertiary-level learning activities such as projects, freedom for students to identify their project titles or topics is very limited. Moreover, because of the common emphasis on the final solution (for instance, the relatively higher weighting on the 'solution'), per the students' feedback above, they often neglect the importance of experience and capability in identifying needs, or prefer to pay little attention to problem-finding.

Secondly, students lack guidance to recognise, discover and invent problems, in particular the latter. As demonstrated by the students' feedback in the questionnaire and interview discussed above, it was not difficult for them to recognise existent problems. However, for discovering problems, the students honestly responded that they had no concrete idea of 'what is a problem?' and 'how to start?' Many of them always had questions on their minds, such as, for instance: 'Is it a problem? It seems so simple.' 'Is it a problem for my learning discipline? I have the impression that it belongs to another discipline and I am not suppose to care about it.' Obviously, it is relatively more difficult for the students to invent potential problems.

The students agreed that one of the major barriers to their inventing a problem is the elaboration from an 'interesting situation' to a 'problem'. Moreover, as stated by the tutors involved in the design subject project, many students always asked the tutors to make decisions for them by asking: 'Is it a good project title (problem)?' This kind of inquiry reflects two common weaknesses of students and one current curriculum constraint. The students have neither the confidence nor the experience to make judgements on an emergent or potential problem, and they do not have enough experience to fine-tune/modify their defined situation. The students always worry about their 'grades' and expect to seek the teachers' 'approval' of their defined problems in order to get higher marks, rather than seeking 'advice' on the problems to gain improvement. It is clear that the current grade-oriented learning attitude limits students' willingness and courage to discover and invent problems.

If the students' judgement relies heavily on the teachers' decisions, and there is insufficient (step-by-step) guidance for students to make decisions by themselves, they will fail to make improvements in problem-finding. With reference to the experience of the project, one of the possible ways for students to start to find a problem is to require them to pay more attention to their everyday life environment (Siu, 1997b). This is because they are familiar with it. Another useful way is to require them to engage in more critical discussions with their colleagues and teachers. They should learn how to accept critical comments, as well as providing them. As Einstein said (Einstein & Infeld, 1938), only through raising more questions can we make real advances in our discipline.

To conclude, to meet the new needs of industry, which requires employees to take more initiative, we need to enhance our students' problem-finding capabilities. This means that the success of a student today lies in not only following and answering, but in asking and identifying. To meet this education goal, we should facilitate a good learning environment, introduce reforms to our curricula, provide more guidance and evaluate students' performance in a more balanced way, in order to encourage them to try not only to solve but also to recognise, discover and invent problems.

Questionnaire

Please tick one response only, unless otherwise specified:

1. Sex: ❒ Female ❒ Male

2. Education level:

   ❒ Cert/Dip ❒ H-Cert/H-Dip ❒ Degree ❒ Other: __________

3. Educational background:

   ❒ Design ❒ Engineering ❒ Other: ______________

4. Did you have any experience of identifying project titles by yourself before taking this subject?

   ❒ Yes ❒ No

If so, when was the first time you had such an experience in school:

❐ pre-primary ❐ primary ❐ secondary ❐ post-secondary

❐ degree ❐ other: ____________

5. Which situation do you prefer in carrying out your design project?

❐ a project title identified by yourself

❐ a project title assigned by your teacher

❐ a set of titles assigned by your teacher, and you select one of them

❐ other:____

6. With regard to your response to Question 5, why?

____

7. What is the most important factor for you in selecting your project title?

❐ interest ❐ ease of finding a solution ❐ others' suggestions

❐ other: _____________

8. Rank the degree of the difficulty of the different stages of a design process provided below. Use '1' to indicate the most difficult, and '5' to indicate the easiest.

( ) identifying problems

( ) confining the problems to a project title

( ) generating ideas

( ) proposing a final solution

( ) presentation

9. Which level is the most appropriate time for students to be introduced to the experience of identifying the problem of a project?

❐ pre-primary ❐ primary ❐ secondary ❐ post-secondary

❐ degree ❐ no need

10. With regard to your response to Question 9, when is the most suitable time for students to gain experience in identifying problems for a project?

❐ as early as possible ❐ final year ❐ other: _____________

11. Do you think that experience in identifying problems is useful for your current job?

❐ strongly disagree ❐ disagree ❐ neutral ❐ agree ❐ strongly agree

12. Do you think that experience in identifying problems will be useful for your future job?

❐ strongly disagree ❐ disagree ❐ neutral ❐ agree ❐ strongly agree

13. Some people say that identifying problems is a conceptual issue. Thus, it is not necessary to have practice in it. Do you agree?

❐ strongly disagree ❐ disagree ❐ neutral ❐ agree ❐ strongly agree

14. Some people say that the experience of identifying problems can be obtained in their workplace. Thus, there is no need to acquire this kind of experience in school. Do you agree?

❐ strongly disagree ❐ disagree ❐ neutral ❐ agree ❐ strongly agree

15. In this (13-week) design project, how many weeks did you spend on identifying the problems and fixing your project title?

____ weeks

16. What was your major difficulty in identifying the problem(s)?

____

17. What was your major difficulty in fixing the project title?

____

18. Any other comments on identifying problems and fixing the project title:

____

____

____

Acknowledgement

The author would like to acknowledge the support of the Project 'Area of Strategic Development: Training for Creativity and Innovation by Product and Process Design', (Industrial Centre and

School of Design), The Hong Kong Polytechnic University, in the preparation of this study and paper.

References

Bunge, M. (1967), *Scientific research* (Vol 1: The search for system (New York: Springer)

Department of Education and Science (1989), *Proposals of Design and Technology for Ages 5 to 16* (Department of Education and Science and the Welsh Office, HMSO)

Department of Education and Science (1990), *Technology in the National Curriculum* (Department of Education and Science and the Welsh Office, HMSO)

Dillon, J. T. (1982), Problem finding and solving, *The Journal of Creative Behavior*, 16, 97–111

Einstein, A., & Infeld, L. (1938), *The Evolution of Physics* (New York: Simon & Schuster)

Fischer, D.H. (1970), *Historians' Fallacies: Toward a Logic of Historical Thought* (New York: Harper & Row)

Getzels, J.W. (1964), 'Creative Thinking, Problem Solving and Instruction', in Hilgard, R. (ed.), *Theories of Learning and Instruction* (63rd NSSE Yearbook, Part 1, pp. 240–267) (Chicago: University of Chicago Press)

Getzels, J.W. (1982), 'The problem of the problem', in Hogarth, R. (ed.), *New Directions for Methodology of Social and Behavioral Science: Question Framing and Response Consistency* (pp. 37–49) (San Francisco: Jossey-Bass)

Getzels, J. W. (1987), 'Problem finding and creative achievement', *Gifted Students Institute Quarterly*, 12(4), B1–B4

Jay, E.S., & Perkins, D.N. (1997), 'Creativity's compass: A review of problem finding', in Runco, M.A. (ed.), *Creativity Research Handbook*, Vol. 1. (Cresskill, NJ: Hampton)

National Curriculum Council (1990), *Non-statutory Guidance - Design and Technology Capability* (National Curriculum Council, HMSO)

Osborn, A.F. (1963), *Applied Imagination* (3rd ed.) (New York: Charles Scribner's Sons)

Polya, G. (1965), *Mathematical Discovery: On Understanding, Learning, and Teaching Problem Solving*, Vol. 2 (New York: Wiley)

Rossman, J. (1931), *The Psychology of the Inventor: A Study of the Patented* (2nd ed.), (Washington, DC: Inventors Publishing)

Siu, K.W.M. (1994), 'A study of pupils' rationale for the selection of topics in the project section of the HKCEE design and technology', unpublished thesis (Hong Kong: The University of Hong Kong)

Siu, K.W.M. (1997a), 'Review the past to plan the future: Setting design education direction through a review of education targets from the 1960s to present', in Kwok, Y.C.J. (ed.), (Re)-*Discovering design* (Hong Kong: A Better Tomorrow Workshop)

Siu, K.W.M. (1997b), 'Criticism and theory studies in design and technology teacher education programs', *Curriculum Forum*, 7(1), 49–58

Siu, K.W.M. (2000), 'A case study of the difficulties and possibilities for students to initiate their project titles', in Volk, K., So, W., & Thomas, G. (eds.), *Science and Technology Education Conference 2000* (pp. 112–120) (Hong Kong: Education Department)

Siu, K.W.M. (2001), 'Meeting the knowledge demands of the new economy: From recognising existent problems to discovering emergent ones', in Beven, F., Kanes, C. & Roebuck, D. (eds.), *Proceedings of the 9th Annual International Conference on Post-compulsory Education and Training: Knowledge Demands for the New Economy* (Volume Two) (Brisbane: Australian Academic Press Pty. Ltd)

Starko, A.J. (2000), 'Finding the problem finders: Problem finding and the identification and development of talent', in Friedman, R.C. & Shore, B.M. (eds.), *Talents Unfolding: Cognition and Development* (Washington DC.: American Psychological Association)

Subotnik, R.F. & Steiner, C.L. (1994), 'Problem identification in academic research: A longitudinal case study from adolescence to early adulthood', in Runco, M.A. (ed.), *Problem Finding, Problem Solving, and Creativity* (Norwood, NJ: Ablex)

Wertheimer, M. (1959), *Productive Thinking* (Enl. ed.) (London: Travistock)

Biographical note

Dr Kin Wai Michael Siu PhD MSc MA MEd lectures in the School of Design and works as Senior Project Fellow in the Industrial Centre at The Hong Kong Polytechnic University. He is a chartered engineer and chartered designer, and a fellow of the CSD, RSA, and College of Preceptors. He has been a visiting professor at universities in China and South Korea, and an academic visitor in the Engineering Design Centre of the University of Cambridge. He is the Chief Examiner of the Design Paper of the HKCE and of the AS levels of Design and Technology, and serves as a committee member of examination boards and curriculum development committees regarding design and technology education. He has also chaired the Hong Kong Association for Design and Technology Education (1997–2000), and was an Executive Committee Member of the Hong Kong Educational Research Association and the Higher Education Research and Development Society of Australasia. His principal areas of research interest are: design and culture, need identification, inclusive design, and user-oriented design.

19

Online learning environments for group-based assessment:

Darrall Thompsons

University of Technology Sydney (UTS), Faculty of Design, Architecture and Building, Australia

Abstract

The impetus to design new learning environments assumes improved economies of scale with subject content delivered to increasingly large numbers of students with minimal face-to-face contact but at no cost to learning outcomes.

Group work and group-based assessment are strategies often adopted to reap the benefits of economy of scale with little reference to relevant educational research. One of the biggest problems with group-based assessment is the students' perception of fairness. Those who work hard are demotivated through lack of acknowledgement and those with minimal contribution to the group task receive the same grade as the rest of the group.

The author was part of a team that designed an online 'Self and Peer Assessment Resource Kit' (SPARK). The system is based on sound educational research and the case studies outlined in this paper provide important clues toward the successful integration of group based assessment.

Introduction

In the educational framework common to most western cultures there is an implicit development with regard to learning abilities:

- dependent (school);
- independent (university); and
- interdependent (work).

This transitional view (developed from Boud, 1988) highlights the university's central and therefore pivotal role. The university learning environment must wean students from teacher dependency, encourage independent learning and develop the collaborative and professional skills vital for an interdependent working life.

The illiterate of the 21st century will not be those who cannot read and write, but those who cannot learn, unlearn, and relearn (Toffler, 1991).

There is a shift in what employers expect the university environment to deliver with regard to 'graduate attributes' or 'transferable skills' (Assiter, 1995). In particular, an excellent study of design graduates and their employers (Garner & Duckworth, 2000) reveals weaknesses that group work is ideally suited to strengthen. They include: graduates need greater ability to take other people's ideas on board; lack of resilience to criticism; weak ability to muster a reasoned defence of their contribution; improve listening skills; higher quality written, graphic and verbal communication; able to be critical of their own work and contributions. To highlight the importance and pivotal role occupied by the university level here is a quote from the conclusions of their study:

> A breadth of skills and knowledge seems vital – as one manager put it, 'we can't afford specialists'. The desired profile seems a broad one: creative and analytical; practical and academic; numerate and literate; able to exploit both divergent and convergent thought processes; sensitive and strong!
> Garner & Duckworth (2000)

The design curriculum has already had to accommodate what could be called the 'digital melting pot' of professions and this continuing convergence adds further pressure as the boundaries of specialism disappear or become blurred.

Concurrent with these demands, curricula must also deliver improved economies of scale with subject content delivered to increasingly large numbers of students with reduced face-to-face contact and ideally at no cost to learning outcomes.

In response to this situation group work projects are often used as an exigent strategy rather than an explicit development of the curriculum. One of the biggest problems encountered with group work using group-based assessment is the students' perception of fairness. Too often those who work hard in a group project are demotivated through lack of acknowledgement and those with minimal involvement receive the same grade as other group members. It is no surprise that the use of assessment that does not adequately address this problem has been a major source of dissatisfaction in student surveys.

These many considerations have prompted the development of an online 'Self and Peer Assessment Resource Kit' (SPARK), which has been applied and refined through a number of pilot schemes since 1998. The SPARK project was developed from a theoretical framework (Goldfinch & Raeside, 1990; Goldfinch, 1994), which addressed a number of perceived problems and challenges associated with group-based assessment.

This paper focuses on the design of a learning environment with specific reference to group work and group-based assessment. It explores the issues surrounding group-based assessment and, in particular, the learning advantages of a Web-based approach with evidence from online statistics and student comments. The SPARK project is explained with analysis of case studies from a four-year B.Design (Visual Communication) degree.

The motivation behind the paper is to impart some confidence in the assertion that group work and group-based assessment can be a practical and valuable strategy in design education.

Issues in the group work learning environment

The term 'group work' is used in this paper to imply a broader coverage than the term 'teamwork' which tends to have a more product-focused and role-based connotation.

Group work is understood to be one of a range of 'peer learning strategies' including discussion groups, parrainage (a form of buddy system), learning cells, peer assessment, student led workshops etc. There have been a number of studies on aspects of peer learning (Boud, Cohen & Simpson 2001; Griffiths, Houston & Lazenbatt, 1995; Falkichov, 2001; Jaques, 2000) in which advantages and disadvantages of these strategies have been identified.

The use of 'peer learning' has been successful in the development of broader graduate attributes (Boud, Cohen & Simpson 2001), but can be treated as peripheral by students if those attributes are not part of the graded assessment. A focus on team skills, self directed learning, self and peer assessment and other peer learning strategies has also been shown to encourage students to be lifelong learners and develop 'reflective practice' and 'critical self-awareness' (Candy & O'Leary, 1994).

Peer learning strategies that imply that important assessable learning can happen without the lecturers' direct involvement represents a challenging leap of trust for all concerned. It is suggested for this reason that the implementation and management of any peer learning strategy is carefully phased (Cohen & Sampson, 2001) and discussed thoroughly with other staff and students.

If the use of group work is to be ratified as part of the assessment process there must be an atmosphere of trust in the learning environment. Group work strategies also need to enhance the learning possibilities for students whilst reducing administrative and assessment loads for design lecturers.

The author's experience over the last four years has led to a growing conviction that carefully integrated Web-based solutions can deliver on these demands. Some of the evidence for this conviction is presented in the section: 'A Web-based approach to self and peer assessment' and the student comments in 'Notes' at the end of the paper.

The need for a 'deep approach' to learning

> We will never know how many plagiarised projects and downloaded dissertations have passed through our degrees unnoticed. The only enduring antidote is to encourage deep approaches in an educational environment that rewards both process and product.
> Thompson (2000)

There is implicit trust in every educational context between those designing or providing a learning experience and those engaging in it. Two main levels of student engagement have been identified and are known as 'surface approaches' and 'deep approaches' (Ramsden, 1992).

If the assessment of group work process through group-based assessment is to be included in individual students graded assessments there must clearly be strong encouragement to adopt a deep approach so that the students' desire to learn is greater than their competition with each other.

There are subtle factors in the design of group work projects that encourage students to adopt a surface approach to their learning. For example, lecturers using group work merely as a labour-saving device can easily encourage students to adopt surface approaches, negating the educational benefits. Students are inadvertently 'trained' through western educational systems to be 'tuned in' to teachers' motivations and preferences on a number of levels. This is particularly important to take account of in design education where there is no 'right answer' and lecturers' subjective design preferences are easily discernible. Group work with a genuine and thorough introduction to the relevance and fairness of well-designed group learning activities is vital to the encouragement of a deep approach.

The motivation of students to engage deeply and take responsibility for their own learning is dependent on the 'characteristics of the learning environment'. The diagram below is a visual representation of some of Paul Ramsden's research results in this area.

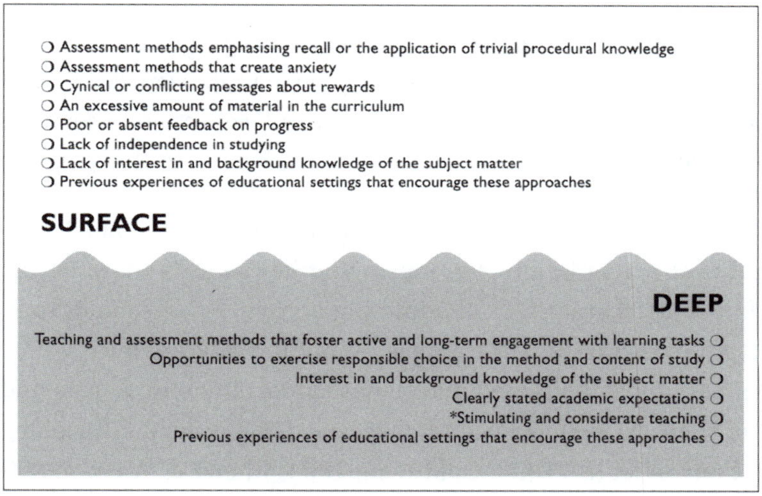

*Especially teaching which demonstrates the lecturer's personal commitment to the subject matter and stresses its meaning and relevance to students

Fig. 1 The author's graphic interpretation of some of Paul Ramsden's research

The design of an assessment process for group work

> Assessment is the single most powerful influence on learning in formal courses and, if not designed well, can easily undermine the positive features of an important strategy in the repertoire of teaching and learning approaches'
>
> Boud, Cohen & Simpson (2001, p. 67)

If reflective practice, critical self awareness, interpersonal skills and other graduate attributes are endorsed as learning outcomes they must become a valued and explicit part of the assessment process. Assessment of group work where all group members receive the same mark regardless of input is clearly unacceptable from the students' perspective and can cause deep resentment to build. It is therefore essential that there is a 'peer assessment' system through which students themselves take responsibility to 'distribute' a group mark using an appropriate range of criteria.

The addition of self assessment to peer assessment has been identified as a refinement with strong educational benefits. The combination of self assessment informed by peer feedback on specific criteria is favoured in preference to peer feedback alone (Sampson et al., 1999). This combination also reinforces 'independent' reflection to complement the 'interdependence' mentioned in the introduction to this paper.

In educational systems where a percentage assessment mark is central to the calculation of grades and other awards there needs to be a fair and accurate way of adjusting a group's assessment to reflect an individual's performance. A number of academic researchers have developed mathematical formulae to do this and most of them have so far been paper based (Goldfinch & Raeside, 1990; Conway et al., 1993; Goldfinch, 1994; Cheng & Warren, 2000).

Further considerations and issues

A major issue in any Web-based solution is equity of access and usability. From surveys it is clear that although most students have computers at home (approximately 80/20 Mac to PC) the majority have slow or difficult Internet access (approximately 12% have no access). We must therefore ensure reasonable times for access using university facilities. There are still a significant number of design students (and staff) who avoid computer use as a matter of principle or preference. It is important to offer online engagement as an enhancement of, rather than a substitute for, studio-based practice.

In a recent survey, 38% of visual communication students indicated that travel to the university was very inconvenient. This is an unexpected result for a university campus that is five minutes from the central rail and bus terminal and highlights our lack of demographic knowledge and appreciation of the students' situation. It does however give good reason to develop further online services on both administrative and academic levels.

The increasing enrolment of those with English as a second language raises the issue of usability and alternative translations. The Web is ideally suited to language variations but it is unclear what the best approach to language support would be in the context of these students attempting to learn English as part of their studies.

There is also an important issue to do with lecturers' fundamental conceptions of teaching and their approach to the learning environment. These have been found to be a major influence in students' adoption of either a deep or surface approach to their learning (Gow & Kember 1993; Prosser and Trigwell, 1999). Conclusions from a phenomenographic study of design lecturers conceptions (Drew, 2000) identified five qualitatively different conceptions of teaching, some of which may preclude the adoption of peer learning strategies: teaching is offering students a range of practical and technical skills; teaching is developing students' practical and technical skills; teaching is developing students' critical, practical and technical skills through student interaction; teaching is developing students' skills and conceptions in the context of professional practice; and teaching is helping students change conceptions. These are constituted as a hierarchy where the more complete conceptions include the more limiting conceptions but not vice versa.

This reinforces the fact that any strategy implemented by different lecturers with different conceptions of teaching can have radically different learning outcomes for students (McKenzie, 2001).

A paper-based approach to group-based assessment

Design lecturers have adopted various methods to cope with variance in student contribution for group-assessed projects. These are intended to give both formative feedback in identifying individual strengths and opportunities for improvement, but summative assessment as a percentage mark is needed in most assessment systems.

There have been a number of problems with paper-based systems not least of which is the disincentive of excessive workloads for lecturers and the lack of anonymity identified by students. In order to explore some of the more subtle problems associated with group-based assessment, the following case study of a design project is used to give a design context.

Case study with paper-based calculations

This example is from a 3rd-year visual communication subject called 'Community Project'. It involved 55 students in groups of 4 to 6 designing live projects for 'not-for-profit' community groups, liaising with the client and taking designs to production. Each group had an academic supervisor meeting for approximately 30 minutes each week during the first 8 weeks.

The groups were expected to devote 9 hours per week to this project and each group presented their project to the whole class in week 9. They received peer and supervisor feedback and assessment forms with which to mark class presentation and overall design solution for each group excluding their own.

Supervisors' guidelines for assessment

Individual mark

The idea here is that each student will get an individual mark from the group but that this mark is related to a mark given by the supervising lecturer after the final client presentation. The students negotiate a fair split of the total mark, and give each other a mark based on the following criteria:

1. participation in project management;
2. contribution to design solution; and
3. contribution to client presentation.

Step-by-step detail: After the client presentation the supervising lecturer gives each group a mark out of 100 based on the overall project in relation to design solution, project management and client presentation. This mark is then multiplied by the number of students in the group. The group then divides this mark up based on the individual mark criteria so that each student gets a percentage mark.

This mark is then returned to the supervising lecturer who then calculates it as a proportional mark out of 60%. This will then be added to other criteria of class presentation, 10%, and design solution, 30%.

Supervising lecturers as a group
At the class presentations the supervising lecturers will give a mark to each grouping according to:
- effectiveness of class presentation, out of 10; and
- appropriateness/effectiveness of overall design solution, out of 30.

Sample marking sheet

Student name:	**Student A**
Project name:	**Project 3**
Supervising lecturers % mark 80% x 5 (no. of students in group) =	**400**
Mark allocated to this student by group:	**74%** = individual mark as a %
Individual mark calculated, out of 60	**44.4**
Class presentation, out of 10	**6** (supervisor + peer averaged)
Overall design solution, out of 30	**18** (supervisor + peer averaged)
Final individual total	**68.4%**

On presentation day, the groups were given a supervisor's percentage mark for their group work which they then had to share as a 60% contribution to their final individual mark. Without exception they gave each other an equal share of the group mark.

Reasons for this result were identified through informal discussion with students:

- students were left to discuss/negotiate the sharing according to three general criteria with no specified mechanism for allocating the marks;

- the three criteria were too simplistic to address the range of contributions involved;
- they were asked to do so at a time of high stress when most were just happy to have made the deadline;
- there was no allocated time within the project for the process, and to get together and organise themselves was too great a hurdle when other projects were pressing; and
- the students would gain no perceived benefit from this discussion/negotiation so the default position of equal shares was adopted.

The peer assessment of the class presentation and overall design solution was also problematic:

- lecturers had an onerous task to collect all the paper, enter the marks from each student and average those with each supervisors mark;
- the students gave over-inflated marks for presentations and project work; and
- there appeared to be collusion between groups to give extra marks if the other group did the same.

One student commented that as collection of the peer assessment papers was not confidential they felt uncomfortable with the process. After the calculations were done, the results were rejected as unusable by the subject co-ordinator and in the end only the supervisors' marks were used.

It is clear that some of these problems do not relate to the simple fact that the assessment was paper-based. However, it was noted by the three supervisors concerned that although there was discussion with students of the benefits of group work, the practicalities of the final assessment process did not encourage a reflective critique of self and peer contributions.

The identified problems of paper-based systems

In summary the problems identified through the use of paper-based systems in two design subjects were:

- lack of time to reflect and change ones ratings after the end of the project;
- small range of criteria did not address contributions leaving graduate attributes non-specific or hidden;
- lack of choice where anonymity is concerned – arising from the practicality of assessment happening when all the students are together;
- the complexities of calculating the contribution of multiple feedback from each group member across a range of criteria;
- lecturers' avoidance of comprehensive criteria owing to the onerous task of calculating a conversion of the group mark into individual marks;
- collusion, and the students' adoption of a surface approach to the whole system, undermining the educational value of group work;
- lack of scalability when extra groups and larger numbers of students are involved;
- difficulty of distribution and collection of assessment particularly with part-time courses and lecturers.

A Web-based approach to group-based assessment

The case studies that follow will show that assessing group work process through Web-based self and peer assessment is educationally valuable and fosters high levels of learning and critical reflection. It should be noted that the use of a phased approach and good preparation (Cohen & Sampson, 2001) is a consistent feature of all successful cases studied. It may be surprising to learn that the assessment task is far less important than the context in which it is set (Samuelowicz, 1994).

This section of the paper focuses on the implementation and evaluation of a Web-based self and peer assessment approach

(SPARK). Case studies and comments come from pilot schemes in a B.Design Visual Communication degree at the third-year level of a four-year course.

The development of this Web-based approach to group-based assessment was the result of a range of concerns and frustrations from staff and students in several faculties at UTS. It was considered that Web mediation of the self and peer assessment process may address some of the problems experienced with paper-based approaches. The need for solutions prompted a successful application for research funding to develop generic templates and databases capable of adaptation to a wide range of group work assessment processes.

The research team developing this system was multidisciplinary and included academics from business, education, law, engineering and the author as a representative of design. It is encouraging to note that the leader of the team Associate Professor Mark Freeman appreciated the strong contribution design can have in the context of educational research, which in this case also included the SPARK logo design and Web interface.

A thorough description and analysis of the iterative design, development, implementation and evaluation of SPARK (Self and Peer Assessment Resource Kit) can be found at: http://cleo.murdoch.edu.au/gen/aset/confs/aset-herdsa2000/procs/freeman.html or in a published paper form (Freeman & McKenzie, 2000). SPARK is based on formulae developed and refined in the UK in the early 1990s (Goldfinch, 1994).

SPARK
Self & Peer Assessment Resource Kit

Fig. 2: The SPARK logo designed by the author to represent self and peer assessment

How does SPARK work?

SPARK is essentially a database accessed through a Web interface with subject set-up operated by the lecturer who can batch enrol students and groups from a class list which must include student numbers. Students can also form their own groups without the lecturer's intervention if this is advantageous to the particular project or learning situation (e.g. for part-time distance education scenarios). The lecturer sets cut-off dates for group formation and the entering of ratings by students and also enters criteria for the self and peer assessment process.

A sample set of criteria is available in SPARK (Goldfinch, 1994) but it is recommended that unique relevant criteria are developed in negotiation with students as part of the group formation process, and according to the learning objectives.

Category: Efficient functioning of group
Helping the group to function well as a team
Level of enthusiasm and participation
Organising the team and ensuring things get done
Performing tasks efficiently
Suggesting ideas
Understanding what is required
Category: Leadership
Chasing and co-ordinating
Deciding who does what and when
Integrating everything at the end to answer the problem
Category: Number crunching
Analysis and cross checking
Data & formula entry and formatting
Finding out how to solve problem
Getting new data
Category: Writing report
Editing format, style, grammar, spell
Getting extra references and appraising their usefulness
Producing diagrams, figures, tables
Typing

Sample criteria (developed from Goldfinch, 1994)

The criteria can be set to be 'prompting' (i.e. not contributing to the SPARK factor but causing students to reflect) or 'final' criteria that are used in calculations. This feature has not yet been explored in the design faculty pilot schemes. Once criteria have been negotiated and set up in the database, students can practise entering ratings with the knowledge that they can be revised up to the cut-off date. The ratings are numerical and can range from -1 to 5 according to the lecturer's intention or through student negotiation. The range used in the design case studies mentioned in this paper was -1 to 3 and an extract from a student handout below describes the meaning ascribed in these particular cases.

> Try entering self and peer assessment ratings for yourself and your team colleagues using the pop-up numbers next to the questions using the guide below:
>
> 3 = a major contribution
> 2 = average contribution 'average' here means much the same as the rest of the team.
> 1 = below average
> 0 = no contribution to this aspect
> -1 = a detrimental effect in this aspect

The students log in to SPARK where they can view frequently asked questions and comments from other students about their experience with the system. When entering ratings they can view a practice form or try a 'live' entry which can be revised later.

This is a sample form from a group of 3 with one section completed using the criteria from a second year typography research subject.

When the rating cut-off date has been passed the lecturer can export a spreadsheet of all the students and groups which includes SPARK factors for Self and Peer Assessment (SPA) and for Self Assessment compared to Peer Assessment (SA/PA).

Please fill out all fields in the self and peer assessment form and then click on submit at the bottom of the form.

Criteria	John Smith	Sarah Ng	Jane Fong
Leadership:			
Understanding and articulating what was required	-1	3	0
Taking a main role in the live debate	3	-1	2
Integrating everything towards a quality result	0	2	-1
Functioning of the group:	John Smith	Sarah Ng	Jane Fong
Suggesting ideas			
Performing tasks efficiently			
Level of enthusiasm & participation			
Helping the group to function well as a team			
Debate Responses:	John Smith	Sarah Ng	Jane Fong
Ideas or preparation for the live debate			
Contributing to the depth of research about the typographer			
Contributing to the clarity and cogency of the online submissions			

Fig. 3: A screen clip showing the ratings entry process

The lecturer then adds the group marks and uses the SPA factor multiplied by the group mark to calculate individual marks. If the SPA factor is 1.0 then the group mark multiplied by this will remain the same meaning that the student has an average performance when all criteria are taken into account by self and peers. A SPA factor above 1.0 will clearly increase an individual's mark and a factor below 1.0 will have a reducing affect. The ratings of each student for every other criteria can also be exported and may be used for formative feedback (careful consideration required).

The advantages and disadvantages of SPARK

This Web-based approach has several advantages when compared with paper-based methods.

For students: the use of multiple assessment criteria can better reflect the variety of group contributions; the flexibility of changing and customising criteria can encourage deep approaches to the learning process; it improves confidentiality as they can access the system from home; it extends time for reflection and re-evaluation as they can change their ratings as often as they wish until a pre-determined cut-off date.

For staff: it saves time by automating the process of collecting and calculating adjustment factors based on complex formulae from multiple entries; there is a reduction in error as data is entered directly by students; there is very little extra work as numbers of groups increase; it has potential to improve student learning from group work tasks; it produces data which can be used fairly for both summative and formative assessment purposes.

The disadvantages identified from staff and student comments are in the areas of technical difficulties and understanding how SPARK factors affect individual marks:

- students and staff need to be familiar with computers and log-in procedures (a significant number of design students and lecturers expressed techno-phobic tendencies and some actively reject involvement with computers);
- students and staff are easily 'turned off' by any instability of the server and database; stability of operation and continuity of access are vital for any system to be effective, particularly when it concerns assessment; and
- students and staff are not usually mathematically inclined and have difficulty in understanding the effect that SPARK factors will have on individual marks.

In all but one case study so far (Freeman & McKenzie, 2000) the advantages have far outweighed the disadvantages. Many of the disadvantages appear to be a result of poor technical planning and support or the lack of preparation in explanation of the process.

The issue of 'teacher conceptions' highlighted earlier in the paper could give SPARK a definite advantage. The fact that criteria have to be identified and negotiated in the context of a learning task encourages the lecturer to consider alignment within the 'eco-system' of learning objectives, learning activities and assessment criteria (Biggs, 1999).

Implementing SPARK for design subjects

The implementation of SPARK in other faculties at UTS has been successful with a number of lessons learned (Freeman & McKenzie, 2000). Recommended conditions for successful implementation include:

- assessment criteria designed specifically for the group assignment, preferably in negotiation with students;
- continuous and reliable accessibility of SPARK from the beginning of the group task;
- thorough appreciation and value by staff for SPARK's usefulness in enhancing group process and encouraging learning opportunities;
- staff able to give students a clear understanding of how it works, why it is being introduced and how it will affect the summative assessment process;
- students regular use of other Web resources for learning in the subject so that SPARK is not the only aspect requiring Web access; and
- staff feel supported at all levels by their colleagues and academic departments and technical support personnel.

It is not surprising that these points are consistent with the results of previous research on the implementation of other educational technologies (Alexander & McKenzie, 1998).

Case studies

Web-based case study 1 – visual communications: design studies research

Staff/student: 2 lecturers – 56 third year students

Mode: groups (3 to 6) met in two 28-student groups, for 2 hours each week with the lecturer for discussions/workshops (40 page reader purchased week 1 of 8)

Outline of brief: students to research an aspect of 'love' in the context of a comparison between design research and sociological research methods. The final research report to include statistical and observational results and outline the design of a 'product' arising from the findings of the research.

Assessment: research task in 3 parts to constitute 70% of the overall subject comprising:

- part 1 – Interim group presentation week 6 assessed 20%;
- part 2 – final presentation 20%; and
- part 3 – final research report 30%

Self and peer assessment (SPARK) was applied at the end of the process (with criteria agreed by week 2), and students then had ten days after the deadline to submit ratings. This group of students had previously used SPARK twice for group-based assessment and it was felt that there was no incentive necessary to encourage the students to enter ratings. The UTS Online system was used to provide announcements and access to SPARK.

Category	Criteria	Criteria Type
Functioning of Group	Consistency of creative input	Final
Functioning of Group	Level of enthusiasm and participation	Final
Functioning of Group	Respect factor	Final
Research	Clarity in group discussions	Final
Research	Contribution to framing the question	Final
Research	Gathering research material	Final
The Final Report	Level of involvement in the final report	Final
The Presentation	Involvement in planning presentation	Final
The Presentation	Preparing material for presentation	Final

Fig. 4: A screen clip of the criteria allocation process

Analysis of results:

Twelve out of the group did not submit ratings. In these cases the students' SPA (self and peer assessment) factor relied on the average of their peers ratings of them.

SPARK caused a variation from the group mark ranging from 0.76 of the group mark to 1.11 and by coincidence both students were part of the same group. The spreadsheet for these two students is shown below and it is worth dwelling on this example to explain one of the formative feedback opportunities with SPARK factors.

Group Name	Time submitted	Date	SA/PA	SPA	Group /100	S&PA Applied	Final / 70
DT3	...	...	0.00	1.11	60.7	67.4	47.2
DT3	22:41	15/10/2001	1.69	0.76	60.7	46.1	32.3

Fig. 5: A spreadsheet example showing SPARK factor calculations

This instance shows that the first student received a credit rather than a pass due to the SPA factor being applied and the second student received a fail mark of 46.1 instead of a pass, which the rest of the group received.

A formative feedback opportunity arises in this example when considering the SA/PA column. This factor is the ratio of the student's own assessment of themselves with that of their peers. It is interesting to note that the first student was one of the twelve who did not submit ratings as can be seen from the blank date and time columns. This student did not take the opportunity to contribute to their own mark but their peers considered them to have performed well against the range of specified criteria. However, the second student rated themselves very highly, perhaps feeling that they had not contributed, or feeling that the group 'ganged up' on them. It is very important that students have the opportunity to do this especially in cases where they feel the group scenario was unfair regarding their contribution (Goldfinch, 1994).

In light of the students' previous exposure to SPARK it was decided to publish both the SPA and SA/PA ratings with the assessment explaining the ways in which they were calculated. The charts shown here are from statistical information from UTS Online (operated using BlackBoard CourseInfo software).

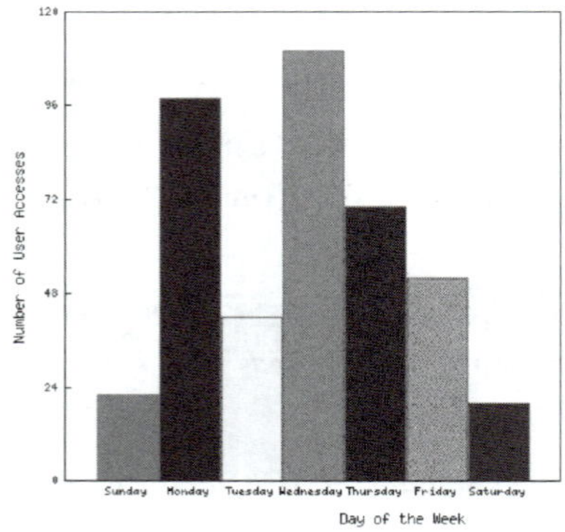

Fig. 6: Chart showing the average number of accesses on each day of the week

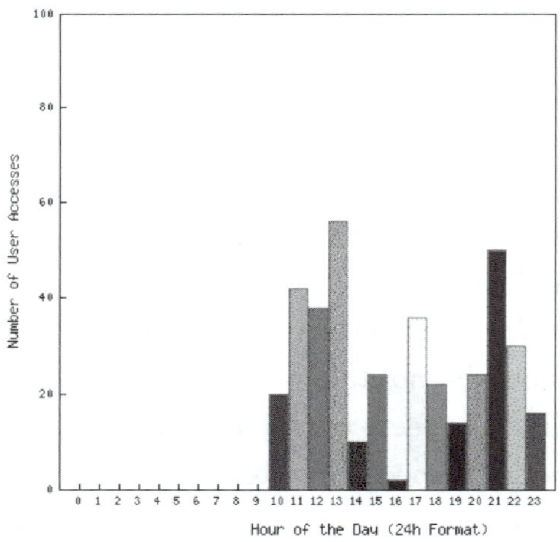

Fig. 7: Chart showing the average number of accesses on each hour of the day

It is clear that 'out of hours' access is important to students in that a significant number of accesses occur at weekends and evening times. The next chart shows three distinct phases of access throughout the project, and because this group of students left the faculty for work experience after the deadline, Web-based self and peer assessment had the advantage of minimal disruption to the completion of marks and feedback.

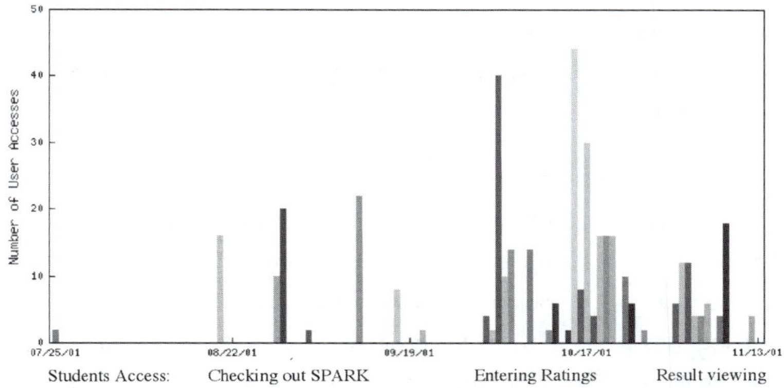

Fig. 8: Chart showing the actual number of accesses over the project period

There were a total of 314 accesses (excluding lecturers) and it appears that 27 students did not access UTS Online at all. However we know that only 12 did not submit ratings, so this means that some groups entered ratings together using one of the groups UTS Online logon accounts to access SPARK.

The students in this project had used SPARK twice previously and the lecturers received no negative comments about the process. The lecturer co-ordinating this subject commented:

> This process has been so easy, we have had no complaints which is unusual in this group situation, and I feel that the fairness and anonymity of the process has allowed students to engage more fully. It has also saved time at the end of semester when there are so many assessments to collate.

One student commented that SPARK allowed her to relax into the group work knowing that extra effort would be rewarded and those who didn't do anything would get fewer marks. Another student had previously put in an official appeal against SPARK which resulted in ten email exchanges, and after an hour-long interview he remarked that he now believed that SPARK should be used for all group-assessed projects. The appeal process was very interesting for the lecturer concerned and resulted in the development of an analogy to explain how self and peer assessment works:

The author's analogy in explanation of self and peer assessment in a group project:

When a group is working together on a complex task the contributions each member makes can vary considerably at different stages and in different aspects of the project. If the group receives one mark then how is it to be shared? The analogy of sharing an apple is useful here. If a group receives an overall mark for the project according to criteria based on the learning objectives for that project, there needs to be a second stage where the group members get a fair share of apple for their efforts in obtaining that group mark according to agreed group work criteria.

It is educationally very important for students to receive feedback from peers, but also that there is the opportunity for self reflection on one's own contributions, and that both of these have an influence on the individual assessment result.

It can then be appreciated that if a group obtained a high mark (big apple) it is still possible for a member of that group to get a lower individual mark (less apple) than someone in a group with a lower group mark (a bigger share from a smaller apple).

Web-based case study 2 - visual communications: community design project

Staff/student: 2 lecturers - 41 third year students

Mode: groups (4 to 7) met in groups for 1 hour (approximately) each week with the supervising lecturer for discussion and progress reporting.

Outline of brief: Students to work in groups on 'live' design projects for not-for-profit groups from client briefs to production. Nine projects were put forward and students self-selected groups according to interest and expertise.

Assessment: as with all projects in the B.Design degree the learning objectives fit into five categories: research; concept; process; communication; and professionalism.

The assessment criteria for each assessment task are developed according to the nature of the project and its potential as a vehicle of learning. In order to give a clear picture of the degree of peer and client involvement in the assessment of this project an extract from the student handout is included here:

Part 1.

Design solution – 60% (assessed as a group and then using SPARK to obtain an individual mark)

Research: information research, understanding of client's needs – 20% (supervisor and client)

Concept: creativity of ideas and solution – 20% (students, supervisor and client)

Communication: effective communication objective to the specified target audience – 20% (supervisor and client). Evidence from actual user testing will be rewarded in this criteria.

Part 2.

Design presentation – to client and class – 30% (assessed as a group)

Professional attitude – 15% (supervisor and client)

Professional and appropriate presentation techniques – 15% (supervisor and client)

Part 3.

Self and Peer Assessment with Reflection statement – 10%

a) SPARK (Web-based self and peer assessment) will be applied to the 60% design solution mark to give each student an individual mark based on agreed criteria for teamwork (see separate handout).

b) Personal reflection is an online survey of multiple choice questions with some short answer questions (e.g. What did I learn about my abilities as a designer in this project? What did I learn about the role of the designer in society in doing this project? etc).

The 10% mark is for completing these two tasks (5% each)

Some of these students had experienced SPARK prior to this project but for a number of reasons the 5% incentive to complete ratings was thought to be appropriate. Assessment criteria for this project were agreed with students as follows:

Analysis of results

In this project, 9 out of the 41 students did not enter ratings, leaving their assessment dependent upon assessment by their peers against the 9 criteria.

It is interesting to note the range of ratings used out of the 1,251 ratings entered: -1 (detrimental to the group on a particular criteria) was used 8 times; 0 (no contribution) 26 times; and 3 (major

SPARK
Self & Peer Assessment Resource Kit

- Subjects
- Students
- Teams
- Assessment Criteria
- Assessment Results
- Passwords

Logout

Criteria for Subject 87552 Design Project.

Category	Criteria	Criteria Type
Client Contact	Offering help in maintaining client contact	Final
Client Contact	Quality of contribution in client meetings	Final
Client Contact	Trying to really understand the clients needs	Final
Functioning of group	Consistency of creative input throughout the project	Final
Functioning of group	Do you respect this person more or less having engaged with them on this project	Final
Functioning of group	Helping the group to function well as a team	Final
Functioning of group	Level of enthusiasm & participation	Final
The Presentation	Help in preparing material for the presentation	Final
The Presentation	Involvement in working out how the presentation should go	Final

Fig. 9: A screen clip showing criteria for the case study project

contribution) 510 times. At the time of negotiating the criteria the students were keen to be able to use the -1 rating. It was thought by staff that this punitive rating could be abused but these figures show that students are using the -1 and 0 ratings responsibly.

The SPARK factors produced ranged from 1.15 times the group mark to 0.81 of the group mark. This means that for a group mark of 80% the highest rated student would have received 92% and the lowest rating student would have received 64.8%. It can be seen from the extent of this range that if the group mark was 90% a high scoring student would have received 103.5%. However, this is a very rare situation because for a group to gain such a high group mark it is likely that all members would need to be fully contributing resulting in equal SPARK factors close to 1.0. In any case it is important to make clear to students what the range can be and the percentage of the total final mark to which SPARK will be applied. In this case study UTS Online was used to explain the Community projects available, negotiate criteria and provide access to SPARK and the online survey. The average number of accesses to UTS Online was 10.73 per student over a nine-week period.

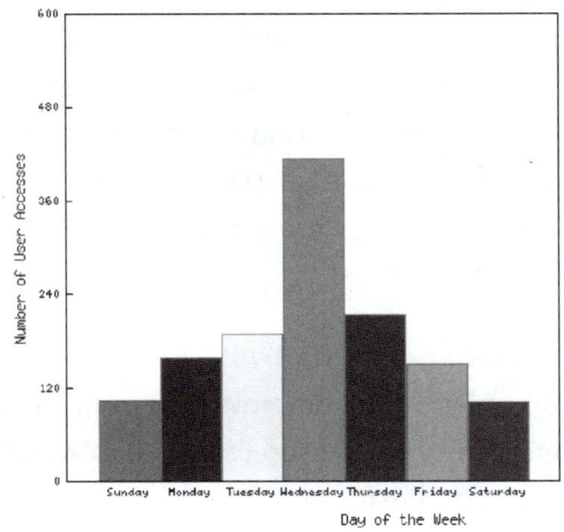

Fig. 10 : Chart showing the average number of accesses on each day of the week

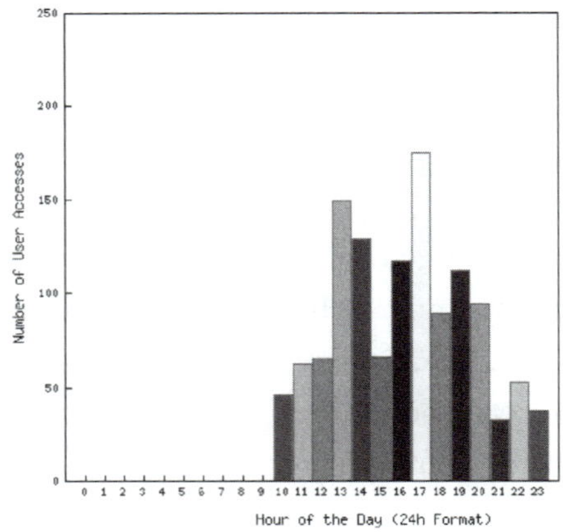

Fig. 11 Chart showing the average number of accesses on each hour of the day

Through the timings of students' access it is possible to measure the degree to which students are using the flexibility that Web solutions offer. The students had sessions with supervisors on Wednesday afternoons between 13.00 hrs and 17.00 hrs which explains the high access rates on Wednesdays during these times, but there are a significant number of off-campus 'hits' at evenings and weekends.

Issues and conclusions

The possibilities of using SPARK for direct formative feedback have not yet been explored in Design subjects. It is apparent that many students rate themselves below their peers ratings of them in a number of criteria and it could be educationally useful for students to be able to access feedback on individual criteria alongside the SPA and SA/PA factors mentioned in the section 'How does SPARK work?' This feature is on the SPARK wish list.

In conclusion, it has been shown here that with an understanding of educational research and careful implementation, group work can provide an excellent opportunity to develop essential graduate attributes in an undergraduate design course.

It is also the author's experience that self and peer assessment is a valid and valuable addition to the learning environment in design education and that paper-based methods of calculation cannot practically accommodate the mathematical complexities needed for the fair distribution of individual marks in group-based assessment.

The careful integration of Web-based self and peer assessment (in this case SPARK) can provide important benefits including anonymity, scalability, broad ranging criteria and a practical solution to many problems associated with group work.

It is also clear that students' perception of the fairness of group-based assessment has improved radically through the implementation of SPARK and this fact has encouraged other design lecturers to begin pilot schemes for the coming year.

It is hoped that some confidence has been imparted to those considering the implementation of group-based assessment and highlighted issues for others. SPARK is not a software product but an on-going educational research project. SPARK is openly available for lecturers or teachers to apply as part of their teaching strategy. Please contact the author for further details.

Notes

The student comments reproduced here are in support of the conclusions mentioned earlier and come from reflection statements (2000) and an online survey (2001). Comments were made in response to open-ended questions about students' learning and their experience of the online services during the Web-based case studies.

The first comment is from a student describing her feelings about a particular member of the group who she named in the reflection statement:

> ... she has been a role model for me in this project and possibly my future career as a designer. I hope that I can still have the chance to

express my gratefulness through SPARK
Spring, 2000

I had to take on a group member's designs and develop them further to meet the client's needs. A sensitivity to their design and the intentions of the original work was important.
Spring, 2000

What I will say, and I don't want to be too harsh ... is that one particular group member must bear some of the responsibility for creating friction between the group as a whole and the client.
Spring, 2000

I just felt that the group would have worked better without ***** and his pre-menstrual mood swings every day. OK, he was a decision maker, but in terms of a contribution, I gave a below average.
Spring, 2000

I learnt that being able to work as part of a group is important, and communication with group members is vital. I discovered that some of my strengths lie in my abilities to work with people. I also felt a confidence in my ability to conceptualise and in my 'visual eye' for what works and what doesn't. I have come through this project, good and bad aspects aside, feeling much more confident in my abilities as a designer.
Spring, 2000

I feel that the online rating is a fair system and that I can be honest about my views on other group members. I also think that at the present this sort of online service is still a 'token' one, because it is only a small aspect of the course that tries to use the Internet in a relevant way.
Spring, 2001 (online survey)

This project helped me understand the role of the designer as a member of a larger team. Through the subject I became aware of the fact that as a designer I needed to be able to communicate and discuss issues with the client, and find a level that both sides could

relate to each other on. It also made we aware that the final decision was the client's rather than the design team.
Spring, 2001 (online survey)

The online service was OK. As I come to use the Internet more and more, this option sits fine ... though sometimes I'm out of contact for a long while, as I don't feel like being computery, and then I feel I'm probably missing stuff ... I will still always want the face-to-face contact.
Spring, 2001 (online survey)

From what I can tell, the online service is much improved from last year and is really accessible. From someone who doesn't as a rule like the Internet, the UTS online facilities are pretty inoffensive and easy to use.
Spring, 2001 (online survey)

I felt somewhat disadvantaged as I do not enjoy Internet access (as my Internet connection is slow) and therefore my impatience does not allow me to fully utilise UTSOnline.
Spring, 2001 (online survey)

I felt it somewhat frustrating that the server was constantly down at the time of assessment. When the service was running I found that it displayed old data, which proved to be quite confusing as we hadn't previously utilised the service extensively, and I wasn't certain if this was my error or that of the program.
Spring, 2001 (online survey)

References

Alexander, S. & McKenzie, J. (1998), *An Evaluation of Information Technology Projects for University Learning* (Canberra: AGPS)

Assiter, A. (ed.) (1995), *Transferable Skills in Higher Education* (London: Kogan Page)

Biggs, J.B. (1999), *Teaching for Quality Learning at University* (Buckingham: SHRE and OU Press) Boud, D. (1988), 'Moving towards autonomy: developing student autonomy in learning' (London: Kogan Page)

Boud, D., Cohen, .R. & Sampson, J. (ed.) (2001), *Peer Learning in Higher Education* (London: Kogan Page)

Candy, P.C.G. & O'Leary, J. (1994), *Developing Lifelong Learners through Undergraduate Education* (Canberra: NBEET, Australian Government Publishing Service)

Cheng, W. & Warren, M. (2000), 'Making a difference: using peers to assess individual students' contributions to a group project', *Teaching in Higher Education*, 5(2)

Cohen, R. & Sampson, J. (2001), in Boud, D. *Implementing and Managing Peer Learning. Peer Learning in Higher Education*, pp. 50–66 (London: Kogan Page)

Conway, R., Kember, D., Sivan, A. & Wu, M. (1993), 'Peer assessment of an individual's contribution to a group work project', *Assessment and Evaluation in Higher Education*, 18(1), 45–56

Drew, L. (2000) , 'A disciplined approach: Learning tyo practice as design teachers in the university' in conference proceedings, Swann, C. & Young, E (eds), Re-inventing Design Education in the University', pp. 187-194 (Perth, Australia: School of Design, Curtin Univesrtiy of Technology

Falkichov, N. (2001), *Learning Together: Peer Tutoring in Higher Education* (London: Routledge)

Freeman, M. & McKenzie, J. (2000), 'Self and peer assessment of student teamwork: Designing, implementing and evaluating SPARK, a confidential, Web-based system', in *Flexible Learning for a Flexible Society*, proceedings of ASET-HERDSA 2000 Conference, Toowoomba, Qld, 2-5 July (ASET and HERDSA.

http://cleo.murdoch.edu.au/gen/aset/confs/aset-herdsa2000/procs/freeman.html)

Garner, S. & Duckworth, A. (2000), *The Employability of Design Graduates: A Study of Competencies Achieved Through Undergraduate Design Education: Re-inventing Design Education in the University* (Perth, West Australia: Curtin University of Technology)

Goldfinch, J. & Raeside, R. (1990), 'Development of a peer assessment technique for obtaining individual marks on a group project', *Assessment and Evaluation in Higher Education*, 15(3), 21–31

Goldfinch, J. (1994), 'Further developments in peer assessment of group projects', *Assessment and Evaluation in Higher Education*, 19(1), 29–35

Gow, L., Kember, .D. (1993), 'Conceptions of teaching and their relationship to student learning', *British Journal of Educational Psychology*, (63): 20–33

Griffiths, S., Houston, K. & Lazenbatt, A. (1995), *Enhancing Student Learning Through Peer Tutoring in Higher Education* (Coleraine: University of Ulster)

Jaques, D. (2000), *Learning in Groups* (London: Kogan Page)

McKenzie, J. (2001), 'Variation in ways of experiencing change in teaching, the development and use of learning technologies and the likely consequences for student learning', paper presented at the 9th Improving Student Learning Conference, Edinburgh, September 2001

Prosser, M., Trigwell, .K. (1999), *Understanding Learning and Teaching: The Experience of Higher Education* (Buckingham: SRHE/Open University Press)

Ramsden, P. (1992), *Learning to Teach in Higher Education* (London: Routledge)

Sampson, J. Cohen, R., Boud, D. & Anderson, G. (1999), *Reciprocal Peer Learning: A Guide for Staff and Students* (Sydney: University of Technology, Sydney)

Samuelowicz, K. (1994), *Teaching Conceptions and Teaching Practice: A Case of Assessment. Phenomenography – Philosophy and Practice*, pp. 343–354. (Brisbane: Queensland University of Technology)

Thompson, D. (2000), 'Learning and teaching in design education: creative holistic approaches and educational theory combined in the design and implementation of a Web-based typography research project', in conference proceedings, Swann, C. & Young, E. (eds.), *Re-inventing Design Education in the University*', pp. 359–366 (Perth, Australia: School of Design, Curtin University of Technology)

Toffler, A. (1991), *Powershift: Knowledge, Wealth, and Violence at the Edge of the 21st Century* (Bantam Books)

Biographical note

Darrall Thompson is currently a full-time lecturer in the visual communication programme at the University of Technology, Sydney. Experience as a designer includes 15 years as a chartered designer in London (MCSD) in the fields of publishing, design and advertising followed by ten years' Australian experience teaching and consulting in visual communication and Web design with clients such as Clemengers and Apple Computer.

Development work in the Centre for Learning and Teaching at UTS led to a number of research projects and pilot schemes resulting in a recent Faculty Teaching Award for innovative use of educational technologies.

Currently completing a Masters by Research in the area of online learning environments and self and peer assessment and teaching in the areas of Web design, visual identity, semiotics, typography, design history and information design.

Understanding learning styles: implications for design education in the university

20

Jenny Toynbee Wilson

Faculty of Design, Architecture and Building, University of Technology, Sydney, Australia

Abstract

In recent years, pressure on the resources of design schools has resulted in significant shifts in approaches to learning and teaching. Schools must emphasise programmes that enable students to become effective learners. One key to achieving this goal is helping students to understand their own learning styles. Another is using this knowledge more effectively to enhance individual potential and help students manage their own learning with access to a large and diverse range of educational resources. A ten-year research programme conducted in the visual communication programme at the University of Technology, Sydney, has resulted in a greater appreciation of how design students learn, and how this knowledge can be applied effectively to extending learning opportunities within the university. This paper discusses the research programme, and how understanding learning styles can be used in curriculum development and the enhancement of teaching and learning in design schools.

Introduction

This paper discusses a research programme conducted over ten years in the visual communication programme at the University of Technology, Sydney. The research has resulted in a greater appreciation of how design students learn, and how this knowledge can be applied effectively in curriculum development and the enhancement of learning and teaching in design schools.

The challenge of change

> It is not as if we can avoid change since it pursues us in every way. The answer is not in avoiding change but in turning the tables by facing it head on. The new mind set is to exploit change before it victimises us. We can learn to reject unwanted change more effectively while at the same time becoming more effective at accomplishing desired improvements.
> Fullan (1991)

In 1989, the School of Design was severed from its symbiotic relationship with the School of Art and became four of many programmes offered by the newly named University of Technology, Sydney (UTS) (CTEC, 1987). Regardless of angry protest, our change of allegiance and status was irrevocable and the future appeared to be daunting as we confronted new challenges (Dawkins, 1988, 1989). Defining the new discipline of design in such a way as to be perceived as authentic to the many sceptics, led to a major re-evaluation of aims, strategies, curricula, and the desired profile of a university graduate with a four-year honours degree in design.

'The most socially useful thing to learning in the modern world is the process of learning, a continuing openness to experience, an incorporation into oneself of the process of change' (Knowles, 1984). A course model developed that substantially increased the role and relevance of research and theory and integrated all inputs by establishing a thematic structure at each progressive stage. To complement this, the creation of a lively, supportive learning environment was agreed to be essential. 'If the students of today are to be the creative managers of change for tomorrow then I believe they need learning environments which are dramatically different from those which currently prevail' (Bawden, 1987).

Change of intake system

Change was constant. In the context of defining Australia as a pluralistic, multicultural society, anti-discrimination legislation was introduced which was rigorously upheld by the university. As a consequence, in 1991, the system of selecting undergraduates was radically overhauled. Entry to all programmes was to be openly competitive regardless of which subjects an applicant had undertaken at senior school. No programme could select students on the basis of essential prerequisite subjects. This meant that we could insist no longer that students had studied subjects such as art or even a sound level of English! Our practice of selecting students on the basis of an interview supported by a visual portfolio was deemed discriminatory and ceased.

Paradoxically, other political agendas were promoting the notion that perceptions of Australia should change from a 'lucky' country to a 'clever' country. This faction successfully lobbied for science and mathematics subjects undertaken at a high level of secondary school education to be preferred for university entry. As a result, applicants for university places from the senior school system in New South Wales were assessed on a competitive tertiary entry score aggregated to favour strong performance in science and mathematics.

Incompatibility of new cohorts and teaching/learning strategies

Although distracted by the immediate issues of physical relocation and technological change, over the next two years it started to emerge that many of the students enrolled under the new intake policy differed significantly from any previously experienced. Individual students were described variously as: over competitive, teacher dependent and poor in time management; unwilling actively to experiment, visually illiterate and lacking ideas; and lazy, disinterested procrastinators who were clever at using avoidance strategies.

Given that the majority of our intake had enrolled from secondary schools with entry scores that placed them in the top 3% of the state education system, none could be accused of inherent laziness. But we had a serious morale problem affecting both staff and students. As Head of the Department of Visual Communication, it was my responsibility to find some solution. In 1993, a student's disgruntled complaint that he did not know how to think like a designer so how could we expect him to start designing[1], was both shocking and intriguing. This complaint provided the impetus and the starting point for research.

Research methodologies

I decided to address the problem by conducting research into the motivations and expectations of the new student cohort. From study of alternative research paradigms a strategy for my research was offered by action research focusing on students' personal experience of learning. The roots of action research lie in the work of Kurt Lewin in the 1940s (Lewin, 1951) whose model demonstrates the process of taking action to promote social change. This spiral methodology of observation, planning, action and reflection to modify and direct further action was later adopted to improve teaching/learning practice (Garr & Kemmis, 1986; Kemmis & MacTaggart 1988; McKernan, 1991; Kember & Kelly, 1993).

Action research starts with the identification of a problem and an incentive to find a solution. The methodology has much in common with the cyclical process of designing. As a designer, problem solving is a constant challenge and the incentive to find a solution was powerful and urgent.

Action research project aims and expectations

The aims of the action research project were to ensure the 'thematic concern' (problem) was well contextualised, defined and presented. This would involve willing participants as the 'critical community' and include a 'critical observer' from the University Centre for Learning and Teaching in the monitoring and reflection process. We would be required to reflect critically on teaching and learning in the context of recent changes with the aim of improving the environment, context or conditions in which our practice took place. As action research is an iterative process of initiation and testing before change can be further evaluated, we expected that ongoing modifications to the methodology may be necessary in that the outcome of research and evaluation could lead to significant rethinking requiring further major change (Kemmis & MacTaggart, 1988).

In developing the methodology, an idiosyncratic range of strategies were employed including the examination of student records, and the use of surveys and student subject evaluations. Information from focus groups, modelled on nominal group techniques, contributed to the anecdotal records compiled from teaching diaries, reflective annotations and notes recording unsolicited casual comments. This approach has been described as, 'narrative-verbatim descriptions of meaningful incidents and events which have been observed in the behavioural setting where the action takes place' (McKernan, 1991).

An additional direction and strategy for the research was offered by approaches which shift the perspective from formal models that embody assumptions about chains of causality, to one which focused on students' personal experience of learning. This method of: 'research rooted in phenomenology which derive from a direct exploration of students' experiences of learning ... involves a shift not just of methodology, but of perspective ... and are illuminating. They present a description of student learning from an unusual perspective – that of the student' (Entwistle & Hounsell, 1975).

Research into students' prior learning

To investigate the root cause of the student's accusation, namely that we had assumed an unreasonable level of experience and prior knowledge, we examined each student's academic transcript. This gave clear evidence that the majority of our new cohort of undergraduates had gained a place by achieving high marks in science and mathematics, often at the expense of subjects in art, humanities and social sciences. Discovering our novices' attitudes to learning and motives for enrolling in visual communication became essential to understanding the breadth of the problem. Focus groups revealed that students' experience of learning consisted predominately of passive involvement requiring quantities of information to be memorised and regurgitated in the stress-laden atmosphere of state-controlled examinations[2]. Our new intake had been highly parent and teacher directed, and had chosen their school subjects strategically to gain a high score and a wide choice of study options. It became clear that the majority had experienced, and had been highly successful in a teaching/learning environment that was diametrically opposite to the student-centred, experiential learning strategy that we were attempting to implement, which aimed to encourage deep learning and student autonomy (Boud, Keogh, & Walker 1986; Boud, 1988; Boud & Feletti, 1991; Candy, 1991; Ramsden, 1991).

Motivation to study design

Although our novice students are highly intelligent high achievers, by choosing to study design each has rejected the subject areas in which they excelled[3]. Their collective experience is well illustrated by Ivan Illich who sceptically attacks the pedagogic traditions of western education by claiming them to be dictatorial, oppressive and dis-empowering:

> The products of our education system don't know how to learn, they only know how to be taught. Traditional pedagogy conditions students to respond to the teacher's stimuli; the initiative in the transaction is almost totally that of the teacher; the role of the student is to react.
> Illich (1973)

First-year students offer many and varied reasons for being motivated to study design, a practice and profession of which they know little and understand even less[4]. With the rejection of a past experience of learning as a primary motive, it became clear that the students were operating in a vacuum of vague expectations with a 'wait and see' attitude[5]. Few had conscious vocational goals and a number revealed that they had not realised that the programme was one of four design programmes, nor could any articulate what had motivated their choice[6]. This group had taken a speculative risk in anticipation of making a successful choice. Their hope that studying visual communication would be exciting and cater to some unspecified needs, was making students highly sensitive and reactive to what and how learning was presented and highly critical if it was failing to meet their ill-defined expectations[7].

Relevance of learning

Many educators state that students must appreciate the relevance of learning if commitment is to be sustained, and that students with distinct vocational goals perform better than those with inarticulate goals (Boud, 1988; Candy, 1991; Ramsden, 1991). Our assumption that enrolling students had an intrinsic desire to study design coupled to the extrinsic motive of finding desirable employment proved to be wrong. The group as a whole was projecting almost total responsibility for the direction of their learning to the content and strategy of the programme and the ability of teaching staff to activate their level of extrinsic and intrinsic motivation (Petri, 1981; Biggs, 1991).

The situation we were facing was as complex as that we demanded of our students. We had to recognise that positive change must operate in both directions. If we expected our students to change their way of learning, we had to move out of our comfort zone of familiar practice which was based on the assumption that first year students were visually literate, had some experience of the design process and awareness of the professional practice to which each might aspire. We had to find a way of beginning the change process by convincing students that learning by designing was different and unfamiliar but had the potential to be personally enriching.

The paradox of learning design without any experience has been examined by Donald Schön:

> He is expected to plunge into designing, trying from the outset to do what he does not yet know how to do, in order to get the sort of experience that will help him learn what designing means. He cannot

> make an informed choice to make this plunge because he does not yet grasp its essential meanings, and his instructors cannot convey these to him until he has had the requisite experience. Thus he must jump in without knowing, indeed, in order to discover-what he needs to learn.
> Schön (1987)

It is certain that our novice students were exhibiting 'the feelings of mystery, confusion, frustration and futility' identified by Schön (1987).

The experiential learning model

Of greatest significance to defining the attributes of learners were the theories of David Kolb who drew on original work of Kurt Lewin (1951). The Kolb/Lewin model of experiential learning presents a cycle of cognitive change in an iterative process that involves the constant movement through four activities. Kolb advocates that:

> ... by combining characteristics of learning and problem solving and conceiving them as a single process, we can come closer to understanding how it is that man generates from his experience, concepts, rules and principles to guide his behaviour in new situations and how he modifies these concepts in order to improve their effectiveness.
> Kolb (1984)

The activities presented by Kolb are termed and described as follows:

- *concrete experience*: learner focus is on personal experience; emphasises feeling states; concern for uniqueness; prefers the complexity of reality rather than theories; operates imaginatively; intuitive thinker; open to difference and change;
- *active experimentation*: learner focus is on influencing change; emphasises practical application; concern for what works rather than absolute truths; prefers active participation; operates actively and is task oriented; sequential thinker; values risk taking;
- *abstract conceptualisation*: learner focus is on using logic, ideas and concepts; emphasises thinking states; concern for neat systems and theories; prefers sequential planning and

quantitative analysis; operates systematically; convergent thinker; values rigour and discipline; and

- *reflective observation*: learner focus is on the meaning of ideas; emphasises understanding through observation and reflection; concern for truths and philosophies; prefers thought to action; operates by examining different perspectives; divergent thinker; values ideas but relies on personal thoughts to form opinions.

Kolb's learning style inventory

Kolb (1976) argues that learners have a preferred learning style, which occupies a position along certain psychological and behavioural dimensions ranging from concrete to abstract and from active to reflective. These learning styles incorporate the four stages of the learning process and are termed and summarised according to a learner's dominant abilities as follows:

- *converger*: abstract conceptualisation and active experimentation – this learner's strength lies in the practical application of ideas as solutions to well-structured problems that have perfect-fit solutions of technical rationality;
- *diverger*: concrete experience and reflective observation – this learner's strength lies in the imaginative ability and excels in viewing a situation from many perspectives through activities such as brain storming;
- *assimilator*: abstract conceptualisation and reflective observation – this learner's strength lies in the ability to create theoretical models and is characteristic of the basic sciences, mathematics and areas of pure research; and
- *accommodator*: concrete experience and active experimentation – this learner's strength lies in carrying out plans and experiments through involvement in new experiences which require some risk taking.

In 1993 I introduced the first-year students to my research project and encouraged the students to discuss their experiences of teaching and learning. Using a questionnaire adapted from Kolb's Learning Style Inventory (Kolb, 1976) the numerical scores from each student were plotted on a single diagram. This indicated the student group's learning style to be narrowly defined and predominantly that of *converger* with some indication of *assimilator*.

I extended the survey to include teaching staff, six graduates and ten non-teaching design colleagues to minimise the anomalies of a small sample. A more diverse span was evident but confirmed a strong bias towards the two remaining learning styles of *accommodator* and to a much lesser extent *diverger*. As there is much evidence to suggest that teaching is most often modelled on the experience of learning (Rogers, 1983), it was not surprising that the practice-based design teachers would prefer this learning style orientation and develop teaching strategies that replicated the master/apprenticeship model of the traditional art and design school. By comparing the results from students and staff, it had become immediately clear that our students' preferred learning styles were incompatible with our teaching strategy which was failing to respond to the expectations and needs of our new intake of learners.

To ensure that further curriculum change would not jeopardise the strengths of the existing programme but would enable deficiencies to be addressed, we examined the four key elements identified as essential for good teaching (Gibbs, 1992). The first key element is a well-structured knowledge base that supports the learning activity by linking new concepts with existing experience and knowledge.

A model for the processes of learning and designing

Thinking about thinking and learning is a new concept for first-year students to understand. The discovery that preferred learning styles may be different and subject to change provokes considerable interest from every student group[8]. As the processes of learning and designing are heuristic and share many characteristics, methodologies and goals it is possible to present a composite model that indicates the parallel processes of learning and designing and identifies the change that must occur when moving from one stage of the design process and learning mode to another:

- **problem identification and definition**; *learning mode*: accommodator/diverger; *requiring* the motivation to start and be open without bias to new situations;
- **task planning and management**; *learning mode*: converger/accommodator; *requiring* active investigation and practical applications;
- **research and evaluation**; *learning mode*: assimilator/converger; *requiring* critical thinking and logical systematic analysis;
- **ideation**; ***learning mode***: diverger/accommodator; *requiring*: creative thinking and the ability to handle unresolved tension;
- **idea selection and decision making**; *learning mode*: accommodator/converger; *requiring* a view from various perspectives with reliance on both research and intuition;
- **action and implementation**; *learning mode*: diverger/accommodator; *requiring* a commitment to take determined action with total involvement;
- **reflection-in-action**; *learning mode*: all combined; *requiring* conscious awareness and self monitoring while acting;
- **evaluation of process and progress**; *learning mode*: converger/assimilator; *requiring* impartial reflection to examine aims and identify improvements; and
- **refinement and completion**; ***learning mode***: accommodator/diverger; *requiring* a willingness to change to achieve aims.

The aim of the model is to help students see the real implications of their preferred learning styles. A further aim is to encourage students to extend themselves with our understanding of the personal risk involved as designing means learning in an unfamiliar way. It has been extremely valuable to have students considering the correlation between thinking, learning and designing[9]. It is clear that a sense of mutual understanding prevails, which alleviates early confusion and also stimulates ongoing discussion.

The usefulness of the composite model can also be illustrated by presenting examples of professional design projects that trace the development of a design concept from original briefing through stages of research, brain storming, client intervention, reflection, evaluation and refinement to final production and user/viewer responses. Each design concept, developmental visuals and finally produced work are evidence of a personally owned designer's approach which makes it possible for participants to describe the 'internal' process of designing as 'feelings' with which students can identify. Among the emotions evident from presentations are excitement and curiosity, frustration and anger, anxiety and stress, surprise and pleasure, disillusionment and disappointment, and pride and satisfaction. The motives for making a commitment to design are explained by participants as both extrinsic (financial income and reputation) and intrinsic (interest, discovery and challenge).

Learning by designing

As a result of the research, it has been possible to make the link between the learning process and that of designing as is indicated in the following observations:

- the individual world of the learner (and designer) is acknowledged in the context of the greater world of personal experiences, events and possibilities;
- the learner (and designer) is encouraged to expose themselves to the world beyond existing experience, through personal interaction and discovery;
- perceptions and understandings (and ideas) of the world are mediated by: personal knowledge, idiosyncratic characteristics, cultural and societal norms and expectations, belief systems, values and ethics;

- conception and perception are ontological processes as each view of the world as understood (and imagined) is predicated on, and informed by, past experience (previous idea or last design) and re-framed progressively (and continually refined);
- new constructions of meaning (improved ideas) are identified (visualised) and defined (synthesised) through a continual process of adaptation and modification of previous knowledge (the design process of reflection in action);
- to construct new meaning (develop imaginative, unique ideas) requires unknown elements (design phenomena and concepts) to be investigated (researched and experimented with) and interpreted (reflected on and critically evaluated); and
- the assimilation of new knowledge enables a new model of reality to be constructed (or designed) which forms the basis of further action (refinement of existing design - reformulated and redesigned; a new, alternative idea; a new design task).

A new teaching and learning strategy

The research findings revealed that the traditional experiential strategy employed in the design studio was alien to our new cohort of students and was potentially becoming dysfunctional. This realisation prompted us to re-conceptualise the design studio as a site for thinking about learning and how this understanding can enhance design thinking[10]. A reader is available to stimulate discussion at tutorials, which are run in rotation with a greatly reduced time spent in the design studio.

The development of the new teaching and learning strategy has been informed by a number of other issues. For some time we have debated whether our approach promotes deep or surface learning (Biggs, 1991). Of significance is that our high-achieving, over-competitive students are reluctant to present unrefined ideas because they risk: being seen not to know, having poor skills or clichéd ideas; being alone with a good idea when attempting to develop a social scene; or confronting possible failure. In addition, these students are strategic learners very geared to assessment outcomes (Entwistle, in Marton et al., 1984). We were concerned that assessment often appeared to emphasise the aesthetic appeal of the final product with the result that students became easily convinced that superficial style was a major factor which they could replicate.

Reflections on learning

To encourage a deep approach and reinforce the idea that our aim is to assess students' leaning rather than their ultimate product we rethought learning objectives and assessment criteria. Our approach was informed by the second of Gibbs' key elements of good teaching which states that learner activity should be active rather than passive and make connections with past learning through reflection which is then processed and related to abstract concepts and new meaning (Gibbs, 1992). Reflective portfolios are now a vital component of assessment. Students are required to provide evidence that they are beginning to understand the relationship between the processes of learning and designing. It has taken time for students to grasp the idea of analytical reflection on what each is learning and how this is progressing rather than producing descriptive ramblings on problems with ideas, skills and technology.

There continues to be signs of resistance[11] and a few strategic learners (Entwistle & Hounsell, 1975) find devious ways of writing what they think we want to read[12]. We also read some hilarious comments which constantly remind us of the naivety of many first-year students[13],[14],[15],[16]. Eventually, as the student group receives assessment feedback that indicates the importance placed on their ability to present evidence of understanding rather than design product, the collective mind set starts to shift.

Motivational context

The final key element of good teaching (Gibbs, 1992) identifies the motivational context which includes personal ownership of learning in an environment of positive encouragement that stimulates intrinsic motivation. The immediate relevance of what is taught to fulfil the learning needs of students is a positive factor that influences intrinsic motivation. By promptly recognising the problems faced by our first-year students and encouraging open discussion, students become more clear about the internal issues each must deal with when the experience of learning is new. We have aimed to develop a level of trust by acknowledging that each student must confront the insecurity of not knowing and the challenge of finding out why and how. We are trying to foster the belief that our role as teachers is to facilitate the process and to support each learner through the stages of transition.

Learning anything new challenges the student to suspend existing beliefs, address personal prejudices and keep an open mind. This demand can promote a sense of excitement and potential discovery or can result in reluctance to start the process. Fear of failure can block any action as the outcome is neither known nor guaranteed to be successful (Koberg & Bagnall, 1976). For our high-achieving students who have the expectation of continued success, overcoming this fear is the greatest problem[17]. Each move through the cycle of learning by designing requires students to be sufficiently motivated to change their attitude and their preferred learning style. In our experience, many of our students have great difficulty moving from the early stage of observation and literature research to that of active experimentation and practical engagement[18]. The tension and cognitive dissonance that the process promotes is often expressed as active resistance to change which is displayed in frustration and procrastination (Maslow, 1973).

However when there is sufficient motivation (too often this is the extrinsic pressure of a deadline) and the action required to overcome this stressful state is committed, students can become energised as new frameworks emerge, perceptions change and anomalies are resolved. This process is discussed frequently and features strongly in the reflective portfolio. At the very least, the open discussion raises students' conscious level of awareness of the process and the expectation that each will be an active participant. Kurt Lewin presents a succinct précis: 'learning occurs as result of a change in cognitive structures produced by changes in two types of forces, one: change in the cognitive field itself and two: change in the internal needs or motivation of the individual' (Lewin, 1951).

Carl Rogers, an inspirational educator, encapsulates this idea:

> Commitment becomes more than an externalised agreement to take action, but an inward functioning of the individual who is searching for the directions that are emerging within himself. It has much to do with creativity involving a trust in one's total reaction rather than one only in the mind. The more one works in this total manner the more confidence is expended in the direction unconsciously chosen. The individual must trust in the experience of which they have only partial awareness.
> Rogers (1983)

Identifying and addressing the needs of students

Continued research indicates that the students' learning style preferences have changed as competition for entry has increased annually. By 1997, students had become even more narrowly focused on **converger** which can be interpreted to mean that they prefer the practical application of ideas as solutions to well-structured problems which have perfect-fit solutions of technical rationality. This is characteristic of students excelling in science subjects at school and who, in the early stages of the course, are the most difficult to convince that alternative strategies of teaching and learning may have any personal value[19]. The idea of open ended 'discovery' through active experimentation is totally alien to these students, and the ill-fit solutions of design are confusing and frustrating. So too are suggestions that they become more divergent in approach and think laterally[20]. For these students who are usually very computer literate, the demand is for the technical rationality of software training. Although uninterested in pursuing a career in science, these students most often retain a genuine interest in the subject, which becomes evident later in the orientation and content of self directed projects[21].

Various strategies for testing the effectiveness of designed visual communication have been introduced including self and peer assessment. Potential users external to the university are specifically identified for testing in a number of projects[22]. The objective is to encourage students to be strategic and analytical thinkers, and also to be accountable for their decisions by taking responsibility for the 'usability' of their work. In this way, claims of subjective judgement based on aesthetic appeal are minimised[23].

Since 1997 we have detected a noticeable shift in the learning style preferences of first-year students towards assimilator. These students have strengths in the ability to create theoretical models which is indicative of higher levels of science, mathematics and areas of pure research (Kolb 1984). They have produced the most interesting and creative response to the study of visual communication, when in later years computer programming becomes a challenge for which they are well prepared. Their talents and interests lie in the abstract conceptions of complex multi-dimensional communication models and systems and they excel in the environment of new converging media.

Applying the learning strategies in external settings

In later years of the course, live projects undertaken for community groups underscore the value of user participation in design decision making. Staff have also responded to the emerging needs of students by increasing involvement with external institutions in collaborative projects that are scientifically and technologically oriented. Students work in interdisciplinary project teams to develop engaging content utilising technologically sophisticated delivery systems and also investigate the possibilities of creating new communication environments.

Conclusion

Few of our enrolling students would have been selected through the old intake system of interview and portfolio[24]. The challenge is that our first-year students are highly intelligent and demand excellence from themselves as learners and from us as teachers. By increasing our understanding of how our students learn, we have been able to acknowledge and accommodate the very different learning experiences and expectations of undergraduates in the early years of study. The findings have impelled us to take an alternative perspective on the unrealised potential of enrolling students in the context of our university's mission and the expanding nature of professional practice. This awareness has also forced us out of the complacent and possibly arrogant view that we knew what we were doing and that there were no better alternatives.

This is not to suggest total success. The attrition rate in the first two years has increased but remains below the university average. But our horizon, limited by past associations and practice, has broadened because the prior knowledge and qualities of our new intake have activated a change in our thinking about design education. The research continues with ongoing modifications to content and teaching strategies as we aim to present a curriculum that is not only sustainable in a climate of harsh economic rationalism, but also more responsive to this new generation of learners. Realigning our perceptions of students to optimise their positive attributes and different learning characteristics has enabled us to recognise the unique potential of the individual which can be directed and nurtured very effectively in later years. Each has the potential to present an exciting, versatile but alternative model of design graduate well able to handle the widening domain for design and the challenges of change.

Appendix

The following comments from students have been extracted from reflective portfolios, focus group minutes and unsolicited comments noted in a teaching diary. For reasons of privacy each student has either selected or been given an alias.

1. 'I have no idea what I am supposed to do, or how to do it and sometimes I wonder why I am doing it at all. I find it so frustrating, I don't know how to think like a designer. I've never done it before so how do you think I know how to

start' (Bob, 1993: noted from a first-year student excelling in science at school but with no experience in art or design).

2. 'School was all about mugging up quantities of stuff for exams; masses to remember; highly stressful time; you know-cram it in spew it out; I never want to work like that again' (Ada, Frank, Maggie, 1993: notes taken at a first-year focus group).

3. 'I took science at school because I was good at it and my teachers told me it would get me good marks to get into whatever uni course I decided on, but it finished off totally stifling personal ideas and any form of imaginative action. I quite liked maths, it made me think but my teacher couldn't convince me that there would be an interesting job at the end. My father is good at maths and he became an accountant. I have no interest in doing what he does or becoming a suit' (David, 1994: written comment by a first- year student reflecting on recent experiences of study).

4. 'I had to concentrate so hard on study for the exams that I gave very little serious thought to what course to take at uni. I had heard Vis. Com. was interesting and that there were no exams' (Sally, 1994: written comment by a first-year student reflecting on choice of study).

5. 'I am a perfectionist but I am not perfect yet so I am hoping I like it and it will do me some good ... but it is very different from school ... so I am prepared to see how the course develops' (Betty, 2001: written in a first-year reflective portfolio).

6. 'I hate exams and wanted to try something different. I had no idea it had anything to do with design ... well, I fancy 3D animation maybe ... I don't know ... maybe film ...' (Ben, 1995: notes from a first- year focus group).

7. 'The course is not what I expected. Two of my friends are in second year and they love it. That was the reason for selecting it. But now I am unclear what I want to study and I am beginning to think it is not design. I have always been good at exams but find design too difficult to be really good at it' (Jo, 1997: written comment by a first-year student reflecting on choice of study).

8. 'Finding out about learning was quite a revelation. I had never thought about it before. My diagram was totally different from the student beside me and I know why because I took design and technology at school and she did Korean, maths and music which are very different subjects' (Samantha, 2001: written in a first-year reflective portfolio).

9. 'I can now understand why I am feeling insecure. I have not done art since year 9 and the idea of thinking through ideas by sketching them is not easy. My drawing skills are so bad that I avoid showing them to anyone. But I can

see that I will have to practise if I want to be a designer. I had no idea that art and design are so different. In art at school you started some work and finished it like making a pot or doing a painting. We were never asked to reflect or evaluate anything and nobody ever did it again to improve it' (David, 2001: written in a first-year reflective portfolio).

10. 'It was helpful hearing that the third-year students could remember what it was like in first year and how strange they felt and how they had changed their way of thinking. What was also useful was seeing their work which looks so professional. I know I can be like that myself if I am serious about being a designer' (Glenda, 2001: written in a first-year reflective portfolio).

11. 'I am writing this in my portfolio because I know you read them. I need to say that I think that telling you what I have learnt is a waste of my time and yours. Surely it is obvious in the way my work has improved. I think that should be enough proof. Nobody asks these questions when you are in the business' (Earl 2001: written in a first year reflective portfolio by a mature age student with some work experience).

12. 'The project was very valuable and I believe I learnt a considerable amount. I did everything wrong which in many ways was useful as I can now do the opposite. For example if your image is bottom heavy, turn it upside down and see if top heavy works better' (Monica, 2001: written in a first-year reflective portfolio).

13. 'I could not complete my work because the art supply shop had run out of white paper' (Rose, 2001: written excuse in a first-year reflective portfolio).

14. 'I am sorry to report that the train had a flat tyre and I was delayed' (Robert, 2001: written in a first-year reflective portfolio).

15. 'I have learnt that working on the computer gives you a realistic and drastic thing' (Jacy, 2001: written in a first-year reflective portfolio).

16. 'This project literally killed me but I have learnt that Moholy Nagy went to Chicago where he died to found the new Bauhaus in America' (Poppy, 2001: written in a first-year reflective portfolio).

17. 'I don't know what I will do if I fail. I have always been at the top of my class and now I don't really know what I am doing so can never judge whether it is good or not. I am enjoying the lectures and tutorials but find my insecurity makes me reluctant to start any project' (Susan, 2000: written in a first-year reflective portfolio).

18. 'I do so much research and thinking that I find it difficult to sort it out and make a start. I feel I always need to know more before I am ready so I live in

the library and hope that inspiration will come' (Ann, 2001: written in a first-year reflective portfolio).

19. 'Just tell me what to do ... I'm bored having to discuss this ... I feel useless and stupid ... just give me the facts and I'll get on with it ...' (Ivan, 1996: noted from a comment made in the first -year studio class); 'I can't get used to working this way. I want information and practical skills' (Ian, 1999: noted in a first-year studio class).

20. 'Having read the notes on lateral thinking I believe that De Bono is a clever manipulator with good marketing skills who promotes aberrant behaviour to Japanese business men' (Charles, 2001: written in a first-year reflective portfolio).

21. 'My primary role in this project has been to apply my science background to assist the team to design a board game to help nursing students understand the basics of immunology' (Jason, 1997: written in a final management report on a third-year community project).

22. 'I chose to design a deck of playing cards for the blind. My user testing was carried out by four members of the Royal Blind Society who gave me interesting feedback on the effectiveness and ease of understanding the systems of pip symbols, numerals and hierarchy. Each wanted to buy a deck and one asked if I could design tarot cards which I might try in the summer break because designing with a particular user in mind presents unique issues to be addressed which makes you think differently" (Patricia, 2001: written in a first-year reflective portfolio).

23. 'Although I thought I had captured exactly the right style and look for my work, when I first tested it on a group of potential readers I found that they did not really understand the diagram or the symbols I had designed which were considered complex and obscure. It was suggested they would prefer larger type and a simpler layout, which was easier to read. Although this feedback was disappointing it was honest and timely as I was able to view my work more objectively and make changes that led to satisfaction all round' (Megan, 1998: written in a final management report on a third-year community project).

24. 'I enrolled in the visual communication course with no experience and little knowledge but some intrinsic interest that kept me involved. It was frustrating at first because I lacked the means to visually express my ideas but gradually I learnt the language. Now I am undertaking postgraduate study and the discourse of design and visual communication in particular, never fails to fascinate and engage me' (Liz, 2001: in response to my request).

References

Bawden, R. (1987), 'Learning Systems and Technological Change', Conference Paper, RMIT, Victoria

Biggs, J.B. (ed.) (1991), *Teaching For Learning, the view from cognitive psychology* (Melbourne: ACER)

Boud, D., Keogh, R., & Walker, D. (eds.) (1986), *Reflection: turning experience into learning* (London: Kogan Page)

Boud, D. (1988), *Developing Student Autonomy in Learning* (London: Kogan Page)

Boud, D. & Feletti, G. (eds.) (1991), *The Challenge of Problem Based Learning* (London: Kogan Page)

Candy, P.C. (1991), *Self-Direction for Lifelong Learning* (San Francisco: Jossey-Bass)

CTEC (1987), T*he Responsiveness of Tertiary Education to the Design Needs of Australian Industry* (Canberra: AGPS)

Dawkins, J. (1988), *Higher Education, A Policy Discussion Paper* (Canberra: AGPS)

Dawkins, J. (1989) *Improving Australia's Training System* (Canberra: AGPS)

Entwistle, N. & Hounsell, D. (eds.) (1975), *How Students Learn* (UK Institute for R&D in Post-Compulsory Education, University of Lancaster)

Fullan, M. (1991), *The (new) Meaning of Educational Change* (New York: Teachers College Press)

Garr, W. & Kemmis, S. (1986), *Becoming Critical: knowing through action research* (London: The Falmer Press)

Gibbs, G. (1992), *Improving the Quality of Student Learning* (New Jersey: Technical and Education Services)

Illich, I. (1973), *Deschooling Society* (London: Pelican Books)

Kember, D. & Kelly, M. (1993), *Improving Teaching Through Action Research*, Green Guide No 14 (Sydney: HERDSA)

Kemmis, S. & MacTaggart, R. (1988), *The Action Research Planner*, Third Edition (Geelong: Deakin University Press)

Knowles, M. (1984), T*he Adult Learner: a neglected species* (USA: Gulf Publishing)

Koberg, D. & Bagnal, J. (1976), *The Universal Traveller: A Soft System Guide to Creative Problem Solving* (California: William Kaufmann)

Kolb, D.A. (1976), *The Learning Style Inventory* (Massachusetts: Technical Manual. McBerand Co)

Kolb, D.A. (1984), *Experiential Learning: experience as the source of learning and development* (New Jersey: Prentice Hall)

Lewin, K. (1951), *Field Theory in Social Science* (New York: Harper and Row)

McKernan, J. (1991), *Curriculum Action Research: a handbook of methods and resources for the reflective practitioner* (London: Kogan Page)

Marton, F., Hounsell, D. & Entwistle, N. (eds.) (1984), *Experiential Learning: experience as the source of learning and development* (New Jersey: Prentice Hall)

Maslow, A.H. (1973), 'Theory of Human Motivation', in Lowry, R.J. (ed), *Dominance, Self Esteem, Self Actualisation: Germinal Papers of A.H. Maslow* (Calif.: Brooks Co)

Petri, H.L. (1981), *Motivation: theory and research* (USA: Wadsworth Publishing)

Ramsden, P. (1991), *Learning to Teach in Higher Education* (Sydney: Law Books)

Rogers, C. (1983), *Freedom to Learn for the 80's* (Columbus, Ohio: Charles Merrill)

Schön, D.A. (1987), *Educating The Reflective Practitioner: toward a new design for teaching and learning in the professions* (San Francisco: Jossey-Bass)

Biographical note

Associate Professor Jenny Toynbee Wilson MHEd (UNSW) Dip Art and Design (ECA) is a member of the Visual Communication Programme in the Faculty of Design, Architecture and Building at the University of Technology, Sydney (UTS). Academic appointments include Head of Department, Visual Communication, Sydney College of the Arts; Sub Dean, Faculty of Design UTS; Programme Director of Visual Communication, School of Design, UTS. External appointments include Visiting Scholar, Sunshine Coast University College, Queensland; Department of Graphic Design, Rhode Island School of Design; National Institute of Design, India. Member, NSW VETAB Course Assessment Panel; NSW Higher School Certificate Examination Committee. Recent professional practice includes interdisciplinary design team member, commission by Australian Government for Australian Service Nurses National Memorial Project, Canberra. Principal areas of research are pedagogy, design education, curriculum development, action research. Publications include papers/book chapters on: curriculum development, problem-based learning, student profiling and assessment, peer learning.

work in practice

Enhancing Curricula:

exploring effective curriculum practices in art, design and communication in Higher Education

21

Research methods curricula for practice-based postgraduate courses (UK): appropriate practice for art and design

Joan Burks

London College of Printing, The London Institute, UK

Abstract

This paper is a 'work in progress' report on research into the issue of what constitutes an effective and appropriate research methods curriculum for underpinning dissertation/major project research within art, design and communication practice-based postgraduate courses. By curricula we refer here to the dynamic interrelationship between content, teaching activities, student learning and assessment (Bradbeer, 1998).

The research project discussed here emerged from an initial staff consultation exercise that was undertaken in 2001 within one London college of art, design and communication. This exercise was designed with a view to developing college guidelines for appropriate practice in research methods curricula within postgraduate courses. As a result of the initial staff consultation exercise, a wider research project into what constitutes effective research methods curricula for art, design and communication postgraduate courses in the UK was initiated in 2002.

The study is located within and informed by the debate relating to what constitutes appropriate research methods training for MPhil/PhD research in art-based practice (Gray & Malins, 1993). It is argued here that the issues within this debate apply also to the research conducted within taught MA courses. What the actual role and intention of research is within postgraduate dissertations, is a question that must, however, underpin that debate. Key themes that have emerged to date within both the initial consultation exercise and the UK research project are presented in this paper.

The context

Practice-based research.

There has been an ongoing debate on the issue of what might constitute appropriate research methodologies and specific methods for art-practice-based practice (Gray et al., 1995, and the online debate on the Art, Design and Media School Web site, University of Sunderland, www.sunderland.ac.uk). 'Research methods generally focus only on what can be made tangible/visible/explicit/observable/evaluated by peers – somewhat limiting for the artistic process' (Web discussion, updated Graham, B., www.sunderland.ac.uk, 2001).

The debate has also covered such issues as what constitutes 'academic rigour', whether the student/artist has a 'right to fail' in unsuccessful projects and whether there is value in applying theory and research methods to practice-research, although there is no concrete solution to a given problem (www.sunderland.ac.uk, 2001). These issues, it is argued, are as relevant to research studies on taught MA courses as to MPhil/PhD research programmes, although the extent to which research projects within MA courses are perceived by the academy as constituting 'real' and valid research (which can and should make a contribution to the knowledge base) is a key issue in defining an 'effective' research methods curricula – 'effective curricula' implying feasibility and fitness for purpose.

Research methods models

In 1992 the Allison Research Index of Art & Design (ARIAD) revealed that artists and designers undertaking formal research drew significantly on the methods of the sciences and social sciences (Allison, 1992). In their paper, 'Artistic Research Procedure', Gray et al. (1995) argued, however, that a shift was occurring in art and design research projects, with greater confidence in alternative research methodologies being demonstrated.

Creative, practice-based MA taught courses that include a research methods curriculum would be likely to offer a range of research methods that are informed by the social and/or natural sciences, ranging from overtly quantitative methods to qualitative methods, each informed by distinctive theoretical perspectives and each using different sources of data. This is particularly common in courses with a media and communication orientation, involving a social, cultural or production focus, where sample populations or cases are studied as the subject of the research. More creatively-orientated, practice-based courses, such as an MA course in screen writing or an MA in typographic design, offer no formal research methods training, reflecting a view that theory and practice are often inextricably intertwined within the overall postgraduate course experience. Some areas of creative media education, on the other hand, encourage 'theorised practice', involving semiotics, psychoanalytic or media theory in the analysis of media practice. The distinctions between these various perspectives on research methods are clear.

Initial staff consultation exercise

Data on what is considered by postgraduate art, design and communication course directors as 'effective research methods curricula', was collected at four group meetings of postgraduate course directors in one London college, held to develop guidelines for appropriate practice in research methods. Initially, a one-day, seven-hour meeting was held, involving staff (course directors) representing courses from schools involved in postgraduate course delivery in publishing, digital imaging, photography, media management, multimedia, graphic design and retail design management. There were three follow-up group meetings to this one-day exercise, at which the course directors again discussed and debated what might constitute an effective research methods curriculum for particular postgraduate courses in art, design and communication.

The course directors were facilitated to 'engage in their own definition of the situation', by which they were encouraged to put forward their views in an open and unstructured context. The first seven-hour meeting started with the staff themselves raising the open questions of what research is and what the actual role and intention of research is within postgraduate dissertations/major projects. These questions were then used as a focus for group discussion and one group member fed through their group comments, which were collated by the facilitator, for the purposes of developing guidelines for appropriate practice.

At these open meetings, three distinctive views on research methods emerged. One group identified with a scientific research methods model (e.g. course directors of MSc Colour Digital Imaging and Publishing Production), another group located their subject focus firmly within the social sciences (e.g. MA Publishing, MA Enterprise and Management for the Creative Arts) and a third group saw themselves primarily as creative practitioners for whom research is inextricably linked with practice, excluding reference to formal social or scientific research methods (e.g. course directors of photography and graphic design).

Research project on an effective research methods curricula

Building upon the initial work described above, a wider cross-institution research project on what constitutes an effective research methods curriculum for postgraduate art, design and communication courses was initiated. It was considered appropriate to extend the research beyond one London college to a selected sample of universities with an art and design focus, in order to establish the broader national picture in the UK.

Research project

The research project referred to above involves a comparative study of university publishing and photography postgraduate courses in art and design orientated faculties, with qualitative interviews conducted with course directors of these courses. Publishing and photography subject areas were selected for research as MA courses in both subjects involve creative practice and the use of technology and each utilises a specific body of theoretical knowledge.

The study is qualitative, using an interactionist concept of the individual's definition of the situation which allows course directors themselves to define their perception of what constitutes an effective research methods curriculum.

A comparative analysis of the data relating to the two subject areas (work in progress), is being conducted to consider the perspectives and experiences of those involved in curriculum developments which centre on research methods in publishing and photography MA taught courses. Key issues that have emerged to date relate to the decision-making process involved in curriculum design development and planning. Themes emerging from the data analysis are: how decisions are made relating to the actual inclusion of research on masters courses; how content is planned and written; whether or not research is required to be original (involving primary data collection); the personal influences of course directors and course team members on the curriculum development process; and the question of what constitutes academic rigour.

It has become clear so far, from this research, that what is considered to be an 'effective research methods curriculum' is based on the complex interrelationship of a vocabulary of individual motives and a set of wider educational imperatives, both of which impinge upon the decision-making process of curriculum design. Photography and publishing course directors are in agreement that a research methods curriculum should be tailored to individual courses, and that all courses should include appropriate research methods training. This is critical if students are to identify an appropriate research topic/question formulation of a conceptual, technological and cultural nature. They also agree that the role of the student in this research process is paramount and that attendance at research methods lectures should be mandatory.

A vocabulary of motives involved in research methods curriculum design include staff interest in research and their subject speciality, recognised student need, institutional desire to stimulate a breeding ground for progression routes to M Phil/PhD, the potential for greater research-led teaching and an opportunity for staff to access current data for extended staff-generated research study within their own institution. In HE environments involving 'efficiency gains', where research time is often constrained, postgraduate student researchers can provide, for teaching staff, current data on relevant teaching interest areas.

The above drivers could potentially affect the decisions made regarding the eventual curriculum design of research methods for new and revalidated postgraduate courses.

A number of firmly held views and tacit assumptions were also expressed regarding the actual role of research methods on MA courses. Furthermore, the personal research experience of the individual course director appears to play an important role in how 'their' particular course curriculum is defined. The most significant factors tend to be the course director's personal knowledge and experience of research and research methods, combined with institutional pressure to offer masters-level courses, with the appropriate research emphasis in the course structure and content. Every course director interviewed conveyed a personal viewpoint which appeared to rest upon their direct and personal experience of research and the confidence which they themselves expressed regarding what constitutes research in their particular subject field. The following sub-themes also emerged:

- a lack of flexibility, in terms of questioning what might be possible outside of the course directors' own subject perspectives; and

- inadequate emphasis on reflective observation and abstract conceptualisation in the stages of curriculum development in terms of establishing the core values and purpose of research within a postgraduate course.

Structural context in research methods curriculum design

The research agenda, driven by current educational directives, is important for new course/curricula development and course revalidation, including those courses with an art and design orientation.

In the UK, the process of subject review of teaching and learning within HE institutions has been recently reviewed (QAA, March 2002), and it has been made explicit in the Quality Assurance Agency (QAA) statement that, in addition to primary evidence and information produced by external examiners, scrutiny will, in the future, make reference to the Framework for Higher Education Qualifications, relevant Subject Benchmark statements and relevant sections of the Code of Practice (QAA statement, point 51, March 2002). The policy statements linked to each of the three initiatives (noted above) all contain references points to the role of research and research methods in higher education teaching and learning.

The rationale for including research methods on courses is underlined by the following statements:

- *The Framework for Higher Education Qualifications*:
  Much of the study undertaken at masters level will have been at, or informed by, the forefront of an academic or professional discipline. Students will have shown originality in the application of knowledge, and they will understand how the boundaries of knowledge are advanced through research. They will be able to deal with complex issues both systematically and creatively, and they will show originality in tackling and solving problems.
  (*QAA, 2001*)

- *Descriptor for a qualification at masters (M) level*:
  Masters degrees are awarded to students who have demonstrated:

  ... a comprehensive understanding of techniques applicable to their own research or advanced scholarship;

  ... conceptual understanding that enables the student ... to evaluate critically current research and advanced scholarship in the discipline; and ... to evaluate methodologies and develop critiques of them and, where appropriate, to propose new hypotheses.

  (*QAA, 2001*)

- *Subject Benchmark Statements for art and design and media, culture and communication.*
  These make reference to the requirement to develop the students' research skills, and there is reference in each statement to the applicability of the statements to postgraduate courses (in the absence, until Spring 2002, of postgraduate Benchmark Statements for these subject areas),
- *Code of Practice for research programmes.*
  The Code of Practice for research makes clear reference to the needs for research methods training, and it is intimated that this is also necessary on taught postgraduate courses.

Institutions of higher education are thus clearly required to prepare students adequately to be able to undertake research and demonstrate their ability to extend knowledge and engage in original enquiry. The monitoring of quality in terms of new course and curriculum development does, therefore, logically involve a scrutiny that focuses on the inclusion of research methods /training in research skills within the curriculum offer. This, in turn, is reflected within internal quality systems that exist in each HE institution and would certainly be relevant in terms of internal scrutiny of new course development and course revalidation submissions. It is clear that the weighting of dissertation/research elements within MA courses signals the significance of research within the overall learning process. Whether this educational directive can be applied to practice-based research must, however, be considered in the context of a range of research methodology options.

The Arts and Humanities Research Board considers research to be a process built around clearly articulated research questions, the specification of a research content and the specification of appropriate research methods for addressing specific research questions, with an associated rational for the use of particular methods. In order to satisfy the QAA requirements pertaining to masters-level education, ways must be sought to accommodate the principle of research methods training for those postgraduate students who, as part of their practice-based masters course, will embark upon a research process leading to the creation of a written dissertation or major project. Hutchings & Saunders (2001) highlight the lack of 'method' for curriculum development and propose a model for large-scale curriculum development.

It is possible that a structured framework for curriculum design may encourage curriculum designers and planners to spend a greater period of time on conceptual thinking before moving into the decision-making process on research methods curricula.

A checklist might, at a minimum level, offer a structure and a means to facilitate this process in designing research methods curricula for specific courses. A checklist could be used in curriculum planning and development, which might include the following items:

- a position paper on the rationale for inclusion of research within the course;
- minuted records of brain storming on the concept of research methods curricula at new course development meetings;
- research methods curricula drafting – as a team activity;
- student feedback comments; and
- external examiner comments.

A check list could also be used to underpin the development of research methods curricula on individual postgraduate courses.

It is the view of the author of this paper, at this stage of the research process, that those involved in curriculum development should be encouraged to adopt a wider perspective on the broader issue of the role of research within particular postgraduate courses and what constitutes an effective research methods curriculum, feasible and fit for purpose. It is clear that a flexible model, informed by academic, educational and creative practice imperatives, is essential in order to meet the needs of students on individual courses.

Scott (2002) stated that in a 'knowledge society', all students today – certainly all graduates – have to be researchers.

> Not only are they engaged in the production of knowledge; they must also be educated to cope with the risks and uncertainties generated by the advance of science. In other words, education and research co-mingle in ways that make their artificial separation destructive of the highest standards in both.
> Scott (2002)

Within this scenario, the need to establish an effective research methods curricula, feasible and fit for purpose, is a priority for postgraduate education. Within practice-based MA taught courses, students who engage in academic research can only benefit from an effective, rationally designed research methods curricula to underpin this activity.

References

Allison, B. (1992), *Allison Research Index of Art & Design* (ARIAD) (Leicester Expertise, UK Art, Design and Media School Web site, University of Sunderland, www.sunderland.ac.uk,accessed April 2002)

Bradbeer, J. (1999), *Imagining Curriculum* (Teachers College Pr, NY)

Gray, C. & Malins, J. (1993), *Research Procedures/Methodology for Artists and Designers*, in Principles and Definitions: Five Papers by the European Postgraduate Art and Design Group (Winchester School of Art)

Gray, C. & Pirie, I. (1995), *Artistic Research Procedure: Research at the Edge of Chaos?* 'Design Interfaces' conference, European Academy of Design, University of Salford, UK, Conference proceedings

Hutchings, T. & Saunders, D. (2001) 'Curriculum Methodology: a casestudy in large-scale curriculum development', *Active Learning in Higher Education ILT Journal*, Dec. 2001 (Sage)

Quality Assurance Agency for Higher Education, *The Framework for Higher Education Qualifications in England, Wales and Northern Ireland, Annex 1* (Jan 2001)

Quality Assurance Agency for Higher Education, *Benchmark Statements for Art and Design, Communication, Media, Film and Cultural Studies* (Web site www.QAA.ac.uk, accessed April 2002)

Quality Assurance Agency for Higher Education, *Codes of Practice – Quality and Standards in Higher Education: Postgraduate Research Programmes* (Web site www.QAA.ac.uk, accessed April 2002)

Quality Assurance Agency for Higher Education, External Review Process for Higher Education in England: Operational Description March 2002 (Web site www.qaa.ac.uk, assessed April 2002)

Scott, P. (2002), 'A lot to learn', *Guardian Unlimited*, 8 Jan 2002 (Guardian Newspapers Ltd)

Biographical note

Joan Burks, PhD is Postgraduate Co-ordinator at London College of Printing (LCP), the London Institute and Programme Director for Media and Cultural Studies at LCP's School of Media. She is currently Chair of the UK Association for Publishing Education (IAPE). Her email address is j.burks@lcp.linst.ac.uk

22

A case study evaluation of task force group peer-assisted independent teaching and learning project

Howard Cannatella

School of Art and Design, Coventry University, UK

Abstract

This completed task force project was designed to facilitate and advance foundation art and design students' capabilities to foster, in a more constructive and conscious manner, their autonomy, independent learning, peer-group learning, critical thinking and life-long learning skills. Essentially, the project was a response to the fact that students are getting less and less direct teaching support. Yet, at the same time, feeling that for various other reasons students were less demanding of themselves when working on their own. The intention was to develop a project that would attempt, in a positive way, to instil a deep rather than a surface approach to learning when working independently. I wanted to promote an approach where more reflection and commitment would manifest assiduously in students' work. In order to implement such a strategy, the project focused on a repertoire of learning skills relating to problem solving, experimentation, creative and critical thinking, personal responsibility, student support and co-operation. Rather than reinvent the wheel, I drew from published research in student-centred learning, colleagues' experiences and my own expertise in running group work projects.

In addition, there were particular social, functional and cultural issues involved in the nature of the design brief that called upon further demanding cognisant awareness than the students had previously encountered, for this was a project that concerned disability. Furthermore, an amalgam of studio, workshop, library and user surveys helped to create a different kind of group dynamic and complexity to this project.

It is hoped that this report will be of some practical use to lecturers and tutors interested in group peer-assisted and autonomous teaching and learning. I will therefore give an account of the major characteristics, problems and successes of this project and outline my recommendations to the school of art and design.

Objectives

- to design a project that involves the development of design skills through a co-operative student group approach;
- to design a project that it is realistically achievable and educationally desirable;
- for students to advance their skills in critical, creative and independent learning;
- for students to demonstrate that they value this kind of experience and can see its relevance in social, economic and employment terms; and
- to produce a project-briefing handbook for use by staff and students.

Key words: independent learning, peer-group learning, critical design thinking, civic values and life-long learning skills.

Project outline

- the project started at week 10 (of the pathway stage of the course) in the academic year and lasted for 4 weeks, involving 3D design students working in groups of 5–6 students (7 groups in all);

- this project experience represented the first pathway choice for students;
- total hours of teaching for this group was 9 hours per week for 4 weeks = 36 hours;
- total hours of student attendance in studios was 20 hours per week for 4 weeks = 80 hours.
- 40 students were involved in this project;
- two members of staff supported the project: the course leader and an MA student from our automotive design course;
- an essential feature of this project was that students had to produce design work guided by group collective decisions; and
- no individual tutorial support was given during the project.

The brief

One aim of the brief was to foster students' interest in design by enhancing their conceptual and practical understanding of this field of inquiry. The project stated the relevant tasks and specifications that students would have to expedite on this assignment. Students had to complete two interrelated but incremental briefs concerned with finding a real solution for a disability design problem.

The decision to do a project relating to disability and design was taken because students up to this point had no prior experience of a social perspective on design. Equally, the course leader had considerable previous experiences in teaching design disability projects over the past ten years. The project itself was challenging and one that required students to consider carefully the functional and ergonomic needs of users, and aesthetic considerations. Thus, it was not possible for students to produce what they liked, creating free-floating imaginative solutions in ad hoc ways. The students were given the following two briefs:

> Dear student
>
> You have just woken-up on the morning 4/11/2K, after a good night's sleep. While still in bed, but not quite yet ready to face the world, you realise quickly that you no longer have the use of your writing hand. It is paralysed.
>
> We now want you to get dressed, make your bed, take a bath, brush your teeth, open doors, make breakfast etc., with only the use of your non-writing hand.
>
> In your sketchbook/diary, record with your good writing hand, the many difficulties that you faced during the day. Note in some detail these specific situations, describing if possible sequentially, many of the problems you faced (allow 4 hours for this exercise).
>
> Having done this, pick out two small but significant problems that you faced during the day and in a graphic storyboard manner (one A1 white mounting board), represent these issues (allow three hours minimum for this exercise). Take care with your presentation.
>
> Present your work/findings at 9 a.m. in your base room, on Tuesday morning, 7/11/2K. The full nature of this assignment will be explained to you on Tuesday.

From the above brief, students went on to tackle the following problem.

> Brief
>
> Working within groups of five-six students, the problem that has been set is to design and make a device that solves successfully one of the difficulties you faced over the weekend's assignment.
>
> Working in groups, your final design solution must be easy to use, uncomplicated, well-made, relevant and creative.

The handbook

To facilitate students' advancement in independent peer-assisted learning and because of the complexity of the assignment a substantial student handbook had to be created. This had to be a handbook that could anticipate many of the difficulties that independent and peer-assisted learning raises. In addition, the handbook needed to be transparent, informative and sequential in order to promote and maximise students' rational and organisational skills. Rather than leave things to chance, resulting in the almost certain development of a superficial and confusing outcome, the handbook would explain to students in precise ways what they needed to do, assisting a more conscientious and targeted approach.

Equally, the handbook was written for staff, so that any staff member teaching on the project would know what to cover and what to discuss with students at any given time during the project. As I further saw it, the advantage of a handbook is that it could be used and developed over time and would represent a permanent record of what went on – useful for inspection purposes, course development and teaching and learning reflection.

Knowing what kind of project handbook one wanted to produce and the degree of information it should contain were important issues to consider. Particular attention was given to the type of key skills that the project would attempt to foster. Furthermore, any handbook needs to consider, among other issues: how long the project is meant to last; the stage when it will be introduced; its relevance to other aspects of the curriculum; the student-staff contact time; the number of students involved; the nature of the assignment; the assignment aims and objectives; knowledge of the student cohort; and the kind of capacities and skills the project wants to instil.

My particular view was that the handbook's content would have to describe the kind of design work that was desirable and help students to organise and record their on-going developments in a more systematic manner. In addition, a further reason for the handbook was to emphasise the process and not the solution to design problems.

It was also felt that this handbook would enable those students who happen to come in late into the project to follow independently at various stages what was required of them.

The tutors' and students' roles and responsibilities

The handbook in some detail clearly stated what the student and staff roles and responsibilities would be for this project. Since roles and responsibilities can and do change depending on the purpose that one has in mind, spelling out to students and staff what their particular roles and responsibilities would be in this project, made it self-evident to everybody the operational nature of this assignment. I personally feel that a factor that contributed to the project success was making explicit what the particular staff and students' roles were going to be in this project.

Definition of group work

The goal of any group work is for group members to unite around a common purpose, one that demonstrates an ability to work together. This project, however, went further than this, and aimed to promote student support, autonomy and peer-assisted learning.

Definition of independent autonomy and learning

A common educational view of independent autonomous learning is as David Little (1995) supposes: 'a capacity for detachment, critical reflection, decision making, and independent action'. A considerable degree of freedom and responsibility is implied in this definition but one might further add to this by stating that autonomy also involves authenticity and community values.

The above two definitions when combined raise a number of issues for teaching and learning and these are as follows:

- establish an effective learning climate;
- encourage learners to demonstrate commitment;
- encourage learners to discuss their work, face obstacles and resolve difficulties;
- encourage learners to identify resources and to devise strategies for using them;
- involve learners in diagnosing their own learning needs;
- involve learners in planning out aspects of their work;
- encourage learners to set their own goals and targets;

- involve learners in continuous self-assessment;
- motivate and enthuse the student groups;
- encourage learners to develop critical thinking skills;
- involve learners in evaluating their own learning and reflective practice;
- promote the nature of group work and independent learning;
- evaluate the strengths and weaknesses of the student groups;
- have a clear picture of what you want to achieve;
- inform all relevant staff and get their support and match, objectives, processes and outcomes; and
- plan and build into project a sequential and logical process of work

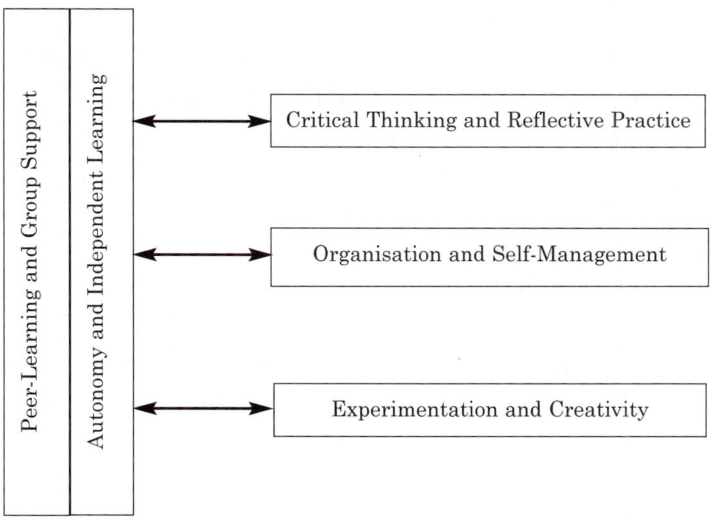

Conceptual and operational map of key skills and learning process

Peer-assisted group learning

As the conceptual and operational map of key project skills illustrates, students were expected to demonstrate competence in a variety of different ways but ultimately in a co-ordinated and co-operative fashion. In order to nurture progress in the project, sufficient attention to these issues and how they relate to each other needed addressing. If students were going to make headway they could only do so by assisting one another and accepting in a positive light that design decisions would have be taken within a consensus and sequential approach. In general, the project aimed to encourage students to develop their skills, capabilities and concepts of design related issues and apply these experiences and ideas to achieve a best solution. In an attempt to help motivate students, a practical orientated design project was designed to give plenty of freedom for students to come up with their own original solutions, to develop their own interests and seek specific solutions that would stimulate them in a peer-assisted group manner. Because this was a group project and because students were expected to work predominately independently, some new ways of learning were for the first time being introduced. However, there would be some transfer of skills from previous assignments important to the success of this project. The way in which these skills were further developed and orientated in different ways, together with the acquisition of new skills such as co-operation, tended to shift the power structure of learning in a different direction. Timing, subtlety and pitch in handling human interactions required particular perceptions and judgements from students.

It is clearly the case that working independently and co-operatively in a team are important skills valued professionally and socially. These skills are often viewed as useful for employment purposes and the advancement of life-long learning skills. Working collectively as opposed to individually would assist other valuable characteristics such as friendship, sensitivity to others, negotiating skills, communication, student peer support and studio and course dynamics.

Project problems

There were two major problems that surfaced during this project that affected students' motivation.

Problem one

Some students felt that if given the choice to begin with they would avoid doing this design disability project altogether because they were uncomfortable with the idea of a design disability project that required them to discuss their designs with disabled persons.

For some other students the problem was that they had an insular automotive view of design. They found it hard to see how a design disability project fitted into a picture of a sexy red sports car.

My approach to tackling these issues was to try to convince students that coming to grips with certain perceived obstacles could open them to different experiences, realities and their rewards. I remarked to them that having a narrow view of what constitutes design would be detrimental to their development and a distorted image of design would affect the outcome quality of the project. I emphasised that having a negative view of this project could have a severe effect on their motivation and with it a more wholesome view of design. Similarly, I pointed out that a good designer has to be able to solve all kinds of problems and think in all kinds of different ways. Indeed, I explained that this was a foundation course and students' design ambitions, whatever they may be, had to be tempered by grasping firstly some of the basic core principles of designing. It was highlighted that design itself must engage knowledge of users' needs and their behaviour patterns and that interacting with their interests in mind and enabling them to make sense of things is good design practice. Furthermore, because it was a disability project students would implicitly be dealing with aspects of equal opportunities as well as making a commitment to understanding the needs of others, both of these things being reasons for action and moral identification.

Problem two

A more difficult issue for me was peer-assisted group learning. All students seemed to agree that it was better for them to decide what groups they wanted to be for this project. Yet, for a small number of students this approach did not work (see student questionnaires), as they wanted the lecturer to decide the nature of the groups. Now in retrospect, I feel that I should have had more discussion with the students over this issue, making sure that everyone was comfortable with their group selection. How students selected their groups seemed hardly rational and seemed for some based purely on their appearances rather than their skills. More prior discussion relating to how compatible groups were and the range of skills individual members can bring to their groups are issues that should not be overlooked.

However, even when students appeared to be happy with their groups it soon became apparent as the project progressed that some tensions regarding laissez-fare attitudes by some members of the groups were beginning to surface. While the project handbook discusses the importance of good group dynamics and I personally spent some time during the introduction to the project suggesting the dangers of conflict within students groups. I was, nevertheless aware and prepared for some unavoidable strains between group members as the project proceeded. Personality and ego clashes were a particular problem with a few students.

Below are ten typical problems that occurred. Some students:

1. were unwilling to co-operate and or compromise;
2. were unwilling to give support;
3. showed a lack of objectivity;
4. were unwilling to meet group deadlines;
5. were unwilling to attended regular group meetings;
6. were having communication problems;
7. were having problems motivating themselves and or other group members;
8. wanted to dominate the group;
9. were producing more work than others; and
10. were finding it difficult to attend group critique sessions and assessments.

It is important to realise, however, that in teaching and learning, problems of the kind so described above are inevitable and to some extent the nature of group project work invites and stimulates these difficulties. How groups tackled and overcame some of these difficulties when they occurred was an implicit problem of the project itself and so in one sense is likely to be seen as beneficial rather than negative.

It was during critique and assessment sessions that I constantly reiterated the importance of good group dynamics.

Student groups were encouraged to solve any problems they had for themselves and only when it became clear that individual students were significantly abusing this freedom would the course leader address the issue.

I had to take aside four students and discuss with them their personal responsibilities to their groups. This was only done with the consent and knowledge of the rest of the group cohort.

Because the groups consisted of five or six members, it only took one member of the group not to carry out their tasks at any one time to delay and frustrate other group members.

Although students did not raise these issues, I feel that more student time should in future be given to debating and reading about design. This in my experience tends to aid a reflective and refined outlook, important to group dynamics.

It is arguably the case, as many have noted, that students now do less reading because they are having to support themselves through college. At one point in the handbook students are asked to debate and discuss a number of design issues, an area that retrospectively should have been more tutor-led because students were clearly ignoring this advice.

Project successes and achievements

The handbook

The relevance of the handbook has been mentioned and the success of this handbook can be gauged in part by what students had to say about it in the student questionnaire forms. The handbook can be found on the School's teaching and learning Web site and on the ADC-LTSN Web site.

Communication

Students wanted concise instructions of the tasks that they were expected to complete, providing clear explanations of any concepts, procedures and techniques that they needed to demonstrate. Those students that were having personal learning difficulties appreciated the lecturer repeating and going over key aspects of the project with them. Many remarked that the project was very clear about what it wanted from students.

I observed that communication in student groups was often very business like, rational, frank, objective and reflective.

The development of critical thinking

During the project there were numerous discussions and challenges that facilitated more abstract, lateral, logical, divergent, experimental, creative, reflective and problem-solving activities. Moreover the ability to think more rigorously was an issue that was encouraged throughout the assignment as the course tutor had noted that some students had a tendency to drift in their thinking and or lower their standards when they got bored. In different ways, lecturers frequently asked students how improvements could be made to their existing design work and what were the current critical issues in their work.

Advancing students' critical design thinking through planning, organisation, research, making skills and the quality and care of the design work itself was particularly given priority.

Thinking and reflecting through action was seen as central to art and design experience by the lecturers involved.

Students were frequently observed discussing the merits of their work and what future action they as a group should take.

However, it was equally obvious through discussion with students that overall many of them lacked historical and contemporary knowledge of design culture. Many aspects of designing depend on articulating and forming critical interpretations of design work.

The students' final results and academic standards

None of the students design work was handed in late for assessment and all students were present for their final presentations. One group achieved a distinction, three achieved merit and three achieved a pass.

Working in groups

It was particularly noticeable, though it was not anticipated, how the international students on the course excelled in this group project. The four international students completing this assignment suggested to me afterwards that this project enabled them to get support from other members of the student group, to develop their friendships with them and to build their self-confidence. While the students were aware that they had language difficulties, with more active group support they were able to play a more positive role in the project. Furthermore, they felt that they were becoming through this support an integral part of the course itself. It was for them a project that seemed to bolster their self-esteem and made them feel less alienated.

The project objectives were to: (1) carry out radical and extensive experimentation with chosen pathway media, techniques and processes; (2) enhance their awareness of their creative intentions when researching ideas; (3) apply understanding when selecting and prioritising to meet identified objectives; (4) outline and propose effective plans for making one's own work; and (5) take an increasing independent role in developing one's skills and in realising the final work. All student groups managed to complete successfully these objectives. The specific issue of working independently is discussed below.

During the project, I found the students more decisive, assertive and questioning than I had previously observed in other projects. The studio atmosphere was dynamic, positively noisy and exciting.

It was apparent that students were developing their own autonomy and taking more responsibility for their own patterns of learning.

Many students appeared to benefit from working in their groups and were personally stimulated by other members in their group in efficacious ways. For example, decisions were often taken in a consensus way and students were given task-specific exercises to complete for the group that they felt they wanted to do and could do. Those students who worked well in these groups tended to produce a greater amount of work and in a more assured fashion. Regular group meetings and strong positive support from its members that was not over judgmental appeared to encourage a productive group ethos and a common work ethic. When everyone shared the same thinking, direction and beliefs, considerable harmony in the groups could be seen. Similarly, when everyone valued everyone else's contribution a feeling of capability, achievement and zest for work was in evidence. A sense of personal realism, enjoyment, focus and what one could do for the group, based on the skills that one possessed also seemed to be a vital factor in those groups that particularly excelled. Groups that particularly worked well were noticeably happier and relaxed.

What seemed to be missing from the groups that did not do as well as the more effective groups could be put down to a number of elements relating to: (1) their inability to develop friendships; (2) an inability to attend regular group meetings; (3) communication was strained because individuals were not prepared to compromise; (4) some individuals behaved very egoistically; (5) some lacked interest in the nature of project itself, (6) some were unprepared to meet agreed group deadlines; (7) some showed an inability to enthuse and support others in their group; and (8) some found it hard to overcome set backs.

Recently, students have started to do more group self-supportive project work and these students have commented that what is transforming their current practice is their reflections upon their previous peer-assisted group disability project. One student who was having problems with peer-assisted group learning has mentioned to me that as a consequence of this project he has since realised its value and is now wary of making some of the same mistakes again.

Creative development

Students were encouraged to experiment, explore, take risks and to imagine. The project aimed to stimulate students to search and discover things for themselves about design, designing and their own personalities. Students were asked to rethink and not simply to accept conventional orthodox views about design.

Students seemed to recognise that in order to develop their creativity, technical skills and an understanding of the design problem relating to user needs were also required.

All student groups clearly wanted to produce design work that was both individual and original. Analysing design objects past and present, recognising how things are made and how they operate, realising how designers think and how users appear to use objects fostered an awareness amongst students of a broader picture of designing.

Concept boards, sketchbook drawing, discussion sessions, surveys and models were introduced to facilitate and enrich students' creative skills.

Scheme of work

All students groups were able to complete their schemes of work stating many of the issues that the student handbook asked them to consider. The students recognised the importance of this, a way of summarising their current project problems and the activities that they were involved with during the project. Having to produce a scheme of work further allowed staff to see what students were getting up to, their reflections and to match and assess their statements against the produced design work.

Group critique and assessment sessions

At regular intervals, students were expected to represent their work and discuss it during critique and assessment sessions. The specifications of what needed to be completed for these collective critiques and assessment presentations could be found in the student-staff handbook. These sessions prompted a reflective period where monitoring, assessing and reviewing the design work stimulated what further action should to be taken in collective ways. In addition, these sessions provided an opportunity for all to see what the other groups were getting up to and what could be learnt from their approaches. Furthermore, it was seen as a time for the lecturer to motivate the student groups and to encourage more critical creative thinking and the development of certain design skills. The regular pattern of these meetings and their demands also seemed to propel students into producing work for these sessions. Receiving feedback that encouraged students to reflect on their performances and experiences was equally essential, as was the questioning nature of staff challenges. Students had to submit a range of work and identify why this work was relevant and the extent to which it was answering certain project requirements. While staff constructive criticism was often voiced these were judged against positive comments of support and recognition of the progress that students had made.

Regular classroom assessment techniques were used to monitor student's awareness, development and reflection. During each teaching session I would encourage students to reflect upon their own perceptions and actions, what they had learnt and the extent of this learning, and to summarise what steps they needed to take next as a group. I would regularly ask students to explain to me what they were doing and whether my advice seemed fair and appropriate. Moreover, I would use student feedback as a way to improve my own teaching, responding to particular on-going problems.

Working independently

All the student groups demonstrated an independent approach. What this project has shown to me is that it is possible for students to advance their learning when working together independently. However, thorough planning is required to make such independent learning a success. Yet, as I found out, the lecturer should be armed with various examples of good student practice, contemporary design solutions and information about where further resource material can be found. With greater emphasis on independent learning inevitable, it is arguably the case that proper guidance must be given if effective student autonomy is to be achieved. Independent learning allows a degree of flexibility in structure, often an appropriate degree of freedom and choice and if properly designed an incremental way to develop one's own self-directed learning.

The students' design work

Much about student work has already been alluded to in this report. Certainly, as one might expect, the quality of the design work produced by the student groups varied between one group getting a distinction, some groups getting merits and other groups getting passes. The quality of the design work not only varied overall but it also varied within each design group. For example, some groups seemed to be better at research, in analysing the specific issues which disability design can cause while for some other groups they appeared better at communicating visually their ideas but without sufficient research to support their design solutions. There were no referrals and in general all student groups produced a broad body of work meeting all the project outcomes.

It was notable how critical reflective thinking about design seemed to affect students' drawing, making and ergonomic development and vice versa. So while the development of technical skills is important in itself, students were encouraged to see the development of such technical skills within a practice: one that was further transformed by the project's own internal goals. Indeed, in a limited way, I wanted students to see that the historical, cultural and various social dimensions of design are crucial aspects that also serve and advance technical skills.

A practical approach was mainly taken and emphasised by staff. However, my thoughts are that this approach needed to be balanced against more experimental, sociological, political and conceptual thinking about design in order for a firmer and more informed creative grip of design to manifest itself. I felt disappointed that I did not personally allow sufficient time to engage students in further discussions relating to design theory and history. Without some rational discourse about design itself, students' motivation, cognition and creative development may suffer. A parochial perspective on design will limit what a student can achieve.

Conclusion

The idea that co-operation and shared responsibility provide some of the best context for human effectiveness in accomplishing social goals, economic prosperity and the idea that close ties of affiliation are beneficial and supportive, if not necessary for living a good life seem somewhat indisputable. In a design way, this project has sought to acknowledge the importance of group work activity, its distinctive situation, certain crucial experiences of it and how students have engaged and interacted.

In this case study report I have tried to produce something of relevance to educational practitioners, information I hope might contribute to improved student learning.

What I feel this project has particular demonstrated is that:

- group work can be seen as less expensive to set up, easy to manage and supervise than individual projects; it is estimated that a minimum of 25% of teaching hours was saved during this project;
- group work clearly can, as this project demonstrated, increase the amount of quality discussion amongst students;
- group work enhances personal contact, friendship, camaraderie and support;
- the development of group work experiences is seen as a key graduate and employment skill;
- academic standards and achievement in learning is maintained in group work activities;
- group work encourages students to value the skills and qualities of others and to work in co-operative ways;
- time management, organisational skills, negotiation, presentation design skills, reflective practice, social skills, critical design thinking and autonomy are important developmental learning activities for students continuous attention;
- group work allows students with different abilities and strengths to tackle more complex problems than they could possibly do on their own;
- group work facilitates more communication amongst students and allows students to express and assert themselves in ways that would not be possible through individual projects or through a more tutor led approach;
- group work facilitates more intimacy and scrutiny of learning and student responsibility;
- group work is an essential student-centred approach;

- group work can facilitate students' learning to learn for themselves quicker than in other approaches; and
- group work can be effective in bringing down absenteeism rates.

How this project could be improved in the future

- further consideration of peer support issues and the blend/cross-section of student groups is needed;
- past students could be asked to come and talk about the difficulties and successes of the project;
- more time for discussing design issues could be more tutor led;
- the findings of the student questionnaires below should be discussed with future students;
- reading about design needs further encouragement;
- a quiz on design could be developed so that students can self-assess their knowledge; and
- student self-assessment and feedback can promote more student-centred thinking and learning could be added.

Recommendations to the School

- that all school modules should work towards producing a student-staff teaching and learning handbook, where specific guidance is given on independent learning;
- that some group work activity could be integrated into all undergraduate courses;
- a structure for the incremental development of self-directed and peer-assisted group learning within the school should be developed;
- more active student reading should be encouraged;
- all modules should involve active on-going student self-assessment and feedback (within classroom/studio teaching);
- for the School to develop and promote more student-centred learning within classrooms/studios; and
- debriefing sessions should be created for each module.

A selection of this project's student feedback quotes

I think we would have done better if we did not spend so much time disagreeing with each other.

Some groups were better able to put their differences aside and work for the benefit of the whole group.

Some groups had strong personality clashes and simply refused to co-operate.

Some groups were more enthusiastic than others.

I think some groups thought about others rather than themselves.Trying to work as much as I could, trying to help others in my group and to pass the unit at any cost.

Meeting deadlines, not only those set by the brief but by those also set by the group. A lot of hard work had to be done that involved the whole group.

We were all very tolerant of each other during the project and we quickly resolved any conflicts.

I boasted about how good I was and this did not go down well with my group.

No one in our group ever stopped working so we had no need to be over critical of each other.

We had problems with the technical drawing but this was resolved by the team putting pressure on one member of the group to do his share of the work.

I have not been very responsible at all, I know I could have been much more responsible and I could of got more involved, I should of made more of an effort.

The most motivated I have been since leaving school.

This was a great project to do as I saw its relevance.

During the first few days of the project I was finding it difficult to motivate myself because I could not generate any ideas but the group encouraged me and this in turn helped me to become more interested and produce lots of good ideas.

I have learnt a lot form the group which helped me to become more critical of myself.

Criticism makes me push for higher standards and goals and I enjoy that.

Perhaps as a group we should have been more critical of each other.

I found the design process and our end disability design solution most satisfying but working in groups taught me a lot about other people some of which is not complimentary.

I have never worked on a group project before but this project was most rewarding and taught me a lot about how working in a group can be very productive.

The project was very worthwhile because it made you interact, compromise and discuss your ideas with others.

I feel we could of done more if we had more teaching help.

I have tried to get on with the male sex in my group but at times this has been difficult because of their egos.

Appendix

Student questionnaires

The student questionnaires raise a number of important concerns for teaching and learning. There were a total of 80 questionnaire form responses from students.

Do you think that you have met all the project expectations?

I think we would have done better if we did not spend so much time disagreeing with each other.
No, I did not feel that I had properly met all the project expectations because at times I may not have been very useful especially in the workshops.
Yes, but I think we could have done more, but because of differences in the group we have only done the minimum amount of work.
On a personal level yes, as a team no.
No, I think that my time management could have been better.
No, some of the work is not as good as it could have been.
No, because as a group we were working far too much independently.

A number of other students had simply put yes or no to this question. A number of students said that they could have done more. A number of students said that they met most of the project expectations.

Why do think some groups got on well with each other and others have not?

Some groups appear to have good communication and spirit.

Some groups appeared more dedicated and hard working while others seem to put in the minimum of effort needed.

Some group members tried to compete with each other instead of working with each other.

Some people find it difficult to communicate with each other.

Far too many different opinions about what the group should be doing.

No one in the group was prepared to compromise.

Lots of ideas but no real agreement on what idea to develop.

Some groups already consisted of friends so the group members knew how to handle each other.

Some people really worked well on communication and I think this was the cornerstone of the groups working effectively.

Maybe some people have found that 3D design is not the subject for them so they have lacked the necessary enthusiasm.

Some groups seemed to have better attendance than others.

Some groups were better able to put their differences aside and work for the benefit of the whole group.

Some people are individuals and cannot work in a team.

Some groups were with friends and this helps.

Some groups had strong personality clashes and simply refused to co-operate.

Groups with different abilities seemed to cause problems.

Some groups were more enthusiastic than others.

The groups that got on well were those who were well organised and who knew exactly what each member of the group was doing.

We were not trying hard at being friendly to each other.

I think some groups thought about others rather than just themselves.

Group communication, attitude, organisation, dedication and working together as a team were frequently mentioned in the questionnaire.

What expectations has this project specifically demanded of you?

Imagination, common sense, problem solving and patience.

Creating ideas, technical drawing, working models.

> Meeting deadlines, not only those set by the brief but by those also set by the group. A lot of work had to be done that involved the whole group.
> The project was essentially about solving a disability design problem.
> Knowing what disability is, researching the topic and thinking in ways that finds solutions to disability problems.
> Learning how to make constructive criticism and not to be afraid to state your point of view.
> The development of ideas and knowing how to present your ideas were important.

Hard work, meeting deadlines, team work and time management were repeatedly mentioned by students.

What personal expectations or aims did you set yourself during this project?

> I aimed to get all my work completed on time.
> To achieve a good grade.
> To improve my drawing skills.
> To improve my knowledge, research and presentation skills.
> Trying to work as much as I could, trying to help others in my group and to pass the unit at any cost.
> To learn about design.

Students in this questionnaire frequently mentioned that making an effort to work in a group, meeting deadlines and getting other members of the group to work hard.

How tolerant have you been of others in your team. State how by giving examples.

> We worked in a well-managed atmosphere. I wanted to work with James on the visual but he pressed to do it himself which after reflection I felt was probably the best thing, given James' drawing skills. I took criticism in a positive way by working harder on the project.
> We were all very tolerant of each other during the project and we quickly resolved any conflicts.
> Even though I did not get on well with my group, I feel that I made an effort to get along with them.
> I think I have been fairly tolerant of others in my group. But I have been irritated by other group members being unreliable and not doing what they said they could complete.
> I have tried to demonstrate to others what has gone wrong and explain what changes we needed to make.

There were times when I wanted to voice my criticism but under the circumstances of not wishing to cause further problems, I kept silent. Perhaps I was just too tolerant.

I have tried to get on with the male sex in my group but at times this has been difficult because of their egos.

I had always tried to explain my ideas and talk it through with others, listening to what others have had to say and responded positively to their criticism and volunteering myself to do extra work.

We used a voting system in our group to get things done.

We had problems with the technical drawing but this was resolved by the team putting pressure on one member of the group to do his share of the work.

I boasted about how good I was and this did not go down well with my group.

One member of the group seemed preoccupied with drawing cars and I was reasonably tolerant of this.

No one in our group ever stopped working so we had no need to be over critical of each other.

A number of students mentioned that they had only partly been tolerant of other group members because a number of them were either refusing to co-operate, seeing themselves as better than others, more intelligent, clever or arrogant.

How responsible do you think you have been?
State whether you have regularly attended team meetings and whether you have always completed tasks to your best ability. Give examples of how you feel that you have worked to your best ability.

During this project I have been in college everyday from 8.30 a.m. and left after 4 p.m. I have completed all the tasks to my best ability and I have even taken on other tasks to help finish off other students' work. I feel that I have had a major part in the organisation of this group and I have taken a lot of responsibility to get things done in the group.

I have always completed the tasks that were assigned to me and I never let the group down.

I think our group started well but we got side tracked and this caused us some problems.

Motivating myself towards the end of the project was difficult as I felt that I had run out of steam.

I have not been very responsible at all. I know I could have been much more responsible and I could have got more involved. I should have made more of an effort.

> I have definitely produced a lot of work and I have worked late into evening on this project.

Many students mentioned that they had completed the work to their best ability, that they had worked effectively and attended college on a regular basis.

How motivated have you been?

> Not very.
> Quite motivated.
> At times, very motivated.
> I was very motivated throughout.
> At the beginning I was motivated but at the end I was loosing interest.
> During the first few days of the project I was finding it difficult to motivate myself because I could not generate any ideas but the group encouraged me and this in turn helped me to become more interested and produce lots of good ideas.
> After the first two weeks I felt motivated and so did the rest of my group as we got more involved in the work we were doing.
> Design briefs always inspire and motive me no matter what they are.
> I was immediately motivated but the hard part was motivating the rest of the group.
> The most motivated I have been since leaving school.
> Incredibly motivated, I have never enjoyed myself so much before.
> Once we got going it got pretty interesting and this motivated me.
> This was a great project to do, as I saw its relevance.
> When the group lacked interest I lacked interest and when the group finally got motivated I got motivated.
> Disagreements in the group affected my motivation.

Other comments from students were of a similar type to the above remarks.

How reflective have you been? In other words, how critical have been of yourself? Give examples that show how you have been critical during this project.

> Very critical, but not a lot of evidence of this.
> The quality of my work shows how critical I have been.
> I have always looked back at my work to see if I could improve upon what I had produced, making corrections as I go along.
> I corrected my research work because I felt I could do better than this.

have not been very critical in this project.
I have been critical in work by rearranging the layout of my sketchbook, storyboard and concept board and adding further information to this body of work when asked to do so.
Avoiding complex ideas.
I try to pick out faults in everything I do.
I try often to analyse and reason through my work and ideas.
I have noticed how my final visual rendering has too much colour and lacks a sense of dynamic form.
I have learnt a lot from the group, which helped me to become more critical of myself.
I regularly did ask my friends to criticise my work and I was particularly critical of my model-making work.
I remade the presentation boards several times before I was happy with the result.
I kept constantly going back to the same piece of work to see if further improvements were needed.
I realised, having completed the drawing that the final visual needed a stronger sense of colour and style.

Other comments from students were of a similar type to the above remarks

Do you feel that you have personally responded well to criticism of your work or your performance during this assignment? Give examples of how you feel that you have responded well to criticism.

When the group told me that the model needed improving I did it.
When asked to produce more work I responded.
Not a lot was criticised.
I was told that I needed to make improvements to my sketchbook and this I have done.
I have tried to respond positively to criticism but I have found it hard to take at times from other group members.
Criticism makes me push for higher standards and goals and I enjoy that.
I find that criticism helps to motivate me.
Perhaps as a group we should have been more critical of each other.
Group criticism helps to get the best out of you.
Knowing that the group would be criticising my work made me work harder.

Other comments from students were of a similar type to the above remarks.

Student second questionnaire for unit 5

Students were asked to grade their responses to the following questions.

1 = very good, 2 = good, 3 = acceptable, 4 = poor

There were 40 questionnaire responses.

		Number of responses to each grade			
	Student self-evaluation of unit 5	**grade 1**	**grade 2**	**grade 3**	**grade 4**
1	*Did you enjoy the project itself?*	8	23	8	1
2	*Did you enjoy working in a group?*	12	18	8	2
3	*Did Howard properly explain the project brief to you and the idea of group work?*	29	11	0	0
4	*Was Howard's limited teaching supportive, challenging and encouraging?*	22	13	3	2
5	*Was the project handbook clear about what was expected from students?*	20	19	1	0
6	*Was the project handbook useful?*	14	21	5	0
7	*Would you recommend for future students this kind of project, one that focuses on group-work learning?*	27	11	2	0
8	*Were your group members supportive and encouraging of your contribution?*	9	19	8	4
9	*Do you feel that you could put to good use what you have learnt from this project experience?*	23	14	3	0
10	*Do you feel that you now understand why group work is important?*	28	11	1	0
11	*Do you feel that learning in a group excels your learning more effectively than if you were having to work on your own?*	19	16	4	1
12	*Do you feel that learning in a group brought out issues and problems faster than if you were working on your own on a project like this?*	23	13	4	1
13	*Do you feel that you have got to know the students in your group better (how they think, their motivation and skills), as a consequence of this group project?*	22	10	6	2
14	*Did you feel there was adequate discussion and co-operation in the group?*	8	17	13	2
15	*Was your group innovative, creative and dynamic?*	13	17	9	1
16	*Did you feel that working in a group was more demanding than working on your own?*	16	15	6	3
17	*Did you feel that working in group helped you to think more effectively?*	14	20	6	0
18	*How would you rate your own contribution to the group?*	6	28	6	0
19	*Teaching input was deliberately reduced on this project did you find this a particular problem to handle?*	12	11	14	3

Students were then invited to write any further comments that they would like to make about this project.

> Maybe in the future groups could be chosen by Howard, so that students would have to work with others they may not already know.
> The project was very enjoyable and interesting.
> A lot of self-motivation was required from the groups.
> This was a very satisfying project, one that I enjoyed thoroughly.
> The project was worthwhile because it made you interact, compromise and discuss your ideas with others.
> I feel that we could have done more if we had more teaching help.
> I found working in groups very difficult.
> I found the design process and our end disability design solution most satisfying but working in groups taught me a lot about other people some of which is not complimentary.
> I cannot think of any criticism.
> I feel that working in groups is a very negative experience.
> I have never worked on a group project before but this project was most rewarding and taught me a lot about how working in a group can be very productive.
> This was a most challenging and interesting project.
> I feel it is unfair to mark the group work as a whole as there were some members in my group who did very little work.

References and further reading

Abercrombie, M. (1979), *Aims and Techniques of Group Teaching*, Research into Higher Education Monographs (Guildford: University of Surrey)

Knight, P. (ed.) (1995), *Assessment For Learning in Higher Education* (SEDA)

Barnett, R. (1996), 'The Limits of Competence, Knowledge', *Higher Education and Society* (The Society for Research into Higher Education)

Barnett, R. (1992), *Improving Higher Education, Total Quality Care* (Buckingham: Open University Press)

Beckett, D. (1999), 'Workplace Learning as Postmodernist Enactment: A Model from Dementia', in *Philosophy of Education Society of Great Britain*, conference paper (Oxford)

Beckett, D. (1998), 'Anticipative Action and Its Contribution to An Emerging Epistemology of Practice', in *Philosophy of Education Society of Great Britain*, conference paper (Oxford)

Bochner, D., Gibbs,, G. & Wisker, G. (1995), *Supporting More Students*, No.6. (The Oxford Centre for Staff Development)

Boud, D. & Higgs, J. (1993), 'Bringing Self-Directed Learning into the Mainstream of Tertiary Education', in Grave, N. (ed.) *Learner Managed Learning-Practice, Theory and Policy* (Leeds: World Education Fellowship, HEC)

Boud, D. & Higgs, J. (1993), 'Bringing Self-Directed Learning Into The Mainstream Of Tertiary Education', in Grave, N. (ed.) *Learner Managed Learning-Practice, Theory and Policy* (Leeds: World Education Fellowship, HEC)

Boud, D. & Miller, N. (1996), *Working with Experience* (London: Routledge)

Boud, D. (1995), *Enhancing Learning Through Self Assessment* (London: Kogan Page)

Boud, D. (ed.) (1995), *Moving Towards Autonomy in Developing Students Autonomy in Learning* (London: Kogan Page)

Boulton, C. & Garth, Y. (eds.) (1983), Learning in Groups (San Francisco: Jossey-Bass Publishers)

Bowden, J. (1988), 'Achieving Change on Teaching Practice', in Ramsden, P. (ed.), *New Perspectives*, (London: Kogan Page)

Brockett, R. & Hiemstra, R. (1991), *Self-Direction in Adult Learning, Perspectives on Theory, Research and Practice* (London: Routledge)

Barnett, R. (1996), *The Limits of Competence, Knowledge, Higher Education and Society* (The Society for Research into Higher Education)

Burgess, T. (1993), 'Can Learners Manage in Fostering Learner-Managed Learning', in Marshall & Rowland (eds.), *A Guide to Learning Independently*

Cryer, P. & Elton, L. (1992), *Active Learning in Large Classes and with Increasing Student Numbers*, Module. 4, parts 1 & 2 (Sheffield: CVCP)

Dam, L. (1998), *Learner Autonomy, From Theory to Classroom Practice* (Dublin: Authentik)

Dewey, J. (1944), *Democracy and Education* (New York: Free Press)

Dewey, J. (1958), *Art as Experience* (New York: Capricorn Books)

Daniel, J. (1999), *Mega-Universities and Knowledge Media* (London: Kogan Page)

Dobes, R & Rawlinson, G. (1993), *Using Synectic Processes in Education*

Dollard, J. & Miller, N.E. (1941), *Social Learning and Imitation* (New Haven: Yale University Press)

Duke, C. (1992), T*he Learning University, Towards a New Paradigm?* (Buckingham: Open University Press)

Ecclestone, K. (1996), *How to Assess The Vocational Curriculum* (London: Kogan Page)

Ellis, R. (1995), *Quality Assurance for University Teaching* (Buckingham: The Society for Research into Higher Education)

Eraut, M. (1996), *Developing Professional Knowledge and Competence* (London: The Falmer Press)

Evans, L. & Abbot, I. (1998), *Teaching and Learning in Higher Education* (London: Cassell Education)

Garvey, C. (1977), *Play* (London: Fontana Open Books)

Ghaye, A. & K. (1998), T*eaching and Learning through Critical Reflective Practice* (London: David Fulton Publishers)

Gibbs, G. (1992), *Assessing More Students*, No.4. (The Oxford Centre for Staff Development)

Gibbs, G. (1992), *Independent Learning with More Students*, No.5. (The Oxford Centre for Staff Development)

Gibbs, G. (1992), *Problems and Course Design Strategies*, No.1 (The Oxford Centre for Staff Development)

Gibbs, G. et al. (1996), *Improving Student Learning, Using Research to Improve Student Learning* (The Oxford Centre for Staff Development)

Habeshaw, T. Gibbs, G. & Habeshaw S. (1992), *Problems with Large Classes* (Bristol: Technical and Educational Services Ltd)

Hager, P. (1999), *Know-How and Workplace Practical Judgement*, Philosophy of Education Society Annual Conference (Oxford)

Hiemstra, R. & Burton, S. (1990), *Individualizing Instruction* (San Francisco: Jossey-Bass Publishing)

Jaques, D. (1995), *Learning in Groups* (London: Kogan Page)

Jarvis, P (1999), *Adult and Continuing Education, Theory and Practice* (London: Routledge)

Journal of Art and Design Education (1991), Vol. 10, No.1

Knight, P. (1995), *Assessment for Learning in Higher Education* (London: Kogan Page)

Knowles, M. (1990), *The Adult Learner, A Neglected Species* (Houston: Gulf Publishing Company)

Kolb, D. (1984), *Experiential Learning* (New Jersey: Prentice Hall Incorporated)

Laycock, L. (1993), 'Enterprise in Higher Education and Learner-Managed Learning: The Use of Learning Contracts', in Graves, N. (ed.), *World Educational Fellowship*

Little, D. (1995), *Learner Autonomy, Definitions, Issues and Problems*, Authentik, Dublin.

Marples, R. (ed.) (1999), *The Aims of Education* (London: Routledge)

Marshall & Rowland. (1993), *A Guide to Learning Independently* (Milton Keynes: The Open University)

McKernan, J. (1996), *Curriculum Action Research* (London: Kogan Page)

Moon, J. (1996), *Generic Level Descriptors And Their Place In The Standards Debate in Modular Higher Education in the UK in Focus* (London: HEFC)

Murray, E. (1986), *Imaginative Thinking and Human Existence* (Pittsburgh: Duquesne University Press)

Norwich School of Art and Design, Quality Audit Report (HEQC, 1997)

Oddi, L. (1987), 'Perspectives on Self-directed Learning', in *Adult Education Quarterly*, Vol.38, No.1, Fall 1987

Piaget, J. (1967), *Six Psychological Studies* (London: University of London Press)

Piaget, J. (1972), *The Child's Conception of the World*, trans. J& A Tomlinson (New Jersey: Littlefield Adams)

Ellis, R. (ed.) (1991), *Quality Assurance for University Teaching* (Buckingham: The Society for Research into Higher Education)

Race, P. (1992), *53 Interesting Ways to Write Open Learning Materials* (Bristol: Technical and Educational Services Ltd)

Ramsden, P. & Marton, F. (1980), 'What Does it Take to Improve Learning?', in Ramsden, P. (ed.) *New Perspectives* (London: Kogan Page)

Ramsden, P. (1980), 'Studying Learning: Improving Teaching in Improving Learning', in Ramsden, P. (ed.), *New Perspectives* (London: Kogan Page)

Boud, D. & Higgs, J. (1993), 'Bringing Self-Directed Learning Into The Mainstream Of Tertiary Education', in Ramsden, P. (ed.), *New Perspectives* (London: Kogan Page)

Rogers, C. & Freiberg (1994), *Freedom to Learn* (New York: Macmillan College Publishing Company)

Ridley, J. (1997), *Learner Autonomy, Developing Learners Thinking Skills* (Dublin: Authenik)

Schön, D. (1987), *Educating the Reflective Practitioner* (San Francisco, Jossey-Bass Publishers)

SEDA Journals 2000

Smith & Brown. (1995), *Research Teaching and Learning in Higher Education*, SEDA (London: Kogan Page)

Smith, F. (1992), *To Think* (London: Routledge)

Stephenson, J. (1993), 'The Student Experience of Independent Study: Reaching The Parts Other Programmes Appear to Miss', in *Learner Managed Learning*, in Graves, N. (ed.), *World Educational Fellowship*

Tait, J. & Knight, P. (1996), The Management of Independent Learning, SEDA (London: Kogan Page)

Thorley, L. & Gregory et al. (1994), *Using Group-Based Learning in Higher Education* (London: Kogan Page)

Tiberius, R (1996), *Small Group Teaching* (London: Kogan Paul)

Tight, M. (1996), *Adult Education and Training* (London: Routledge)

Torrance, E. (1964), *Guiding Creative Talent* (New Jersey: Prentice-Hall, Inc)

Ushida, E. (1996), *The Role of Motivation*, No.5 (Dublin: Authentik Books)

Walford, G. (ed.) (1991), *Doing Educational Research* (London: OUP & Routledge)

Walker, L. (1994), 'The New Higher Education System, Modularity and Student Capability', in Jenkins, A. & Walker, L. (eds.), *Developing Student Capability Through Modular Courses* (London: HEC)

Wilks, M. & Gibbs, G. (1994), *Course Design for Resource Based Learning, Art and Design* (The Oxford Centre for Staff Development)

Winfred, F. (1980), *Learning, a Survey of Psychological Interpretations* (London: Methuen)

Wragg, E. (1994), *An Introduction to Classroom Observation* (London: Routledge)

Vygotsky, L. (1962), *Thought and Language* (Massachusetts: MIT Press)

23 The role of art and design graduate employment research in informing curriculum development and review

Hardip Gosal, John S Pearson and Paul L Squires

Department of Textiles, University of Huddersfield, UK

Abstract

The curriculum review and development of the Textile Design degree at the University of Huddersfield is informed by changes in the UK and international textile industry, particularly in relation to the increase in overseas sourcing and use of IT. These factors will affect the nature of present and future graduate employment and job opportunities. The skills that students acquire while on a degree course must reflect those required by a potential employer.

Although single-year 'snap shots' are taken of graduate employment, it is important to take a long term view of how higher education should bridge the skills gap between university and the work place. This paper is based on a longitudinal study into textile design graduate employment, involving over 600 graduates and their employers over a ten-year period and addresses issues related to curriculum development raised by this research.

Introduction – the current state of the UK textile industry

The UK textile and clothing industries have suffered a significant downturn in recent years, in terms of employment. Table 1 shows that employment levels have decreased by 28% over the past five years and this trend would seem to be a continuous one. Manufacturing output in the textile industry has decreased by around 50% in the past ten years (Table 2), imports of textiles are increasing (although so are exports) (Table 3) and the number of manufacturing sites is rapidly decreasing (Table 4).

	1996	**1997**	**1998**	**1999**	**2000**	**2001**
Textiles	174	173	166	152	143	134
Clothing	150	148	145	122	103	89
Total	313	311	297	262	246	223
Year-on-year % decrease	-	0.6	4.5	11.8	6.1	9.3

Table 1 Employment levels in the UK textile and clothing manufacturing industries (thousands) Source: Annual Abstract of Statistics (2002a)

	1990	**1991**	**1992**	**1993**	**1994**	**1995**	**1996**	**1997**	**1998**	**% decrease 1990–8**
Yarn	58.0	42.0	35.6	41.1	40.1	37.6	36.1	30.9	27.2	53.1
Fabric	428.9	386.2	372.1	331.0	303.4	288.5	294.5	262.2	245.8	42.7

Table 2 Manufacture of cotton and man-made fibre yarns (thousand tonnes) and woven fabric (million linear metres) Source: Annual Abstract of Statistics (2002e)

	1991	1992	1993	1994	1995	1996	1997	1998	1999	2000	% increase: 1991–9
Imports	3586	3778	3974	4401	4806	5075	5003	4864	4382	4382	22.2
Exports	2337	2444	2661	2950	3282	3471	3421	3261	3018	3055	30.7
Deficit	1249	1334	1313	1451	1524	1604	1582	1603	1364	1327	6.2

Table 3 UK imports and exports of textiles (£million) Source: Annual Abstract of Statistics (2002c)

Number of employees	Number of units: 1998	Number of units: 2001	% decrease: 1998–2000
0–9	4135	3705	10.4
10–49	1630	1360	16.6
50–99	370	330	10.8
100–199	320	245	23.4
200–499	170	110	35
500+	20	15	25
Total number of units	6645	5765	13.2

Table 4 Number of local units (UK textiles, excluding clothing) Source: Annual Abstract of Statistics (2002d)

The reasons for this decline are well documented – it is becoming increasingly less cost effective to manufacture textiles and clothing in the UK than in countries with much lower wage costs and other overheads. Although the cost of producing textiles and clothing in the UK is relatively cost effective compared to the general costs of manufacture (Table 5), this country (and, indeed, most developed countries) cannot compete in the bulk production market with many of the developing countries. Table 6, for instance, shows that the cost of manufacturing textiles in the UK is three times greater than in the Philippines, 20 times greater than in China, 30 times greater than in India and 60 times greater than in Turkey.

	1993	1994	1995	1996	1997	1998	1999	2000
Textiles	88.6	91.6	100.0	99.1	95.8	93.4	88.4	89.8
Clothing	89.6	92.9	100.0	99.5	97.0	94.6	90.2	90.6
All manufactured goods	92.0	94.0	100.0	100.3	97.0	93.2	92.5	96.8

Table 5 United Kingdom producer price index numbers of textile and clothing manufacture – purchase Source: Annual Abstract of Statistics (2002b) (1995 = 100)

Country	Labour cost ($/h)
Germany	17.35
United States	13.63
Italy	12.51
United Kingdom	11.04
Hong Kong	10.45
Australia	8.49
Israel	7.90
Thailand	5.42
North Korea	0.00
Philippines	3.50
Mexico	2.88
Latvia	1.92
China	0.52
India	0.37
Turkey	0.18

Table 6 Comparative labour costs (2000) Source: Textile Manufacture Yearbook of Labour Statistics (2000)

Nevertheless, consumers in the UK and other developed countries still need to purchase textiles and clothing. Consumer spending continues to increase year-on-year as does average earnings and domestic demand (Table 7).

Year	Domestic demand	Consumer spending	Average earnings
2000	3.6	4.1	4.0
2001	2.8	3.9	4.8
2002	2.7	3.5	3.6
2003	3.2	3.0	4.6
2004	3.2	3.0	4.4
2005	2.9	2.5	4.7

Table 7 Forecasts for the UK economy (% changes on previous year) Source: Ernst & Young (2002)

Textile education in the UK

Currently, there are a huge number of diploma and degree courses in the UK related to textile design. UCAS (2002) data show that there are 24 HND courses and 69 degree courses. However, of the 4591 graduates in design studies in work in 2000, fewer than 100 found employment as textile designers – a significant decrease compared to 1999 (Table 8). We who operate in further and higher education have a moral duty to provide our graduates with the academic and personal skills required for them to obtain worthwhile employment. In addition, with students paying a substantial tuition fee, they are behaving more as consumers, demanding value for money from their post-school education. Clearly it is incumbent upon those who work in colleges and universities to be very much aware of these factors and to respond to the fact that employment opportunities in design in general and in textile design in particular are very different from what they were only a few years ago.

The nature of the research in this paper

It is easy to say that the above issues must be addressed, but how exactly can it be done? The Association of Graduate Careers Advisory Service and the Higher Education Statistics Agency produce annual first destination statistics. However, these produce, at best, a four-year review, utilising very broad subject categories within the design studies area. For instance, at the University of Huddersfield, our

Employment type: design studies	% of total: 2000	% of total: 1999
Employment	71.5	72.0
Further study	9.6	9.5
Not available for employment	6.4	5.3
Not employed	12.5	13.2
Total number of graduates working	4591	4864
Number employed in clothing design	87	112
Number employed in textile design	138	n/a

Table 8 Graduate employment on design studies Source: Association of Graduate Careers Advisory Service (2002)

experience is that there are vast differences in employment opportunities and prospects between, textile, fashion, product and multi-media design, for instance. In order successfully to develop existing curricula and new courses, it is essential to know what employment destinations graduates from specific courses enter, what skills they require and the extent to which existing courses provide these skills. Although student feedback on courses is obtained regularly via course committees, tutorials, personal tutors, annual course evaluation and from Student Services and the Careers service, a longitudinal study provides a longer term framework of trends. Hence the nature of the research presented in this paper, a study of Huddersfield textile design graduates over the period 1990–9.

The objectives of the research, relative to the Department of Textiles at the University of Huddersfield, can therefore be summarised as being to:

- inform curriculum development in existing courses and the development of new courses;
- provide a database of graduates for use in developing an alumni association;
- provide information for potential and existing students on types of graduate employment possible;

- provide information on how changes in the textile design course over a ten-year period have affected graduate employment prospects; and
- dentify new skills and working priorities required in the future in the textile and clothing industries with the aim of informing future developments in the department.

Methodology used

600 questionnaires, consisting of 23 questions, were sent to University of Huddersfield students who had graduated from the textile design course between 1990–9; 138 replies (23%) were received and analysed. The questionnaire related to:

- the nature of the course itself, particularly its structure;
- reasons for choosing the University of Huddersfield to study at;
- the image of the Department of Textiles;
- the workshop environment in the department and the equipment used;
- academic/practical skills learned on the course related to employment;
- transferable/problem-solving skills learned on the course;
- suggested improvements to the course;
- staff support on the course;
- importance of career management skills;
- experience/present work after graduation;
- employer details; and
- importance of personal skills and training in employment.

An even distribution of questionnaires from the different years of graduation was obtained. A selection of employers was sent similar questionnaires, covering aspects such as:

- reason for choice of a graduate from Huddersfield;
- numbers of employees plus changes over the years;

- skills/strengths/weaknesses brought by graduates;
- importance of management/personal skills; and
- training in employment.

A sample of responding graduates was selected for in-depth structured interviews (comprising 57 questions) covering:

- the course that they studied in more detail;
- their perception of the textile industry;
- the type of employment that they had experienced;
- details of skills obtained on their course; and
- effectiveness of the University Careers Service.

The importance and effectiveness of personal development during the course and in employment was an important feature of the interviews.

Interviews were recorded for further analysis of the transcribed texts. Questionnaires were analysed using SPSS (Statistical Package for Social Science), which enables investigations to be undertaken of any relationships between two variables, by use of cross tabulation.

The work was undertaken in association with CAPITB (Clothing and Allied Products Industrial Training Board), the National Training Organisation for the Clothing Industry, and was supported by grants from the European Social Fund and the University of Huddersfield.

Enforced changes to the textile design course

A number of factors, other than responding to needs of potential students and employers, have effected change to the textile design course since its inception in 1977. Responding to these factors has had some effect on the usefulness of the course to these students and employers. To date, there have been six versions of the course: 1977; 1983; 1988; 1993; 1999; and 2002. The reasons for developing new versions are shown below (Table 9):

Version of course	Reasons for changes
1977	CNAA quinquennial review process
1983	CNAA quinquennial review process
1988	CNAA quinquennial review process
1993	Incorporation as a university; modularisation
1999	Introduction of BA and MText routes
2002	Changes to University CATS system – assessment/semesters

(CNAA = Central Council for Academic Awards; MText = Master of Textiles).

Table 9 Changing Structure of the Textile Design Course

In addition, the following factors have driven changes to the course:

- need to increase student numbers (Government);
- need to increase staff:student ratio (university);
- demise of HND courses (Government/colleges);
- changes to student funding mechanisms (Government);
- nature of entrants/need to widen participation (Government/university); and
- changes to entrance qualifications: Curriculum 2000 (Government).

The main changes to the course, as a result of both reactive and proactive initiatives, can be summarised as follows:

- the course is still based on design supported by/integrated with technology;
- the technology content has decreased as a percentage of the course;
- technology teaching has become more 'hands on' and less theoretical;
- the design content has increased as a percentage of the course;
- design elements/teaching have become more integrated;
- contribution of supporting studies (business; marketing; management; careers guidance) has increased;

- CAD/IT has become increasingly important and has been increasingly integrated into modules;
- optionality between modules has decreased while that within modules has increased;
- course administration has been simplified;
- new exit routes have been introduced:
- BA;
- BSc;
- MText;
- Cert HE; and
- Dip HE.

The delivery and assessment of the course has also changed:

- greater use of group work, including tutorials;
- multi-purpose use of studios;
- 'hot-desking' of studio space;
- use of peer assessment;
- use of formative and summative assessment;
- decrease in overall assessment load;
- decrease in class contact hours/increase in non-contact, student-directed hours;
- move away from examinations towards continuous assessment;
- increased use of CAD and IT; and
- increased use of electronic methods of delivery/presentation.

Each of the above re-validations of the course has provided an opportunity to examine the effectiveness of the course overall; this can be summarised in terms of the present philosophy of the course:

- the course aims at enabling learning rather than teaching knowledge;

- the importance of study skills and interpersonal skills is recognised;
- the importance of self-directed learning is recognised;
- the importance of widening participation is recognised;
- the relevance of course material needs to be constantly addressed;
- the relevance of facilities, including equipment, needs to be constantly addressed; and
- the relationship to industry is still seen to be of central importance.

There have clearly been significant changes to the course as a result of these factors and of the implementation of their consequences. The extent to which these imposed changes (reactive) and deliberate changes introduced by the course team (proactive) affected the students' and employers' perception of the course was of interest to the research.

Results of the graduate questionnaires

70% of the graduates in employment were working in textile or textile-related positions, 20% were in education, the remaining 10% being employed in other areas.

Most were employed in design positions, others were in technology, sales, accounts, CAD/IT, consultancies or training. Many reported that significant changes had occurred to the company(ies) for whom they worked. Many reported on how useful the placement experience had been in preparing them for the world of full-time employment. Most realised that opportunities for textile design graduates to work as designers in industry were diminishing.

Graduates recognised the importance of non-academic skills gained on the course, such as:

- teamwork;

- communication;
- personal;
- presentation;
- commercial;
- research;
- time management/working to commercial briefs;
- transferable; and
- decision making.

In fact, many graduates said that personal skills were of more importance in employment than textile skills.

The need for students to take control of their own career development whilst at university was clearly expressed. Aspects seen to be of particular importance included:

- self awareness;
- self promotion;
- exploring and creating opportunities;
- action planning;
- decision making;
- coping with uncertainty;
- transfer of skills; and
- self confidence.

It was interesting to note that employers tended not to rate most of these skills as highly as graduates. It was not surprising that, given the present state of the textile industry, employers rated 'coping with uncertainty' very highly. 'Self confidence' and 'transfer of skills' were rated very highly by employers.

Graduates identified the following personal attributes as being very important in the workplace:

- willingness to learn;

- commitment/dependability;
- self-motivation;
- communication skills; and
- co-operation.

Employers also highlighted the importance of commitment/dependability; employers rated 'computer literacy' less highly than graduates.

Students had positive comments about the following aspects of the department and of the course studied:

- practical focus of teaching;
- facilities;
- the placement year;
- new environment;
- general image/impression;
- group teaching;
- design, CAD, technology, quality control, marketing found useful in employment;
- industry links;
- relevance/usefulness of course content to employment; and
- analytical skills developed.

Negative comments, related to experiences in employment, included:

- in group teaching, large group sizes made learning difficult;
- some equipment outdated/doesn't relate to industry/not used/not relevant to employment;
- CAD equipment not 'state of art' (graduates from the early 1990s);
- some aspects of art, art history, mathematics, not relevant to employment;
- insufficient teamwork experience; and
- insufficient experience of problem solving.

Possible areas for improvement included:

- increased emphasis on computing/CAD (early 1990s graduates);
- more careers advice/interview skills;
- more on garment production, languages; and
- more industrial visits.

Responses from graduates over the ten-year period were very similar, apart from an increased awareness of the importance of CAD by later graduates.

Conclusions

- Questionnaire responses from graduates over the ten-year period of the study were broadly similar, apart from an increasing awareness of the importance of CAD by later graduates.
- Employability skills identified as being important continue to be relevant as textile design graduates increasingly gain employment in non-design areas such as retail.
- Links with industry, particularly the placement year, are seen to be of high importance with regard to potential employability.
- The major review of the textile design course at Huddersfield in 2002 (as a result of the university implementing a new CATS assessment strategy) was helped considerably by the present research.
- This resulted in the formal inclusion of study skills and career-management skills as compulsory components of the course, together with a more integrated approach to delivery of all subjects.
- Major reviews of department facilities and equipment since 1997 have resulted in the removal of irrelevant equipment and an increased emphasis on CAD/CAM.
- The development of the new BA Global Textile Sourcing and Management course in 2001–2 relied heavily on the findings of this research, in terms of:

(i) the philosophy of the course;

(ii) establishment of an industry advisory panel re course development; and

(iii) structure and delivery of the course.

- This research has shown the value of undertaking longitudinal studies into graduate employment. This research should not be regarded as a 'one-off', but should be continuous, not just for the textile design course at Huddersfield, but for all university courses.
- This is of particular urgency with respect to initiatives such as Widening Participation and the move towards allowing 50% of all 18–30 year olds access to higher education, if we are to provide the optimum courses for all our students.

References

Annual Abstract of Statistics (2002a), 'Employment Levels in Manufacturing Industries', Section 7.5, p. 87 (The Stationery Office)

Annual Abstract of Statistics (2002b), 'Producer Price Index Numbers', Section 16.1, p. 254 (The Stationery Office)

Annual Abstract of Statistics (2002c), 'UK Imports and Exports', Section 182/18.3, pp. 296–7 (The Stationery Office)

Annual Abstract of Statistics (2002d), 'Number of Local Units', Section 21.3, p. 352 (The Stationery Office)

Annual Abstract of Statistics (2002e), 'Manufacturing Output', Section 21.17, p. 365 (The Stationery Office)

Association of Graduate Careers Advisory Service (2002), *What do Graduates Do?*, pp. 34–5 (Cheltenham)

Ernst & Young (2002), Economic Outlook for Business, Issue 19, p. 3

Yearbook of Labour Statistics (2000), *Comparative Labour Costs*, Section 6A (International Labour Office, Geneva)

Biographical notes

Hardip Gosal BA is a Research Assistant in the Department of Textiles at the University of Huddersfield. Her first degree was in Business Studies; she undertook placement at the Bradford and District Training and Enterprise Council (TEC) before taking up her present post.

Dr John Pearson BSc MPhil PhD C Chem MRSC C Text ATI is Head of the Department of Textiles at the University of Huddersfield. Professional experience includes membership of the Council, the Professional and Educational Affairs Committee and the Events Committee of the Textile Institute, membership of the Huddersfield Textile Society, Association of Professors and Heads of Textiles, Yorkshire and the Humber Regional Innovation Strategy, Textiles and Clothing sector, Confederation of British Wool Textiles Awards Committee and the Yorkshire Section of the Royal Institute of Chemistry. Research interests include flammability of textiles, textile finishing, foam treatment of textiles, diversified uses of jute, and environmental disposal of textile waste. Dr Pearson has publications in these areas and in the area of developments in education. He has considerable experience of research supervision and examination and of external undergraduate examination.

Paul Squires is a Senior Lecturer in the Department of Textiles at the University of Huddersfield. He has been Course Leader for the BSc Textile Design course and is now responsible for publicity and recruitment for all courses in the department. Professional experience includes Print Production Manager at Coats Viyella Home Furnishings Ltd, Director of own design and production business, Consultant Designer for Weverij De Ploeg in Holland and several part-time lecturing posts. Paul Squires has exhibited his design work widely in the UK and Europe. His research interests include screen printing techniques, CAD/CAM related to small scale production and curriculum design and development in higher education.

24 Student mentor project

Daphne Hampton

**School of Marketing and Management,
London College of Printing, The London Institute, UK**

Introduction

The student mentor project described here took place at London College of Printing (LCP), one of the constituent colleges of The London Institute. The LCP is strongly committed to personal tutorial and learning development support because they link the college's retention and achievement policy with its desire to widen student participation. The author is also passionately concerned with mentoring and peer tutoring.

Two mentor projects for two different undergraduate groups are in place. The first project targets 'at risk' students early on in their year-one Marketing and Management undergraduate programme. The second mentor project targets the direct-entry students into year two of the Retail Design Management undergraduate programme.

The project aim is to enhance integration, academic development, learning and retention throughout the remainder of the course by the use of student mentors.

Earlier small-scale internal college research by the author has shown the important role of personal tutorials in improving retention. Case studies from learning development tutors also show how study support improves the learning experience of the students involved. Student mentoring is seen as one of the strands in this all-important area of overall student support in its role of enhancing the curriculum and aiding retention.

Selection and training of mentors

Second- and third-year student groups from the relevant courses were informed of the projects and volunteers were requested. Mentors were selected from these students. A training session was designed and run, based on a mentor handbook that was produced for this project. This handbook describes the role of the mentor, gives advice on carrying out this role and offers sources of support. In particular, both the training and the handbook emphasise the boundaries and responsibilities of the role. The training involved going through the handbook together, followed by questions and answers and further discussion. The mentors were also each given a copy of the Tutor Handbook, the guide that is given to all personal tutors in the college. The mentors were to treat the position in a professional manner, as they would treat a full-time job. They were to keep a written record of all contact. Mentors were not to do work for their mentees, i.e. they were not to write any part of their mentees' assignments, but could give advice in the planning period and then read drafts and advise again.

Mentors would be paid for each hour's mentoring, with an initial maximum of ten sessions to be spread across the academic year by mutual agreement between each pair. Where mentors felt that extra sessions above the initial ten would be beneficial to their mentee, this would be discussed with the author in the Spring term. Payment was seen as a good incentive to attract good quality mentors to the projects at the outset. It also encouraged mentors to act professionally. Mentors were also attracted to the project for the skills it gave them to add to their CVs.

The project is felt to be excellent value as it aids retention. Preventing the loss of an international student is a huge saving for the institution, making the project very cost effective in the eyes of management.

The author supported the mentors throughout the year, maintaining regular informal contact with them by telephone and e-mail. Queries about the role and how to perform it were encouraged and answered. Specific questions about sources of help for mentees were also addressed. Mentors were encouraged to fill in their personal record of all contact with their mentees.

Selection of mentees

In the Marketing and Management (M&M) project, personal tutors from year one of the programme were asked to identify 'at risk' students in their personal tutor groups and ask them if they would like to take part in the project. In the Retail Design Management (RDM) project, all direct-entry year-two students on the course were offered the opportunity to have a mentor.

Meetings between mentors and mentees

An initial meeting took place, with all mentors and mentees in the same room. Here, the purpose of the project was explained again and then each mentor paired up with their mentee for a 'getting to know you' session, during which the author was also available to answer any queries.

Following this initial meeting, the students were free to set their own agenda regarding meetings, within the overall number of ten sessions. Some met face to face all the time, while others interspersed face-to-face contact with telephone and/or e-mail contact.

Participant profile

In the first year of the M&M project, most mentees were second language home students. There was also one single parent, who was a refugee. In year two of this project, mentees were a mix of international students, second language home and EU students and 'first generation' university students.

Mentees were 100% female in year one, and 78% female and 22% male in year two. Mentors were 43% male and 57% female in year one and 22% male and 78% female in year two.

One interesting feature was that mentors had often volunteered for other things too, for example, course representative, student union representative.

Results

Interviews with mentors and mentees took place at the end of the pilot year. The results were very positive for both groups.

Mentees

Mentees all reported that they felt that they had benefited greatly from mentor help. They remarked that they had gained in self-confidence. Mentoring had also improved their study techniques.

They felt that they had settled into college life quicker than many peers ('It was all very helpful, both with the assignments and settling into the course'), learning the college and course conventions and culture through their mentors ('Useful and helpful. My mentor has also given me the lowdown on the lecturers, what they are like, what sort of feedback they give and what not to say to them.'). Some mentees from the first year's project became mentors in year two.

Mentors

The mentors all stated that they had really enjoyed the role, with several adding that they wished that the project had been available to them the previous year.

The most valuable result for the mentors was seen to be the academic benefits for the mentees: one mentor noted that, 'I was able to pass on my knowledge of the course and the college, and give other less obvious advice and tips, such as what I thought that tutors were expecting of her.'

However, mentors also felt that their own studies had profited from their increased focus on study skills and techniques, with their own work benefiting from re-visiting their previous year's topics. One mentor noted that the project 'has given me further insight into the problems that students experience and will I hope help me in my prospective teaching career.' The whole 'experience as a mentor has been helpful and fulfilling for both my mentee and myself.' The process had enabled mentors to observe and realise their own academic progression and maturation during the course of the year.

Mentors also reported increased confidence and self-esteem, together with the 'feel good' factor associated with helping others. One mentor was dyslexic, reflecting the confidence she had gained from the college dyslexia support in her first year. Some mentors never claimed their payment, as thy felt that the satisfaction of helping others was reward enough.

Problems

Two issues surrounding the mentor scheme arose early on. One involved the cases of two mentees who tried to 'save up' their mentoring sessions for use as the end of term and the exams approached. This was seen to be a problem as the main point of the project was to provide support throughout the year, and especially during the first term.

The second issue was more problematic. In the M&M project two mentees were not using their mentors after two sessions. When challenged and asked if they would relinquish their mentors for a newly identified needy student, they both refused and immediately set up meetings with their mentors. However, their meetings still ended up being very irregular over the year.

It became apparent that these two students were actually skilled users of the education system. They had managed to persuade their personal tutors that they needed a mentor while also tapping into student services, study support and other college help. They saw the mentor scheme as another 'safety net' for them, in case they needed the extra help.

Solutions

The first issue, the 'saving up' of mentor sessions, was easily resolved by explaining that the main point of the project was to provide support throughout the year, and especially during the first term, to enable students to settle in and learn more effectively throughout the year. A promise was made to provide extra sessions at the end of the year if they were needed.

The second issue, the irregular use of mentoring sessions, provoked greater care and thought in the selection of mentees for the second year of the M&M project.

The solution for the extra 'at risk' student who was identified was to recruit and train an extra mentor and emphasise the need for intensive meetings when they first met in order to catch up.

Recommendations

All mentees in the second year of the project have fully utilised their mentors but it has become apparent that there were more students in the M&M project who could have benefited from having a mentor than there were mentors. One idea to overcome this is to set up peer tutoring groups for the others.

It is intended to develop a free-standing unit as part of the Personal and Professional Development (PPD) scheme, whereby student mentors could gain credit for mentoring and other activities, such as being a course rep or working for the Student Union. One issue that needs resolving here is that the mentoring project is set up as a paid activity whereas the other activities are voluntary and unpaid. Can a student gain credit on a course unit and be paid for it?

25

'Quick, act like an art director!' Role playing in the graphic design classroom

Deborah Huelsbergen

University of Missouri-Columbia, USA

Abstract

This work in progress looks as how role playing can be used in a studio classroom setting to enhance student engagement and learning. Objectives for the course included helping students in their ability to work under strict time constraints, to develop effective communication skills and to work productively members of a design team. This course was an attempt to structure an experience that had both the benefits of real world client-designer relationships with the comfort of a classroom and teacher-student relationships. The environment established enabled students to relate to each other as fellow designers rather than fellow students and to their teacher as a variety of clients.

Introduction

This paper is a case study of an innovative course design. It began as a pedagogical experiment in the form of a packaging design course taught at the University of Missouri, Columbia in the summers of 1998 and 2000. Role playing was used to produce a 'real world' experience which is often difficult to duplicate in traditional classroom settings. This work is certainly work in progress. This initial work has opened up many possibilities for further study.

First it is important to look at the problem that brought about the study. The students lacked the 'real world' experience that is often difficult to duplicate in a classroom setting. Some university situations such as internships and practicums give the students experience at functioning in practical settings but because of the size of our department, these situations are not as prevalent as they should be. I therefore set out to design a class experience that had both the benefits of real world client-designer relationships with the comfort of a classroom and teacher-student relationships. When working out the syllabus for this course, I first considered getting volunteer clients to come in and deal with the students directly. While I still think this idea could work and be beneficial for the students, it was clear early on that this would not work for this particular class. The decision was made then to line up someone I knew would be available and relatively easy to work with to perform the duties of client – myself.

My objectives for this study were as follows:

- to help students develop the ability to work productively and effectively under very strict time constraints;
- for students to leave the class with a greater ability to communicate their ideas effectively to others; and
- for students to develop the ability to function as members of a design team.

In the syllabus for the course the students were also given objectives which acted as a set of goals for their experience. Eight objectives were listed. These objectives were to:

- develop the ability to work creatively and effectively under strict time constraints;
- learn to budget time effectively and keep track of design time;

- develop the ability to communicate ideas clearly;
- learn to work in a design studio atmosphere;
- develop the ability to maintain good client-designer relationships;
- develop and stick to a budget;
- learn to include solid research in your conceptualisation and design phases of projects; and
- leave this class with three solid portfolio pieces or series.

The basic idea was to structure an environment where the students related to each other not as fellow students but as fellow designers. I relied on my training as an actor to become not the teacher, but many people, their clients each one with a unique identity, personality and agenda. This meant that for the next four weeks we would not be ourselves but we would be playing roles to learn about functioning in the atmosphere of a design studio. In essence, I put the students in an uncomfortable environment but in a comfortable setting. The uncomfortable part was dealing with real and demanding clients, but the students were secure that when I took my client 'hat' off we would be able to discuss what just happened.

The course met for four hours daily for four weeks. Days had different focuses: Mondays were work days; Tuesdays were client meeting days; Wednesdays and Thursdays were group to group critique days; and Fridays were problem solving and work days. There were five design/studio teams each consisting of five to six people. Students in the class ranged in age from 18 to 38. On each team someone played the role of the art director and someone else the secretary/research co-ordinator in addition to their jobs as team designers. Each design/studio team created a name and logo for themselves that helped to add to the feeling that they were actually playing the roles of 'professional designers'.

Ideas in this project stem from elements of my teaching philosophy. The first is the importance of establishing an environment of trust in the classroom. Students need to feel comfortable enough to take risks and experiment while knowing that they are safe and secure with their classmates and teacher. I believe in making the classroom a place where no idea is overlooked and nothing is too far-fetched or outrageous to try. I encourage interaction and communication among all students. Interaction and trust become especially relevant when dealing with group projects as we were in this course. The second element that can only happen when the element of trust is in place is risk. I often describe learning to my students as being like a potluck dinner. If only one person brings something to the table - even though the dish may be tasty - it is rarely enough to feed everyone or for people to leave satisfied. On the other hand when everyone brings a dish there is usually a diverse selection. Therefore, when everyone contributes not only is the meal more interesting by nature of the variety of dishes, people are also better fed and more satisfied. I believe that learning about graphic design is very similar to this diverse potluck dinner: students learn from participating, taking risks and trying new things. Students, however, are not usually willing to do this without a little push.

This brings in the third element of my teaching philosophy, which is balance versus imbalance. I believe that my role as a teacher is related to controlling balance and imbalance in the learning environment. Everyone likes balance and the overwhelming preference people have for symmetry is an inclination that goes back to infants' preference for contrast and symmetry in their environment. It is, however, the role of the teacher strategically to bring imbalance to the learning environment. When learners are thrown out of the ordinary, when there is a slight bit of confusion, discomfort, newness and imbalance then the struggle begins to return to the familiarity of balance. It is in this struggle that learning and risk-taking occur. The element of trust must be present because if the learner is fearful or distrustful, unsure of the atmosphere and what is expected of them, then any imbalance or taking of risks is impossible. When the learner is sure of themselves and the environment they are in, then risk taking and imbalance become a wonderful challenge.

Design projects

Each design team was given three projects to complete by the end of the four-week session. Two of these three projects had clients and the third was conceptually driven with no client.

- **Problem one**: design systems – the problem here is to develop a system of packages for a beverage company. This could be for juice, soda, water, beer, wine etc. By a system I mean that one company wants a recognisable style of labels and/or containers for a variety of similar products. For example, a juice box company wants boxes for grape, cranberry, and apple juice but wants the customer to be able to recognise visually that these are all from the same company. There needs to be a minimum of three packages in this system.

project 1 image 1

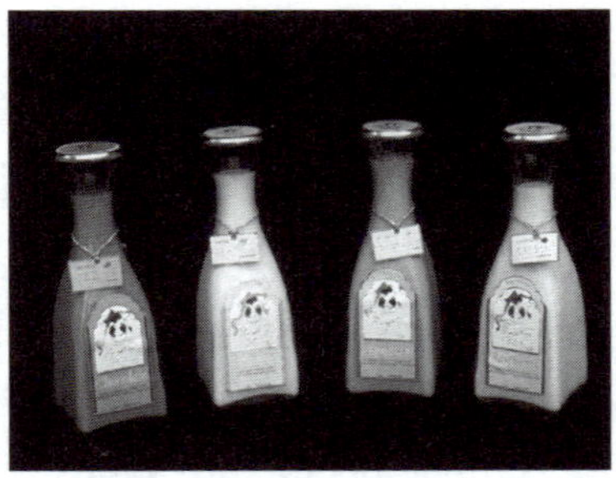

project 1 image 2

project 1 image 3

project 1 image 4

- **Problem two**: green design – the basic problem here is to go out and find something that is over-packaged and redesign the packaging to make environmental sense. The student needs to be concerned not only with how many materials are used but also what the life cycles of the materials are. The company has recently made a commitment to the environment and, therefore, wants to redesign its product, packaging and logo to reflect its new environmentally friendly attitude. The students will need to undertake significant research when tackling this problem, in order to inform themselves about issues of green design.

project 2

- **Problem three**: conceptual design - this is a highly conceptual problem. The student is asked to package something intangible, such as fear, love, hate, sadness, tranquillity, confidence etc. This is all about concept and form and how this thing will look, feel, taste, sound or whatever it takes to get the idea across. The final package can take any form the student wishes and materials are unlimited, but the final piece must fit into the classroom. Students are encouraged to give the problem a good deal of thought before settling on an idea, to be creative and to stay away from the obvious. The students also need to figure out what goes in this package to support their concept. Perhaps this is the time to think in terms of metaphors.

project 3 image 1

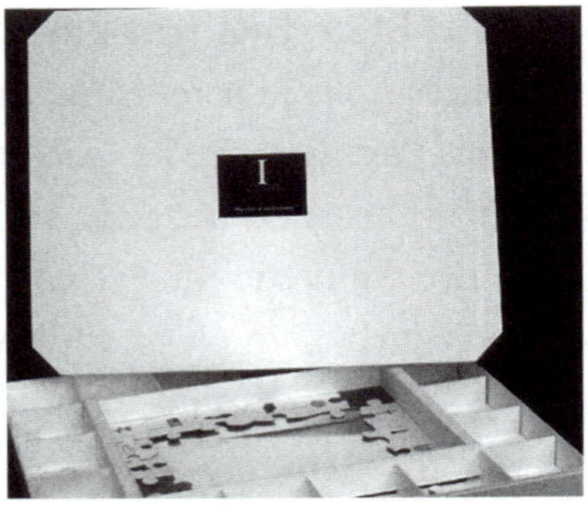

project 3 image 2

In terms of student research the first thing that the students tackled was a company profile for project one. In a real situation the designers would not be determining the client, company or product but in this class situation I decided to give the students this level of freedom. But, once they set the guidelines for the company nothing could change. They were set in stone.

It was important for students to think this through clearly and know as much about the company as they could. For example, in the first project they could say the beverage company was a small- to medium-scale company located in Washington State. They were a group of college friends that were interested in creating a beverage company that sold organic teas. The company gives a portion of their proceeds to environmental groups.

Once they had decided upon the company profile, students then wrote out product profiles. These included information not only on the product and the packaging but also on the market. At this time students also did contemporary research in shops by taking photos of related products.

With all of the research in place students began the work of designing. The art director oversaw all of the work, while also acting as a designer and was called upon to settle any design disputes. In the creative research part of the role-playing exercise students were called upon to work not by themselves at their desks but actively as members of their groups. Students worked together in brainstorming sessions and on conceptual matrices to come up with creative solutions to the problems. This research was documented in the form of process books that were controlled by the group secretary. Each team member would sign and date every piece of paper they generated and the secretary organised all of this information. This is a way to look back at the team's ideation process and see how their ideas came together. Students also used sheets to estimate their costs and time use.

My part of the role-playing was that of ten different clients. When studio teams met with clients the meetings were outside of the classroom and ranged from very casual to quite formal depending on the personality of the particular client. Meetings were set up in advance and the moment we entered the meeting room I was no longer the teacher but the client and studio teams addressed me accordingly. This was the toughest aspect for the students to learn but they did so rapidly. It was difficult at first to embrace the role playing but physically having a different environment for these meetings helped. Several students had trouble with maintaining their role playing in the first client/designer meeting but after that were able to stay 'in character' for the full meeting. When the meeting was concluded we left the room and immediately talked about what happened in the meeting.

The clients

Before beginning this research I interviewed several designers to find out if I would be able to condense some basic client personalities for use here. Designers gave me descriptions of what they would consider average clients including some of their behaviors and methods of communication. I then took this information and determined that we would work with three types of clients. This does raise issues that I am making stereotypes but in this situation it seemed to be the best way to condense an infinity of client personalities into a workable chunk.

- **Client number one** – the 'I think I am smarter, more powerful, wealthier that you so obviously I know more about design that you do' client. This client tends to be gruff, abrupt and not on time, cuts things short when they think you are done not when you think you are done, does not look at everything, changes ideas midstream, and makes rash judgments.
- **Client number two** – the 'wishy washy, I know what I want but I just can't explain myself' client. This client changes their mind several times, keeps asking what you think, does not ever seem to be able to make a concrete decision, wants it to be different or better but can't explain, probably has an idea but can't describe it, but nothing you do seems to fit this idea that they have in their head.
- **Client number three** – the 'I am unsure of myself and my company and therefore want everything I do to look like another company that is doing really well but, of course, I will not admit that to you, myself or anyone else' client. This client keeps referring to other existing logos, packages etc., will keep going along with an idea and then suddenly decide that something major should be changed for no apparent reason. Many times the change will stem from a talk with a spouse. For example, 'I know that we said that the bottle should be blue but I think my wife really prefers green.'

There are many variations of these general types of clients and I would vary the specific personalities of the client based on the company and product profile that the students provided me with. By using these client profiles and varying them to fit the individual teams I tried to give students a variety of situations that might happen to them in the working world. Each situation provided the student with insight in how to deal with clients they might face in their future.

Course conclusion and evaluation

The four-week session ended with a reception where all design/studio teams set up displays of their prototypes for an invited audience which consisted of parents, friends, professors and local designers. This enabled the students to present their hard work in a formal setting with informal conversation rather than a typical critique. It was my intention that after a four-week period where students were thrown in and out of tough situations with clients that they deserved a chance to be totally in control. Students set up elaborate displays of their work and chatted with invited guests about the process and the final product.

Student projects were evaluated on the following criteria:

- did the project solve the problem?
- was the final presentation carried out in the most professional manner possible?
- was the problem solved in a highly creative manner?
- in their interaction with the 'clients' did the students handle themselves in a professional manner? Were they on time, prepared and professional in their presentations?

Following the conclusion of the class I informally interviewed students to get their responses to the use of role playing. I was pleased to get only positive feedback but feel that this is not the ideal way to evaluate the study. Perhaps it is better to re-visit this question after a student has entered the work environment and actually had interaction with clients so that they can see if this experience made a difference in their ability to communicate with clients.

Conclusion

In conclusion, I believe that this is really just the beginning of my research in role playing. I think that there are many ways that this idea can be used in graphic design. Again, I would also like to say that this does not take the place of actual client/designer interaction but it could be used to ease students into this. If you use role playing in more beginning classes and then use actual clients in more advanced classes I believe the students will be more prepared. This would also allow the research to take place over a longer time frame so that the results could be studied.

Biographical note

Deborah Huelsbergen is Assistant Professor of Art, Graphic Design, at the University of Missouri-Columbia, USA. She teaches graphic design and calligraphy and is also the director of Undergraduate Studies for the Department of Art. In addition to teaching, Deborah maintains an active practice of graphic design and illustration with clients in the USA and UK. She works mainly with clients who are in areas related to child welfare. She also exhibits fine art work in the areas of digital printmaking and artist books. Principal areas of research interest are: design pedagogy, theories of design learning and innovative curriculum development.

The development of an art curriculum for part-time adult students

26

David Jones and Gillian Perkins

School of Continuing Education, University of Nottingham, UK

Abstract

The paper describes the findings of a research project aimed at developing a curriculum for part-time adult arts students. The research identified four areas of development concerned with visual perception, exploiting the potential of a medium of expression, creativity and relevant supporting knowledge. The paper goes on to describe the curriculum that was developed within a university department of continuing education based on these four areas of development. This represents a part-time course in the visual arts leading to a Bachelor's degree for adult students. By adults we mean those who have had a break between compulsory education and this course; the course is not aimed at school leavers. The research and the curriculum have a wider application to university teaching and learning in the visual and other arts.

Introduction

This paper outlines the development of a visual arts curriculum for mature students. Originally, the intention was to devise a curriculum for non-vocational adult education students who wanted something that involved more than copying post-cards. In an attempt to cater for those who wanted to take their studies seriously, but who could only attend on a part-time basis, a curriculum was designed which was based on research carried out in the early 1970s. This curriculum was offered by a university continuing education department and was a level one course; it was equivalent to the first year of a degree course. Subsequently, level two and level three curricula have been devised and there is now a progression route from an open studies programme through to degree-level work.

We will begin by outlining the research on which the curriculum is based and continue by describing how it was developed, evaluated and amended. David Jones, who is writing this section of our joint paper, carried out the original research. I say this to clarify who is writing when the first person singular is used.

Whilst studying for a Diploma in Adult Education I began to research the area of evaluation and assessment in adult art classes. I later extended this original study by undertaking research for a Master's degree at the University of Manchester (Jones, 1988). It is this research that subsequently informed the curriculum design.

The terms evaluation and assessment are used here in their conventional sense: the term assessment refers to identifying the student learning that has taken place and the term evaluation refers to making judgements about the success or otherwise of a course of study. One assesses students and evaluates courses.

At the time, the convention was to base one's assessment on an exhibition of students' work. In conversation with students, and it must be remembered that these were mature students, I became increasingly concerned that all we were doing was comparing students' work to a culturally based notion of what constituted a good painting or artwork.

The history of art demonstrates that values in the arts are not constant: they are constantly changing and developing. There are numerous examples of an avant-garde being rejected by the dominant academy, and later becoming the new orthodoxy. When assessing students, I couldn't help seeing myself as a member of the Salon that rejected the Impressionists. Hence my wish to research the subject.

I devised several research instruments that included interviews, participant observation and questionnaires. I visited a range of fine art classes in adult education institutions and colleges of art. From the data I collected I was able to identify four areas of development that art students undertook. This was the first stage in developing a means of assessing their progress in these four areas of development.

The four areas were:

- the development of visual perception;
- the development of an ability to exploit the potential of a medium of expression;
- the development of an ability to become involved in the creative process; and
- the cognitive development of a relevant conceptual framework.

I will briefly look at these four areas but for a more detailed version the reader should consult Jones (1988).

The development of visual perception

The majority of the people I spoke to were concerned to improve levels of perceptual acuity. Exercises were devised to make students look harder at the world they inhabited. The literature on the subject suggested that, under normal circumstances, we perceive minimally: we perceive as little as we need to perceive in order to live our everyday lives.

There is also a lot of evidence from Holmes (1964, p. 65), Gregory (1973), and Bruce and Green (1985) that perception is culturally determined: the way we perceive the world is dependent on where we learned to perceive the world.

It became clear that in helping people to develop as visual artists a great deal of effort went into overcoming these constraints by trying to ensure a high level of perceptual awareness. Similar arguments can be made for other senses or perceptual systems in relation to other art forms and in relation to crafts.

The development of an ability to exploit the potential of a medium of expression

Many of the people I spoke to in my research project were keen to point out that they wanted to help students to be inventive in their use of media. They didn't want to adopt a 'how-to-do-it' approach; how to paint in oils – how to use watercolour. They wanted a more inquiring approach.

They felt the key to this area of development was about attitudes. It was about developing a willingness to be experimental. It was a question of weaning students away from an attitude that led them to ask the tutor 'how to do it' and towards an attitude that led them to want to find out for themselves what they could do with a new medium. The development of this experimental attitude was seen as important for the student of art. Again this area of development can be seen to relate to other art forms as well as to the crafts.

The development of an ability to become involved in the creative process

This area of development was felt to be the most difficult by many of my interviewees. They all recognised something they referred to as 'the creative process'. It was described in a variety of ways but usually they referred to 'being involved in the painting to the extent that they were unaware of what was going on around them'.

If one begins by asking how do we recognise creativity when we see it, the literature suggests there are at least three answers.

There were those researchers like Symes (1983, p.85) and Child (1970, 390-404) who saw it as a characteristic of a work of art – *this is a very creative painting/sculpture.* There were those like Rogers (1961), Hudson (1966), and Ross (1978) who saw it as an aspect of personality – *they are very creative people.* Finally, there are those like Maslow (1968, pp. 135-45), Ehrenzweig (1968, p. 102), May (1975) and Stumbo (1970, p. 466) who see it as a process – *artists get involved in the creative process.* Again, the evidence to support these assertions and a more detailed description of the three approaches to creativity can be found in Jones (1988).

For the purposes of my research, I felt it most appropriate to focus on the creative process. This has been described many times by artists and psychologists and is, increasingly, understood as a behaviour that involves what, in Western terms, are referred to as conscious and unconscious processes. In the East they might talk about tapping the inner self and many aboriginal peoples talk about the Spirit. What they all seem to be referring to is a state of being where the artist is not in conscious control of what is going on but rather trusts intuitive judgement to help decide what to do next.

The process also involves more conscious critical analytical activity. It is like a dialectical process that swings between states of consciousness and unconsciousness. It is from the unconscious processes that the artist derives images and visual metaphors. It is here that he derives his ability to get in touch with an inner self, a cultural history that informs and influences the creative activity.

It was the development of an ability to become involved in this process that was seen as central to a creative education in the arts.

The cognitive development of a relevant conceptual framework

This last area of development is about knowledge and there was much discussion of what knowledge was appropriate or necessary. Whilst a knowledge of the history of art was seen as important by some, others felt it was not entirely necessary. In any event, there were questions about 'which' or 'whose' history of art. There was agreement about the need for some sort of cultural contextualisation.

It was also felt important to develop a vocabulary that would enable students to discuss their work. Additionally it was felt important for them to know about the nature of the creative process and to understand more about how perception works. It became possible to identify the sort of knowledge that was felt to be important to the practising artist.

The role of drawing

Before moving on it is necessary to say a word about drawing. The vast majority of respondents stressed the importance of drawing. However, when they were asked why drawing was important, their answers fell into two distinct categories. There were those who felt it was important in order to make people look harder. In other words, it was a teaching method for developing visual perception. Others felt it was a way of being expressive and of working out ideas. Here drawing was seen as contributing to the development of an ability to become involved in the creative process.

In designing our curriculum, therefore, drawing was seen not as an educational objective but rather as a teaching method. It was a way of either developing perception or of developing creative ability.

Moving forward

In this area of research and scholarship, nothing has happened since that original research was carried out to lead us to reassess or reconsider the findings. Indeed, one might have arrived at a similar list of areas for development, simply by asking what skills; abilities and knowledge are required by an artist working in the visual arts. Now that the headings have been generated they seem to be self-evident. However, they arose from empirical research in the field and we feel that this gives them a certain validity.

Initially, the curricula I planned for the art courses would concentrate upon one or more of the above areas of development. As they were taught and developed, however, they were changed and amended. I was eventually joined by my colleague Gillian Perkins and together we developed the three-stage degree course presented below.

Research into practice

The introduction of accreditation into the area of adult and continuing education provided the opportunity to redesign the curriculum and the delivery of courses to adult learners. In response to this, in 1996 the School of Continuing Education at the University of Nottingham launched what was then called an Advanced Certificate in Visual Arts Studies. The structure of this course drew directly from the research described above and has since been amended to reflect developments in the possible progression routes on offer. Both the original course, the subsequent version and additional levels have all remained grounded in this research. We will explain how the knowledge gained from the research informed the curriculum at level one and go on to describe the changes that have taken place.

Firstly, it will be helpful to describe briefly the types of students that make up our groups. When we refer to mature we are usually meaning about 25 years and older, although there are signs of younger students starting to apply for such courses. Their motivation for attending art and design courses includes managing a life change, curiosity, a need for qualifications, and fulfilling a long-held desire to study art. They cover the usual range of employment status and domestic complications encountered by all educators of adult students. We have more female students than male. Because of our open access policy the majority of our students enter our courses with little or no formal qualifications traditionally required by schools of fine art or design. If we are to offer them an honest alternative to conventional art and design courses we have to move them through a foundational level of work to a point of criticality appropriate for degree-level study at level one.

Originally the two-year, part-time Advanced Certificate in Visual Arts was devised as a stand-alone package. The programme was broken down into 12 modules. These were delivered over 20 hours of study, usually in 2-hour teaching blocks. Students attended on one day per week during which they studied one module in the morning and one in the afternoon. They were expected to do about 10 hours of work at home between class meetings.

The opportunity to develop a level-two course allowed us to reflect on the strengths and weaknesses of the original programme. The strong features of that course were seen to be the ideological structure of the four areas of learning, the commitment and professionalism of the part-time tutors and the desire of the students to learn. The main pitfalls appeared to be the number of modules, all worth ten credits each, which had to be accommodated in the two-year time period. One of the main effects of this was a working day where students had to change from one module to another, and an assessment procedure that inherently encouraged students to concentrate on product at the expense of the processes involved.

The plan we subsequently devised built in the following:

- *flexibility of delivery* – most modules are worth 20 credits that can be time-tabled as one large module or two smaller ones;
- *coherent progression* – each module at level one feeds into an advanced version at level two; and
- *triangulation of assessment procedures* – equal weighting for evidence from observation of process, product and verbal evidence.

The programme reflects the four areas of learning described above, namely perception, manipulation, creativity and cognition. In order to help students develop their visual perception we subdivided this part of the curriculum, allowing us to focus on colour and form as discrete areas of study. Further, because of the fundamental importance of these two learning outcomes, we maintained the amount of time spent on each at both levels one and two, encouraging students to revisit the issues of colour and form as they developed artistically.

Similarly, the type of media that can be explored by our students encompasses both two and three-dimensional forms, so we divided this area of the curriculum into two separate modules. The inclusion of a specific three-dimensional module provided us with the opportunity to direct students to deal with, often unfamiliar, issues of space whilst at the same time exploring a new medium. If students have learnt some strategies at level one to approach a new medium, they should be able to apply these skills in relation to any new media confronted later. However, because all learning is reinforced by repetition we included these two modules at level two but reduced the amount of time spent on their study.

The changing balance of modules was an important factor in the construction of our programme, so as we reduced the formal exploration of materials we increased the amount of time allocated to developing the students' creative abilities. The students have to revisit this area of study, as the credit rating increases, but each time bringing more awareness and understanding of the elements of the process to bear.

The visual arts programme is largely of a practical nature but is underpinned by a theoretical component. This comprises the 'Psychology and philosophy of the arts', 'Cultural studies' and 'Contemporary issues of art and design'. Students' cognitive development also happens through the informal tutorials and discussions that take place between tutor and student and amongst the students themselves

Our programme is now at the stage of further development. In July 2001 the first level two cohort completed their Diploma in Visual Arts, the majority of whom are continuing on to their degree level studies. At this final level we have attempted to draw together the various threads that have run through the previous levels. There are three modules that invite the students to work across the boundaries of the previously highly structured modules to begin the process of producing a cohesive body of work. The first of these we have called,

Module category	Area of learning	Credits at level 1	Credits at level 2
A	Creative development	20	40
B	Development of visual perception – colour	20	20
C	Development of visual perception – form	20	20
D	Two-dimensional design	20	10
E	Three-dimensional design	20	10
F	Psychology and philosophy of the arts	10	-
G	Cultural studies	10	10
H	Contemporary issues in art and design	-	10

Table 1: The model devised for the delivery of levels one and two

after much discussion, 'Visual composition'. The focus for this module is the combining of all the formal elements in the production of an art work, and it therefore continues with issues and ideas generated in the field of visual perception and the manipulation of various media.

The other two practical modules, 'Creative development' and 'Introduction to research in the visual arts', are designed to build towards the student's dissertation, a 30-credit module of personal research. Students are challenged to work out where they and their work stand in relation to the current issues and practices in the art world of their time. In addition to this, we have introduced a module on professional development in order to support their transition from education into practice, whatever their chosen field of work. In this way we have a programme that moves from an equal distribution of structured time for each of the four fields of learning to one that equips the student to 'go it alone'.

As this programme is put into action it will be monitored and evaluated. The current cohort of students is aware that they are the first group to complete this programme. As adults, they are frank in both their praise and criticism. In two years' time we will be able to report on the completion of the whole course and to present evidence in the form of student work, evaluations and assessment results. Until then, we will continue to monitor progress and to make whatever adjustments appear to be necessary.

Module title	Area of learning	Credits at level 3
Visual composition	Visual perception	20
Creative development	Creative development	20
Introduction to research in the visual arts	Creative development	20
Contextual studies	Cognitive development	10
Theoretical perspectives on culture and the visual arts	Cognitive development	10
Professional development	Cognitive development	10
Dissertation	All four fields	30

Table 2: The model devised for the delivery of levels three

References

Bruce, V. and Green, P. (1985), *Visual Perception, Physiology, Psychology and Ecology* (New Jersey: Lawrence Erlbaum)

Child, I.L. (1970), 'The problem of objectivity in esthetic value', in Pappas, G. (ed.), *Concepts in Art and Education* (London & New York: Macmillan)

Ehrenzweig, A. (1968), *The Hidden Order of Art* (London: Weidenfield and Nicolson)

Gregory, R.L. (1973), *Eye and Brain, the Psychology of Seeing* (London: Weidenfield and Nicolson)

Holmes, A.C. (1964), *Health Education in Developing Countries* (London: Nelson)

Hudson, L. (1966), *Contrary Imaginations – A Psychological Study of the English Schoolboy* (London: Methuen)

Jones, D. (1988), *Adult Education and Cultural Development* (London: Routledge)

Maslow, A.H. (1968), *Towards a Psychology of Being* (New York: Van Nostrand Reinhold Company)

May, R. (1975), *The Courage to Create* (London: Collins)

Rogers, C.R. (1961), *On Becoming a Person* (London: Constable and Company)

Ross, M. (1978), *The Creative Arts* (London: Heinemann Educational Books)

Stumbo, H.W. (1970), 'Three bases for research and teaching in the arts: subjective objective and projective', in Pappas, G. (ed.), *Concepts in Art and Education* (London & New York: Macmillan)

Symes, C. (1983), 'Creativity: A divergent point of view', *The Journal of Aesthetic Education*, Vol. 7, No. 2, Summer 1983, pp. 83-96

Biographical notes

David Jones is a senior lecturer in Adult and Continuing Education at the University of Nottingham. He originally trained as a painter and a potter at Leeds College of Art and studied at the Goldsmith's College for an Art Teacher's Certificate awarded by the University of London. He was awarded a Diploma in Adult Education and an M.Ed. by the University of Manchester and a Ph.D. by the University of Nottingham. He writes extensively on Lifelong Learning and the Arts and has acted as a consultant to government departments and arts funding bodies both in the UK and abroad. He has been a co-organiser of seven international conferences on Lifelong Learning and the Arts.

Gillian Hugman Perkins is a University Teacher in the School of Continuing Education at The University of Nottingham. She trained as a painter and photographer at Bretton Hall College and taught for many years in adult and continuing education before completing her MA in Art & Design Education at De Montfort University and her PhD at Leicester University. She is a practising painter and the focus of her research is women artists, their art and their educational development.

27 Tangible to intangible

Filiz Klassen

Faculty of Communication and Design, School of Interior Design, Ryerson University

Abstract

This paper focuses on curriculum development through a series of design investigations in a second-year interior design studio. The studio investigations consist of three related projects: a women's shelter, a personal shelter, and transformable furniture. The theoretical and practical design issues addressed in these projects were informed by a case study of a unique built project in Toronto – Strachan House: Special Needs Housing – that the author participated in as part of the design team for Levitt Goodman Architects.

The structure and implementation of these projects in a design studio setting demonstrate the fusion of specific curriculum goals and expectations with student needs and learning objectives as well as current design issues with diverse research topics. Specifically, these design investigations emphasise an individual programmatic response by each student to the generic design criteria presented within each project to encourage a less prescriptive and a more collaborative studio atmosphere.

Introduction

My approach to teaching and learning emphasises design as a continuous creative/research process that does not simply culminate or finish with a specific project but continues as part of a larger scope of investigation into the current and future state of design. Within this design/research process I emphasise educational projects that encourage students to engage in a critical debate about the interaction of related (or distant) design disciplines as a direction for the future of built environments. This expanded outlook on design broadens students' imagination and helps them see the activity of building/making as a cultural construct that extends far beyond the perception of built spaces as merely the product of physical and commercial activity.

My personal input into the curriculum development process derives from my own research interests and projects as well as my professional experience. I continually integrate results of my research into the design studio. In turn, I also develop research or paper proposals associated with learning in design. Some of these projects include; 'Pro-fusion: A Cross-disciplinary Exhibit Design'; an article entitled 'Transformable Personal Space Within a Communal Setting' to be published in an upcoming book on transportable environments; and other design investigations related to transformability.

Stimulating critical thought, design debate, and inquiry in the studio teaching and learning environment constituted a guideline for me, as a design instructor, in redeveloping the second year design curriculum over the past two years at the School of Interior Design, Faculty of Communication and Design, Ryerson University.

A design exercise: the project brief

This paper argues that project briefs prepared for students in an educational context should go far beyond functional statements to present a sphere of cultural investigation. Presented with this goal in mind, the design projects in second-year studio acknowledge that design projects cannot be created in a cultural vacuum and that student-designed spaces or objects are not mere translations of bubble or block diagrams representing functional and economic requirements. Through the design project briefs, the context of our cultural, social and intellectual concerns should be addressed and open to discussion.

Within this approach I also encourage the development of a student-inspired project brief, a complementary component to the generic project criteria presented by the instructor, as an alternative to the studio projects that are fully conceived by design instructors. I have found out that this approach requires direct involvement, responsibility and more rigor on students' behalf, demanding that they develop a personal design attitude by way of seeing, questioning and commenting on the situations and environments that they observe and experience. The result is more satisfaction and enjoyment of the design process, the final outcome, as well as the educational experience.

Research and design investigations centred around diverse issues, such as social and environmental responsibility in design, gender, private, public and transitory spaces, home and shelter, flexibility, adaptability and mobility, provide an opportunity in the studio environment to discuss and evaluate current as well as historical design developments. My emphasis on these issues challenges the conventional assumptions and approaches to spatial design as set within fixed professional boundaries, thus encouraging students to think outside the norm. In return, design studio and research projects that question or re-examine the traditional ideas of shelter, space and permanence all contribute to the debate about the future of interiors, industrial design, furniture making and architecture.

The catalyst: Strachan House by Levitt Goodman Architects

Strachan House is a special needs housing project[1] in Toronto, Canada, where 70 chronically homeless men and women were actively involved in the planning and construction of their 'home' between 1993 to 1996. This project demonstrates the need to change traditional notions of what constitutes belonging to a community as a positive social attribute.

The design, while accommodating the basic programmatic requirements such as a reception, meeting areas, living spaces, bedrooms, kitchen and bathrooms, a community kitchen, a bank, staff areas, and health houses for short term care, also provides un-programmed transitional spaces as a means of meeting the alternative communal needs of a transient group of users.

Built within a former furniture factory, the spatial concept is based on the analogy of city streets, a town hall, courtyards, private houses and threshold spaces such as the porches and passages to encourage social interaction and also to create a sense of territory, social awareness, community, and feelings of comfort and security for the residents. Transitional and threshold spaces utilise raw and unfinished materials such as rough lumber and two by four studs to promote the idea of appropriation and transformation of space for the changing individual or group needs of the residents (Klassen, 2001).

Fig. 1: Strachan House: view towards the communal spaces of a 'house' unit

This built project has acted as a catalyst in the generation of several studio projects that help position the second year interior design curriculum in a culturally, environmentally and socially conscious design context. Through discussions of the issues around this built example, the concepts of sheltering and place making (as opposed to generating functional spaces) are emphasised as a way to develop a theoretical base for all interior design projects.

A jig saw puzzle

Piece 1: Women's Shelter Project[2] T(individual project, 5 weeks/60 hours)

The issues of homelessness and the transformation of personal and communal spaces, discussed in relation to Strachan House, are used as the basis of this hypothetical design studio project to initiate a reflection on the theoretical and practical issues of sheltering in downtown Toronto.

The *project context* is the east corner of Strachan House, designated by the Ministry of Health as a refuge and transitional place for homeless women. There are no standardised prototypes that address the specific needs of this group of homeless women. Therefore, the design resolutions to this project must sensitively respond to the highly experimental nature of its mandate; that is, to house a group of women who might have extreme emotional and psychological reaction to communal and/or confined spaces due to their past or present trauma.

The *design objective* is to develop an appropriate built form and communal environment as an alternative model that bridges the extremes of spatial experience defined by the fixed rooms and spaces of a house and the nomadic existence of street life. Students are encouraged to question and investigate the theoretical and pragmatic issues of what constitutes a home, private/public/transitory space as well as to provide practical design solutions and details for notions of sheltering, screening, blocking, veiling, shuttering and transforming a space within an existing environment.

As a facilitator for the project discussions and design debate in a studio setting, *my teaching philosophy* emphasises my commitment to creating an active learning environment. Inquiry, critical thinking and creative problem solving are on-going *learning methods* that involve students' consideration of multiple viewpoints and approaches. The objective of active learning is to stimulate lifetime habits of creative thinking and problem solving that involves imagination, analysis and synthesis of alternative design issues and/or solutions to interior design problems.

In collaboration with the Learning and Teaching Office at Ryerson, the active learning and inquiry methods are used to promote a way of asking questions that lead students to develop a concept and a thesis in a design project context. These methods help students to unravel the intangible design process and to take a more active role by way of methodical questioning from the most simple questions over observations to the most complex interpretative ones (Thorpe, 1997).

Owing to the stressful nature of undertaking a creative process, student feelings of unrest and anxiety are common in the design studio environment. I have observed that these methods help reduce students' anxiety levels and the natural defensiveness they feel regarding their projects. Within this learning context, the project reviews are perceived as an extension of the design questioning process rather than passing of favourable or unfavourable personal judgements. This approach to project reviews encourages an exchange of ideas about design attitudes that students develop as a response to specific project criteria and constraints.

The project *research objectives* are used as an opportunity to generate discussions about the topic of homelessness in both the global and the local perspective, focusing specifically on women's homelessness issues. Secondly, the issue of gender and space is used to encourage readings on the women's perception of space, design of confined spaces, as well as the psychology and fear of spaces. Finally, in an attempt to address the context of the large number of female students in the studio, students are encouraged to examine the history of female designers as part of the initial research phase to develop an understanding of the role of the design and feminism in the current debate.

The *programme information* includes private sleeping arrangements for the residents of this facility with an emphasis on the need to address confinement and privacy. Students are asked to interpret the idea of sleeping nooks as a means of accommodating those residents who have a fear of confined spaces, and come up with the functions they want to incorporate into these open yet personal spaces. Further, they are asked to address the spatial arrangement of the personal areas within the context of the entire social group as a form of community. Shared facilities include an adequate number of barrier free bathrooms, wash areas, kitchen, cleaning and storage facilities, appropriate shared living spaces, as well as staff rooms. Other support facilities located in the main portion of Strachan House, such as the community kitchen, town hall, bank and the health unit, are also accessible for these residents.

The *design process* in the studio involves an introduction to the project, site and the Strachan House as a reference for students' work. Through lectures they are further introduced to the complexity of issues about homelessness in a global and local context. Then in teams, they are asked to research, brainstorm and come up with a concise list of questions that would guide them through the development of a design thesis statement and a project concept. In their research and work they are asked to address whether, through interior design, one could achieve a healthy and safe dwelling alternative for a group of homeless women, and to explain how.

Following the research and questioning process, a hybrid use of sketching, computer graphics, modelling, photography and collage techniques are used for the generation of ideas. A similar hybrid approach to visualisation and representation is used through the design development and presentation phases to document student's observations, research and design growth.

Student projects at first resembled dormitories with small cubicles for personal living arrangements. Overtime this changed drastically as they started developing the communal spaces and articulated the connective transitional spaces from the most public to the most private. This resulted in an increasing degree of flexibility and adaptability for the private living arrangements that corresponded with the unique situation of the residents.

Quite a few examples of student projects such as the Force of Light, Apple Tree, Monarch Place[3] and Life Capsule, named mostly after nature, concentrate on creating spaces that heal, nourish and provide spiritual balance and harmony for the self and the community. Life Capsule's design concept, based on creating situations but no rooms, offers open personal space cabins that move on a track to address individual and group needs/desires to increase or decrease personal privacy and social contact. Translucent sliding panels give control over light and visibility to the individual in the capsule.

Fig. 2:
Life Capsule by Irene Marianne Tolvanen

Another personal nook design demonstrates a sensitivity to the design of small and confined spaces by addressing the need to sleep, stand, sit and socialise in one's private domain as part of the larger social space.

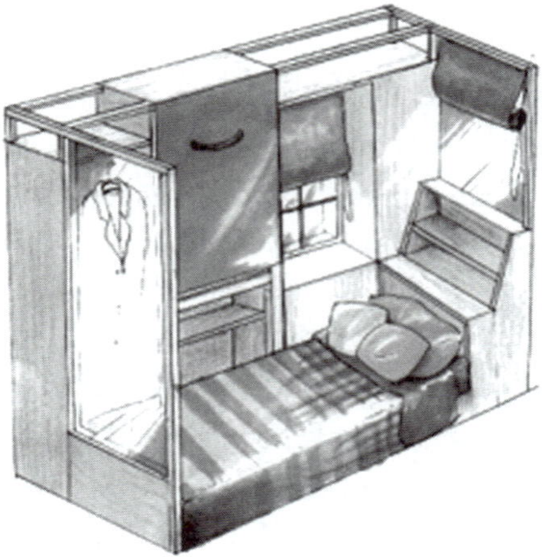

Fig. 3: Personal Nook by Satomi Tabei

Another project, entitled Resurgence, contemplates achieving solitude in a social space through sculpting and carving small niches that is a-typical of hostel, shelter or dormitory designs.

Fig. 4: Resurgence by Jayson Irizawa

Puzzle pieces 2, 3, 4 .... : Transformability and Design

Conceptually in line with the women's shelter project, I have initiated a number of other projects such as the Personal Shelter, Transformable Furniture and the Human Body in Design that deal with the issues of transformability, transportability and adaptability in a broader cultural context. These projects allow students to deal with a variety of conceptual and technical issues ranging in context from spatial design to body architecture, virtual environments, and furniture and product design. Involving research, design experimentation and the actual fabrication process, these projects provide an opportunity to discuss and present recent developments relevant to interior design and design learning to encourage greater social responsibility and environmental entrepreneurship. In order to provide a concise discussion I will concentrate primarily on the personal shelter project.

Puzzle piece 2: Personal Shelter[4] (team project, 4 weeks/36 hours)

Students are given a challenge to design and build an ergonomic personal shelter that demonstrates sensitivity towards contemporary cultural, social and technical conditions. The personal shelter project fuses together spatial design, furniture making, clothing and product design by encouraging the exploration of interdisciplinary ideas and interests as a creative base.

In an *educational context*, the design of small environments or objects propose a more approachable and tactile quality for students than the design of large-scale buildings, especially in the early years of their design education. Through the design and actual construction of life-size objects or environments, students directly address the issues of human scale and multiplicity of functions in the process of experimenting with space and construction on a reduced scale. This type of a project further provides them with an opportunity to devote greater attention to detailing and innovative material usage.

The *research objectives* for this project are aimed at developing an understanding of the issue of transformability/transportability in architecture, interiors, furniture and fashion design through readings of the works of current and early modern designers. This research extends into unique examples of lightweight and portable furniture and industrial design with specific emphasis given to the research of sustainable materials and construction methods that are readily available to everyone.

The personal shelter project addresses the observed, experienced or inherited conditions of our urban and suburban cultural landscape as a rich context for student design investigations. Students are challenged to conceptualise, design and fabricate a working prototype for a shelter in a context of their choice. The generic project criteria emphasise the requirement for the design solution to be able to vary its size, shape and function in an attempt to address notions of flexibility, adaptability and portability.

Students are encouraged to think conceptually in order to develop a practical design solution that demonstrates competency in using structural principles and methods of assembly and deployability as found to be relevant to the shelter design. Students are also encouraged to experiment with soft, flexible and/or rigid materials, investigating the inherent capabilities of these materials in relation to the collapsibility, assembly, disassembly and changeability requirements. A maximum of two dominant materials are required to provide shelter and act as support for the final structure.

Prerequisite to the design investigation is the writing of a creative programme brief that guides the student's research concept, design and construction of a personal space/shelter/structure. The fabrication method and material choices are required to be appropriate for the environmental and climactic conditions that the students set forth in their programme brief.

Following the introduction of generic project criteria and research topics, students are asked to individually articulate the relevance of their proposed formal investigations within the project context. After producing individual scale models of their ideas, students are asked to brain storm in groups and come up with a collective project brief that clearly identifies their research direction, project concept and goals, intended functions, applications, site and environmental requirements, and also the proposed materials and structural choices.

The students then proceed to develop ergonomic charts for the intended uses and activities. The final concept and design development sketches, modelling, material and joinery investigations, and fabrication drawings or patterns are documented in a design process book that guides the production of the final, finished prototype and it's presentation.

The proposed design resolutions range in context from wearable, carryable shelters for diverse uses such as the students' own need to sleep in the design studio or at an unexpected place, protection from the sun or other weather hazards or pollution, protection from the invasion of the media to homeless or emergency shelters. The Water Bottle and Tarp project proposes building a personal homeless shelter with recycled materials collected by the individual such as commonly found water bottles and sheet materials (tarp or industrial grade bubble wrap) salvaged from construction sites.

Figure 5:
Water Bottle & Tarp Project by Michael Steele, Connor Molloy & Gianni Toto

Design Student's Sleeping Shelter proposes a knapsack that unfolds into a sleeping bag providing a comfortable personal space to sit, read and sleep in.

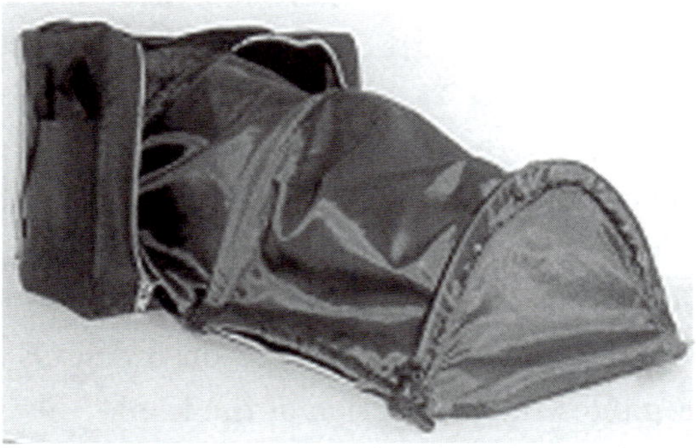

Fig. 6: Design Student's Sleeping Shelter by Hyun Ju Lee, Jeung-Min Hong & Hyun Jung Park

Endnotes

[1] Strachan House, designed by Levitt Goodman Architects has won the prestigious Governor General Award of Excellence in Architecture in 1999 and was published in the following design magazines and books:

Baniassad, E. (ed.), (2000), *Architecture Canada 1999: The Governor General Medals for Architecture* (The Royal Architectural Institute of Canada & TUNS Press), pp. 4–59

Vansittart, K. (1997), 'No place like home', *Azure*, March & April 1997, pp. 20–22.

Jonson, L. (1997), 'En fraga om vardighet: Streetcity project, Toronto', *Form 5* (Sweden) Fall 1997, pp. 46–49.

Kapusta, B. (1996), 'Street City, Strachan House', *Canadian Architect*, August 1996, pp. 26–27

[2] This project was taught with Barbara Clewly-Gagnon and Caroline Robbie-Montgomery in Spring 2001 and by Arlene Dougall and Viz Saraby in Autumn 2001. Generous contributions in lecture format was received from John Thorpe, Center for Student Development and Counselling on Active Learning Methodology, Dr Joseph Springer, School of Urban and Regional Planning and Angela Robertson, Executive

Director of Sistering on homelessness, David Warne and Brock James, Levitt Goodman Architects on various shelter projects in Toronto.

[3] Student Projects: Force of Light by Mirella Iurescu, Apple Tree br Starlyn Cag, and Monarch Place by Adam Crabe.

[4] This project was taught with David Johnston and Paul Mezei in Spring 2002. Dr Kathryn Woodcock from the School of Occupational and Public Health at Ryerson University also made invaluable contributions on the topic of ergonomics that enhanced students' sensitivity and understanding of dynamic human dimensions and needs.

References

Klassen, F. (2001), 'Transformable Space Within a Communal Space' in Lim, J. (ed.), *Transportable Environments 2001, Proceedings of the 2nd Conference on Portable Architecture*, 17–18 May, (Singapore: Center for Advanced Studies in Architecture, Singapore), pp. 81–90

Thorpe, J. (1997), *Method of Inquiry Book for Students and Faculty* (Toronto: Ryerson University, Student Development and Counselling)

Biographical note

Filiz Klassen is currently working as assistant professor at Ryerson University, sharing her ideas in the design studio and workshop with interior design students. She is also an independent curator. Her most recent exhibition titled 'Pro-fusion: A Cross-disciplinary Design Exhibition' presented a diverse body of work by various artists and designers that contribute to a more pluralistic, interactive understanding of design (www.ryerson.ca/~fusion).

Specialising in exhibit design, museum re-structuring and multi-functional cultural spaces, her professional work since 1993 has focused on the interface of Architecture and Interior Design. Strachan House, a special needs housing project that she consulted on as part of the project team for Levitt Goodman Architects, won the Governor General Award, Medal of Excellence in Canadian Architecture, in 1999.

Her research interests lie in the social and cultural dimensions of built and un-built environments and in their material realisation. Her research includes projects and work in urban issues involving transformability and sustainability in a hybrid practice of fashion, interiors, architecture and graphics. She recently presented a paper at the 'Transportable Environments 2001 Conference, 2nd International Conference on Portable Architecture', held in the National University of Singapore, School of Design Environment, Singapore, May 17&18, 2001.

28

Effective multimedia contents developing for moving image design on Web-based instruction

Chang-Hyun Kwon

Department of Design, Goldsmiths College, University of London, UK

Abstract

In Korea (as of April 2002) there are 12 cyber universities and three colleges that have no campus. There are just some offices to operate Web-based instruction (WBI), with various developed contents by new education technologies, the so-called 'Internet learning', 'e-learning', 'Web-based training', 'computer-based training', 'WWW-learning' and 'cyber education', etc. It is possible to reach the whole of Korea and all over the world if there is the Internet connection line. They started with text-based documents using HTML, then tried to develop and produce multimedia content: text, graphics, video, audio, video/audio streaming and animation on the Web. There are numerous different developments and implementations in each institution.

At most of the institutions, meetings are held to discuss how to develop, produce and organise the curriculum effectively with various technologies in different subjects. The curriculum should be developed and produced to be suitable according to the major subject's characteristic.

This case study considered effective Web-based multimedia contents for the Moving Image Design (MID) course. It was hoped that this would provide an up-to-date guide for the development and production of contents in other related subjects.

The project discussed in this paper shows the current patterns and contexts of use of multimedia contents on WBI in higher education. It also suggests an effective multimedia contents for development on the Web and one of the practice-based courses in both cyber and traditional higher education.

Introduction

The educational environment has been changed very fast by computer and network technologies. At present, it is possible to offer distance and Web-based online education with the Internet, wireless network system and personal mobile phone. Multimedia systems of Web-based instruction (WBI) are used in a wide variety of education fields, including teaching and learning materials and other study support.

This trend has affected all kinds of educational institution, from the traditional campus, to industry-based education systems, and to adult and life-long education centres throughout the world. Institutions are investing to develop Web-based instruction for the first time or to develop and expand upon early models. Some of them have begun to run a range of courses, from short courses to degree courses in higher education.

Some institutions run practice-based design courses on the Web. However, there is very little Web-based instruction in moving-image design and guidelines for WBI in this field are less well developed than in some other fields.

It was important that this case study should carry out some primary research on WBI models that use multimedia contents. The models would be analysed in detail, looking at the contents, design and structure. This analysis would suggest how effective multimedia contents could be developed for WBI in two MID courses in particular – Film Language Directing (FLD) and Digital Character Animation (DCA). Both of these were developed for use as part of an academic degree course for first-year students in colleges and universities.

Context review in WBI education

Khan (1997) defined different concept of the WBI as 'a hypermedia-based instructional program, which utilises the attributes and resources of the World Wide Web to create a meaningful learning environment where learning is fostered and supported' (p.6). He also mentioned that WBI could be viewed as 'an innovative approach for delivering instruction to a remote audience, using the Web as the medium' (p. 5). He emphasised the 'hypermedia-based' and 'remote' nature of WBI.

There are many different methods for distance education, using different media including letter, telephone, videotape, cassette tape, videoconference and television. However, distance education has been changing rapidly since Internet technology has become part of education. The 'cyber education system' has also changed social and cultural communication in the real world. The following terms have become important features of education: collaboration, connectivity, student-centredness, unboundedness, community, expoloration, shared knowledge, multisensory experience, authenticity and so on (Kearsley, 2000). The Internet provides a magnificent information supply for study – unlimited by space and time. It is possible for contact between students and the instructor to take place anytime and anywhere.

This can be an opportunity for students to maximise the effectiveness of their education, using rather than the traditional one-to-many traditional education.

However, Crossman (1997) indicates a question, 'many teachers whose students use the Web are concerned about the question of authenticity and reliability of information on the Internet in general and the Web in particular' (p. 22).

Next, who should develop the instructional model? Ideally, instructors would develop course models for their own subjects, using the latest relevant technologies. However, in reality this is not possible because Web technologies change so rapidly. Instructors should choose the most suitable methods and technologies and specialists with the skills to apply these to the development of the Web-based instructional model. Sometimes a team is formed for new course development on the Web. It depends on the time and cost.

Assessment and analysis of WBI model

When assessing and analysing the WBI model, it is necessary to consider all the various factors that affect students' studying: personal characteristics, personal background knowledge, contents structure, interface design, networking system and feedback with instructor. Furthermore students' progress in their studies should be monitored. For example, this can be through interactions between student and student, student and instructor and students and the contents.

It is important to develop a model for learner-centred Web-based education. Instructors, who usually develop the models, often think that learners should navigate everything in the contents provided in order to master the subject through the interactively structured model. A student's understanding can be determined by assessment of the student's learning.

WBI models

Models of WBI vary according to the subjects and institutions. They also depends on fast-changing computer technologies mentioned above. In the models below the production technologies involved and design layout are considered , but not the actual content itself (Fig. 1).

WBI using multimedia contents consist of the elements: text, video, audio, animation and graphics.

Contents	Features
VOD + TEXT VOD (optional) + TEXT Virtual Studio + TEXT	Instructor's video/audio clips, summaries and detailed teachingdocuments, other information about tutorial
AOD + TEXT AOD (optional) + TEXT Electronic board (optional)	Instructor's audio clips (no video), summaries and detailed teaching documents, other information about tutorial
TEXT or HTML Audio (optional) Video (optional)	All documents based on text
FLASH + HTML *Flash animation mostly contains audio	Flash animation clips with HTML documents
Screen captured clips + TEXT	Usually for application tutorial

Fig. 1 (VOD=Video on Demand, AOD=Audio on Demand, TEXT=word document, HTML=Hypertext Markup Language, FLASH=computer program)

Text with video/audio (VOD)

This model is mainly text-based to provide a list of all tutorials. Video clips are an option. The model starts with 'how to use' guide information. Then the learner can open video clips for more information and detailed instructor's explanation.

A limitation is the size of video streaming window, which depends on video compression quality when it was transferred from analogue to digital data.

Video/audio (VOD) with text

This model is mainly based on video/audio clips. Then text-based window shows more detail about teaching. The learner can click other buttons to access various information about the course. It is usually very helpful for learners to access the information by interactive navigation.

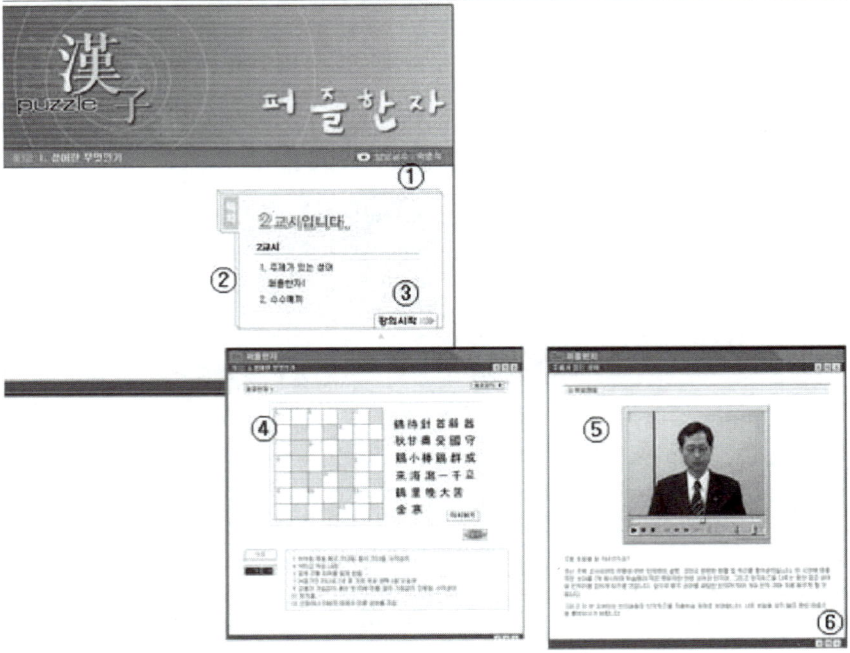

Fig. 2 Video/audio (VOD) with text
1. video window: it shows instructor teaching material related to the subject; 2. teaching plan: showing text-based teaching plan synchronised with video clip; 3. navigation bar: can access directly other teaching plan and detail teaching lists; 4. subject information: I: basic information about subject (text-based); R: reference (text-based); D: download from the teaching lists and materials (various format); L: link (hypertext).

Virtual studio with text

This is mainly based on a virtual studio where an instructor sits in his office to give a tutorial. When shot by the camera, it produced a small angle with the instructor, and then it was digitally mixed with virtual computer graphics studio.

Text with screen-captured image

This model is used usually practice-based course. Instructor presents the subject based on text or/and video/audio style which is not very different with previous shown examples. It usually practice-based course needs to learn tools that are computer applications. At this time learner needs how to use and apply the suitable application programs. So, instructor provides a program tutorial session which has to be recorded by special program (screen capture program).

Fig. 3 Video/audio (VOD) with text
1. video window: it shows instructor teaching material related to the subject; 2. teaching plan: showing text-based teaching plan synchronised with video clip; 3. navigation bar: can access directly other teaching plan and detail teaching lists; 4. subject information: I:basic information about subject (text-based); R: reference (text-based); D: download from the teaching lists and materials (various format); L: link (hypertext).

Fig. 4 Virtual studio with text
1. video window, showing the instructor teaching; 2. playing control panel: rewind, play, pause, stop and forward; 3. teaching board, synchronised with video tutorial; 4. instructor's profile; 5. teaching chapters; 6. shows index; 7. when mouse click the button, learner can download teaching material data files.

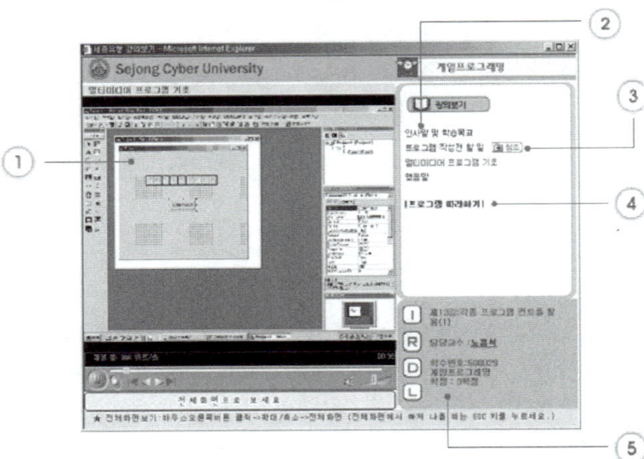

Fig. 5 Text with screen-captured image
1. video window: shows instructor or teaching material related to the subject; 2. teaching list: shows text-based teaching lists; 3. reference button: links relational materials (text-based, video clip(s), still image(s)); 4. application program tutorial: goes to a new pop-up window showing how to use a computer application tool for the subject, recorded by special screen capturing program; 5. subject information: I: basic information about subject (text-based); R: reference (text-based) D: download from the teaching lists and materials (various format); L: link (hypertext).

Flash animation

This is recent popular model using the Flash computer application program to make animation. The feature of Flash is for making vector images for processing image data. So, its file data is not big on the Web against bitmap style.

The program is used broadly, in online education courses for children and adults.

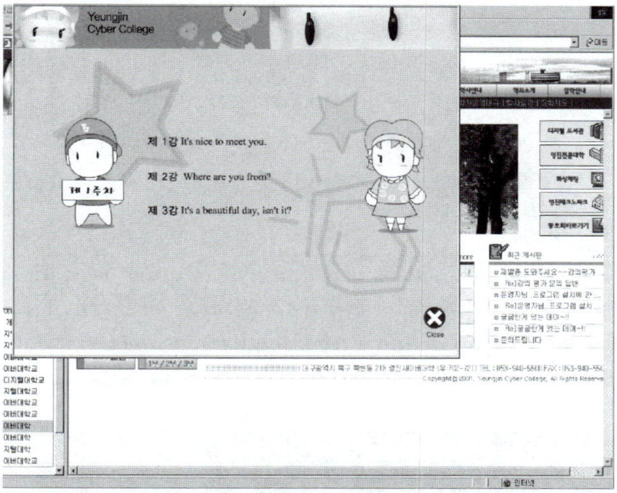

Fig. 6 Flash animation

Text

This model is not entirely text based, but it is developed and produced with audio or audio, video/audio. It gives priority to text, and other features are optional for learners, depending on whether they want to click or not. Sometimes it is boring, but it depends on design and tree structure of contents. It is also, easy to update the teaching data for learner.

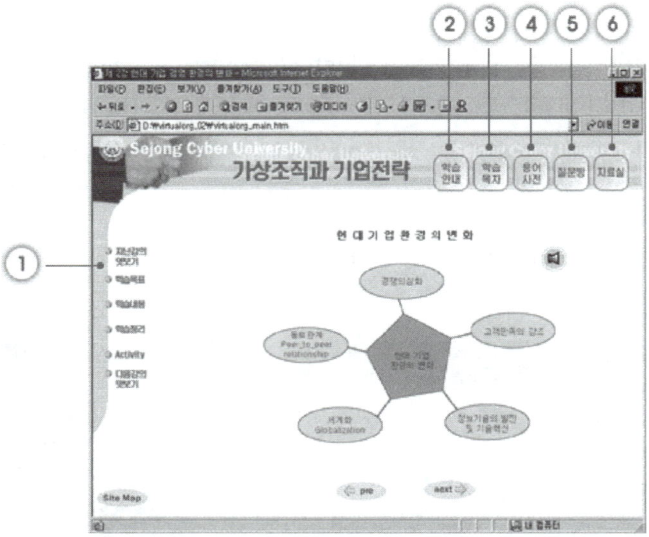

Fig. 6 Text
1. tab function: shows teaching lists in order or randomly; 2. learning information: provides instructor profile, teaching plan, objectives; 3. teaching lists: shows all detailed teaching lists for the term; 4. explanation of teaching terms; 5. Q and A button; 6. teaching materials and discussion room.

Fig. 6 Video/audio and electronic board with text
1. teaching lists; 2. summary of the chapter; 3. instructor's profile; 4. teaching processing and instructor's board writing; 5. text-based teaching board with instructor's action playing recorded; 6. playing control panel; 7. teaching time-bar (meaning video clips running).

Video/audio and electronic board with text

This model is very specially produced. While video/audio clips are shot by the video camera, the instructor's explanation on electronic board is recorded. The instructor's explanation and the electronic board were shot simultaneously by video camera, so the learner can watch instructor and electronic board together on same video/audio window.

The above models are the seven different basic formats of Web-based online education. There are some other additional styles, but they are variations on the basic formats, using some special functions.

These are all recent up-to-date models developed and produced in higher education, Korea. So, which kind of model is the best for a subject that has not yet developed a fixed form of Web-based instruction?

A case study of new WBI for MID education

Contents structure

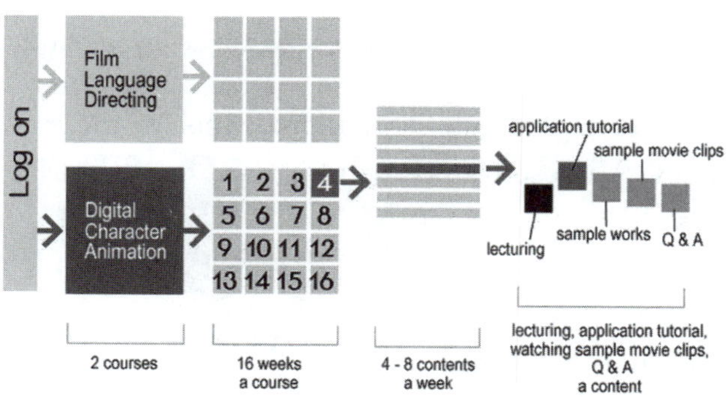

Fig. 7 Contents structure

This WBI course has mainly two parts. One is a main window with a control panel to show video streaming source of tutorials and sample works. The other is a menu for the learner to navigate through the contents. Also, the menu is divided into two different functions. On the right of the page is a description of the weekly study – the content of tutorials – and at the bottom is the title of the course and a weekly navigation function by pop-up window. All contents can be used interactively using learner-centred functions.

Lecturing

The main window shows two instructors who give the course lectures, giving details about basic concepts and discussing samples of students' work (Fig. 8).

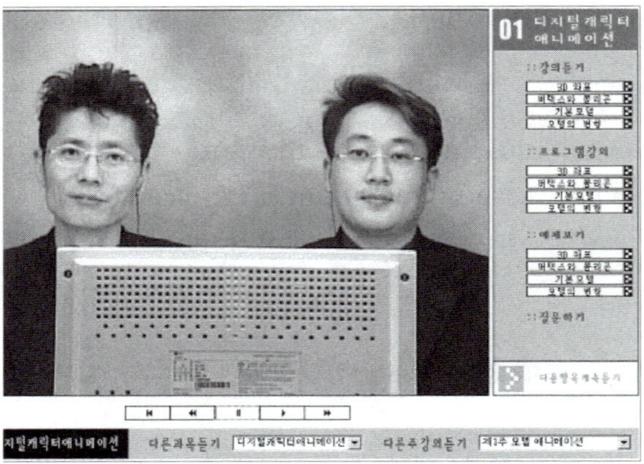

Fig. 8 Main page: lecturing with two instructors on main window

There are several application programs for the main video streaming window. Microsoft Powerpoint is used for a tutorial for preparing the course lists (Fig. 9).

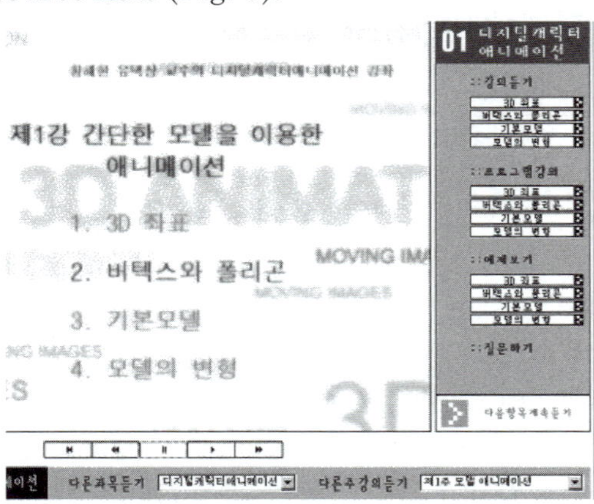

Fig. 9 Use of Microsoft Powerpoint

A program for instruction of a knowledge concept is Microsoft Paintboard in Window 2000 OS program. It uses a board instead of the traditional white board used in the classroom (Fig. 10).

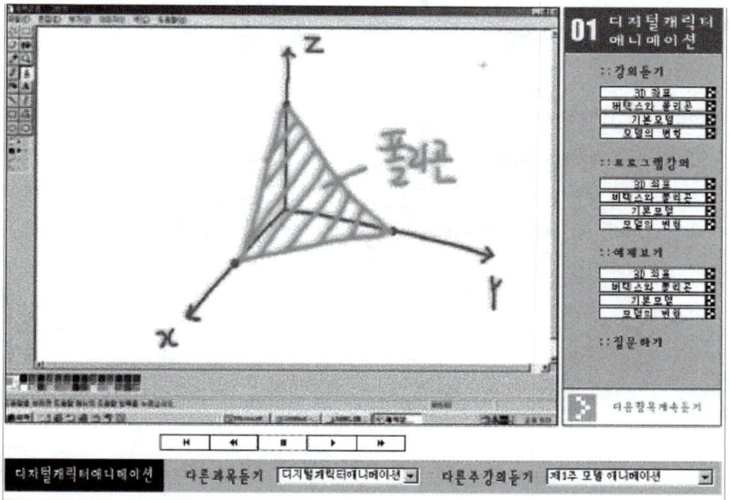

Fig. 10 Use of Microsoft Paintboard

Two instructors were recorded by an ENG camera in the studio with a sound mixer. Then simultaneously, Digital Video (DV) recorder was used to record two separate materials – computer and camera output sources. Then computer-captured DV tape and transferred to digital data for video streaming files with audio Web-based on Microsoft Windows Media.

Application tutorial

Learners can click the application program tutorial menu button whenever they want to know how to use the application or need help with how to search through the files already screen-captured and recorded. The learner's experience is like a one-to-one lesson with the instructor. Learner can open and close this menu whenever they want. Also, they can click and listen to any point on the file, playing repeatedly if they wish (Fig. 11).

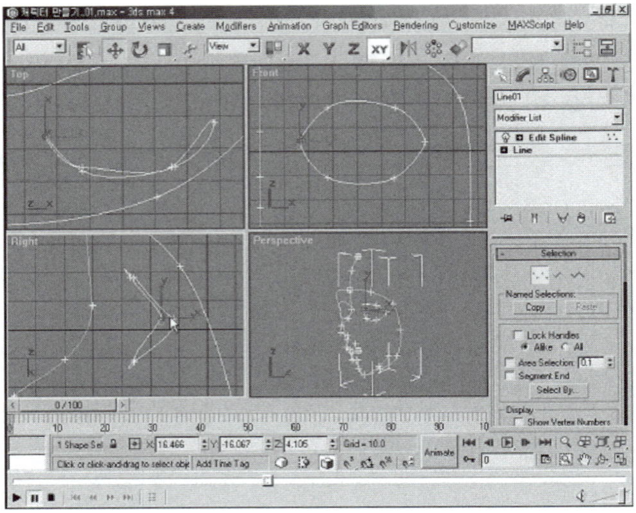

Fig. 11 Application tutorial window: this window will be opened new pop-up window.

Sample movie watching

The learner can click and watch sample pieces with tutorial with new pop-up windows whenever they want. There are two kinds of sample movies files on the menu. One is sample pieces of professional work related to the lecturing. The other is related to the work of students. Usually it runs two to five minutes long (Fig. 12).

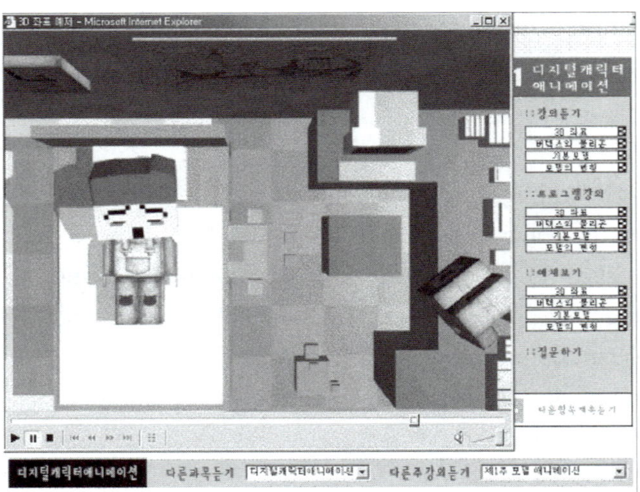

Fig. 12. Sample movie watching: learner can watch repeatedly by pop-up window

Q & A

Learner can use this function anytime anywhere when they need to ask anything about all contents and tutorials. They can access via e-mail to instructor and communicate with other learners through the Web board service.

Tutorial features

This project has two courses, Film Language Directing (FLD) and Digital Character Animation (DCA). FLD is about directing to use film languages through the production line. The key elements over 16 weeks include camera angle, lens, shooting, lighting, shot composition, editing and so on. DCA is about producing character animation using an application of 3-dimensional computer graphics. It is also divided into 16 weeks, with contents about creating and developing character, modelling, mapping, lighting, camera moving, rendering, animation, computer editing and so on. In both FLD and DCA, each weeks' tutorial contains several elements that run 10 to 15 minutes video clips. For FLD, the application programs used for learners to practise were Adobe Premiere (for video and audio editing) and Sonic Foundry's Vegas (for sound effects). For DCA, Discreet Logic company's 3D Studio Max was used.

Tutorial features		
Course	Film Language Directing	Digital Character Animation
Contents	shooting, editing, sound mixing, analysis, directing etc.	character creation and developing, modelling, mapping, lighting, camera moving, rendering, animation etc.
Application programs	Premiere, Vegas	3D Studio Max

Fig. 13 Tutorial features

Discussion and conclusion

It was important to think about how learners study and what they want to achieve through the WBI as the above new case developed. MID education is not simple to provide in traditional campus-based higher education institutions. A lot of facilities and teamwork are required to provide learning opportunities for design in studios or special labs. Although it cannot be easy to study on the Web, using the contents provided by a specialist, the author tried to cover all possible problems that learners might have.

The most important thing is that there were two instructors for each course. The courses tried to mix entertainment and education to help to prevent learners' feelings of isolation while studying on the Web. Sometimes one of the instructors can ask a question and the other answer it, instead of just having questions from the learner.

In practical design education, a Web-based course should use tool(s). Recently, the majority of design-related courses have involved computer application programs. It is difficult for first-year design course students to use some applications. In Web-based courses it is important for instructors to provide the application tutorials themselves. This can help to solve design-process problems that students might meet when learning how to use an application.

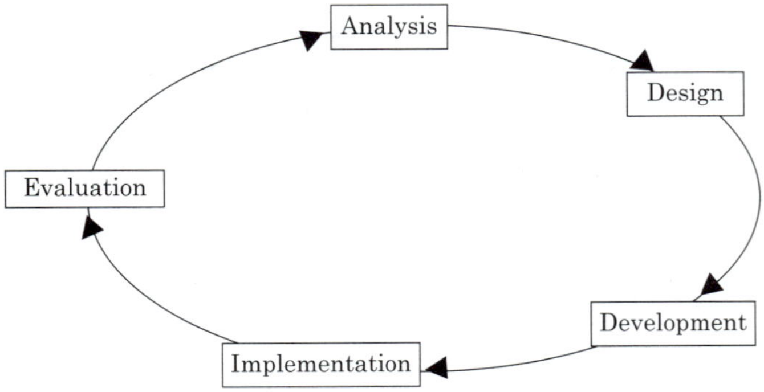

Lee & Owens (2000)

Lee and Owens (2000) presented their five phases in Multimedia-Based Instructional Design. They mentioned that the design phase is 'probably the most important factor in the success of your project. Projects often founder because of failure to adequately plan' (p. 83).

However, success also depends on how the contents of WBI in MID education are designed and developed. Thus researchers should consider effective evaluation and analysis in the future. Whenever the evaluation and analysis of problems and needs occur, the contents should be updated constantly.

29 'Creatives' and 'suits': developing an interdisciplinary course for design and management students

Nicky Ryan

London College of Printing, The London Institute, UK

Abstract

This paper reviews the development of an interdisciplinary unit within the School of Retail Studies. The original delivery was from a single discipline perspective using traditional methods of lectures and seminars. The revised approach synthesises several disciplines to create alternative theoretical frameworks. The pedagogic strategies employed places more emphasis on collaborative, process-oriented and experiential forms of learning. The impetus for reinterpreting the unit came from recognition that the multidisciplinary needs of the changing workplace for the designer and manager were not being met owing to limitations imposed by a single discipline approach. The separate cultures of designer and manager appeared to be increasingly polarised within the higher education system. This resulted in graduates missing out on lifelong learning opportunities. The paper describes the aims of the unit, its underpinning philosophy and the student response to its implementation.

Introduction

The unit is called 'Managing Retail Concepts' and forms part of the third year curriculum of the combined programme in retailing at the London College of Printing, School of Retail Studies. Students graduate from this programme with a BA (Hons) in Retail Design Management, Visual Merchandising Management or Retail Management depending on the individual pathway selected. Managing Retail Concepts was introduced as part of the re-validated programme in 1997. It is a core unit taken by all students with a content focused on design management. The unit was taken over by two new tutors in 2000, one from a design and one from a management background. It was decided that within historically designated parameters the content would be re-focused toward a more holistic view of design and retail situated within a cultural, social and political context. To encourage active and deep learning a range of more radical learning and teaching strategies were experimented with.

The cultural divide

On the combined programme in retailing, design and management students work together from year one with various levels of interaction. By the time they enter the third year they have a strong self-image and have developed a range of preconceived ideas and prejudices about each other. An early session in the managing retail concepts unit explored the issue of personal identity and each group was asked to characterise the other. Polarised and stereotypical perceptions emerged from this discussion. The personality traits of managers were identified as 'logical, organised, rational, precise, analytical, critical and concerned with control and profits'. On the other hand designers were characterised as 'pictorial, intuitive, experimental, holistic, disorganised and concerned with innovation and creativity'. These definitions fit neatly into the 'left brain, right brain' neurological theory developed from Roger Sperry's Nobel prize winning discovery of two separately functioning hemispheres of the brain (Sperry: 1968). Managers demonstrate the dominant, logical left-brain thinking while designers are right-brain thinkers, in the sway of the imaginative and suppressed cerebral hemisphere. Whether this particular interpretation is rooted in science or phrenology it provides a useful metaphor signifying the differences between the two cultures.

Difference is encoded within the students' clothing, language and set of shared interests. Whilst there are students who bridge the divide, as Walker (1990, p. 152) argues, 'The divergence between managers and designers can be detected in personality traits, in habits of thought and work, as well as in educational background.' The concern is that Higher Education reinforces polarities instead of closing the gap between them. Teaching and learning strategies in design and management have traditionally been very different. In design, pedagogy predominantly takes place in the studio, is centred on practical activity and artefacts are assessed rather than the written word. The 'hero' culture (Jackson, 1997, p. 2) still prevails where the individual 'name' is valued above the collective effort. Management teaching employs a variety of techniques including case studies and simulations but is based on formal methods of transmitting information and involves study rather than practice. Organisations and teams are privileged above the individual. Callaway (1990, p. 415) suggests that the effect of 'two parallel, non-convergent educational tracks, one about controlling and one about creating' is potentially divisive. He argues for the need to develop business-oriented designers and design-aware managers by shifting the current educational boundaries.

Industry context

Commercial organisations adapt and restructure to survive in an increasingly competitive environment. Retail design companies have diversified into strategy, branding and research and have set up departments or teams to reflect these changes. Retailers recognising the value of design as a means to competitive advantage need managers who are visually literate and design-aware. Surveys have proved (Foreman & Johnston, 1999, p. 375) that employers place a high value on non-sector specific 'soft' skills such as oral and written communication, team working, listening and problem solving. This broadening of perspectives can also be detected in the type of business and design literature currently being published. In addition to the discipline-specific books on offer is a range of literature drawing on a broader theoretical framework. Popular examples include No Logo (Klein, 2000), Funky Business (Ridderstrale & Nordstrom, 2000) and The Harvard Design School Guide to Shopping (Koolhaas et al., 2002). These books are symptomatic of the lateral and creative thinking now being demonstrated by international academics and practitioners.

Interdisciplinarity

Accelerated cultural change, increasing flexibility in the labour market and the current requirements of industry suggest that graduates need a broader world view than is offered by a narrow single discipline approach. It has been argued (Robles, 1998) that interdisciplinary approaches to teaching are well suited to producing the outcomes demanded by society and especially the workplace, as they tend to be characterised by collaboration, interactivity, development of team-building skills, and development of critical thinking and problem-solving skills. Interdisciplinary learning has been defined as 'the synthesis of two or more disciplines, establishing a new level of discourse and integration of knowledge. It is a process for achieving an integrative synthesis that often begins with a problem, question, or issue.' (Klein, 1990: 5). The problem identified in the case of the Managing Retail Concepts unit was to attempt to bridge the knowledge gap between managers and designers and to provide a broader educational perspective and promote a deep approach to learning. Life is interdisciplinary and the problems experienced in the commercial world today are often so complex that they cannot be answered from a single perspective. The term interdisciplinary as DeZure argues (2001, p. 1) can be used as '...a concept, a methodology, a process, a way of knowing and even a philosophy.'

Unit rationale

The 'invisible paradigm' or philosophy underpinning the unit was to create balance within the bodies of knowledge of design and management. The intention was to integrate and synthesise the perspectives of several disciplines in order to set commercial activities within a social, political, economic and cultural context. Retailing like all human activities is situated within society and can best be understood when viewed as part of a broader picture. The aims of the unit and its mode of assessment were to consider commercial design and management within the context of the forces, which shape its development and visual manifestations. Content was focused on contemporary and topical issues, which transcended the disciplines. The issues were deliberately intended to destabilise preconceived assumptions and be challenging and thought provoking. Examples included 'Tate as Brand', 'Holocaust as Product', 'Interpreting the Zeitgeist: Science or Alchemy?' and 'Shopping in an Age of Moral Uncertainty'. Guest speakers were invited and visits made where appropriate. An authoritarian educational style was rejected in favour of a collaborative and student oriented approach.

Learning and teaching strategies

The promotion of interdisciplinary learning can be associated with active learning. Newell (1994. p. 35) argues that it encourages higher-order critical thinking skills such as analysis, synthesis, application and evaluation. Student co-operation and teamwork, the connection of knowledge and insight, more creative original thinking, development of cognitive and affective skills, preparation for work and a holistic and integrated approach can result from its application.

The learning and teaching strategies of the Managing Retail Concepts unit were centred on student reflection and group work. The underpinning structure for each taught session incorporated a visit, an image and a text. The students read the text and carried out the visit prior to contact sessions where the images were introduced through PowerPoint presentations. The intention was to stimulate a range of sensory experiences within the learning process. Workshops provided a forum for the exploration of ideas, group reflection and the sharing of personal experiences. Textual and visual analysis were given equal precedence within the unit and the links between images and the written word explored.

The pedagogic methods employed within the unit emphasised process-oriented and experiential forms of learning. Reflection on learning and self-directed study was encouraged through the introduction of reflective journals. This provided the opportunity for students to reflect on topics raised in class, demonstrate their ability to relate their learning across other units, to include personal experience and engage with issues at a deeper level. Students were asked to produce a reflective log according to specific guidelines. The intention was to encourage free writing but within a given structure. In addition to reflecting on the taught sessions they were given specific tasks to complete within their log in order to focus and guide their reflection. The mixed group presentations were intended to promote collaboration, the sharing of experiences and provide experience of peer assessment.

Davies (1997, p. 1) has argued that familiarity with the discourse of learning theory is necessary for students to take a deep approach to learning. Students were introduced to reflective writing with reference to Boud (1985), Schon (1987) and Moon (1999), to theories of deep and surface learning, Bigg's Solo Taxonomy and Kolb's experiential learning cycle. The intention was to help the students make sense of their learning and render transparent the pedagogic theories underpinning the unit.

Student feedback

Student feedback was obtained from a range of data over a two-year period. Extracts from reflective logs and questionnaires including unit evaluations and self-evaluations were analysed. Other research methods included tutor reflection, a focus group video and informal discussion with colleagues and students. The main points emerging from the evaluations in the academic year 2001/2 were:

Strengths of unit

Approximately 80% of students made positive comments about the unit:

- taught sessions (interactive lectures and workshops) were considered stimulating and thought provoking;
- content and delivery encouraged students to look at the bigger picture, to make links with other units and take a more holistic view of their learning;
- student group presentations were challenging and provided freedom of choice to explore issues of interest; peer assessment was useful and constructive; the benefits of managers and designers working together was strongly endorsed; students were able to learn from one another, appreciate each other's skills and strengths and experience teamwork;
- students particularly enjoyed the visits they were asked to undertake and reflect on; management students commented that this was not something regularly programmed into management units;
- the reflective log was acknowledged as a different and challenging mode of assessment which encouraged a deeper approach to learning, raised self awareness, valued personal input and allowed a more emotional and 'creative' approach to writing; the log provided a means of tailoring the assignment to the individual's interests;
- management students commented on the unusual nature of the log as an assignment in contrast to the more formal reports with which they were familiar; they welcomed the freedom of this approach at the same time as expressing concerns about their competence to work effectively within this framework.

Areas for improvement

- 60% of students commented on the time consuming nature of the reflective log particularly in the third year where the main emphasis should be on the final project;
- 40% suggested the use of a reflective log (and in some cases the unit) should move to the first or second year where there would be more time to explore issues in depth; they thought that to gain lasting benefit from reflection these skills should be taught to students earlier.
- the workload demanded of the unit was problematic for design students as they felt it interfered with time spent on the final project and exhibition; they were encouraged to see the log as a useful addition to their portfolio that demonstrated an ability to intellectually engage with and articulate ideas in written as well as visual form; however, for many students acceptable portfolio work was limited to that produced in the studio as a result of practical activity;
- management students wanted more time to concentrate on their written dissertation;
- 50% of managers expressed concern about the presentation of their reflective logs – they felt they lacked the appropriate skills to visually communicate their ideas effectively;
- 20% of the managers felt uncomfortable with the more abstract nature of the unit and were unsure how it fitted into the degree programme as a whole – although this did not detract from their enjoyment of topics raised it did not fit into their preconceived idea of what a useful management subject should be.

Tutor reflection

The Managing Retail Concepts unit has been an enjoyable and challenging experience for the tutors involved. The opportunity to compare student verbal response and written feedback year on year has ensured the continual improvement of practical teaching management strategies. Student feedback resulted in the introduction of accompanied visits supported by worksheets. An increased number of tutorials were timetabled to support the students with their self-directed study and preparation of mixed-group presentations. A more detailed explanation of reflective writing was given and previous examples of logs shown by former students who returned to talk about their experience of the unit. An interim hand in of the logs was instigated to provide formative feedback. These changes addressed some of the concerns initially highlighted.

The heavy workload of the unit appeared to be the main area of concern. A heavy workload can be associated with surface learning. The students were not being asked to do more than students in the previous year but the perception of time invested had grown. The intention was that the log should be completed on a continual basis and the number of contact sessions was restricted to allow time for self-directed study. Tutor workload was heavy in terms of marking and session preparation. The mixed group presentations had to be marked and peer comments analysed. The log, which had no word limit, required formative and summative assessment. Sourcing of images for the interactive presentations on PowerPoint and the preparation of handouts with appropriate texts and designated visits was time consuming. Topics discussed in contact sessions necessitated extensive background research, owing to their contemporary and interdisciplinary nature.

Attendance was good throughout the unit and the few students who regularly missed sessions were those with a history of poor attendance. Continual involvement was required in order to complete the reflective log. The atmosphere during sessions was relaxed and enjoyable and workshop discussions were generally lively and engaging. These discussions, however, did require close observation and facilitation in order to avoid the natural separation of groups into single discipline clusters. The level of intellectual engagement during these discussions did not match the standard achieved within the logs.

Overall the unit appeared to provide an enhanced learning experience for design and management students although there were specific concerns in relation to both groups that require further discussion and development. The students evaluated their learning experience as one which developed critical thinking, enabled them to explore their view of the world and encouraged creativity. Qualitatively this is confirmed by the standard of the logs, the value placed on them by the students and the comments contained within the written feedback completed over a two-year period.

> Although I have always known that you don't take things at face value, the unit has taught me to look even deeper within and to think more broadly than I have before.
> Management student

> I think this is the most creative subject I have experienced on the course. I feel safe and trusted, I am encouraged to ask questions and put down thoughts and experiences into words. I believe this is called deep learning.
> Design student

> I got experience of places I had never been to and the chance to express my feelings.
> Management student

> Through the process of writing the reflective log I learnt about myself as well as the world around me.
> Design student

Conclusion

The initiatives described above have led to a greater sense of involvement on the part of the students in their learning experience. Higher education has the potential to be an agent of change in bridging the cultural divide between managers and designers. Key issues highlighted by this project are:

- design students need to develop their written and oral communication skills; the workshops and use of reflective logs were intended to facilitate this development; they must be prepared to increasingly engage in theoretical discussion in order to improve their interpersonal skills and the ability to operate in a business environment;
- management students need to be more open-minded about their interpretation of business and explore their chosen field within a broader context; introducing cultural/contextual studies from the first year would facilitate this development and familiarise the students with a more conceptual, synthetic and visual learning experience; they would also benefit from being taught design skills which Jackson (1997, p. 3) argues are as important as literacy and numeracy: 'Design skills could be identified as fundamental visual literacy – the ability to understand and to use visual mechanisms for making sense of the world.'

Lessons learned and questions raised by this action research will prove invaluable in future discussions about the continuing development of the Combined Programme in Retailing.

References

Boud, D. (1985), *Reflection: Turning Experience into Learning* (London: Kogan Page)

Callaway, W. (1990), 'New directions in design and management education', in *Design Management* ed Mark Oakley (Oxford: Blackwell Reference)

Davies, A. (1997), 'Using learning journals to identify critical incidents of understanding', http://www.linst.ac.uk/cltad/resea/papers/ISLlearning%20journals.pdf (accessed December 2002)

DeZure, D. (2001), 'Interdisciplinary teaching and learning centre for teaching excellence', http://www.inform.umd.edu/EdRes/FacRes/CTE/library/podresourcepackets/alternatives/interdisciplinary.html (accessed December 2002)

Foreman, J. & Johnston, T. (1999), 'Key aspects of teaching and learning in business and management studies', in *A Handbook for Teaching and Learning in Higher Education* ed Heather Fry et al (London: Kogan Page)

Jackson, B. (1997), 'Values and traditions in teaching and learning art and design in deliberations on learning and teaching in higher education', http://www.lgu.ac.uk/deliberations/Subjects/art_design/intro.html (accessed December 2002)

Klein, J. (1990), *Interdisciplinarity: History, Theory and Practice* (Detroit: Wayne State University Press)

Koolhass, R. et al (2001) *The Harvard Design School Guide to Shopping* (Taschen, Cambridge MA)

Moon, J. (1999), *Reflection in Learning and Professional Development* (London: Kogan Page)

Newell, W. (1994), 'Designing interdisciplinary courses', in *Interdisciplinary Studies Today* ed Thompson Klein, J. and Doty, W., pp. 35-52 (San Francisco: Jossey-Bass)

Ridderstrale, J & Nordstrom, K (2000) *Funky Business* (Financial Times, Prentice Hall, UK)

Robles, H. (1998), 'Interdisciplinarity TCC '98 Online Conference', http://leahi.kcc.hawaii.edu/org/tcon98/paper/robles.html (accessed December 2002)

Schön, D. (1987), *Educating the Reflective Practitioner* (San Francisco: Jossey-Bass)

Walker, D. (1990), 'Managers and designers: two tribes at war?', in *Design Management* (Oxford : Blackwell Reference)

Biographical note

Nicky Ryan is a senior lecturer in retailing at the London College of Printing where she teaches design and business theory in the School of Retail Studies. Previously she was a visiting tutor at the London College of Fashion. Before teaching she worked in the retail sector in marketing, buying and merchandise management. She remains involved with industry through consultancy and training. Her academic background is in history of art and she is a PhD student at Birkbeck College. Her principal area of research is an interdisciplinary investigation into the convergence of commerce and culture. The current focus of her thesis is an examination into the collaborative attempt by Prada and Rem Koolhaas to 'refashion the shopping experience'. Pedagogic research interests include interdisciplinarity and the relationship between theory and practice in design.

workshops

Enhancing Curricula:

exploring effective curriculum practices in art, design and communication in Higher Education

30

Embedding new technologies in language learning for art, design and media in higher education: from invisibility to transferability with ALLADIN

Alison Kennard

Surrey Institute of Art & Design, University College, UK

Abstract

This paper, based on a workshop at the CLTAD conference Enhancing Curricula (April 2002), explores the ways language learning can contribute to the undergraduate experience in art, design and media disciplines, both through current key debates (key skills, student-centred learning, employability) and individual qualities in subject and delivery (linguistic acquisition, inter-cultural understanding and communication). It reviews the work of the ALLADIN project, the applicability of a range of information and communication technologies (hereafter ICTs) in subject-focused/non-specialist language learning, approaches to learning, staff development and course design issues. It also identifies current challenges facing language delivery in art and design courses, as well as changes in culture and perception needed by sectors of the creative professions in order for the full exploitation of language expertise beyond higher education.

Introduction: languages 2002

Language learning in art, design and media education takes many forms and can contribute to the overall student experience in a variety of ways – both through its specific characteristics as well as within key generic debates, such as employability, inter-cultural understanding, key skills, learning difference and communication. Its forms may be in joint or combined honours, contextual studies or a completely separate opportunity within the educational structure. Whatever the delivery format and outcomes, since the development of early CALL (computer assisted language learning), technology-based resources have been used effectively to enhance language acquisition as well as add value to the learning experience in Higher Education.

Recently, however, struggles in language departments to recruit or stay viable have led to a diluted appreciation (in the broader community) of the value of languages or, if not this, a nervousness about financing them in times of stretched budgets. This has meant that, increasingly, languages have a tendency to appear in the curriculum as an additional subject, and one which is often considered as a skill, rather than an academic discipline in its own right in relationship to the major subject, which has been incorporated in the role of 'service industry' to round out the profile of the undergraduate. As a result, language professionals have seen the emergence of a parallel universe in terms of how the importance of second language capability may be stressed in HE while what an institutional culture (staff and students) is prepared to sustain is often somewhat different. It is furthermore often the case that the extent of what really happens in a language classroom, beyond the acquisition of vocabulary to carry out practical functions, is not fully understood by those outside it.

ALLADIN: 1998–2002

A prime aim of the ALLADIN project was to tackle the invisibility of language learning in art and design institutions in the UK, and to support the opportunities presented by the diverse delivery formats through more effective use of new technologies by staff and students. This aim was achieved through an audit of national practice, the creation of a Web site with sample materials, subject-related links, online learning resources, training documentation and background reading. In the last two years of the project, specific emphasis was laid on providing staff and student training workshops in house.

Language use in art and design and participant interests

Participants brought a variety of perspectives to the workshop – interests in negotiating meaning, use of technology, exploring creativity and supporting specific learners such as those for whom English was a second language.

By and large, participants had expertise in a second language, 50% of whom were skilled to some extent in a minority/ethnic language or fluent in a non-European language such as Chinese, Russian or Japanese. Discussion revealed that second-language capability that is subject related and the value of personal contact were felt to be the most important contributing factors provided by language learning. This latter echoed a point made in Stephen Farthing's opening keynote speech which underlined the importance of relationships in artistic marketing and production.

Further ways in which languages can enhance the graduate profile and employability were in:

- acquisition of information and development of attitudes of mind (cf Tide Frater, 1998);
- transmission of product or concept;
- transacting business functions (purchase, sales, management, administration);
- fulfilling practical requirements abroad;
- health and safety issues, particularly with a multilingual workforce;
- social interaction;

- describing and promoting creative output (aesthetics, output, processes, theories, meaning and ideas; and
- through a specific subject alliance (e.g. textiles and Italian) or skills required for a certain field such as reading skills for art historians.

Languages are also seen to play a part in transferable skills acquisition, to support the accessibility agenda and as part of staff development. Finally, and not to be underestimated, is the value of learning a language just for the pleasure of it.

Resource building and exploitation

It was already apparent at the start of ALLADIN that language learning courses for art and design subjects in the UK were woefully under-resourced in terms of existing, comprehensive commercial courses or any other body of materials available to staff and students. The quickest and most economical way of destroying the resource lacunae was to develop approaches for using existing, shared tools such as the Internet and Word applications.

However, investigation revealed that the majority of language tutors were sessional and often not included in staff development opportunities or even dialogues with main programme staff. Many tutors interviewed at the start of the project and throughout felt inexperienced or unconfident about teaching students using ICT and nervous of the potential for technological downfall within the electronic environment. Significant staff development was an evident need in terms of enabling both full-time and sessional staff to commence or consolidate skills, working with ICT tools to produce up-to-date, real-life, context-based tasks and scenarios – not least to maintain the motivation and interest of students wishing to learn a subject-related language.

Use of ICT in art and design language learning

These contextualising factors made the use of a range of information and communication technologies essential in language learning in art, design and media contexts. A key example is access to subject-related materials that can be adapted for language learning purposes e.g. those on the Web. Activities were designed involving computer tools in use on an everyday basis (e.g. Word, Web, e-mail etc.) or of resources that facilitated the drawing together of the creative and linguistic. This may be on a primary level, e.g. in an electronic document combining words and graphics or on a secondary level through the digital recording of student submissions, through photography or video. Use of such tools tended also to cater well for the auditory or visual learner, rather than the text-based, who also benefit from multi-sensory delivery and practice. Examples of these technologies and their uses are as follows:

- voice recognition products – of interest to some learners who benefit from seeing visual representations of their sound waves or matching voice patterns with the speaker on screen;
- Internet resources including audio-visual teaching online; these have helped provide limitless subject-related raw materials with significant visual elements that can serve as the basis for evaluative or questioning activities, comprehension or simulation; online galleries and interactive maps, say, of the Pompidou Centre, appeal to the visual and allow discursive activities, ranging from how to reach somewhere, what is there when you get there, to the nature of the artwork. Infinite levels of language capability can be supported by the critical use of such materials;
- communications technologies, e.g. e-mail for discussion groups, keypal exchanges, submission of work or the freer environment of the second-language chat room used within specific parameters;
- creative or visually oriented language learners have also made use of virtual environments such as MOOs to explore & create physical environments and objects, make contact with other users in an unusual setting; educational MOOs allow learners to

work individually and collaboratively, with and without a teacher; as well as working towards specific pedagogical objectives, MOO offers learners a social (and at best, international) experience in a constructive and entertaining environment (Laxton, 2001);

- authoring software such as Hot Potatoes which provide flexible online exercises which can be created by learners as well as tutors and which may incorporate sound and image;
- mind-mapping tools such as Inspiration which allow visual representation of ideas with layered info, expandable graphics libraries, sounds, videos and hyperlinks for use as a solo and group tool; these lend themselves to organisational activities as well as vocabulary building or networking terms, phrases and functions around a topic area;
- generic software (e.g. Word, Powerpoint and the adjustment of controls on the PC to reframe the screen, allow voice recording or change settings to another language; and
- multimedia self-study courses with audio-visual materials, exercises and adaptable narratives which allow for the recreation of a story with an element of user decision-making.

Learning support and ICT

Resources to support the development of meta-cognitive skills also featured extensively in materials tested and produced: ones that would enable a student to develop independent learning skills or improve their understanding of their own learning style. Lateral thinking, visualisation and association were all skills drawn on through the use of ICT based resources. These were perhaps particularly in evidence in the work of language learners exploring virtual environments or using mind-mapping tools. The latter were particularly useful to tutors inducted into strategies to support learning differences, especially with dyslexic students wishing to learn a language, in terms of boosting memorisation and providing a logical structure for ideas. This is one illustration of the cross fertilisation of theories and approaches to learning shared between the different disciplines.

Synthesising the language learning experience

Through the language lesson, therefore, the learner has an opportunity to use ICT-based resources they may not use so extensively in their creative programme, develop their personal learning style in a environment complementary to their main subject, progress their second language capability and add to identifiable transferable skills through the tasks they accomplish. A number of different elements interweave and overlap: the employment of multi-sensory teaching methods to serve visual and auditory learning preferences, the incorporation of the visual and textual, machine-driven (computer-based) and man-made (the creative output of student) with the linguistic. Collaborative, constructivist experiences of working with and around the computer terminal are negotiated between tutor and student/student and student through elements of choice, assumption of responsibility and delegation of control. The student will lead certain activities – select the topics, resources and mode of presentation. The tutor will facilitate the use of resources and interact in electronic exchanges where welcome. Many elements of the key skills agenda are also apparent in the languages classroom, through the development of communicative or presentational skills – here enhanced by the use of ICT to achieve outcomes.

In addition, many language activities at all levels whether through developmental games, roles or simulations, will involve an element of the creative and the theatrical through play. West (1997) defines creativity as the creation or discovery of any new idea technique form or pattern that can be successfully applied to a particular need. In language learning terms this can be games, pictures, textures, music, physical displacement, presentation of concepts and personal meaning with creative support which can be manual or electronic. For the art and design language learner, the demonstration of language acquisition through personal production and/or use of ICT resources has led to the submission of CD Roms, spoof documentaries on video, models, clothing incorporating text, wall hangings, graphics and typographical work, paintings and countless other modes of expression.

The challenges of implementation

A further expression of this creativity and of the common challenge faced in any learning environment which incorporates human and electronic elements is as follows:

> The key to successful use of technology in language teaching lies not in hardware or software but in 'humanware', our human capacity as teachers to plan, design, and implement effective educational activity. Language learning is an act of creativity, imagination, exploration, expression, construction and profound social and cultural collaboration. If we use computers to fully humanise and enhance this act, rather than to try to automate it, we can help bring out the best that human and machine have to offer.
> Warschauer & Meskill (2000)

We see here both the special nature of the language contribution and also the generic challenge faced by anyone wishing to promote learning through electronic means. Given the endless permutations when art and design talents, language competency and ICT capability are brought together the question of what to include when designing a language component for a creative discipline, or any other major subject, needs to be clearly and strictly defined. In some cases, this takes the form of highly focused, subject-specific modules (such as French for Fashion) which cater for homogenous groups of learners and embed the use of ICT as implicit within tasks. Many more institutions have opted to develop language courses which are either generic in theme or that focus on inter-cultural issues at all levels of ability, with topics of communal interest for mixed cohort classes from a range of programmes. Alternatively, to provide outlets for self-expression on art- or design-related topics, tutors focus on the students' subject ownership within the language classes and turn the spotlight onto the learners' communication of their personal discipline interests, expertise and production.

Conversely, there is also the danger that an extremely enthusiastic advocate of language acquisition and all the possibilities inherent within its learning environment may over-reach and commit to too much. Selectivity in defining what can and is being measured is imperative from the outset: is the ICT component of the experience simply implicit or assessable? Are key skills merely to be identified or is more required? In terms of the creative discipline, what levels of linguistic achievement, context and function for that speciality compared to communicative competence of a generic kind? Is the design element of a language submission to be evaluated and by what criteria? What are the learning outcomes? Obvious stuff, but in a climate where there is increasing pressure to add value and make it visible the challenge is to make it realistic and achievable without doing a disservice to your subject.

Whether free-standing classes or subject-aligned language provision, the need for communication and support between the range of different departments involved cannot be under-estimated. (The ALLADIN model of course design in 'Elements of Course Design', the final project publication, illustrates these relationships.) Goodwill within the general culture may not be sufficient to promote the fruitful collaboration between the specialist programmes and the chosen language(s). In this, art and design may differ from other discipline areas such as business studies, law or engineering, where the stimulus to acquire a second language may be more immediate and organic and the employment correlation more obvious. The views of creative departments may be ambivalent; both keen for students to round out their talents and concerned that learners whose main programme time is already full, and who may need to work as well as study, may not be sufficiently good at time management and prioritisation to give a complementary or additional subject attention.

However, it will not be enough to simply make space for language learning in the curriculum and expect the momentum to self generate and the relationship to survive. The language staff alone can only do so much. There has to be ownership and belief in the relationship potential on the part of programme and departmental (as well as language) staff. A sense of direction and active support for the subject within its art and design context is key for relationships to be fostered and developed, perhaps through joint events, exchanges, business connections and an underpinning sense of the place that second language has in the creative environment. This is also fundamental to ensuring student engagement – any intimation of half-heartedness or a conflict of interests in terms of commitment to the subject and the learner will lose the momentum to work towards any goal other than the most pressing, i.e. their main qualification.

Some of this ambivalence may also be due to the block that exists in some sectors of the creative industries concerning the value of language capability in art and design employment. Divergence of opinion swings from profound enthusiasm for the positive influences second language competency bring to the workplace, to the belief that English is the only language necessary for doing business in. This is not an argument that linguists can turn around on their own, even with staunch support from other practitioners within the creative community as voiced here:

> Language communications in their various forms have been central to and informed my work. I have always believed in the integration of image, word and voice when presenting new concepts. How we, as makers of designs for clothes, buildings, interiors, consumer products, describe these projects to others is successful on the basis of how well the description is managed and sold to a potentially sceptical audience.
> Chaloner (1998)

We have seen the range of existing and potential benefits offered by combining languages, a creative discipline and ICT competence. We have also seen that to be fruitful, this combination requires balance and commitment in curriculum design, shared goals and long-term vision, ownership on all sides (even if the nature of this may vary), understanding of employability prospects, appreciation of personal development opportunities within the experience, a true perception of what takes place in language learning and a nurturing communal culture.

Inevitably the success of this combination will be dependent on how far institutions and students subscribe to its value. Without a shift in institutional and industrial culture the full possibilities inherent within the triangle of language learning, ICT and art and design will not be achieved on a significant scale. Anything is possible within the combination of languages, ICT and art and design – the only limitations will be local parameters and constraints and a failure to make the most of the opportunity.

Post script: the ALLADIN legacy

Although ALLADIN as an active project concludes in July 2002 the Subject Centre for Languages, Linguistics and Area Studies (LLAS) will continue to disseminate the project's findings. The final project publication - Elements of Course Design; A Practical Guide to Integrating ICT into Languages for Specific Purposes in Higher Education – and all other materials, will continue to be available for downloading for the foreseeable future from the website at http://www.alladin.ac.uk.

References and further reading

ALLADIN, http://www.alladin.ac.uk

Chaloner , D. (1998), Creative Director Conran Design Group, speech to launch ALLADIN at the Royal Institute of British Architects

Kennard, A. and Laxton, J. (2001), 'Integrating learning technologies to support the acquisition of foreign languages for specific disciplines', in Wisdom, J. and Macdonald, R. (eds.), *Educational Development: Research, Evaluation and Changing Practice* (London: Kogan Page)

Laxton, J. (2001), 'What are MOOs?', available on ALLADIN Web site: http://www.alladin.ac.uk/support/moo/about.html

Kenard, A. and Laxton, J. (2001), *Elements of Course Design: A Practical Guide to Integrating ICT into Languages for Specific Purposes in Higher Education* (ALLADIN)

Richards, M (2002), 'Mind Your Language', *Building* magazine, March 1, 2002, available at http://www.building.co.uk (accessed September 2002)

Tide Frater, S. (1998), Fashion Director Selfridges, speech to launch ALLADIN project at the Royal Institute of British Architects

Warschauer, M. and Meskill, C. (2000), 'Technology and second language Learning', in Rosenthal, J. (ed.), *Handbook of Undergraduate Second Language Education*, (Mah Wah , NJ: Lawrence Erlbaum)

West, T.G. (1997), I*n the Mind's Eye: Visual Thinkers, Gifted People with Dyslexia & Other Learning Difficulties, Computer Images & the Ironies of Creativity* (New York, Prometheus Books)

Bibliographical note

Alison Kennard is currently languages co-ordinator and ALLADIN project co-ordinator at the Surrey Institute of Art & Design, University College. Her interest in languages for specific purposes (LSP) developed through using languages in business and interpreting in areas as diverse as architecture, natural medicine and harbour management. Since 1991 her LSP focus has been the design and delivery of language programmes for art, design and media disciplines, both in subject-specific and mixed programme form. Her research interests include the use of ICT to support language study, student learning styles and strategies, and the creation of Web-based tools for independent learning.

31 Workshop: extending education and career opportunities for the Deaf community with particular reference to developing generic and subject specific language skills

Judith Mole, Direct Learn Services Ltd, UK

Diane Peacock, School of Art and Design, University of Wolverhampton, UK

Abstract

Deaf[1] students learn differently to hearing students. Depending on the onset and severity of deafness, preferred communication mode, parental and educational background and motivation, the student will require adaptations to the learning environment in order to succeed in completing a degree course.

Experience in the School of Art and Design at the University of Wolverhampton has shown that many Deaf students were missing out on specialist art and design terms and concepts due to a lack of available reference materials in BSL for art and design for use both by the student and their interpreter.

The paper will focus on language and literacy issues of Deaf students. Many Deaf students use British Sign Language (BSL) as their first and preferred language. Many technical, critical and contextual terms used in art and design education do not exist or are not in common use amongst Deaf people. The Wolverhampton University project has produced a web based BSL/English glossary for art and design education.

1 'deaf' written in lower case denotes the medical condition of hearing loss. Upper case 'Deaf' is the political and social term for belonging to the Deaf community. It is used in the same way other nationalities and groups would be spelt with uppercase letters, e.g. Spanish or Muslim.

Introduction

The University of Wolverhampton (UW) currently works with large numbers of profoundly Deaf[1] students studying a number of undergraduate and postgraduate courses. Within the university there is considerable expertise in working with Deaf people and teaching English as a second language to Deaf people for whom sign is their first language. The university's Communication Support Unit is the largest educational support unit for Deaf people in Britain in terms of numbers of permanent staff and established expertise.

Within the university, the largest number of registered Deaf students, study in the School of Art and Design. The percentage of Deaf students entering the School has risen steadily since 1996. The School is one of the few specialist providers to accommodate a community of Deaf students.

Purpose of the session

- Sharing information about the project with delegates.
- Exploring and reflecting on working with Deaf students and the impact of doing so upon teaching and curriculum delivery.

The workshop will concentrate on the BSL/English Glossary for Art and Design Education and the language issues affecting Deaf students and academics in teaching, learning and assessment.

The University of Wolverhampton innovations projects

The School of Art and Design and the School of Humanities, Languages and Social Sciences aim to complete six projects by October 2002. The project outcomes are as follows:

- The research and production of an interactive Web site which uses current art and design Deaf students and Deaf professional practitioners to promote positive role models for Deaf students wishing to enter higher education. This will include factual and evaluative material and will be available to schools and colleges, relevant societies and organisations.

- The research, development and accreditation of a BSc/BA Combined Studies (Communication Supported Route) that includes an introductory year in English for Deaf learners and introduces specialist subject orientation in art and design.
- The research and production of a 'specialist' British Sign Language glossary to support undergraduate art and design study. This glossary will be developed to cover technical, critical, contextual and professional practice terminology. The glossary will be produced on a Web site and be available for use in other institutions (this will be a model for a specialist glossary development which can be applied to a variety of subject areas).
- The preparation and production of a guidance and support pack and code of practice for lecturers working with Deaf students.
- Linked with the above will be a series of structured staff development programmes for teaching and technical staff. Initially, these will be available for UW staff, but will be offered externally once project outcomes are more advanced.
- Dissemination of project information and a special event within the 'Deaf Film and Video Festival 2002' in the form of an Art and Design Careers Forum to include employers, practitioners and prospective employers, students and teachers.

Background

A study of English language literacy skills of Deaf people conducted by Conrad (1979) concluded that the average Deaf person left school with a chronological reading age of between 8 and 12 years. Research commissioned by the DfEE in 1998, carried out by Durham University and Birmingham University, looking specifically at attainment achieved by Deaf children, found no significant change in these levels of literacy (Powers, 1998). In the case of Deaf people, a low reading age is emphatically not a measure of intellectual incapacity, rather it is a reflection of the need to hear a spoken language in order to be able to learn it with ease.

Deaf students have another language, British Sign Language (BSL), which they can utilise to access information and concepts. However, their attainment in English must be further developed alongside their language ability in BSL in order to maximise education and career opportunities for this group. Furthermore, to gain equality with hearing learners, subject specific, standardised glossaries are required as a matter of urgency.

The online BSL/English glossary for art and design

Rationale

Experience in the School of Art and Design at the University of Wolverhampton, has shown that many Deaf students miss out on specialist art and design terms and concepts owing to a lack of available reference materials in BSL for art and design, for use both by students and their interpreters.

Target audience

The glossary aims to assist Deaf students, sign language interpreters, communication support workers, note-takers for Deaf people and advanced BSL students. It is hoped that foreign language learners who wish to be able to access clear English definitions of art and design terms will also find the glossary useful.

Communication and British Sign Language

Deaf and hearing-impaired students use a variety of communication methods to gain access to education. Some students use English or British Sign Language, and others may use lip reading and the services of a note-taker to be able to follow what is being said. Partially hearing students may require specialist equipment; others may not seem to have any additional needs. The communication method that the Deaf or hearing-impaired student uses depends largely on the onset of their deafness, parental and social background, and schooling. Most Deaf people use a variety of communication modes, sometimes simultaneously.

No communication method used by Deaf and hearing-impaired people is inherently better or more effective than any other – it depends on the individual and the precise nature of their hearing loss.

British Sign Language

BSL is not a signed interpretation of English or a collection of gestures. It is a fully functioning language with its own grammar and syntax. The grammatical structure of BSL is similar to German in that the verb is placed at the end and it has an object/subject/verb structure. For example, in BSL the sentence 'The boy goes to the shop' would be signed as 'Shop boy goes'. Just because BSL does not use articles and prepositions, does not mean that the language is simple, in the same way as one would not say that Russian is simple, although it has these same linguistic characteristics (Crystal, 1987). Another feature of BSL is that, like spoken language, it has regional accents and dialects.

BSL can express complex and complicated concepts and ideas as effectively as any other language can. Although its development has suffered from linguistic oppression in education and in the community, and although it has no written form, the language has continuously evolved over centuries. Since the advent of video technology and television, it can now be recorded and reference materials can be produced.

BSL uses a variety of 'types' of signs. Some signs are iconic in that they show what something looks like. (e.g. the sign for 'drink', 'grinder', 'throwing'). Other signs are more abstract, like the signs for 'metaphor' or 'concept'. Some signs use explanation, rather than one sign (e.g. the sign for 'anthropology'). BSL also 'borrows' from English in using finger-spelling and signed English (for example for proper names and places).

Other communication tools

There are other methods of communication that are often confused with BSL. These are Signed Supported English, Signed Exact English, Makaton, Paget-Gorman and others. These forms either use sign with English (like speaking French words but using English word order) or are a collection of gestures used with people with communication difficulties. They do not have the vocabulary, grammar or linguistic richness that theoretically defines a language. Most of the above have been created as an educational tool in order to aid Deaf people in accessing education or learning English. They are not, however, commonly used outside education and serve as a communication aid, rather than a language.

Whist lip reading is often seen as the most effective communication tool for Deaf people, in fact only 30% of English is lip-readable (NATED, 1998). Any sounds produced in the throat or by intakes or releases of air, cannot physically be seen by a lip-reader. Lip-reading previously unseen words is particularly problematic.

The language of art and design

Much of the 'language' use associated with art and design centres on describing, discussing, evaluating and ascribing meaning and purpose to the wide variety of creative practices that constitute our subject area. As with other specialist discourses, art and design language, terminology and vocabulary relies heavily on the prior understanding and linguistic ability of the communication receiver to interpret what can often present as complex and contradictory. Communication is clearest when art and design specialists from the same or similar disciplines address each other. This shared understanding can be challenged by the inclusion of communications contexts that require differing methodologies, practice bases and/or value systems. In all forms of communication understanding is achieved through explicit and implicit exchange of meaning. In the case of art and design we therefore expect the receivers to 'test' and 'contest' meaning in relation to their own creative practice. When any such complex communication is 'translated' by an individual without having first acquired the necessary vocabulary and specialist understanding, it is inevitable that inaccuracies and misunderstandings occur. In our discipline, in particular, conceptual, critical polemical and metaphorical language alongside inferences of tacit knowledge and changes in language context can be baffling, disorientating and open to misinterpretation to all students new to undergraduate study. If we add to these factors the language of current higher education, and we consider the situation of the Deaf student acquiring meaning via a sign language interpreter, we can perhaps begin to comprehend the challenges to our prevailing approaches to teaching, learning and assessment.

Interpreting the language of art and design

Currently, there is a national shortage of interpreters in Britain (current estimates suggest that there is one qualified or trainee interpreter per 166 Deaf sign language users). Particularly, there is a problem of recruitment in higher education:

> The difficulty, certainly in Britain, is that few of the best or most qualified interpreters regularly accept any educational interpreting assignments, and as a result the majority of these assignments are undertaken by those who have not undergone interpreter training or whose skills are less advanced. In reality then, not only do students have a limited choice of interpreters to work with them, with often quite varied degrees of skill and ability. Finding an interpreter whose language skills match the needs of the student is a most difficult thing to achieve.
> Harrington (2000)

Whilst interpreting specialist language in a higher education setting:

> Interpreters need to consider their role in an educational environment, and the fact that Deaf people may be disadvantaged when compared to other university students. Although all university students may attend lectures without any background knowledge to the subject, and thus have lack of familiarity with subject-specific terminology, the interpreter is faced with the task of deciding how to provide an interpretation that is linguistically and culturally sensitive, incorporating meaningful equivalents, while still providing Deaf students with the opportunity to access specialised terminology that may be important for them to know in order to fully understand the subject of the lecture and pass examinations ... this context presents sign language interpreters with a dilemma of whether to freely interpret the content of

> a lecture, or whether to establish a language contact situation that occasionally relies on the finger-spelling of English words and possible use of literal interpretation. In the context of their relationship with Deaf consumers, and the negotiation of language needs, interpreters need to use their judgement to decide what vocabulary should be interpreted conceptually, and what should be interpreted literally. In making decisions as to whether Deaf students need to access subject-specific terminology, interpreters should not perceive their role as educators, but rather as linguistic decision-makers.
> Napier (2001)

When sign language interpreters become linguistic decision-makers, they affect the quantity and quality of the information the student receives:

> ... there is no guarantee that an individual interpreter has attended university themselves, or that they are knowledgeable in the subject areas for which they may be expected to interpret. In fact it has been suggested by the Council for the Advancement of Communication with Deaf People (CACDP), which is the examination and assessment board for interpreters in England, Wales and Northern Ireland, that as few as 5% of people interpreting in educational settings in Britain currently posses appropriate language skills and a graduate-level qualification. Such a lack of awareness on the part of educational interpreters, either of the environment in which they are working or the subject they are interpreting, combined with lower language skills, is bound to have an impact on the student's ability to learn.
> Harrington (2000)

Many terms commonly used in art and design have been transliterated directly into signed English (rather than BSL). This has meant that the translation has conveyed the literal, not semantic, meaning. For example, 'modernism' was translated using the same sign as 'new'; 'Postmodernism' was often signed as 'after-new'. While this method enabled a translation of the words it wholly failed to convey the meaning and richness of the terms.

Similarly, much initialisation (finger-spelling) is used when interpreters are unfamiliar with a specialist term. For example, 'aesthetic' is often signed as 'a' with the appropriate accompanying lip pattern. This translation method works if it has been previously agreed with the Deaf student and the student has a firm grasp of both the subject matter and English. It is not useful when deploying the same initial to a number words with very different meanings, all of which, however, look very similar on the lips. For example, the same initialisation could be used for 'aesthetic', 'aesthetics', 'aestheticism' or 'aesthetic movement'. By this method it would also be impossible to distinguish whether a word was being used as an adverb, adjective or noun.

Art and design subjects also utilise many homographs, where a word is spelt the same, but has a different meaning – for example, 'form'. This means 'to form' as in to shape, 'a form' as in a shape or 'a form' as in a type. All these have different signs. Similarly, 'edit' has a multitude of different signs, depending upon whether one is referring to a video, written text or computer text.

Additionally, art and design subjects often borrow existing words and give them new, very specific meanings in a subject context. For example, multimedia uses 'rendering', ceramics uses 'bat' and photography uses 'pushing' and 'pulling'. In BSL there are separate signs for terms depending on each meaning of the word. If the interpreter is unsure of the context and therefore the meaning, then they may use the wrong sign.

British Sign Language features many iconic signs and most concrete objects have a sign that describes how something looks or, alternatively, shows the function of what the object does. When a sign language user is unsure of either, it is difficult or impossible to provide an accurate description. For example, if the sign language user does not know the meaning, function, feel or shape of a fish eye lens, a linisher or cloque, then it is not possible to sign these.

Because there has been no available reference material or BSL glossary for art and design there is little recorded BSL vocabulary for the subject area. Interpreters working in one institution or co-working in one lecture may share the same signs, but often interpreters will use different signs for specialist terminology. This can add to the confusion of Deaf students when they have to learn many different signs for one concept, depending on who their interpreter is for one course or module.

Learning art and design terminology for Deaf students

Anecdotal evidence from the University of Wolverhampton suggests that many Deaf students find it difficult to relate the signs seen in a lecture to their lecture notes (usually taken by a note-taker for Deaf people) and sometimes have difficulty using the correct words in assignments, if initialisation or signed English (a direct, literal translation) has been used. Students could utilise the services of a language support tutor, but these tutors may not use the same signs as the interpreters in the lecture, often adding more confusion.

Many profoundly, pre-lingually Deaf people use BSL as their first language and English as a second language. As with many second language users, first language interference often hinders the student translating effectively from one language to another. When using a sign language interpreter, Deaf students can have two-way, real-time access to what is happening around them. However, they then have to relate what they have seen in one language to what they can read in books, handouts and notes that are written in another. For example, to illustrate the problems some profoundly Deaf sign language users face, it is if a hearing person was to undertake a degree in Saudi Arabia, with all their lectures being simultaneously translated from Arabic into English. Having accessed all the information contained in the lecture in English, for assessment they would be required to submit all their essays and exams in Arabic. This requires a high degree of bilingualism.

Selection of terms

Research for the selection of terms to make up the glossary entailed the documentation of over 2000 terms specific to subjects in art and design. The terms were selected by a hearing researcher and a Deaf researcher, both being art and design graduates and the latter using sign language interpreters to access lectures and tutorials.

This project has required much discussion around methodology and around the rationale for choosing appropriate terms for inclusion. We recognise that it is impossible to include all terms required for first-year study across all subjects in art and design, and some method for selecting terms and concepts therefore had to be developed. Initially, terms were sought using Internet and library reference materials, subject guides, module guides, assignment briefs, the benchmark statement, other glossaries and art and design dictionaries. The research team also held a number of staff consultation sessions during which subject specialists were interviewed. Subject glossaries were also sent to external academics for consultation and feedback.

Words were initially categorised under five headings: technical, contextual, critical, professional and historical. A further category, conceptual, was added at a later date. Further research in the area of professional practice and consultation was undertaken with the Careers Advisory Service.

There was also a section added for general words that were used frequently in higher education and that were perceived to be useful to Deaf learners. Some examples of terms included in the glossary:

3 D Design	Digital Media	Painting	Art History	General
Anthropometrics	Algorithms	Charcoal	Art Brut	Articulate
Circular saw	Bandwidth	Fixative	Avant Garde	Commission
Hand cut mortices	Clips	Mahl stick	International Style	Costings
Plexi-glass	Dialogue box	Portraiture	Jacobean	Innovative
Rivet	Showreel	Intaglio	Medievalism	Paradigm

Bearing in mind that it is essential that students learn new concepts for their subject, the project will focus only on the language used at level 0 and level one of a degree subject. To include terms commonly used at higher level study would have exceeded the resources and time scale of the glossary project. (N.B. additional funding is currently being sought to extend the glossary on the basis of feedback from the users and to develop a science glossary for higher education.)

The glossary will also feature links to other general art and design glossary Web sites so that students can look up new terminology not included in the BSL glossary and interpreters conduct preparation more easily.

Selection of signs

Given the situation outlined above, many signs in art and design are not commonly known or shared in the Deaf and interpreting community, all the signs included in the glossary have had to be found. This has been achieved by interviewing Deaf artists, Deaf art and design undergraduates and graduates, sign linguists, BSL lecturers and interpreters who work in art and design.

In order to present authentic vocabulary that is used in real situations, rather than using artificially created signs, hours of video footage has been taken and analysed. In many cases more than one sign has been found for one word and this reflects the regional variation of sign language. Where this is the case, each variation has been included.

During the selection of signs a number of philosophical and ethical queries have had to be addressed. For example, when there is an established and widely used sign, but it doesn't strictly cover the meaning of the word in an art and design context, should this still be included in the glossary? For example, the sign for 'modern' is the same as the sign for 'new'. However, can we also use the sign 'new' for the art movement 'Modernism', as is commonly done?

In the end the criterion for inclusion have been the following:

- to present as many regional variations as possible;
- to ensure that signs are correct in context and meaning;

- to separate homographs and show different meanings with different definitions;
- to include different communication modes: (finger-spelling, signed English, iconic signs, abstract signs and explanations); and
- to present lip patterns accurately to aid partially hearing students.

The aim of the glossary is not to standardise sign language in the area of art and design, but to provide an effective communication tool in the academic setting. Taking and collating different signs from different institutions and settings will, we hope, enable us to do this. It is important to note that glossary users will not see a sign in isolation. They will know the subject area to which it belongs, be offered a (plain) English definition and (where appropriate) an image or photograph to illustrate the term.

Although, to date, it has not been possible to provide all terms with signs, terms without signs have been included, in the hope that an explanation and image will still be useful to the glossary user.

The glossary Web site

It is essential that the information provided is appropriate, accurate and accessible for the glossary user. As the glossary is aimed at Deaf people who use BSL as their first language, it is important to ensure that all English definitions are accessible to a second language user. The project aims to present definitions in clear, rather than academic, English. If a student wishes to seek a more in-depth explanation of a term, at present these are only available through existing written reference materials for art and design.

Another consideration is the usability of the Web site. It is essential that the site can be navigated easily and quickly. Freelance interpreters may work in a variety of settings each week and will not be able to devote much time to preparation of one individual assignment. Being able to access the required information quickly will allow interpreters to maximise their time and expertise.

The glossary will be illustrated and original artwork and photographs have been commissioned. Image libraries have also been approached to provide more known and recognisable images to illustrate art historical terms. The issue of copyright and royalties has been an important consideration for the project. While some copyright free images have been found, a number of terms will not be able to be illustrated owing to lack of affordable source material.

During the project consideration has been given to providing both an English and signed version of the definitions. However this has been abandoned due to the download time that would be required. The project team has also been asked to consider producing a dictionary, rather than a glossary of terms. Unfortunately, the team could not find a way to search for signs, other than using finger-spelling, which would be the same as searching using the written A–Z search.

Searching the Web site

The Web site will be searchable by various means: A-Z, by subject, department, keyword, abbreviation and possibly category. The search facility will utilise fuzzy logic: users will not have to be able to spell a word completely correctly, or will need to input only the first few letters of a word in order for it to appear. The project team feels sure this essential to enable the resource to be useful to a target audience of Deaf people for whom English is their second language.

References

Conrad, R. (1979), *The Deaf School Child* (London: Harper and Row)

Crystal, D. (1987), *The Cambridge Encyclopaedia of Language* (Cambridge: Cambridge University Press)

Harrington, F. (2000), in Roberts, R., Carr, S.A., Abraham, D. & Dufour, A. (eds.), *The Critical Link 2: Interpreters in the Community* Benjamins Translation Library 31, US, ISBN 90 272 1636 3

Napier, J. (2001), 'Linguistic coping strategies of sign language interpreters', unpublished doctoral dissertation, Macquarie University

NATED (1998), *Deaf and Hard of Hearing Students: Guidance for College Lecturers* (National Association for Tertiary Education for Deaf People)

Powers, S. & Gregory, S. (1998), *The Educational Achievements of Deaf Children* (DfEE Publications)

Biographical note

Judith Mole is a freelance consultant in d/Deafness and disability issues. She has worked as an interpreter, lecturer and support service manager. She now advises national organisations and further and higher education institutions on accessibility issues.

Diane Peacock is an experienced art and design educator and manager who has worked in the compulsory, tertiary and higher education sectors for the last 30 years. She has a particular interest in art and design learning styles and language. She is currently Associate Dean in the School of Art and Design, University of Wolverhampton where she first became involved with supporting Deaf students.

Curriculum integration of a visual digital learning unit, with reference to *SeeingDrawing* and *Seeing Colour*

32

David Rowsell

Information Technology Research and Development Unit (ITDRU), The London Institute, UK

Abstract

Drawing is central to all that is produced within the broadest spectrum of art and design. It is the core around which the conceptual and intellectual development of students is built .

The *SeeingDrawing* DVD, funded under a Higher Education Council TLTP initiative, formed a three-year project aimed at providing an interactive learning environment for the exploration of drawing and its contexts by art and design students. The focus of the project is not 'how to draw'; it is rather the fundamental and crucial skills of visual literacy. *SeeingColour* is a related digital product (funded by the London Institute), that enables students to explore colour and colour relationships.

This interactive workshop aims to enable participants to experiment with *SeeingDrawing* and *SeeingColour*. The intention is to identify methods and means of integrating such digital products into the art and design curriculum, and extending student learning through the use of digital learning materials.

Broader issues connected with art and design educational technology will be addressed in relation to both examples.

The Added Value of Digital Learning Materials

A visual digital learning unit may supplement or enhance an art or design curriculum either through extending curriculum content (covering new or neglected content) or by complementing existing curriculum content (elaborating contexts and paralleling non-digital units and learning). At the same time, a digital learning unit offers the possibility of expanding the students' learning experiences and giving them increased control over the direction, pace and content of their learning. This may in future lead to the possibility of students, not staff, choosing how to enhance the art and design curriculum.

Aside from the direct impact on learner experience and the substance of a curriculum, digital learning materials have a number of peripheral advantages. Firstly, they provide a means of capturing and sharing information and content. Secondly, digital materials are often flexible enough to allow repositioning or reuse, in contexts or according to structures perhaps not originally imagined.

For example, a digital learning unit initially designed and intended as functioning within a one to one relationship (between the software and a student user) could be deployed just as easily in other circumstances. This might include lectures, demonstrations and seminars; or it could involve group learning and group projects.

For current purposes, a visual digital learning unit will be defined as: a specific and bounded set of learning experiences accessed through material with a visual bias, available in a digital medium and typically stored on a DVD or CD. A portable disk format enables asynchronous learning – at more or less any place or time - but it does not in and of itself enable networked communication between users. A networked learning unit generally carries significantly different functions, aims and objectives from those of the units considered here (*SeeingDrawing* and *SeeingColour*).

A student using a digital learning unit, according to the above description, will usually be able to produce work that is capable of capture in an appropriate format, accessible and viewable in a number of other contexts. Output of this kind obviously provides evidence of learning progress and will probably be central to any subsequent learner assessment.

Feedback and interaction with software comprise the important means by which the student user is engaged in learning when using a digital unit. This interaction between learner and software is likely to centre on tasks contained within the product, although a tutor or facilitator is equally likely to guide or select specific tasks for their students. In the absence of facilitation or tutor guidance, a thoughtfully constructed piece of software should support a student when they seek to identify their own goals and any subsequent tasks. Ideally software should complement the student's choices and broadly operate within the expected parameters set by a student's self-determined projects. In this sense, the software functionality should be as transparent as possible in order not to damage a student's motivation or confidence.

Digital Learning Materials in Use

Characteristically and generally, a digital learning unit has multiple entry and exit points along with associative links between content. All of which tends to promote non-linear pathways of exploration. Non-linearity and inherent complexity can lead to problems of navigation. Difficulties with navigation, or understanding of the functionality of a piece of software, combine in hindering learning when time and energy are wasted on negotiating the software at the expense of learning. In general, the larger the digital unit, the more critical navigational and functional choices become. The difficulty for the student learner may be in matching their learning objectives with whatever they can find through the software interface (Nunes & Fowell, 1993). This is an issue of navigational means, terminology, menu design, content categorisation and function interpretation. But most importantly, it means mapping anticipated learning objectives to navigational means.

Assessment mechanisms, tools or devices may also form part of a digital learning unit, thereby increasing the independence of the learning experience. However, in this instance, neither of the products referred to, either *SeeingDrawing* or *SeeingColour*, contain explicit assessment tools. It is self-evidently the case that some degree of reflexive and self-assessment follows from the conditions of interaction by virtue of built-in feedback channels but there is no internal monitoring of this activity in *SeeingDrawing* or *SeeingColour*. Ordinarily, a reliable and objective mark of learning is the success or otherwise achieved by a learner in managing a task. Output, in the form of a completed task, is therefore (as always) the primary evidence in any assessment of learner progress.

In most educational circumstances, a tutor or facilitator is required to be an expert in the subject matter in question, someone able to supply contexts of understanding relevant to the area of study. This is no less the case with many digital units. *SeeingColour*, for example, as it stands at present, certainly requires such expert contextualisation. However, it is perhaps a measure of the maturity, breadth and depth of *SeeingDrawing* that it can operate as more or less autonomous learning material that does not necessarily require the guiding presence of an expert in drawing.

SeeingDrawing

All learning arguably contains cognition determined by the explicit subject or content under study together with meta-cognitive activities associated with reflection, abstraction, learning about learning and the like (Kolb, 1984). *SeeingDrawing* provides some tools for capturing meta-cognition, which enables it to be used by tutors who are not specifically experts in drawing. This is the case at the London College of Printing, where *SeeingDrawing* will be used as part of the Professional and Personal Development component of first-year degree courses. The most valuable component of *SeeingDrawing*, for these purposes, is the notebook tool – which allows students to capture text, screen grabs and write their own notes as they visit the different sections of the product.

SeeingDrawing was a TLTP-funded project that spanned three years. The project was brought to completion in June 2001. *SeeingDrawing* was a collaboration between the London Institute (represented by the IT Research and Development Unit – as primary developers – Camberwell College of Art and the London College of Fashion), together with Falmouth College of Art, Ravensbourne College of Design and Communication and the University of Ulster.

The final product was a complex collection of interactivity and content, stored on a DVD and providing something in the order of 25 hours of learning activity. The content of the DVD spans:

- Drawing as instrument (measured drawing conventions, methods and terminology);
- Drawing as method (the creative process, problems and issues, drawing practice);
- Drawing as reflection (context and interpretation, representation, evaluation of drawing);
- Drawing as understanding (mechanics of perception, interpretation and culture, analysis of drawings);
- Drawing as fashion (drawing and the fashion design process, examples of fashion drawing, communicating ideas by drawings);
- Drawing as exploration (visual thinking, cognition and perception, the vocabulary of drawing discourse).

SeeingDrawing is distinguished by the range of viewpoints on drawing that it offers. Students have found this variety particularly stimulating and have enjoyed exploring the differing approaches and uses of drawing outside their own discipline. At the same time, *SeeingDrawing* supports a number of learning approaches and methods of exploration. This includes, among others, video interviews with experts, descriptions of drawing processes, games, simulations and exercises.

The aim of *SeeingDrawing* was not to provide a computer drawing tool or replacement for pencil and paper. It was instead conceived of as a means of accessing overviews of how drawing is used, what drawing means and how drawings are made and perceived. The pedagogy underlying *SeeingDrawing* was broadly constructivist and experiential, whereby the student, given the appropriate means, could make their own sense of the many contexts of drawing.

SeeingColour

SeeingColour, in contrast to *SeeingDrawing*, was developed by a much smaller team (internally to the London Institute) and with more prescribed and simpler learning objectives. *SeeingColour* is an ongoing and evolving project that aims to provide a basic colour course, with the main objective of sensitising students to colour relationships through the provision of more or less standard colour exercises. The project has grown out of and alongside a colour course taught by Garth Lewis at Central Saint Martins. Much of the content, embedded through the colour exercises, derives from the familiar Albers colour course (the Bauhaus and Yale). The development work for *SeeingColour* has been the sole responsibility of the London Institute's IT Research and Development Unit.

Whereas *SeeingDrawing* was designed to run from a DVD, *SeeingColour* was designed from the beginning to be accessible over a network. The result is a product that can also readily be stored on a CD, making for a potentially cheaper and more flexible digital resource.

SeeingColour is perhaps best thought of as a collection of software tools – tools that are specific to the intended colour exercises. The result is software that foregrounds colour manipulation over, for example, software that relies upon metaphors of image manipulation. *SeeingColour* software consequently provides some novel methods for mixing and using colour. An important aspect of the software is that it employs colour swatches similar to Albers' colour papers – a collection of screen-printed papers that remains available through the Color Aid Corporation. The specific colour swatches used in *SeeingColour* were produced as part of another London Institute project: *Chromafile*.

Chromafile swatches provide a finite collection of colours that stress colour relationships over tonal ones. In this fashion, they accentuate colour choices as made by the student, leading to very different colour work when compared with that produced using more standard colour mixing software tools.

Although *SeeingColour* was initially planned as a straightforward collection of colour exercises, students have quickly grasped how to use exercise output in other contexts – and with other software. The need to have exercise output in standard image formats (GIF or JPG) has therefore become increasingly important.

At the present time *SeeingColour* exists as a small set of director movies. This, as has been mentioned, forms something like a software resource. Unlike *SeeingDrawing*, there is little in the way of contextualisation and the colour exercises still need to be embedded and contextualised by an expert tutor. However, once a student has reached even an elementary understanding of the how and why of the exercises, the software is sufficiently flexible and portable to be used in a variety of circumstances (at home or at college) and for a number of purposes. The analogy with paper swatches and how they are used in collage, which formed the basis for the software tools of *SeeingColour*, has resulted in methods of working that are quick, easy to use and independent of accurate drawing. Again the emphasis is on colour over photographic representation (which forms the underlying metaphor of Photoshop, for example).

Future Directions

Although *SeeingColour* consists of a collection of exercises (loosely termed), the common features and functions by means of which colour is applied, delimited and organised in the software unifies the appearance of the exercises and tools. Behind this visual unity (of the interface), there is a consistent set of concepts and assumptions relating to colour and its use.

We have done some work in sketching out prototype software that encapsulates the thinking about colour embedded in the

SeeingColour exercises. Our prototypes not only suggest how the software could be extended (for example, through additional applications) they also highlight the role that software can play in a more general sense and across the curriculum.

Learning through using software is sometimes overlooked as simply a matter of acquiring some particular software skills. Software skills are viewed as driven entirely by needs and goals external to the software. Whereas in practice, learning software usually proceeds as a learning dynamic, where software tools are investigated alongside a developing understanding of the concepts underpinning the software.

Most software works by means of analogy and simulation, and it is through this that software encodes information and concepts appropriate to the intentions and goals of users. In this sense, software is always located within a context of use, clearly relating skills and knowledge to that context and, as such it situates the learner in an environment of practice. Understood in this way, software tools begin to have a strategically important relationship with the curriculum and learning.

Even the simplest of software is, to some extent, a simulation of working contexts: Photoshop implies the photographer's studio as does AutoCAD the architect's and designer's. Which is to say that the working practices, tools, assumptions, terminology and knowledge contexts of those professions are intrinsic to the software. In learning the software, the student acquires an understanding of the contexts of practice that amounts to a "cognitive apprenticeship" (Black *et al* 1994). The inherent learning possibilities of this are rarely overtly acknowledged or recognised.

When we first developed the *SeeingColour* exercises we were satisfied with simply emulating the processes of previously well-defined studio exercises. These processes consisted of selecting and juxtaposing colours for the purposes of revealing the perceptual logic of colour relationships as well as generally sensitising students to colour and colour relationships. The resulting digital versions worked well but perhaps their real value was in re-directing our attention to the possibilities of software built upon non-standard analogies and specific (colour studio) working practices.

Bibliography

Black, J., Thalheimer, W., Wilder, H., de Soto, D. and Picard, P. (1994). *Constructivist Design of Graphic Computer Simulations:* http://www.ilt.columbia.edu/publications/cdgcs.html (accessed December 2002)

Duffy, T. and Jonassen, D. (1992). *Constructivism and the Technology of Instruction: a conversation* (Hillsdale, NJ: Lawrence Erlbaum Associates)

Kolb, D. A (1984). *Experiential learning: Experience as the source of learning and development* Englewood Cliffs (NJ: Prentice-Hall)

Lally, V. (1999). *Analysing Teaching and Learning Interactions in a Networked Collaborative Learning Environment*: http://www.mmi.unimaas.nl/euro-cscl/Papers/97.doc (accessed December 2002)

Laurillard, D. (1993). *Rethinking University Teaching: a Framework for the Effective Use of Educational Technology*, New York: Routledge.

Nunes, J. & Fowell, S. (1993). 'Hypermedia as an experiential learning tool: a theoretical model': http://informationr.net/ir/2-1/paper12.html (accessed December 2002)

Papert, S. (1993). *Mindstorms: Children, Computers, and Powerful Ideas*, 2nd edition (New York: Harper Collins)

SeeingDrawing: http://www.SeeingDrawing.com (accessed December 2002)

Suchman, L. (1988). *Plans and Situated Actions: The Problem of Human/Machine Communication* (Cambridge, UK: Cambridge University Press)